Holistic Game Development
with Unity

Holistic Game Development with Unity

An All-in-One Guide to Implementing Game Mechanics, Art, Design and Programming

Third Edition

Penny de Byl

CRC Press
Taylor & Francis Group
Boca Raton London New York

CRC Press is an imprint of the
Taylor & Francis Group, an **informa** business

CRC Press
Taylor & Francis Group
6000 Broken Sound Parkway NW, Suite 300
Boca Raton, FL 33487-2742

Printed on acid-free paper

International Standard Book Number-13: 978-1-138-48073-5 (Hardback)
                                      978-1-138-48062-9 (Paperback)

Library of Congress Cataloging-in-Publication Data

Names: De Byl, Penny, author.
Title: Holistic game development with Unity : an all-in-one guide to implementing game mechanics, art, design and programming/ Penny de Byl.
Description: Third edition. | Boca Raton : Taylor & Francis, 2019.
Identifiers: LCCN 2018058220 | ISBN 9781138480629 (pbk. : alk. paper) |
ISBN 9781138480735 (hardback : alk. paper)
Subjects: LCSH: Unity (Electronic resource) | Computer games--Programming. | Video games--Design.
Classification: LCC QA76.76.C672 D42 2019 | DDC 794.8/1525--dc23
LC record available at HYPERLINK "https://protect-us.mimecast.com/s/Ij6pCG6Y9jf1gp21yiQBwxB?domain=lccn.loc.gov" https://lccn.loc.gov/2018058220

Visit the Taylor & Francis Web site at
http://www.taylorandfrancis.com

and the CRC Press Web site at
http://www.crcpress.com

Contents

Preface..xi
Acknowledgments... xv
Author xvii

Chapter 1: The Art of Programming Mechanics.......................1
  1.1   Introduction 1
  1.2   Programming on the Right Side of the Brain 3
  1.3   Creating Art from the Left Side of the Brain 8
       1.3.1   Point 9
       1.3.2   Line 9
       1.3.3   Shape 10
       1.3.4   Direction 11
       1.3.5   Size 12
       1.3.6   Texture..13
       1.3.7   Color 14
  1.4   How Game Engines Work...............................17
       1.4.1   A Generic Game Engine.........................17
       1.4.2   The Main Loop 18
  1.5   A Scripting Primer 27
       1.5.1   Logic...28
       1.5.2   Comments 31
       1.5.3   Functions 33
       1.5.4   Variables 34
             1.5.4.1   C# Variables 37
       1.5.5   Operators 43
             1.5.5.1   Arithmetic Operators.................43
             1.5.5.2   Relational Operators 43
       1.5.6   Conditional Statements........................ 46
       1.5.7   Arrays 54
       1.5.8   Objects..57
  1.6   A Game Art Asset Primer 62
       1.6.1   The Power of Two Rule..........................63
       1.6.2   Using Other People's Art Assets 68
  1.7   Summary 72

Chapter 2: Real-World Mechanics 73
  2.1   Introduction 73
  2.2   Principles of Vectors....................................74
  2.3   Defining 2D and 3D Space.............................79
       2.3.1   Cameras... 80

	2.3.2	Local and World Coordinate Systems	87
	2.3.3	Translation, Rotation, and Scaling	87
	2.3.4	Polygons and Normals	91
2.4	Two-Dimensional Games in a 3D Game Engine		95
	2.4.1	Quaternions?	100
	2.4.2	Quaternions to the Rescue	103
2.5	The Laws of Physics		113
	2.5.1	The Law of Gravity	114
	2.5.2	The First Law of Motion	116
	2.5.3	The Second Law of Motion	120
	2.5.4	The Third Law of Motion	121
2.6	Physics and the Principles of Animation		123
	2.6.1	Squash and Stretch	125
	2.6.2	Anticipation	131
	2.6.3	Follow-Through	132
	2.6.4	Secondary Motion	134
2.7	2D and 3D Tricks for Optimizing Game Space		137
	2.7.1	Reducing Polygons	138
		2.7.1.1 Use Only What You Need	138
		2.7.1.2 Backface Culling	138
		2.7.1.3 Level of Detail	140
	2.7.2	Fog	143
	2.7.3	Textures	143
		2.7.3.1 Moving Textures	144
		2.7.3.2 Blob Shadows	145
	2.7.4	Billboards	146
2.8	Summary		149

Chapter 3: Animation Mechanics ... **151**

3.1	Introduction	151
3.2	Sprites	153
3.3	Texture Atlas	153
3.4	Animated Sprites	157
3.5	Baked 3D Animations	163
3.6	Biomechanics	173
3.7	Animation Management	177
	3.7.1	Single 2D Sprite Actions	177
	3.7.2	Single-Filed 3D Animations	182
3.8	Secondary Animation	184
3.9	Summary	187

Chapter 4: Game Rules and Mechanics ... **189**

| 4.1 | Introduction | 189 |
| 4.2 | Game Mechanics | 190 |

4.3 Primary Mechanics.................................... 192
    4.3.1   Searching................................ 192
    4.3.2   Matching................................. 193
    4.3.3   Sorting 193
    4.3.4   Chancing 194
    4.3.5   Mixing................................... 195
    4.3.6   Timing 195
    4.3.7   Progressing.............................. 196
    4.3.8   Capturing 196
    4.3.9   Conquering............................... 196
    4.3.10   Avoidance 197
    4.3.11   Collecting 197
4.4 Developing with Some Simple Game Mechanics...... 198
    4.4.1   Matching and Sorting...................... 198
    4.4.2   Shooting, Hitting, Bouncing, and Stacking....217
    4.4.3   Racing................................... 223
    4.4.4   Avoidance and Collecting.................. 227
    4.4.5   Searching................................ 235
4.5 Rewards and Penalties 238
4.6 Summary 242
Reference 242

Chapter 5: Character Mechanics................................... 243
5.1 Introduction 243
5.2 Line of Sight 245
5.3 Graph Theory...................................... 250
5.4 Waypoints 251
    5.4.1   Searching through Waypoints.............. 252
5.5 Finite State Machines 269
5.6 Flocking 292
5.7 Decision Trees 301
5.8 Fuzzy Logic....................................... 306
5.9 Genetic Algorithms 317
5.10 Cellular Automata................................. 322
5.11 Summary 323

Chapter 6: Player Mechanics 325
6.1 Introduction 325
6.2 Game Structure.................................... 326
6.3 Principles of Game Interface Design 334
    6.3.1   User Profiling 334
    6.3.2   Metaphor................................. 335
    6.3.3   Feature Exposure 336
    6.3.4   Coherence................................ 337
    6.3.5   State Visualization 338
    6.3.6   Shortcuts................................ 338

	6.3.7	Layout	339
	6.3.8	Focus	340
	6.3.9	Help	340
6.4	Inventories		343
6.5	Teleportation		358
	6.5.1	Implicit Teleports	358
	6.5.2	Explicit Teleports	360
6.6	Summary		362

Chapter 7: Environmental Mechanics **363**

7.1	Introduction		363
7.2	Map Design Fundamentals		364
	7.2.1	Provide a Focal Point	364
	7.2.2	Guide and Restrict the Player's Movement	364
	7.2.3	Scaling	366
	7.2.4	Detail	366
	7.2.5	Map Layout	367
		7.2.5.1 Open	369
		7.2.5.2 Linear	369
		7.2.5.3 Branching	370
		7.2.5.4 Spoke and Hub	370
	7.2.6	Other Considerations	371
		7.2.6.1 Player Starting Position	371
		7.2.6.2 Flow	371
		7.2.6.3 Trapping	371
		7.2.6.4 Use the Third Dimension	371
		7.2.6.5 Vantage Points	372
7.3	Terrain		372
	7.3.1	Drawing a Terrain	373
	7.3.2	Procedural Terrain	378
	7.3.3	Procedural Cities	383
	7.3.4	Infinite Terrain	389
7.4	Camera Tricks		391
	7.4.1	Depth of Field	391
	7.4.2	Blur	392
	7.4.3	Grayscale	393
	7.4.4	Motion Blur	394
	7.4.5	Sepia Tone	394
	7.4.6	Twirl	394
	7.4.7	Bloom	394
	7.4.8	Flares	395
	7.4.9	Color Correction	395
	7.4.10	Edge Detection	395
	7.4.11	Crease	395
	7.4.12	Fish Eye	396
	7.4.13	Sun Shafts	396

	7.4.14	Vignette	396
	7.4.15	Screen Space Ambient Occlusion	396
7.5	Skies	....	401
	7.5.1	Skyboxes....................................	402
	7.5.2	SkyDomes	404
	7.5.3	Clouds	407
7.6	Weather	....	409
	7.6.1	Wind.......................................	409
	7.6.2	Precipitation	412
7.7	Particles	....	412
7.8	Summary	....	419
Reference	....		419

Chapter 8: Mechanics for External Forces **421**

8.1	Introduction	....	421
8.2	Mobile	....	422
	8.2.1	Design Considerations........................	422
		8.2.1.1	Text.....................................	423
		8.2.1.2	Icons and User Interface Elements ...	424
		8.2.1.3	Gameplay............................	424
	8.2.2	Haptics......................................	434
	8.2.3	Accelerometer	434
	8.2.4	Orientation..................................	436
	8.2.5	Web Services	439
	8.2.6	GPS	445
8.3	Gestures and Motion		450
8.4	3D Viewing	....	454
	8.4.1	Side-by-Side	454
	8.4.2	Anaglyphs	456
	8.4.3	Head-Mounted Displays	457
8.5	Augmented Reality	....	458
8.6	The Social Mechanic	....	462
	8.6.1	External Application Security Matters	463
	8.6.2	Twitter	465
	8.6.3	Facebook	466
8.7	Platform Deployment: The App Store, Android Market, and Consoles.		466
	8.7.1	Publishing for the App Store and Android Market	466
	8.7.2	Console Publishing	467
	8.7.3	Download Direct to Player	468
8.8	Summary	....	468
8.9	A Final Word	....	469

Index **471**

Preface

About This Book

I first decided to write this book in 2010 when I found existing literature for budding game designers, artists, and programmers tended to focus on only one specific vein of games development, that being either a design, artistic, or programming book. Those with artistic talents and ideas for games could not find a good resource to ease them into programming. On the other hand, programming texts tended to be dry and ignore the visual aspect.

At the time, the face of the game development industry was rapidly changing from a small number of large development teams to much more of a cottage industry consisting of small multi-skilled teams. And today, some eight years later, it is more imperative than ever that individuals are skilled in both art and programming.

Game development tools are also not what they used to be, and rapid game development tools such as Unity are making it a possibility for individuals to make complete games from scratch. It's also becoming almost impossible to write a book about software and have it published before the software is updated. Year after year we see advancements that quickly make printed material obsolete.

To address all these issues, this book is written for the artist who wants to program and the programmer who wants some pointers about using game art. In the beginning, I started writing just for artists, but soon came to realize the content was equally as relevant to those wanting to learn how to start programming games. In addition, the content inside these pages is organized by theory first, followed by application and practice in Unity. While the theory will remain relevant long into the future, the versions of Unity and how the interface changes will not, although, to Unity's credit, the interfaces from one version to another are mostly the same. What you'll find inside these pages are code and techniques that work from versions 5.6 through to 2019.

How This Book Is Organized

This book has been written with *artists who want to learn how to develop games* and *programmers who want to learn about using art in games* in mind. It approaches game development in a unique combination of teaching programming that keeps design in mind, because programming a games graphical user interface is entirely different from making it look good.

Learning about how design impacts programming and vice versa is a logical way to introduce both sides of the game development coin to game creation.

All chapters focus on sets of mechanical functions existing within games:

- Chapter 1, The Art of Programming Game Mechanics, explains the roles both art and programming play in creating games and explores the limitations of having one without the other. In addition, the complementary nature of digital art and programming is established.
- Chapter 2, Real World Mechanics, examines the branch of physics dealing with the study of motion. Motion is a fundamental idea in all of science that transcends the computer screen into virtual environments. This chapter examines kinematics, which describes motion, and dynamics, examining the causes of motion with respect to their use in computer games. It introduces the physical properties of the real world and demonstrates how a fundamental understanding of mathematics, physics, and design principles is critical in any game environment. Composition, rules of animation, and design principles are introduced in parallel with technical considerations, mathematics, and programming code that controls and defines the movement of characters, cameras, environments, and other game objects.
- Chapter 3, Animation Mechanics, studies the technical nature of 2D and 3D animated models. The reader will develop skills with respect to the programmatic control of their own artwork, models, and/or supplied assets in a game environment. Elementary mathematics, physics, and programming concepts are introduced, demonstrating the concepts of keyframes, animation states, and the development of dynamic character movement and sprite animation.
- Chapter 4, Game Rules and Mechanics, introduces common generic game mechanics such as matching, sorting, managing, and hitting. Examples of how each of these is visually represented in a game and the programming that controls them are explained in depth. Common algorithms and data structures used for each mechanic are worked through with the reader, integrating the key art assets where appropriate.
- Chapter 5, Character Mechanics, explains simple artificial intelligence algorithms to assist the reader in creating their own believable non-player characters. Animation states and techniques covered in Chapter 3 are integrated with game-specific data structures and algorithms to control the behavior of characters, from the flocking of birds to opponents that follow and interact with the player.
- Chapter 6, Player Mechanics, presents the code and artwork that will be deployed to develop graphical user interfaces and maintain player states. It includes details about the development of inventory systems, heads-up displays, and character–environment interaction.

- Chapter 7, Environmental Mechanics, reveals the fundamental concepts in creating and optimizing game environments. It covers techniques that range from adding detail to environments to make them more believable to tricks for working with large maps and weather simulations.
- Chapter 8, Mechanics for External Forces, examines issues related to developing games while keeping in mind the new plethora of input devices, social data, GPS locators, motion sensors, augmented reality, and screen sizes. Practical advice is included for using Unity to deploy games that leverage touch screens, accelerometers, and networking to the iPhone, iPad, and Android mobile devices.

The Companion Website

The website accompanying this book is http://www.holistic3d.com. It contains all of the files referred to in the workshops, finished examples, and other teaching and learning resources.

More Holistic3D Resources

Join Penny's students online on Discord at https://discord.gg/su2zar2 or Facebook at https://www.facebook.com/groups/hgdev.

To accompany this book, there is also a YouTube channel updated constantly with new techniques and game development examples in Unity. This can be found at https://www.youtube.com/c/holistic3d. There are also several high-quality online video courses produced by the author, which you can access at a heavily discounted rate with the following coupons. These courses cover a vast range of topics from animation to procedural terrain generation to machine learning. You can find each here:

Augmented Reality:
https://www.udemy.com/augmented_reality_with_unity/?couponCode=H3DGAMEDEVBOOK
Procedural Terrain Generation:
https://www.udemy.com/procedural-terrain-generation-with-unity/?couponCode=H3DGAMEDEVBOOK
Machine Learning:
https://www.udemy.com/machine-learning-with-unity/?couponCode=H3DGAMEDEVBOOK
Shader Development:
https://www.udemy.com/unity-shaders/?couponCode=H3DGAMEDEVBOOK
Artificial Intelligence:
https://www.udemy.com/artificial-intelligence-in-unity/?couponCode=H3DGAMEDEVBOOK
Minecraft Voxel Worlds:
https://www.udemy.com/unityminecraft/?couponCode=H3DGAMEDEVBOOK

C# Programming:
https://www.udemy.com/naked_cs/?couponCode=H3DGAMEDEVBOOK
Networking:
https://www.udemy.com/unet_intro/?couponCode=H3DGAMEDEVBOOK
Animation:
*https://www.udemy.com/mastering-3d-animation-in-unity/?couponCode
=H3DGAMEDEVBOOK*

Acknowledgments

First, I'd like to thank my editor, Sean Connelly, who has kept my project on track. His encouragement and enthusiasm for the book have been highly motivating. In addition, thanks must go to Mark Ripley of Effervescing Elephant Interactive, who acted as the initial technical editor and provided valuable insight on game programming with Unity, as well as Rachel, Ramesh, and Joy from the Unity educational team, without whose enthusiasm this third edition of the book wouldn't have materialized.

Next, I'd like to acknowledge Unity3d, who have helped shape the content of the book through their reviews and the development of a truly inspirational game development tool; as well as all of the forum contributors who have freely shared their ideas and code to answer all conceivable game development questions. The forums at http://forums.unity3d.com are an invaluable knowledge base.

Finally, I'd like to thank my family, Daniel, Tabytha, and Merlin (my labrador). Daniel has been an absolute rock. His knowledge of Microsoft Word formatting still leaves me amazed, and his proofreading and testing of all the workshops have saved so much time, which has been an invaluable contribution to this work (i.e., if the code in this book doesn't work for you— blame him! ☺). Tabytha has also been a source of inspiration, as she's now at an age where programming and mathematics are becoming fascinating to her. Her journey with Unity is just beginning. As always, Merlin has provided constant companionship and copious amounts of fur by sitting constantly under the desk at my feet, snoring and snuffling.

I should also thank my close friends, Kayleen and James, who've provided editorial, art directing, code testing, and rewriting support over the years; and especially Adrian, who's been a hard-working little minion for me over the final few weeks of pulling this third version together. His dedication to the project and occasional comic relief have been greatly appreciated.

To me, game development is the quintessential seam where the tectonic plates of programming and art meet: It is where both domains really start to make sense. If you are reading this, I hope you feel the same.

Author

Dr. Penny de Byl, former university professor of games and multimedia, is the founder of Holistic3D.com, an online education provider for all things games related. She has researched and taught computer science, computer graphics, animation, artificial intelligence, and mobile game development for over 25 years and has students working for Ubisoft, Apple, The Binary Mill, and Unity. Penny hosts the popular Unity development YouTube channel, Holistic3D.

CHAPTER 1

The Art of Programming Mechanics

Everyone can be taught to sculpt: Michelangelo would have had to be taught how not to. So it is with the great programmers.

Alan Perlis

1.1 Introduction

In 1979, art teacher Betty Edwards published the acclaimed *Drawing on the Right Side of the Brain*. The essence of the text taught readers to draw what they saw, rather than what they *thought* they saw. The human brain is so adept at tasks such as pattern recognition that we internally symbolize practically everything we see and regurgitate these patterns when asked to draw them on paper. Children do this very well. The simplicity in children's drawing stems from their internal representation for an object. Ask them to draw a house and a dog and you will get something you and they can recognize as a house and dog (or, more accurately, the icon for a house and dog), but something that is far from what an actual house and dog look like.

FIG **1.1** Dogs in the yard of a castle, by Tabytha de Byl, age 4.

This is evident in the child's drawing in Figure 1.1. The title of the book, *Drawing on the Right Side of the Brain*, also suggests that the ability to draw should be summoned from the side of the brain traditionally associated with creativity and that most *bad* drawings could be blamed on the left.

Different intellectual capability is commonly attributed to either the left or the right hemispheres, with the left side being responsible for the processing of language, mathematics, numbers, logic, and other such computational activities, whereas the right side deals with shapes, patterns, spatial acuity, images, dreaming, and creative pursuits. From these beliefs, those who are adept at computer programming are classified as left brained and artists as right brained. The segregation of these abilities to either side of the brain is called *lateralization*. While lateralization has been generally accepted and even used to classify and separate students into learning style groups, it is a common misconception that intellectual functioning can be separated so clearly.

In fact, the clearly defined left and right brain functions are a *neuromyth* stemming from the overgeneralization and literal isolation of the brain hemispheres. While some functions tend to reside more in one side of the brain than the other, many tasks, to some degree, require both sides. For example, many numerical computation and language activities require both hemispheres. Furthermore, the side of the brain being utilized for specific tasks can vary among people. Studies have revealed that 97% of right-handed people use their left hemisphere for language and speech processing and 70% of left-handed people use their right hemisphere.

In short, simply classifying programmers as left brainers and artists as right brainers is a misnomer. This also leads to the disturbing misconception that programmers are poor at art skills and that artists would have difficulty in understanding programming. Programming is so often generalized as a logical process and art as a creative process that some find it inconceivable that programmers could be effective as artists and vice versa.

When Betty Edwards suggests that people should use their right brain for drawing, it is in concept, not physiology. The location of the neurons the reader is being asked to use to find their creative self is not relevant. What is important is that Dr. Edwards is asking us to see drawing in a different light—in a way we may not have considered before. Instead of drawing our internalized symbol of an object that has been stored away in the brain, she asks us to draw what we see—to forget what we *think* it looks like. In the end, this symbolizes a switch in thinking away from logic and patterns to images and visual processing.

There is no doubt that some people are naturally better at programming and others at art. However, by taking Edwards' *anyone can draw* attitude, we can also say *anyone can program*. It just requires a little practice and a change of attitude.

1.2 Programming on the Right Side of the Brain

While it is true that pure logic is at the very heart of all computer programs, it still requires an enormous amount of creativity to order the logic into a program. The process is improved greatly when programmers can visualize the results of their code before it even runs. You may liken this to a scene from *The Matrix* where the characters look at screens of vertically flowing green numbers and text, but can visualize the structure and goings on in a photorealistic, three-dimensional virtual reality. To become a good computer programmer, you need to know the language of the code and be able to visualize how it is affecting the computer's memory and the results of running the program.

Learning a computer language is one key to being able to program. However, understanding how the language interacts with the computer to produce its output is even more important. Good programmers will agree that it is easy to switch between programming languages once you have mastered one. The fundamental concepts in each language are the same. In some languages, such as C, C++, C#, JavaScript, Java, and PHP, even the text and layout look the same. The basic code from each aforementioned language to print *Hello World* on the computer screen is shown in Listings 1.1 through 1.6.

Listing 1.1 C

```c
#include <stdio.h>
main()
{
    printf("Hello World");
}
```

Listing 1.2 C++

```cpp
#include <iostream>
using namespace std;
void main()
{
    cout << "Hello World" << endl;
}
```

Listing 1.3 C#

```csharp
public class HelloWorld
{
public static void Main()
    {
        System.Console.WriteLine("Hello World");
    }
}
```

Listing 1.4 JavaScript (in bold) embedded in HTML

```html
<html>
    <head>
        <title> Hello World </title>
    </head>
    <body>
        <script type = "text/javascript">
            document.write('Hello World');
        </script>
    </body>
</html>
```

Listing 1.5 Java

```java
class helloworld
{
    public static void main(String args[])
    {
        System.out.println("Hello World");
    }
}
```

Listing 1.6 PHP

```php
<?php
    echo "Hello World";
?>
```

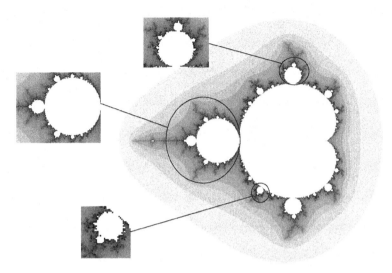

FIG 1.2 The Mandelbrot set and periodicities of orbits.

Umberto Eco, the creator of *Opera Aperta*, described the concept of art as mechanical relationships between features that can be reorganized to make a series of distinct works. This is true of programming, too. The same lines of programming code can be reorganized to create many different programs. Nowhere is this shared art/programming characteristic more obvious than in fractals.

Fractals are shapes made up of smaller self-similar copies of themselves. The famous Mandelbrot set or *Snowman* is shown in Figure 1.2. The whole shape is made up of smaller versions of itself. As you look closer, you will be able to spot tens or even hundreds of smaller snowman shapes within the larger image.

A fractal is constructed from a mathematical algorithm repeated over and over where the output is interpreted as a point and color on the computer screen. The Mandelbrot set comes from complex equations, but not all fractal algorithms require high-level mathematical knowledge to understand.

The Barnsley fern leaf is the epitome of both the creative side of programming and the algorithmic nature of art. Put simply, the algorithm takes a shape, any shape, and transforms it four times, as shown in Figure 1.3. It then takes the resulting shape and puts it through the same set of transformations. This can be repeated ad infinitum; however, around 10 iterations of this process give a good impression of the resulting image (see Figure 1.4).

Creating images with these types of algorithmic approaches is called *procedural* or *dynamic generation*. It is a common method for creating

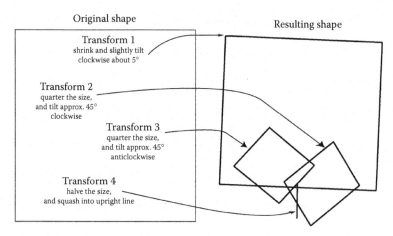

FIG 1.3 Transformations of Barnsley's fern leaf.

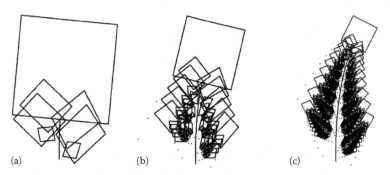

(a) (b) (c)

FIG 1.4 Three iterations of Barnsley's fern leaf transformations after (a) 2 iterations, (b) 5 iterations, and (c) 10 iterations.

assets such as terrain, trees, and special effects in games. Although procedural generation can create game landscapes and other assets before a player starts playing, procedural generation comes into its own *while* the game is being played. Programming code can access the assets in a game during run time. It can manipulate an asset based on player input. For example, placing a large hole in a wall after the player has blown it up is achieved with programming code. This can only be calculated at the time the player interacts with the game, as beforehand a programmer would have no idea where the player would be standing or in what direction he would shoot. The game *Fracture* by Day 1 Studios features dynamic ground terrains that lift up beneath objects when shot with a special weapon.

◉ For Research

Procedural Generation in Unity

The Unity website has a project with numerous procedural generation demonstrations. At this point in your game-development learning journey, you may not be able to understand the underlying code, but the examples will show you what is possible and the types of things you will be able to achieve by the end of this book. The Unity project can be downloaded from https://assetstore.unity.com/packages/essentials/tutorial-projects/procedural-examples-5141.

A purpose-built programming language for creating art is *Processing*. The syntax of the code is not unlike JavaScript or C# and contains all the fundamental programming concepts you will learn about in Section 1.4. A book entitled *Creating Procedural Artworks with Processing: A Holistic Guide* by Dr. Penny de Byl that teaches these techniques is available on Amazon. The image in Figure 1.5 was created using Processing by randomly plotting circles and drawing a series of curves from a central location to each circle. Art created by Casey Reas, shown in Figure 1.6, programmed with Processing, has been displayed at the DAM Gallery in Berlin.

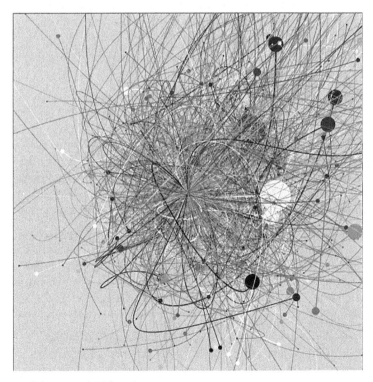

FIG 1.5 An image created with Processing.

FIG **1.6** Artwork created by Casey Reas using Processing, as exhibited at DAM Gallery, Berlin.

● For Research
Getting Started with Processing
If you're interested in learning more about Processing and drawing images with programming code, you can download the open source language and find tutorials at http://processing.org.

1.3 Creating Art from the Left Side of the Brain

Most people know what they like and do not like when they see art. However, if you ask them why they like it, they may not be able to put their thoughts into words. No doubt there are some people who are naturally gifted with the ability to draw and sculpt and some who are not. For the artistically challenged, however, hope is not lost. This is certainly Betty Edwards' stance.

A logical approach to the elements and principles of design reveals rules one can apply to create more appealing artwork. They are the mechanical relationships, alluded to by Umberto Eco, that can be used as building blocks to create works of art. These fundamentals are common threads found to run through all good artwork. They will not assist you in being creative and coming up with original art, but they will help in presentation and visual attractiveness.

The elements of design are the primary items that make up drawings, models, paintings, and design. They are *point*, *line*, *shape*, *direction*, *size*, *texture*, *color*, and *hue*. All visual artworks include one or more of these elements.

In the graphics of computer games, each of these elements is as important to the visual aspect of game assets as they are in drawings, painting, and sculptures. However, as each is being stored in computer memory and processed by mathematical algorithms, their treatment by the game artist differs.

1.3.1 Point

All visual elements begin with a point. In drawing, it is the first mark put on paper. Because of the physical makeup of computer screens, it is also the fundamental building block of all digital images. Each point on an electronic screen is called a *pixel*. The number of pixels visible on a display is referred to as the *resolution*. For example, a resolution of 1024 × 768 is 1024 pixels wide and 768 pixels high.

Each pixel is referenced by its *x* and *y* Cartesian coordinates. Because pixels are discrete locations on a screen, these coordinates are always in whole numbers. The default coordinate system for a screen has the (0,0) pixel in the upper left-hand corner. A screen with 1024 × 768 resolution would have the (1023,767) pixel in the bottom right-hand corner. The highest value pixel has *x* and *y* values that are one minus the width and height, respectively, because the smallest pixel location is referenced as (0,0). It is also possible to change the default layout depending on the application being used such that the *y* values of the pixels are flipped with (0,0) being in the lower left-hand corner or even moved into the center of the screen.

1.3.2 Line

On paper, a line is created by the stroke of a pen or brush. It can also define the boundary where two shapes meet. A line on a digital display is created by coloring pixels on the screen between two pixel coordinates. Given the points at the ends of a line, an algorithm calculates the pixel values that must be colored in to create a straight line. This is not as straightforward as it sounds, because the pixels can only have whole number coordinate values. The *Bresenham line algorithm* was developed by Jack E. Bresenham in 1962 to effectively calculate the best pixels to color in to give the appearance of a line. Therefore, the line that appears on a digital display can only ever be an approximation to the real line, as shown in Figure 1.7.

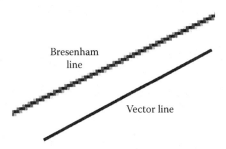

FIG 1.7 A real line and a Bresenham line.

1.3.3 Shape

A shape refers not only to primitive geometrics such as circles, squares, and triangles, but also to freeform and nonstandard formations. In computer graphics, polygons are treated as they are in geometry: a series of points called *vertices* connected by straight *edges*. By storing the coordinates of the vertices, the edges can be reconstructed using straight-line algorithms. A circle is often represented as a regular polygon with many edges. As the number of edges increases, a regular polygon approaches the shape of a circle.

Freeform objects involve the use of curves. To be stored and manipulated by the computer efficiently, these need to be stored in a mathematical format. Two common types of curves used include Bezier and non-uniform rational basis spline (NURBS).

A Bezier curve is constructed from a number of control points. The first and last points specify the start and end of the curve and the other points act as attractors, drawing the line toward them and forming a curve, as shown in Figure 1.8. A NURBS curve is similar to a Bezier curve in that it has a number of control points; however, the control points can be weighted such that some may attract more than others.

In computer graphics, a polygon is the basic building block for objects, whether in two dimensions (2D) or three dimensions (3D). A single polygon defines a flat surface onto which texture can be applied. The most efficient way to define a flat surface is through the use of three points; therefore, triangles are the polygon of choice for constructing models, although sometimes you will find square polygons used in some software packages. Fortunately for the artist, modeling software such as Autodesk's 3DS Studio Max and Blender do not require models to be handcrafted from triangles; instead, they automatically construct any objects using triangles as a base, as shown in Figure 1.9.

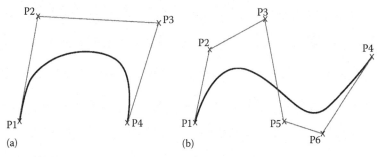

(a)   (b)

FIG 1.8 (a) A Bezier and (b) a NURBS curve.

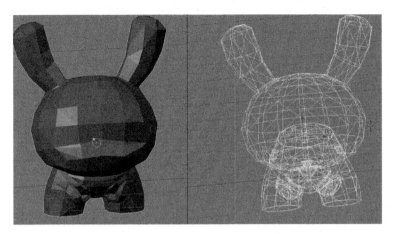

FIG 1.9 A 3D model constructed from triangles in Blender.

The wireframe model that represents a 3D object is called a *mesh*. The number of polygons in a mesh is called the *polycount*. The higher the polycount, the more triangles in the model and the more computer processing power required to render and manipulate the model. For this reason, computer game artists must find a balance between functionality and visual quality, as a high-resolution model is too costly with respect to making the game run slowly. The models must be dynamically processed and rendered in real time. In contrast, animated movie models can be of much higher quality, as they are not rendered in real time. Next time you are playing a game, take a closer look at how the models are constructed.

1.3.4 Direction

Direction is the orientation of a line. Depending on its treatment, it can imply speed and motion. A line can sit horizontal, vertical, or oblique. In computer graphics, physics, engineering, and mathematics, a *Euclidean vector* is used to specify direction. A vector stores information about how to get from one point in space to another in a straight line. Not only does it represent a direction, but also a distance, otherwise called its *magnitude*. The magnitude of a vector is taken from its length. Two vectors can point in the same direction but have different magnitudes, as shown in Figure 1.10a. In addition, two vectors can have the same magnitude but different directions, as shown in Figure 1.10b. A vector with a magnitude of 1 is *normalized*.

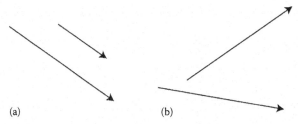

(a) (b)

FIG 1.10 (a) Vectors with the same direction but different magnitudes and (b) vectors with the same magnitude but different directions.

Vectors are a fundamental element in 3D games as they describe the direction in which objects are orientated, how they are moving, how they are scaled, and even how they are textured and lit. The basics of vectors are explored further in Chapter 2.

1.3.5 Size

Size is the relationship of the amount of space objects take up with respect to each other. In art and design, it can be used to create balance, focal points, or emphasis. In computer graphics, size is referred to as *scale*. An object can be scaled uniformly in any direction. Figure 1.11 shows a 3D object (a) scaled uniformly by 2 (b), vertically by 3 (c), horizontally by 0.5 (d), and vertically by −1 (e).

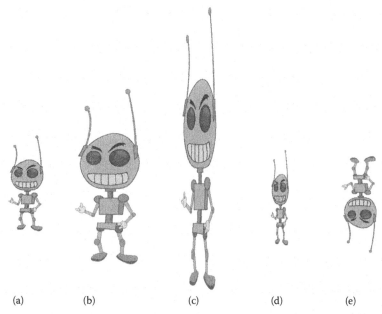

(a) (b) (c) (d) (e)

FIG 1.11 A 3D object scaled in multiple ways (a) the original object, (b) scaled uniformly by 2, (c) scaled vertically by 3, (d) scaled horizontally by 0.5, and (e) scaled vertically by −1.

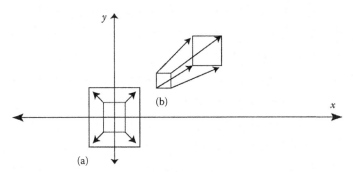

FIG 1.12 How can scaling move an object? (a) When vertices of an object around the origin are scaled, negative values become bigger negative values and the same with positive values. But the original center (0, 0) will remain (0, 0) when scaled. (b) If the vertices are all positive, then scaling them up will just make them bigger. And the final object moves location.

Note in Figure 1.11e how scaling by a negative value flips the object vertically. This can also be achieved uniformly or horizontally using negative scaling values.

Depending on the coordinates of an object, scaling will also move it. For example, if an object is centered around (0,0), it can be scaled remaining in the same place. However, if the object is away from (0,0), it will move by an amount proportional to the scale. This occurs as scaling values are multiplied with vertex coordinates to resize objects. A vertex at (0,0) multiplied by 2, for example, will remain at (0,0), whereas a vertex at (3,2) multiplied by 2 will move to (6,4). This is illustrated in Figure 1.12.

1.3.6 Texture

In art and design, texture relates to the surface quality of a shape or object. For example, the surface could be rough, smooth, or highly polished. In computer games, texture refers not only to the quality, but also to any photographs, colors, or patterns on the surface where the surface is defined by a polygon.

In games, textures are created using image files called *maps*. They are created in Adobe Photoshop or similar software. The image that gives an object its color is called a *texture map*, *color map*, or *diffuse coloring*. All images are mapped onto an object, polygon by polygon, using a technique called *UV mapping*. This aligns points on an image with the vertices of each polygon. The part of the image between the points is then stretched across the polygon. This process is shown on a square polygon in Figure 1.13.

To add a tactile appearance to the surface of a polygon to enhance the base texture, *bump mapping* is applied. This gives the object an appearance of having bumps, lumps, and grooves without the actual model itself being changed. Bump mapping is often applied to add more depth to an object

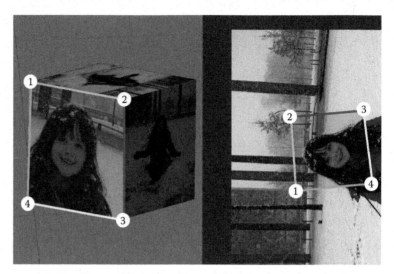

FIG 1.13 The UV mapping process. Vertices of a polygon on an object are mapped to locations on a 2D image.

with respect to the way light and shadow display on the surface. Figure 1.14 illustrates the application of a color and normal map on a soldier mesh taken from Unity.

A variety of other effects also add further texture to a surface. For example, *specular lighting* can make an object look glossy or dull, and *shaders*, small programs that manipulate the textures on a surface, can add a plethora of special effects from bubbling water to toon shading.

1.3.7 Color

In the theory of visual art involving pigments, color is taught as a set of primary colors (red, yellow, and blue) from which all other colors can be created. The color perceived by the human eye is the result of light being reflected off the surface of the artwork. When all of the light is reflected, we see white. When none of the light is reflected, we see black. The resulting color of a mixture of primaries is caused by some of the light being absorbed by the pigment. This is called a *subtractive* color model, as the pigments subtract some of the original light source before reflecting the remainder.

The light from a digital display follows an additive color model. The display emits different colors by combining the primary sources of red, green, and blue light. For this reason, color is represented in computer graphics as a three- or four-numbered value in the format (red, green, blue, and alpha). In some formats, the alpha value is not used, making color a three-value representation.

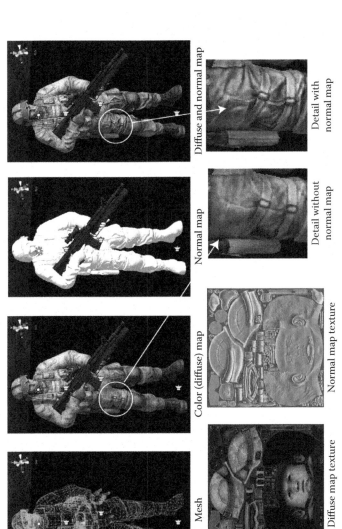

Mesh

Color (diffuse) map

Normal map

Diffuse and normal map

Detail with normal map

Detail without normal map

Normal map texture

Diffuse map texture

FIG 1.14 A soldier mesh with and without a color map and a normal map.

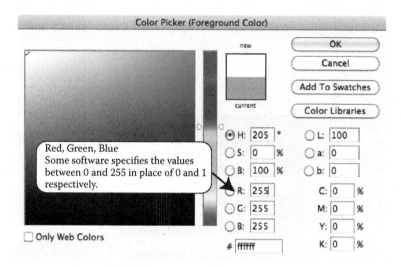

FIG 1.15 The Adobe Photoshop color picker.

Alpha represents the transparency of a color. When a surface has a color applied with an alpha of 0, it is fully transparent; when it has a value of 1, it is totally opaque. A value of 0.5 makes it partially transparent. Values for red, green, and blue also range between 0 and 1, where 0 indicates none of the color and 1 indicates all of the color. Imagine the values indicate a dial for each colored lamp. When the value is set to 0, the lamp is off and when the value is set to 1, it is at full strength—any values in between give partial brightness. For example, a color value of (1,0,0,1) will give the color red. A color value of (1,1,0,1) will give the color yellow. The easy way to look up values for a color is to use the color picker included with most software, including MS Word and Adobe Photoshop. The color picker from Adobe Photoshop is shown in Figure 1.15.

Also included with most color pickers is the ability to set the color using different color models. The one shown in Figure 1.15 includes a Hue, Saturation, and Brightness model, as well as a CMYK model. For more information on these, check out http://en.wikipedia.org/wiki/Color_model.

● **Note**

An alternate way to set the value of a color is with values between 0 and 255 instead of between 0 and 1. It depends on the software you are using. In programming, values are usually between 0 and 1, but more commonly between 0 and 255 in color pickers.

1.4 How Game Engines Work

A game engine takes all the hard work out of creating a game. In the not so distant past, game developers had to write each game from scratch or modify older similar ones. Eventually game editor programs started to surface that allowed developers to create games without having to write a lot of the underlying code.

The game engine takes care of things such as physics, sound, graphics processing, and user input, allowing game developers to get on with the creation of high-level game mechanics. For example, in Unity, physical properties can be added to a ball with the click of a button to make it react to gravity and bounce off hard surfaces. Driving these behaviors, embedded in the engine, are millions of lines of complex code containing many mathematical functions related to real-world physics. The game developer can spend more time designing what the ball looks like and even selecting the type of material it is made from without having a background in Newtonian physics.

1.4.1 A Generic Game Engine

To understand how a game engine works, we will first look at a simple illustration of all its components. A conceptualization is shown in Figure 1.16.

The game engine is responsible for the running of a variety of components that manage all the game resources and behaviors. The *Physics Manager* handles how game objects interact with each other and the environments

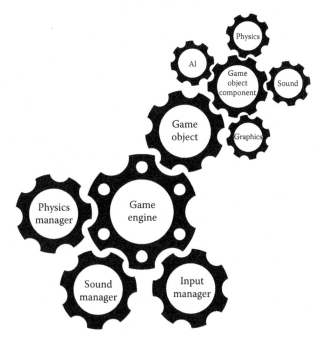

FIG 1.16 Parts of a generic game engine.

by simulating real-world physics. The *Input Manager* looks after interactions between the player and the game. It manages the drawing of graphical user interfaces and the handling of mouse clicks and the like. The *Sound Manager* is responsible for initializing and controlling how sound is delivered from the game to the player. If 3D sound is called for, it will ensure that the right sound at the right volume is sent to the correct computer speaker.

In addition to these managers are game objects. Game objects represent all the assets placed in a game environment. These include the terrain, sky, trees, weapons, rocks, nonplayer characters, rain, explosions, and so on. Because game objects represent a very diverse set of elements, they can also be customized through the addition of components that may include elements of artificial intelligence (AI), sound, graphics, and physics. The AI component determines how a game object will behave. For example, a rock in a scene would not have an AI component, but an enemy computer-controlled character would have AI to control how it attacks and pursues the player. A sound component gives a game object a sound. For example, an explosion would have a sound component whereas a tree may not. The physics component allows a game object to act within the physics system of the game. For example, physics added to a rock would see it roll down a hill or bounce and break apart when it falls. The graphics component dictates how the game object is drawn. This is the way in which it is presented to players on the screen. Some game objects will be visible and some will not. For example, a tree in a scene is a visible game object, whereas an autosave checkpoint, which may be a location in a game level, is not.

1.4.2 The Main Loop

All games run in the same way, as illustrated in Figure 1.17. There is an initialization stage in which computer memory is allocated, saved information is retrieved, and graphics and peripheral devices are checked. This is followed by the *main game loop* or *main loop*. The main loop runs continuously over and over again until the player decides to quit the game. While in the main loop, the game executes a cycle of functions that processes user input messages; checks through all game objects and updates their state, including their position; updates the environment with respect to game object positions, user interaction, and the physics system; and finally renders the new scene to the screen.

Essentially each loop renders one frame of graphics on the screen. The faster the loop executes, the smoother the animation of the game appears. The more processing that needs to be performed during the main loop, the slower it will execute. As the number of game objects increases, the amount of work the main loop has to do also increases and therefore slows down the time between frames being rendered on the screen. This time is called *frames per second* (FPS).

Game developers strive for very high FPS, and for today's computers and consoles, FPS can extend beyond 600. In some circumstances, however,

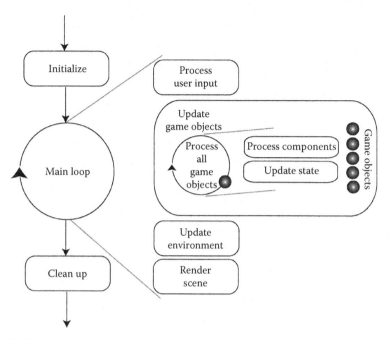

FIG 1.17 How a game runs.

such as on mobile devices with less processing power, FPS can become very low with only several game objects, and the animation will flicker, and user controls will be nonresponsive. Having said this, beginner game developers need to be aware of this issue, as even on a very powerful computer, adding a lot of highly detailed game objects can soon bring the FPS to a grinding halt. Anything below 25 FPS is considered unacceptable, and as it approaches 15 FPS the animation starts to flicker.

◁ Unity Specifics
Game Objects
Game objects are the fundamental building blocks for Unity games. It is through the addition, modification, and interaction of game objects that you will create your own game. After adding a game object in Unity (which you will do in the next section) a variety of components can be added to give the game object different functionalities. In all, there are seven components categories. These will be thoroughly explored throughout this book. In short, they are *Mesh*, *Particles*, *Physics*, *Audio*, *Rendering*, *Miscellaneous*, and *Scripts* as shown in Figure 1.18. A game object can have all, none, or any combination of these components added. The game object exemplified in Figure 1.18 has at least one of each of these component types added.

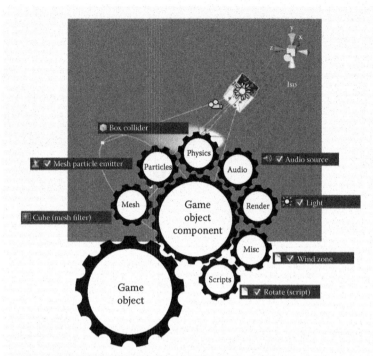

FIG 1.18 Components that can be added to a game object in Unity.

A Mesh component handles the drawing of an object. Without a Mesh component, the game object is not visible. A Particles component allows for a game object to have a particle system added. For example, if the game object were a jet fighter, a particle system could be added to give the effect of after burners. A Physics component gives the game object real world physical properties so it can be collided with and affected by gravity and other physics effects. An Audio component adds sound or sound effects to a game object. For example, if the game object were a car, the noise of a car engine could be added. A Rendering component adds special effects to a game object such as emitting light. Miscellaneous components include a variety of affects for the game object that do not fit within other categories. In Figure 1.18 the Wind Zone component is shown as a type of miscellaneous component. In brief, this causes the game object to become a source of wind for interaction within the physics system. Last, Scripts are components that contain programming code to alter the behavior of a game object. Scripts can be used for a large variety of purposes and are fundamental to developing game mechanics and tying an entire game together.

In Unity, scripts added to game objects can be written in C#.

In addition to this traditional method of game engine use, Unity has also introduced (in 2019) methods to support multithreading and multicore processing. It is called the Entity-Component System (ECS). Such methods of programming depart heavily from the traditional object orientated or procedural methods that better facilitate beginners starting out and therefore will not be explored in this book. However, if you are interested in what's possible then check out the author's YouTube tutorials for this system at:

- https://youtu.be/Awf_Y4hBhBM
- https://youtu.be/Vg-V5G2JJNY

☺ Unity Hands On
Getting to know the Unity3D development environment
Step 1: To begin, download Unity by visiting http://unity3D.com/ and clicking on *Download*. Unity has a free version that lacks some functionality, but never expires. The free version is still quite powerful and certainly enough for the first time game developer. Once you have downloaded the software, follow the installation instructions to get Unity up and running.
Step 2: Running Unity for the first time reveals the multi-windowed editing environment shown in Figure 1.19. The tabs and windows can be dragged around to suit your own preferences.

☺ On the Web
Navigating the Unity Editor Interface
Visit the website for a short video demonstrating some best practices for finding your way around in the Unity Editor.

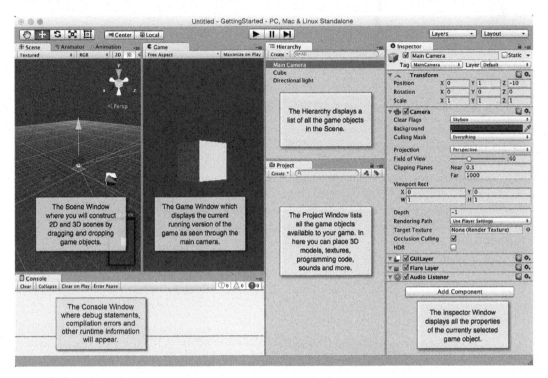

FIG 1.19 The Unity editing environment.

Step 3: After starting Unity, create a new project by selecting File > New Project. Note that the project name and directory used to save the project are one and the same; by default, this is "New Unity Project." The dialog box for creating a new project will allow you to choose 3D or 2D. For now select 3D.

Step 4: To create a simple scene, select GameObject > 3D Object > Cube from the main menu. All objects added to the game scene are called game objects in Unity. A cube will appear in the Hierarchy, Scene, Game, and Inspector windows.

● Note

From this point in the text, these windows will be referenced just by their capitalized names.

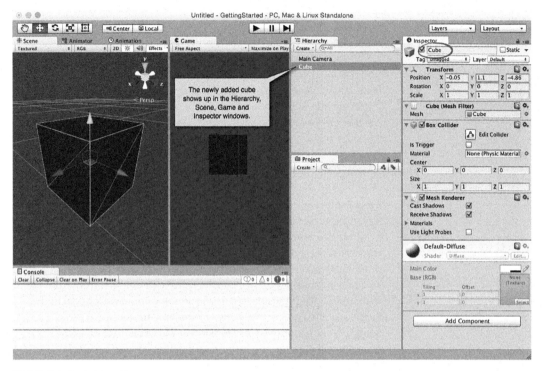

FIG 1.20 A single cube in a scene.

Step 5: If the cube appears very small, place your mouse in the Scene and use the scroll wheel to zoom in. You can also focus the scene on the cube by double-clicking it in the Hierarchy or selecting it in the Scene and pressing the F key. Note that your viewing position and angle in the Scene do not affect the look of the final game or change the attributes of any game objects. This initial Scene is shown in Figure 1.20. The Inspector shows all the properties of the cube. This includes its position, rotation, scale, the 3D mesh representing it, and a physics collider. We will look at these properties in more detail later.

Step 6: At this time, press the play button. As you have not added any functionality at this stage when running, all the game will do is display a static cube.

⚙ **Note**

Unity allows you to edit your game as it is running. This is great if you want to test out an idea to see how the game will react. Be careful though, because any changes you make in the editor, while play is on, will revert back to their previous value when you press stop. This can be very annoying if you've made large changes not realizing you are in play mode, as they will be wiped away as soon as you press stop. The only exceptions to this are script files, because they are edited and saved externally to the editor. Changes you make in script files are independent of the play button.

Step 7: Although lighting is a subject usually delayed for more advanced topics in game development, the author always likes to add a light to scenes to give them more depth and bring them alive. In the Scene, the cube is already shaded, as this is the default method of drawing. However, in the Game, the cube is a lifeless, flat, gray square. To add a light, select GameObject > Light > Directional Light from the main menu. A light displaying as a little sun symbol will appear in the Scene and the cube in the Game will become brighter.

Step 8: Now, because we are looking at the cube front on in the Game, it still appears as a little square. Therefore, we need to transform it for viewing. A transformation modifies the properties of position, rotation, and scale of a game object. The specifics of transformation are discussed later, but for now you can transform the cube quickly using the W key for changing position, the E key for rotating the objects, and the R key for scaling it. Before pressing any of these keys, ensure that the cube is selected in the Hierarchy window. When it is selected, it will have a green and blue wireframe displayed on it.

Step 9: In W (position) mode, the cube will be overlaid with red, green, and blue arrows. These represent the x, y, and z axes of the object. Clicking and dragging from any of the arrowheads will move the object along that axis. To move the object freely, click and drag from the central yellow box.

Step 10: In E (rotate) mode, the cube will have red, green, and blue circles drawn around it. Click and drag any of these circles to rotate the cube in the associated directions.

Step 11: In R (scale) mode, the red, green, and blue axes will include small cubes on the ends. Clicking and dragging any of these will change the scale of the object in the respective direction. You may also click and drag the central small cube to resize the object in all directions uniformly. Note that while you are moving, rotating, and scaling the cube, its appearance changes in the Game window. You will also notice that values in the Transform part of the Inspector change too. Move and scale the cube so that you can see it clearly in the Game window.

Step 12: The color of a GameObject comes from an associated material. To create a material, click on Create in the Project window and select Material. New material will appear in the Project window and, when selected, its properties in the Inspector are as shown in Figure 1.21.

Step 13: To change the color of this material, click on the white box next to Main Color in the Inspector. Select the color you want from the Color Popup and then close it. The large sphere view of the material in the Inspector will change to your chosen color. To change the name of the material, click on New Material once in the Project window. Wait a moment and then click on it again slowly. This will place you in editing mode for the material name. Type in a new name and hit the Enter key.

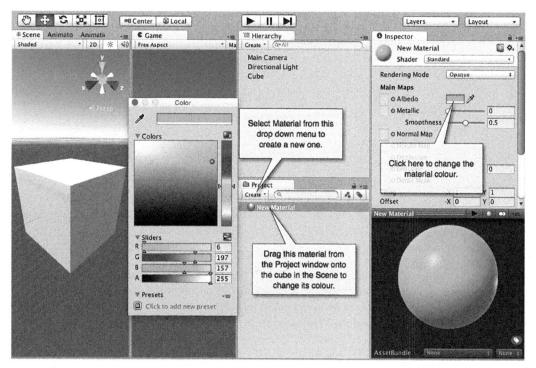

FIG 1.21 Creating a new material.

Step 14: To add material to the cube, drag and drop your material from the Project window onto the cube in the Scene. Alternatively, you can drag and drop the material from the Project window and drop it onto the cube listed in the Hierarchy window. Both will achieve the same effect. The cube will be colored.

Step 15: In the Project window, select Create and then C# Script. The C# script created will be called *NewbehaviorScript*. Change this, by slowly clicking on it, as you did with the material, to *spin*.

● **Note**
Naming C# Files
When you create a new C# Script, you only give it a name. Do not add *.cs* on the end. Unity will do this for you automatically. However, in the Project, *spin.cs* will only appear in the list as *spin*, without the *.cs* on the end.

Step 16: Double-click on it and a code/text editor will open for entering code. In the code editor type:

```
using System.Collections;
using System.Collections.Generic;
using UnityEngine;

public class spin : MonoBehaviour {

    // Use this for initialization
    void Start () {

    }

    // Update is called once per frame
    void Update () {
        transform.Rotate(Vector3.up * 10);
    }
}
```

The code must be EXACTLY as it appears here. Ensure that you have the correct spelling and capitalization; otherwise, it may not work. For large spaces, for example, before the word *transform*, insert a tab. When you are done, save your code in the text editor.

● **Note**
The code in Step 15 contains the Unity function *Update()*. Whatever code you place inside *Update()* will be run once each main loop. Therefore the code in Step 15 will run over and over again for the entire time the play button is down.

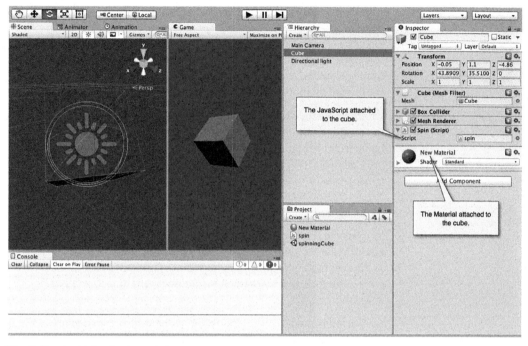

FIG 1.22 The cube with the spin script attached.

Step 17: Return to Unity and drag and drop the spin code from the Project window onto the cube in the Hierarchy window. You will notice that if you select the cube, the spin script will appear as a component added to the cube in the Inspector, as shown in Figure 1.22.

Step 18: Press the play button and watch as the cube spins.

Step 19: To save the application, select File > Save Scene from the main menu. In the dialog that pops up, give the scene a name such as *spinningCube*. Next, select File > Save Project from the main menu.

Each project you create can have multiple scenes. Scenes are saved inside projects. For example, an entire game application would be a single project. However, inside the game there would be multiple scenes, such as Main Menu, Help Screen, Map View, and 3D View. Single scenes can also be imported from one project to another.

1.5 A Scripting Primer

Hard-core programmers do not strictly consider scripting as programming, as it is a much simpler way of writing a program. Scripting languages have all the properties of programming languages; however, they tend to be less verbose and require less code to get the job done. For example, the

JavaScript and Java shown in Listings 1.4 and 1.5, respectively, demonstrate how the scripting language JavaScript requires much less code to achieve the same outcome as Java. The major difference between programming and scripting is that programming languages are compiled (built into a program by the computer) and then run afterward, and a scripting language is interpreted by another program as it runs.

When a program is compiled, it is turned into machine code the computer can understand. Compilation checks through the code for errors and then builds it into a program. Do not worry if you get lots of errors when you start programming. It is a normal part of the learning process. Some of the error messages will also seem quite vague and ambiguous for what they are trying to tell you. However, a quick search on Google will often reveal their true meaning.

C# is used in this book as the primary means of programming. Its syntax and constructs are closely related to C++, C, and Java; therefore, it is ideal to learn as a beginning language. It also provides a very powerful and yet simple way to develop game mechanics in Unity and many other game-editing environments.

Several fundamental constructs in programming are required to fully understand a programming language. These are variables, operations, arrays, conditions, loops, functions, and objects. However, the most fundamental and important concept that underlies everything is logic.

1.5.1 Logic

At the heart of all computers are the electronic switches on the circuit boards that cause them to operate. The fact that electricity has two states, on or off, is the underlying foundation on which programs are built. In simplistic terms, switches (otherwise known as relays) are openings that can either be opened or be closed, representing on and off, respectively. Imagine a basic circuit illustrated as a battery, electric cable, light switch, and light bulb, as shown in Figure 1.23.

When the switch is open, the circuit is broken, and the electricity is off. When the switch is closed, the circuit is complete, and the electricity is on. This is exactly how computer circuitry works. Slightly more complex switches called

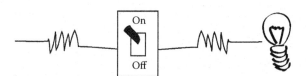

FIG 1.23 A very basic electric circuit.

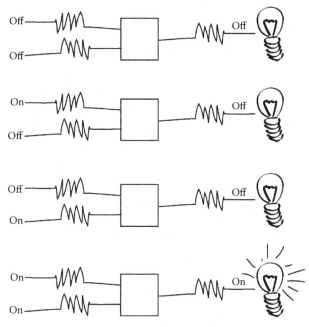

FIG **1.24** A conceptualization of an AND logic gate.

logic gates allow for the circuit to be opened or closed, depending on two incoming electrical currents instead of the one from the previous example.

In all, there are seven logic gate configurations that take two currents as input and a single current as output. These gates are called AND, OR, NOT, NAND, NOR, XOR, and XNOR. The AND gate takes two input currents; if both currents are on, the output current is on. If only one or none of the input currents is on, the output is off. This is illustrated in Figure 1.24.

In computer science, mathematics, physics, and many more disciplines the operation of combining two currents or signals into one is called *Boolean algebra (named after nineteenth-century mathematician George Boole)* and logic gate names (i.e., AND, OR) are called *Boolean functions*, although the *on* signal in computer science is referred to as TRUE, or the value 1, and *off* is FALSE, or 0. Using this terminology, all possible functions of the AND gate can be represented in *truth tables*, as shown in Table 1.1. It should be noted from Table 1.1 that truth tables can be written in a number of formats using 1s and 0s or TRUEs and FALSEs.

Each Boolean function has its own unique truth table. They work in the same way as the AND function does. They have two input values of TRUE and/or FALSE and one output value of TRUE or FALSE.

TABLE 1.1 Truth Table for the Boolean Function AND

Format 1			Format 2		
Input		*Output*	*Input*		*Output*
A	**B**	**A AND B**	**A**	**B**	**A AND B**
1	1	1	TRUE	TRUE	TRUE
1	0	0	TRUE	FALSE	FALSE
0	1	0	FALSE	TRUE	FALSE
0	0	0	FALSE	FALSE	FALSE

If you are just learning about programming for the first time right now, these concepts may seem a bit abstract and disconnected from real programming. However, as you learn more about programming, you will realize how fundamental knowing these truth tables is to a holistic understanding. It will become much clearer as you begin to write your own programs.

● Quick Reference

Boolean Algebra

Function	Boolean Algebra Syntax	C#	Truth Table		
AND	A · B	A && B	**Input**		**Output**
			A	**B**	**A AND B**
			0	0	0
			0	1	0
			1	0	0
			1	1	1
OR	A + B	A || B	**Input**		**Output**
			A	**B**	**A OR B**
			0	0	0
			0	1	1
			1	0	1
			1	1	1
NOT	Ā	! A	**Input**		**Output**
			A		**NOT**
			0		1
			1		0

● Quick Reference

Boolean Algebra (Continued)

Function	Boolean Algebra Syntax	C#	Truth Table		
NAND	$\overline{A \cdot B}$	!(A && B)	**Input**		**Output**
			A	**B**	**A NAND B**
			0	0	1
			0	1	1
			1	0	1
			1	1	0
NOR	$\overline{A+B}$	!(A || B)	**Input**		**Output**
			A	**B**	**A NOR B**
			0	0	1
			0	1	0
			1	0	0
			1	1	0
XOR	$A \oplus B$	(A && !B) || (!A && B)	**Input**		**Output**
			A	**B**	**A XOR B**
			0	0	0
			0	1	1
			1	0	1
			1	1	0
XNOR	$A \odot B$	(!A && !B) || (A && B)	**Input**	**Output**	**Output**
			A	**B**	**A XNOR B**
			0	0	1
			0	1	0
			1	0	0
			1	1	1

● **On the Website**

Interactive Boolean Algebra Logic Gates

Navigate to the book's website for an interactive Unity version of Boolean Algebra.

1.5.2 Comments

Comments are not actually programming code. They are, however, inserted lines of freeform text totally ignored by the compiler. They allow you to insert explanations about your code or little reminders of what your code does.

They are *very* useful when you write some groundbreaking code, leave it for six months, and then come back to it, having forgotten what it does. The author's advice is to use comments as frequently as possible. It is common practice to place comments at the top of each program file to give an overview of the entire code, as well as above each function. Another programmer may also insert comments if he makes a change. Some examples are shown in Listing 1.7.

Listing 1.7 A short program with comments

```
/*Program: Spin.cs
Description: Will rotate any game object around the y axis
Author:  Penny de Byl
*/
using System.Collections;
using System.Collections.Generic;
using UnityEngine;

public class Spin : MonoBehaviour {

    // Use this for initialization
    void Start () {

    }

    // Update is called once per frame
    void Update () {
        transform.Rotate(Vector3.up * 10);
    }
}
```

There are two types of comments. The first is a way to block out an entire paragraph. It begins with a /* and ends with */. You can write anything you want between these characters and it will be totally ignored by the compiler. The second type is a one liner. A line starting with // will also be ignored by the compiler but only until the end of the line. Therefore, you could write this:

```
/* Here are some comments about my program I wrote
to control a spinning cube in Unity. I used the code
I found in the Script Reference after doing a search
for the word Rotate.*/
```

or this:

```
//Here are some comments
//about my program I wrote
//to control a spinning cube
//in Unity. I used the code I
//found in the Script
//Reference after doing a
//search for the word Rotate
```

Use comments wisely and as you see fit. It is quite legitimate to write an entire program without comments; however, be warned, when you come back to code several months later you will be glad if you did leave them.

1.5.3 Functions

A *function* is a block that bundles a number of lines of code together to form a specific operation. It contains prewritten code that can be reused over and over again, saving programmers the stress of reinventing the wheel each time they write a program. Programmers can also write their own functions.

Whenever the author thinks of functions, she visualizes them as food processing machines. You put vegetables in, they get processed, and you get chopped, mashed, or minced vegetables out.

The most common newbie function taught is print() or a derivative thereof. This function takes input and prints it to the screen. For example,

```
print("Hello Unity");
```

will print

```
Hello Unity
```

on the screen or console.

The functions available to you as a programmer will depend on the programming language. JavaScript has numerous standard functions, but also takes on added ones depending on the context. For example, when JavaScript is embedded into the HTML of a web page,

```
document.write("Hello Unity");
```

will display the text on the web page when viewed inside a browser.

◁ **Unity Specifics**
Functions
Several essential functions need to be included in your code to talk to Unity. As Unity is running your game, it will look through code attached to all game objects for functions it needs to execute at any particular time. For example, the *Update()* function runs once each main loop. If there are five game objects each with *Update()* functions in their scripts, then all five *Update()* functions will be executed.

Another useful function is *Start()*. This function runs just once during the lifetime of the game object. Think of it as an initialization method for a game object. You can use it to set initial states and values for a game object. It does not run over and over again like the *Update()* function and therefore is a good place to put code that does not need to run for the life of the game object. For example, if you want to constantly rotate an object like that in Listing 1.7, then it makes sense for the rotation to occur each loop. However, if you want to set the color of a game object to red, coding it in an *Update()* function will just cause the same command to run over and over again. Once the object is red, there is no need to keep setting it to red. A more suitable place to make an object red would be in the *Start()* function. It is set to red just once.

Remember, code inside *Update()* runs each main loop and each line of code in the main loop will cause it to run slower, albeit a minute amount, but superfluous code can soon add up to huge drops in frame rates.

⚫ **For Research**
More Unity Functions
More Unity-specific functions will be revealed throughout the book as needed. If you are interested in the other available functions, go to the *Script Reference* at https://docs.unity3d.com/ScriptReference/MonoBehaviour.html and have a look at the *Public Methods, Static Methods and Messages*. These are the ones you can use in your C# Script.

1.5.4 Variables

A *variable* is the name of a piece of computer memory allocated for your program. Think of it as a storage box that you can put things into, take things out of, add to, and change. A variable in programming is similar to a variable in algebra that holds a numerical value. However, in programming, pretty much anything can be placed into a variable. In the line of code,

```
x = 50;
```

x is the name of the variable and it has a value of 50. If you continued with

```
y = x + 30;
```

another variable called *y* is being given the value of *x* (50) plus 30. The value of *y* in this case would be 80.

The differing types of information that can be stored in variables are called *data types*. These include integers (whole numbers, e.g., 5), floating-point numbers (numbers with decimal values, e.g., 3.14), characters (a single alphanumeric value), strings (words and texts, e.g., "hello"), Boolean values (e.g., true and false), and other data types made from mixtures of the aforementioned.

Variables do not just exist automatically in computer memory. They must be *declared*. The process of declaring a variable gives it a name, initial value, and a size. Some examples are shown in Listing 1.8.

Listing 1.8 An example of declaring variables of differing types

```
int x = 10;              // an integer called x with the
                         value 10
float y = 5.6f;          // a float called y with the
                         value 5.6 v
bool isSpinning = true;  // a Boolean value set to true
char ch = 'a';           // a character called ch with a
                         value 'a'
string myName = "Penny"; // a string called myName with
                         the value Penny
```

If you do not know what value should be placed into a variable, you do not need to assign one. For example,

```
int x;
```

will create an integer variable called *x* and the value will be set to 0 automatically.

Variables in computer memory can be conceptualized as boxes in a large storage space. The different types of variables have different sized boxes. The smallest box is a Boolean, as you only need to store a value of 1 or 0 inside it. A character is the next size up. It would hold all the alphanumeric characters such as those appearing on the keys of your keyboard and a couple of miscellaneous others. The integer size box is even bigger, holding numbers between −32,768 and 32,767 and a float box bigger again holding numbers with seven decimal digits of significance between 0.000000×10^{-95} and 9.999999×10^{96}. The exact size of the boxes will change depending on the operating system and computer processor, but the relative sizes remain the same. A conceptualization of memory allocation from variable declarations is shown in Figure 1.25.

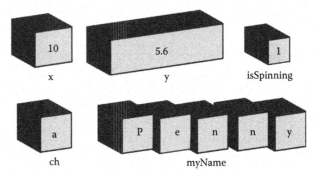

FIG 1.25 A conceptualization of the memory allocation that occurs from Listing 1.9.

One thing to note from Listing 1.8 is the way characters and strings are given values. A single character is enclosed in single quotes and a string is enclosed in double quotes. The reason being that if they were not, the compiler would consider them to be other variable names.

This brings us to another matter about naming variables. Variables can be named anything you like, keeping in mind the following.

Variable names

- Must start with a letter or number (e.g., myNumber, x, 7number, name10).
- Cannot contain spaces (e.g., my Number)
- Cannot be the same as a reserved word [these are the keywords used in the programming language (e.g., var, for, function, transform)]
- Cannot be the same as another variable unless it is in a different function, so this is not valid

```
void DeclareValues()
{
    int x = 10;
    char x = 't';
}
```

However, this is acceptable

```
void CreateAValue()
{
    int x = 0;
}
void CreateAnotherValue()
{
    char x = 't';
}
```

Also keep in mind that variable names can make your code more readable and can reduce the need for comments. For example,

```
x = 10;
```

is ambiguous, whereas

```
accountBalance = 10;
```

has more meaning.

You will notice the use of capital letters in some of the variable names shown beforehand. This is just one convention of using several words in one name. The capital makes the variable name more readable as single words are easier to read. A variable name could also be written

```
account_Balance
```

using the underscore to separate words. This is totally a personal preference and makes no difference to the compiler; however, naming conventions* are recommended. For example, if programming in C#, camel casing for variable names is recommended with the first letter being in lowercase. Because conventions can vary slightly between languages, they will not be covered in this book.

● On the Website
Code Naming Conventions

1.5.4.1 C# Variables

Variables in Unity C# usually appear near the top of the code file. Although they could be placed in a variety of locations, the best place is at the top because they are easy to find and they must be declared before they are used. We will examine other types of variables in later sections.

Consider the script in Listing 1.9.

Listing 1.9 C# to change the x-axis scale of a gameobject on game start

```
private float objScaleX = 0.5f;
void Start ()
{
    transform.localScale = new Vector3 (objScaleX,
    transform.localScale.y, transform.localScale.z);
}
```

---

* For more information about naming conventions, see http://en.wikipedia.org/wiki/Naming_convention_(programming).

The line showing the variable declaration is shown in **bold**. Note, do not use bold in your own code; this is for illustrative purposes only. The keyword *private* forces the variable to remain hidden for use inside the C# file in which it is declared. It cannot be seen for use by other code files. You can add many C# files into the same Unity application, and sometimes you will want to be able to share the variable contents between these. In this case, you would declare an *exposed* variable. In this example, the code would be the same as Listing 1.9, except the *private* keyword would be replaced with *public*.

When a variable becomes exposed, it also appears in the Inspector of the Unity Editor where values can be entered manually. The difference is illustrated in Figure 1.26.

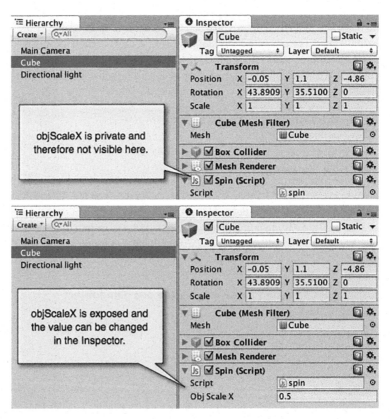

FIG 1.26 A private and exposed variable in the Inspector.

☺ Unity Hands On

C# Variables

In this hands-on session, you will create variables of your own to modify the scale of a cube and explore the differences between private and exposed variables. The starting file is supplied on the website for download.

Step 1: Download *Chapter One/Variables.zip* from the website; unzip. Run Unity and open the project using File > Open Project, select *Open Other*, and browse for the *Variables* directory. In the Project, double-click on *cubeResize* to open the scene. In the Scene you will see a white cube. Attached to the cube is the script from Listing 1.9. The objScaleX variable is private and therefore not visible in the Inspector when the cube is selected.

Step 2: Highlight Cube in the Hierarchy and look at the resize script in the Inspector at the very bottom. You will notice that there are no variables visible. Press play to watch the *x* scale of the cube change. Remember to press stop when finished.

Step 3: Double-click on *Resize.cs* in the Project to open with a code editor. Note that the objScaleX variable has the keyword *private* at the beginning of the declaration.

Step 4: Replace the *private* keyword with *public* and save the file.

☺ Note

When saving a script in the external editor there is no need to close the editor. If you keep it open and click on the Unity window to switch back, it becomes quicker to edit and re-edit script files. You only need to click back and forth between the Unity and script editor windows to move between programs. Just remember to save the script file before switching back to Unity. Unity will automatically reload any script changes you have made.

Step 5: Highlight Cube in the Hierarchy and look at the *resize* script in the Inspector at the very bottom. You will notice that the variable has become exposed.

☺ Note

Remember variable names cannot have spaces. However, because the variable name in this case is constructed with capital letters in it, Unity has made it look like three separate words in the Inspector. *objScaleX* has become *Obj Scale X*. This is only for readability purposes. Your variable is still called *objScaleX* in the script.

Step 6: In the Inspector, click on the 0.5 value for Obj Scale X. This will put the variable into editing mode. Change the value to 0.1 and press play. The cube will now become very narrow.

◉ Note

When a variable's value is changed in the Inspector, it does not change in the script. Opening the Resize.cs in the script editor will review the *objScaleX* variable to still have an initial value of 0.5. Any value you type into the Inspector for a variable will override what you have initialized for the variable within the script. This can quickly become confusing when you start changing variable values in the script and expect them to affect the game when nothing seems to happen. If this occurs, it is most likely because the variable is exposed and has a value set in the Inspector.

Step 7: Switch back to the script editor. If you have closed this window, it can be reopened by double-clicking on *Resize.cs* in the Project. Change the value of *objScaleX* to 2.0f. Do not forget the semicolon after the value.

Step 8: Save the script and switch back to Unity. The Inspector will still have 0.1 as the value. Playing at this point will give the same results as before. The Inspector value of 0.1 will override the value in your code.

Step 9: To update the Inspector values to those in the script file, click on the wheel/cog icon, drop down to the very right next to *Resize (Script)*, and select from the list *Reset*. Note that the value of *objScaleX* has been synchronized with the code in the script file.

◉ Note

Should a variable remain private or exposed? If you only require the value in the variable inside a single script file, then private is fine if you don't want to be able to change the values of the variables in the Inspector. If at some stage you need to access the value of a variable from another C# file, which will be covered later in the book, the variable needs to be exposed. My advice is to keep the variable private until necessary, that way you can mess around with setting its values in the code file and you don't need to keep resetting the script in the Inspector.

Step 10: Play the application to see the cube resized to double its width.

Step 11: Switch back to the script editor. Take a look at where the value of *objScaleX* is being used. It is changing the *X* value of the *Scale* in the *Transform* component of the game object the script is attached to, which in this case is the cube. This linkage is illustrated in Figure 1.27 showing Unity in play mode and the modified *X* scale in the Inspector.

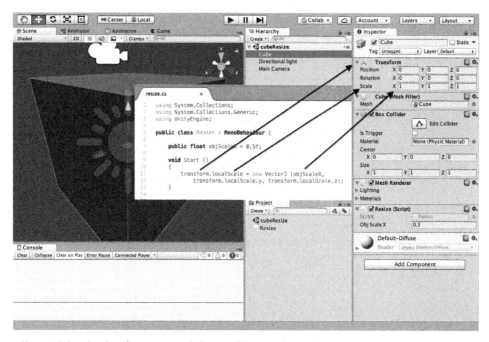

FIG 1.27 How script links to the values of components attached to game objects.

Step 12: In the script, add two more variables for adjusting the Y and Z scales and some code to link these values to the cube's transform component. The full listing of the new code is shown in Listing 1.10. Modifications are shown in **bold**.

◉ Note

Do not use **bold** in your own code. Scripting should have no font effects whatsoever. Any coloration or bolding put in by the editor is for your own readability. It is put in automatically. Make use of this coloration and bolding to check you have keywords spelled correctly.

Listing 1.10 A script to modify x, y, and z scales of a game object

```
public float objScaleX = 2.0f;
public float objScaleY = 0.2f;
public float objScaleZ = 0.5f;

void Start ()
{
    transform.localScale = new Vector3
                        (objScaleX, objScaleY,
                            objScaleZ);
}
```

Step 13: Save the script, return to Unity, and play to see that the changes take effect. Change the values of these scales in the Inspector to experiment with the shape of the cube as the differing scales are changed.

◉ Note

When you start programming, it is extremely common to make typing errors and to leave out parts of code such as semicolons on the end of lines or brackets. If you make a mistake, Unity will detect it and give an error message. It shows up in red at the very bottom of the Unity window as shown in Figure 1.28. If you get an error, double-click on the red message and Unity will take you to the line in the script editor where the error occurred. From there you can fix it, save the file and return to Unity to try again.

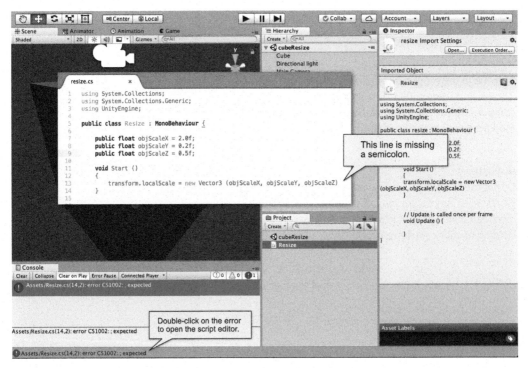

FIG 1.28 The Unity error message displayed when a semicolon is missing from a line of code.

1.5.5 Operators

There are two main types of operators in programming: *arithmetic operators* perform mathematical operations between variables and values, and *relational operators* compare variables and values.

1.5.5.1 Arithmetic Operators

Basic math operators are shown in Table 1.2.

The assignment operator you may be more familiar with is an equal sign, and the multiplication and division operators are a little different to those used in traditional math. Note from the C# examples in Table 1.2 that values are placed into variables using the assignment operator. To use values already stored in a variable, you simply refer to them in the equations using their name. It is the same as high school algebra. More complex equations can also be created, such as

```
x = (y + z) / 3 + 8;
```

where parentheses work for order of operations as they do in traditional algebra (e.g., the y + z between the parentheses would be calculated first).

1.5.5.2 Relational Operators

Unlike arithmetic operators that can calculate a plethora of values, relational operators make comparisons that result in Boolean values (TRUE or FALSE). The most common operators are given in Table 1.3.

An important thing to note in Table 1.3 is the use of = versus ==. One equal sign means *assign* or place a value into a variable, and the double equal sign means *compare* two values. First-time programmers often get these mixed up, but with practice the differences become clear.

TABLE 1.2 Common Math Operators Used in All Programming Languages

Operator	Arithmetic Performed	Example in C#	Value of x from Example
=	Assignment	X = 2;	2
+	Addition	Y = 5; X = y + 3;	8
−	Subtraction	Y = 15; Z = 5; X = z−y;	−10
*	Multiplication	Y = 15; X = x*3;	45
/	Division	Y = 15; Z = 5; X = y/z;	3

TABLE 1.3 The Common Relational Operators Used in All Programming Languages

Operator	Arithmetic Performed	Example in C#	Value of x from Example

>	Greater than	y = 5;
		z = 2;
		x = y > z;
			TRUE

<	Less than	y = 10;
		z = 3;
		x = y < z;
			FALSE

>=	Greater than or equal to	y = 4;
		z = 4;
		x = z >= y;
			TRUE

<=	Less than or equal to	Y = 3;
		z = 1;
		x = z <= y;
			TRUE

==	Equal to	y = 12;
		z = 16;
		x = y == z
			FALSE

!=	Not equal to	y = 12;
		z = 16;
		x = y != z
			TRUE

◉ Unity Hands On

Operators

Step 1: Download *Chapter One/Operators.zip* from the website, unzip, and open in Unity. In the Project, double-click on *dynamicResize* to open the scene. In the Scene, you will see a small white sphere. Attached to the sphere is the script called *Grow.cs*.

Step 2: Double-click on *Grow.cs* in the Project to open the script editor. Note that there is already a variable added called *growthRate*. Modify the script to reflect the one in Listing 1.11.

Listing 1.11 Script to grow a game object by 0.05 in scale in each game update

```
float growthRate = 0.05f;
void Update ()
{
    transform.localScale = new Vector3(transform.
        localScale.x + growthRate, transform.
        localScale.y + growthRate,
    transform.localScale.z + growthRate);
}
```

Step 3: Save the script and play in Unity. Note how the sphere grows slowly in size. This will continue until you stop playing. The Update function continues to run over and over again while the application is playing. Functions will be explored in depth later. For now, a simplistic explanation of what is happening is that the growthRate is continually being added to the current value of the localScale, thus updating it. Change the exposed variable of Growth Rate of the Grow script attached to the sphere to 0.005. It will grow more slowly.

Step 4: Click on the Sphere in the Hierarchy. Ensure that you can see the Scale part of the Transform component in the Inspector. Now press play and watch as the *x, y,* and *z* values of the scale change constantly.

Step 5: In the Project, select *Create* and add a new C# Script file. Call it *Revolve*. To the file, add the code in Listing 1.12.

Listing 1.12 A script to move a game object in a circle

```
float radius = 5;
void Update ()
{
    transform.position = new Vector3(radius *
    Mathf.Sin(Time.fixedTime), radius *
    Mathf.Cos(Time.fixedTime), 0);
}
```

Step 6: This new C# Script file can be added to the Sphere while the *Grow* script is still attached. Select *Revolve* in the Project and drag and drop it onto the Sphere in the Hierarchy. Select Sphere in the Hierarchy and check the Inspector to see that *Revolve* is attached. If it is not attached, try the drag and drop process again.

Step 7: Play the application. The Sphere will resize slowly while moving in a circular motion.

⊜ **Note**

The parametric form for a circle is used in Listing 1.12 to move the sphere around the circumference of a circle. These equations are based on modifying the *x* and *y* positions with cosine and sine functions and the time. The value of *Time.fixedTime* is a built-in Unity variable holding the time in seconds since the application started running. It is therefore dynamic and constantly changing value. Unity also contains functions for all mathematical operations such as *Mathf. Sin()* and *Mathf. Cos()*.

It is not expected at this early stage in learning Unity to know this type of information. However, it can be handy to know where to find it, and the most **invaluable resource** you should have at your disposal is the *Unity Scripting Reference*. To access this information, while in Unity, select Help > Scripting Reference from the main menu. In the website that opens, try searching for *Mathf* and *Time* to see what is available to you.

1.5.6 Conditional Statements

Conditional statements allow the flow of a program to change when certain conditions are met (or not met). They rely on Boolean algebra for making decisions on which way code should flow. Conditional statements can divert code to other parts of code or can make the same statement of code repeat over and over.

Conditional statements, which are essentially the programmed form of Boolean algebra, cannot operate on their own. They need constructs around them to assess their value. The simplest form of these is an *if-else statement*.

Used quite a lot in simple artificial intelligence programming, if-else statements make an assessment of a statement and do one thing if that statement is true and another (or nothing) if it is false. The if-else statement was used in the logic circuit application mentioned earlier in the chapter. Think of it as the type of logic you might use in deciding whether or not to wear a raincoat, thus:

```
if it is raining
wear a raincoat
otherwise
don't wear a raincoat
```

The if-else statement in C# looks like that in Listing 1.13.

Listing 1.13 An if-else statement

```
if(test)
{
        //if the value of test is true, do this bit;
}
else
{
        //if the value of test is false, do this bit;
}
```

For example, consider the script in Listing 1.14.

Listing 1.14 An example script using an if-else statement

```
int x = 5;
int y = 10;
if(x > y)
{
    Debug.Log("X is greater than Y");
}
else
{
    Debug.Log("Y is greater than or equal to X");
}
```

This program will print out "Y is greater than or equal to X" because the conditional statement inside the parentheses of the if statement will equate to false. If X were given a value of 20, the program would print out "X is greater than Y".

◎ Unity Hands On
if-else Statements

Step 1: Download *Chapter One/ifelse.zip* from the website, unzip, and open in Unity. In the Project, double-click on *falling* to open the scene. In the Scene, you will see a small white sphere. Attached to the sphere is the script called *FallAndGrow.cs*.

Step 2: Play the application. The sphere will appear to fall as its *y* position is changed constantly by the script.

Step 3: Open the *FallAndGrow.cs* script and make the changes, as shown in Listing 1.15.

Listing 1.15 Making a game object fall to a certain position and then stop

```
float speed = 0.1f;
int groundLevel = -4;
void Update ()
{
    if(transform.position.y > groundLevel)
    {
        //keep moving down
        transform.Translate(0,-speed,0);
    }
}
```

Step 4: Save and play. Watch as the sphere moves down the screen until it stops. What is occurring is that the *y* position is constantly being reduced by 0.1. While the value of the *y* position remains larger than −4, the code inside the if statement will continue to be processed. As point *y* becomes greater than or equal to the *groundLevel*, that line of code is skipped and thus the sphere no longer has its *y* position modified.

Step 5: We are now going to modify the code to make the sphere start to grow when it stops moving. We know it will stop moving when the conditional statement in Listing 1.15 becomes false; therefore, by adding some growth code into an else statement we can have it execute, but only when the sphere stops moving. Update the FallAndGrow.cs script to reflect Listing 1.16.

Listing 1.16 A script to make a game object fall down to a certain height and then grow

```
float speed = 0.1f;
float growthRate = 0.01f;
float groundLevel = -4;
void Update ()
{
        if(transform.position.y > groundLevel)
        {
            //keep moving down
            transform.Translate(0, -speed, 0);
        }
        else
        {
            transform.localScale = new Vector3(transform.
                localScale.x + growthRate, 1, 1);
        }
}
```

Step 6: Save and play. When the sphere reaches a *y* position of −4, it will stop moving and start to grow along its *x* axis.

The other programming construct that handles condition statements is a *loop*. A loop is a segment of code that runs over and over again until an ending condition is met. There are several types of loop constructs, but for now we are going to have a look at just one, the *for loop*.

Consider the code in Listing 1.17.

Listing 1.17 C# for printing numbers between 1 and 5

```
int i = 1;
Debug.Log(i);
i = i + 1;
Debug.Log(i);
i = i + 1;
Debug.Log(i);
i = i + 1;
Debug.Log(i);
i = i + 1;
Debug.Log(i);
i = i + 1;
```

The output from this code in the console would be

```
[time] 1
UnityEngine.Debug:Log(object)
[time] 2
UnityEngine.Debug:Log(object)
[time] 3
UnityEngine.Debug:Log(object)
[time] 4
UnityEngine.Debug:Log(object)
[time] 5
UnityEngine.Debug:Log(object)
```

as the variable *i* starts with a value of 1, is then printed, has one added to the value, and is printed again five times. Imagine printing out all the numbers between 1 and 100. It would be a lot of code.

Enter the for loop. The for loop reduces such repetitive tasks down into a few simple lines. The basic format of a for loop is shown in Listing 1.18.

Listing 1.18 A for loop

```
for(initialize variable; test value; update value)
{
    // perform some action while the test is true
}
```

The first part of the for loop declares a variable and gives it an initial value. The second part performs a Boolean test on the value of the variable. If the test comes back true, the loop performs the code inside the parentheses. After the contents of the parentheses are finished, the variable value is updated, and the test is performed again; if true, the inside part runs again. This continues until the test becomes false and the loop quits.

A for loop to perform the same action as Listing 1.17 is shown in Listing 1.19.

Listing 1.19 A for loop to print out numbers between 1 and 5

```
for(int i = 1; i <= 9; i++)
{
    Debug. Log(i);
}
```

◉ Note

Listing 1.19 introduces a new type of arithmetic used as a shortcut in programming. Writing

```
i++
```

is identical to writing.

```
i = i + 1
```

It is a shortcut for adding one to the value of a variable. You can also write

```
i--
```

which will take one away from the variable i. More shortcut arithmetic is shown in Table 1.4.

TABLE 1.4 Shortcut Arithmetic Operations and Their Equivalent Longhand

Shortcut	Longhand	Description
i++	i = i + 1	Adds one to the value of the variable and replaces the original value with the new one.
i--	i = i - 1	Takes one away from the value of the variable and replaces the original value with the new one
i += 2	i = i + 2	Adds two to the value of the variable and replaces the original value with the new one.
i -= 2	i = i - 2	Takes two away from the value of the variable and replaces the original value with the new one.
i *= 2	i = i * 2	Multiplies the value of the variable by two and replaces the original value with the new one.
i /= 2	i = i / 2	Divides the value of the variable by two and replaces the original value with the new one.

◎ Unity Hands On

for Loops

Step 1: Download *Chapter One/forloop.zip* from the website, unzip, and open in Unity. In the Project, double-click on *stacked* to open the scene. The Scene will appear empty. Attached to the Main Camera is the script called *StackedSpheres.cs*. Play the file. A vertical stack of spheres will appear in the Game.

Step 2: Open *StackedSpheres.cs* with the script editor. The code used to create the stack of spheres is inside the Start function. Each sphere is created individually, and its *y* position is changed by 1 with each new sphere.

Step 3: Modify each line like this

```
sphere = GameObject.CreatePrimitive(PrimitiveType.Sphere);
```

to this

```
sphere = GameObject.CreatePrimitive(PrimitiveType.Cube);
```

Step 4: Save the script and replay the application. The stack of spheres will be replaced with a stack of cubes.

◎ Note

Although the sphere is being changed to a cube, notice the variable called *sphere* that is being assigned to the game object does not need to be changed. This is because the name of a variable as far as the compiler is concerned is not important. It is only named sphere in this case for readability. It could have easily been called *aPrimitive* or *aP*.

Step 5: Imagine that you now need to add another 50 cubes on top. This would be a big cut and paste and editing job as the *y* position would need to be incremented for each new cube. Instead we will replace all the code with just three lines (and a couple of parentheses) that will allow you to make the stack any height you like. Modify *StackedSpheres.cs* to the code shown in Listing 1.20.

Listing 1.20 Creating a stack of cubes with a for loop

```
void Start ()
{
    GameObject aP;
    for(int i = 1; i <= 9; i++)
    {
        aP = GameObject.CreatePrimitive(PrimitiveType.
            Cube);
        aP.transform.position = new Vector3(0, i, 0);
    }
}
```

◉ Note

Although the variable, *aP*, in Listing 1.20 does not have the keyword *private* included, it **will not** become exposed. Variables declared inside functions are called *local variables* and are only visible inside the function that created them.

Step 6: Save and play the application. It will produce the same result as the previous version. Note how the value of the variable *i* is being used to set the *y* position of each cube? Just another advantage of using a for loop.

Step 7: To put even spaces between each cube, change the line

```
aP.transform.position = new Vector3(0, i, 0);
```

to

```
aP.transform.position = new Vector3(0, i*2, 0);
```

Step 8: Save and play to see the spaces created between the cubes.

Step 9: To create another set of cubes horizontally in the Game, add another for loop as shown in Listing 1.21. Note the use of the new variable *j* as the *x* position.

Listing 1.21 A script that creates one column and one row of cubes

```
void Start ()
{
    GameObject aP;
    for(int i = 1; i <= 9; i++)
    {
        aP = GameObject.CreatePrimitive(PrimitiveType.Cube);
        aP.transform.position = new Vector3(0, i * 2, 0);
    }
    for(int j = 1; j <= 9; j++)
    {
        aP = GameObject.CreatePrimitive(PrimitiveType.Cube);
        aP.transform.position = new Vector3(j*2, 0, 0);
    }
}
```

Step 10: Save and play. The result will look like that in Figure 1.29. You may need to move the camera around to see all the cubes.

Step 11: A few readjustments to this code can give you the power to create a matrix of 9 × 9 cubes. By placing one for loop inside the other,

FIG 1.29 A column and row of cubes created entirely with script.

the nine repetitions of the horizontally placed cubes are compounded by the nine repetitions of the vertical cubes. Modify your code to that in Listing 1.22. On the first pass of the outer loop, the inner loop runs nine times. Then the outer loop moves onto its second pass. At this time the inner loop runs nine times again. This continues until the outer loop has finished its nine passes.

Listing 1.22 A matrix of cubes created entirely with script

```
void Start ()
{
    GameObject aP;
    int numRows = 9;
    int numCols = 9;
    for(int row = 1; row <= numRows; row++)
    {
        for(int col = 1; col <= numCols; col++)
        {
            aP = GameObject.CreatePrimitive(PrimitiveType.
                Cube);
            aP.transform.position = new Vector3(col*2,
                row*2, 0);
        }
    }
}
```

Step 12: Save and play to see the matrix of cubes as shown in Figure 1.30.

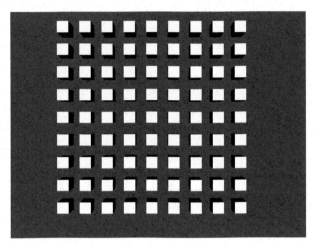

FIG 1.30 Game view of a matrix of cubes created with Listing 1.22.

1.5.7 Arrays

Sometimes a single variable is a less efficient way of storing data and objects. For example, consider changing the color of each of the cubes created in Listing 1.20, not initially at the beginning of the program, but randomly and constantly while it is running. In Listing 1.20, a single variable is used to create nine cubes. However, the variable itself only ever holds one cube at a time. Each time a new cube is created, the variable is overwritten with a new one. This means that after a new cube is created and assigned to *aP*, it is no longer possible to access the properties of the previous cube. Even the ability to change its position is gone. Therefore, we need the variable *aP* to hold not just one game object, but nine.

This can be achieved by making *aP* into an *array* as shown in Listing 1.23.

Listing 1.23 Storing game objects in an array

```
void Start ()
{
    GameObject[] aP = new GameObject[9];
    for(int i = 0; i < 9; i++)
    {
        aP[i] = GameObject.CreatePrimitive
            (PrimitiveType.Cube);
        aP[i].transform.position = new Vector3(0, i + 1, 0);
    }
}
```

In Listing 1.23, the variable *aP* is no longer a single game object but an array. An array can store anything, including integers, floats, and game objects.

If the original *aP* was a single storage box in memory, this new *aP* is a row of storage boxes, where each box has its own index number.

The first box in the array is indexed with a 0. To refer to each box individually, their names are *aP[0]*, *aP[1]*, *aP[2]*, *aP[3]*, *aP[4]*, *aP[5]*, *aP[6]*, *aP[7]*, and *aP[8]*. This is the reason for changing the for loop in Listing 1.23 to begin counting at 0. The variable *i* can be used as the array index. The first time the loop runs, *aP[i]* is equivalent to writing *aP[0]*.

Because the *y* position of the first cube was initially 1 and *i* now starts at 0, the position must be set with *i* + 1 to keep this consistent.

☉ Unity Hands On
Arrays
Step 1: Download *Chapter One/Arrays.zip* from the website, unzip, and open in Unity. In the Project, double-click on *coloredCubes* to open the scene. The Scene will appear empty. Attached to the Main Camera is the script called *StackedColors.cs*. Play the file. A vertical stack of colored cubes will appear in the Game as shown in Figure 1.31.
Step 2: Open *StackedColors.cs* in the script editor. Note that in the Update() function, only four of the cubes are assigned a color. Also, the array declaration has been moved to the top of the script. This is to make *aP* a global variable available to all functions, not just Start().

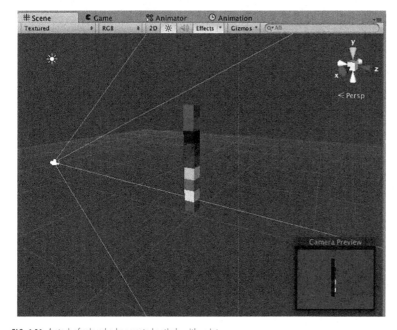

FIG 1.31 A stack of colored cubes created entirely with script.

Step 3: Modify *StackedColors.cs* to the code shown in Listing 1.24.

Listing 1.24 Setting an array of cubes to the color red

```
using System.Collections;
using System.Collections.Generic;
using UnityEngine;

public class StackedColors : MonoBehaviour {

    GameObject[] aP = new GameObject[9];
    void Start ()
    {
        for(int i = 0; i < 9; i++)
        {
          aP[i] = GameObject.
              CreatePrimitive(PrimitiveType.Cube);
          aP[i].transform.position = new Vector3(0, i+1, 0);
        }
    }

    void Update ()
    {
        for(int i = 0; i < 9; i++)
        {
          aP[i].GetComponent<Renderer>().material.
              color = Color.red;
        }
    }
}
```

Step 4: Save and play. The cubes created will have turned red. If you want to keep the cubes red, the code in the Update() function of Listing 1.24 would be better served inside the bottom of Start() as there would be no need to keep setting them to red in each main loop. However, we are now going to modify them to change to random colors.

Step 5: Modify the Update() function in your code to that in Listing 1.25.

Listing 1.25 Script to change cubes to random colors in each main loop

```
void Update ()
{
  for(int i = 0; i < 9; i++)
  {
    aP[i].GetComponent<Renderer>().material.color = new
    Color(Random.Range(0.0f, 1.0f), Random.Range(0.0f, 1.0f),
    Random.Range(0.0f, 1.0f));
  }
}
```

Step 6: Save and play. The cubes will change colors constantly. An explanation of the Color function is given in later sections.

1.5.8 Objects

Objects are complex data types. They consist of a bunch of variables (sometimes called *properties*) and functions (sometimes called *methods*). In most of the previous examples, you have already worked with objects. A GameObject is an object. A cube is an object. Most of the items you work with when coding that are not integers, floats, strings, or characters are objects. A *class* defines the data type of an object.

Let us assume that we have a simple class called *Square*. The class definition acts as a template for making many *Square* objects. Figure 1.32 illustrates how the variables of the class can be set to create differing objects. Each object is called an *instance* of the class. In this case, setting the variable values for *Square* allows for a variety of *Square* objects to be created. Although they all look different, they are still squares and retain the essence of a square, which is to have four equal sides and 90° angles.

The functions of an object can be used to set the values of the variables or change the behavior. For example, the *Rotate* function in the *Square* class might update the *rotation* variable and thus change the orientation of the object.

⊙ **Unity Hands On**
Objects
Step 1: Download *Chapter One/objects.zip* from the website, unzip, and open in Unity. In the Project, double-click on ChangeObjects to open the scene. The Scene will appear empty. Attached to the Main Camera is the script called *CreateObjects.cs*. Play the file. A capsule will appear in the Game.
Step 2: Open *CreateObjects.cs* in the script editor. Note that *gameObj* is a private variable created to hold a game object. In the Start() function,

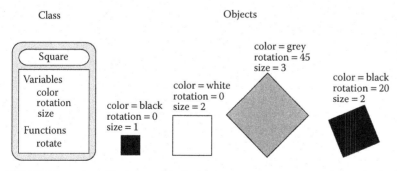

FIG 1.32 A Square class and four instances of the class.

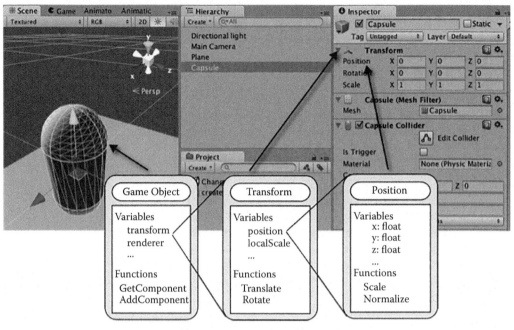

FIG 1.33 The Game Object class containing a transform class that contains a position class.

it is assigned as a *PrimitiveType. Capsule*. The capsule is a complex game object where the attached components are also objects. For example, *Transform* is an *object. Position*, which is a part of *Transform*, is also a *structure* (this is another data type with complex variables and functions. It acts so much like an object that we will just treat it as one rather than complicate matters). Visualizations of the Game Object, Transform, and Position classes, along with their locations in the Unity Editor, are shown in Figure 1.33.

⬤ **On the Website**
Game Object Definition
All of the variables and functions attached to a game object are listed in the script reference at: https://docs.unity3d.com/Manual/class-GameObject.html.

Step 3: To change the location of the capsule you can access the *x*, *y*, and *z* position coordinates via the Transform component of the Game Object. Modify the script to that in Listing 1.26. Save and play.

Listing 1.26 Changing the location of a game object with script

```
using System.Collections;
using System.Collections.Generic;
using UnityEngine;

public class CreateObjects : MonoBehaviour {
    GameObject gameObj;
    void Start()
    {
        gameObj = GameObject.CreatePrimitive
            (PrimitiveType.Capsule);
        gameObj.transform.position = new Vector3(1, 5, 2);
    }
}
```

◉ Note

You can always change the location of a game object by typing values into the Transform component in the Inspector, although this can't be done after the game has been built, while the game is playing. That is why scripting is more powerful.

Step 4: One of the functions available to the game object is AddComponent(). This script performs the same task as selecting the Game Object in the Editor and choosing an item from Component in the main menu. To add a physics component to the game object, modify your code to that in Listing 1.27. Save and play.

Listing 1.27 Adding a Rigidbody to a game object using script

```
using System.Collections;
using System.Collections.Generic;
using UnityEngine;

public class CreateObjects : MonoBehaviour {
    GameObject gameObj;
    void Start()
    {
        gameObj = GameObject.CreatePrimitive
            (PrimitiveType.Capsule);
        gameObj.transform.position = new Vector3(1, 5, 2);
        gameObj.AddComponent<Rigidbody>();
    }
}
```

Step 5: The Rigidbody component is used by the physics system. As you play your new script, the capsule will fall due to gravity until it hits the plane in the scene. The collision event will cause the capsule to stop dead in its tracks. If you examine the capsule in the Inspector while the script is playing, you will notice that the capsule has a Collider component. This is used by the physics system to determine the boundary area of the object in order to calculate collisions. You can access the collider and change its values in the script. Modify your script to that in Listing 1.28.

Listing 1.28 Modifying the physics material of a game object

```
using System.Collections;
using System.Collections.Generic;
using UnityEngine;

public class CreateObjects : MonoBehaviour {
    GameObject gameObj;
    void Start()
    {
        gameObj = GameObject.CreatePrimitive(PrimitiveType.
            Capsule);
        gameObj.transform.position = new Vector3(1, 5, 2);
        gameObj.AddComponent<Rigidbody>();
        PhysicMaterial material = new PhysicMaterial();
        material.bounciness = 1;
        gameObj.GetComponent<Collider>().material =
            material;
    }
}
```

Step 6: Save and play. We will examine physics in more depth later in the book. For now, just accept that this new code makes the capsule bouncier, and the physics engine will cause it to bounce when it collides with the plane. *PhysicsMaterial* in Listing 1.28 is another type of object. Note the use of the keyword *new* as it is being assigned. On this line a new variable called *material* is being created and assigned a new *PhysicsMaterial*. The *new* keyword creates an instance of the object. After an instance is created the values can then be manipulated via referencing the variable to which it has been assigned—in this case, *material*.

Step 7: So far we have modified a game object via a script attached to the camera. Scripts can also be attached directly to a game object. From the main menu, select GameObject > 3D Object > Sphere. A sphere will appear in the Scene. Select the sphere in the Hierarchy and press the W key. Use the axes in the Scene to move the sphere above the plane.

Step 8: In the Project, select Create > C# Script. Rename the script *SpherePhysics*, attach it to the sphere by dragging and dropping it from the Project onto the sphere in the Hierarchy, and open it in the script editor. Add the script in Listing 1.29.

Listing 1.29 Script to modify properties of a game object to which it is attached

```
using System.Collections;
using System.Collections.Generic;
using UnityEngine;

public class SpherePhysics : MonoBehaviour {

    public Color myColor = Color.red;
    void Start()
    {
        this.gameObject.AddComponent<Rigidbody>();
        PhysicMaterial material = new PhysicMaterial();
        material.bounciness = 0.5f;
        this.GetComponent<Collider>().material = material;
        this.collider.material = material;
        this.GetComponent<Renderer>().material.color =
            myColor;
        this.renderer.material.color = myColor;
    }
}
```

Step 9: Save and play. Now the script is attached to a game object; it can directly reference the object with the keyword *this*. There is no need to create the object because it already exists in the scene. Because the variable *myColor* is exposed, you will be able to change it in the Inspector.

Step 10: From the main menu select GameObject > 3D Object > Cube. A cube will appear in the scene. Position it above the plane and to one side of the sphere. Attach the *SpherePhysics* script to the new cube.

Step 11: Play. Note that the new cube behaves in the same way as the sphere. This is because the script in *SpherePhysics* applies itself to the object to which it is attached. As a result, the cube turns red and falls with the same physics attributes at the sphere. Generic script like this can be added to any game object.

Step 12: Because the *myColor* variable is exposed, it can be changed in the Inspector before playing. Select the cube from the Hierarchy and change *myColor* in the Inspector to green.

Step 13: Play. Note that the sphere remains red but the cube is now green. Both are using the same script but different versions of it. You could also expose the variable for the bounciness and set it to different values for the sphere and cube in the Hierarchy, as shown in Listing 1.30.

Listing 1.30 Exposing a variable for bounciness

```
using System.Collections;
using System.Collections.Generic;
using UnityEngine;

public class Bouncy : MonoBehaviour {

    public Color myColor = Color.red;
    public float bouncyAmount = 0.5f;
    void Start()
    {
        this.gameObject.AddComponent<Rigidbody>();
        PhysicMaterial material = new PhysicMaterial();
        material.bounciness = bouncyAmount;
        this.GetComponent<Collider>().material =
            material;
        this.GetComponent<Collider>().material =
            material;
        this.GetComponent<Renderer>().material.color =
            myColor;
        this.GetComponent<Renderer>().material.color =
            myColor;
    }
}
```

◉ Note

Bounciness in the physics engine is a float that only takes values between 0 and 1 where 0 is not bouncy and 1 is fully bouncy.

1.6 A Game Art Asset Primer

This primer *will not* teach you how to *create* game assets. Such topics are books on their own. It will, however, point you in the right direction to get started creating your own assets, as well as where to find ready-made ones. Most importantly, this primer will introduce you to the different types of assets and how to get them into a Unity game.

When it comes down to it, there are two types of art assets used in games: 2D and 3D. Two-dimensional art assets are the most used, as everything in the game has a 2D visual element. From trees to buildings, terrain to explosions, and characters to user interfaces they all include 2D art. In addition, normal maps and shading maps are also 2D images.

1.6.1 The Power of Two Rule

Since the inception of computer graphics, people have been trying to create superior and higher resolution images. The quality has not been restricted by the ability of the artist to create, but by the computer hardware's ability to process. Computer games need to quickly render frame after frame of real-time animation that changes with game flow influenced by user input. Unlike an animated movie, in which the contents of each frame are known from the outset, the interactive nature of a computer game means that the artist will never know what will be in any particular frame. The game itself needs to render frames on the fly. This requires a lot of processing power. This is why, over the years, as hardware performance has improved, so too has the quality of game graphics.

However, as a game developer you will still want to push the boundaries of quality, and knowing a few simple tricks can help you optimize your art assets to get the best out of the graphics processing. One such trick is to follow the *power of two* rule.

Computers continuously process data in cycles in order to push it through the processors, whether it *be* the central processing unit or, more commonly for graphics, the graphical processing unit. Processors can only handle so much data in one cycle and therefore it is chunked into packages of certain sizes.

Earlier in this chapter we examined the most elementary values in computing. They were 0 for on and 1 for off. These values are the basis for binary code that is used to encrypt all values in computer memory. The smallest amount of computer memory is a *bit*. It can store either a 0 or a 1. If we put two bits together, they can store four values: 00, 01, 10, or 11. Three bits can store eight values: 000, 001, 011, 010, 011, 100, 101, or 111. In fact, the number of values that can be stored is 2 to the power of the number of bits or 2 number of bits. Therefore, eight bits (called a byte) can store 2^8 or 256 values.

A computer processor has a limited number of bytes it can push through in one cycle. By making an image file a power of two in dimensions, it optimizes the number of cycles required to process it. For example, if an image were nine bytes in size and the processor could process four bytes per cycle, the first eight bytes of the image could be processed in two cycles. On the third cycle the ninth byte would be processed. This would mean three whole empty bytes of space wasted during the third cycle.

Imagine it as though you have a dishwasher that can hold four plates. You need to wash nine plates. You would do two full cycles and then have only one plate in the third cycle. For the same amount of dishwashing you could have invited another three guests to dinner! This illustration is exacerbated as file sizes become larger.

If you sacrifice processing cycles, you will sacrifice quality and speed. Ideally, images should have width and height values that are a power of two, for example, 2, 4, 8, 16, 32, 64, 128, 256, etc. The image does not need to be square; for example, the width could be 16 and the height could be 128. Making an image this size in dimension will lead it to occupy a space in computer memory that is also a power of two in size.

A digitized image is not just the size of its width and height, but also its depth—its *color depth*. The color depth is defined as the number of bits required to store the color values of each pixel. When a pixel is colored according to its red, green, blue, and alpha values that take up 8 bits (1 byte) each, it is said to have a color depth of 32 bits.

Therefore, an image that is 16 × 32 pixels with a color depth of 32 bits is 16,384 bits in total size. This is equal to 2^{14}; a power of two! Because computer memory processes in chunks whose sizes are also a power of two, it will result in an optimized use of each processing cycle.

But what happens if your texture is not a power of two? Your image will be resized or rescaled. If it is rescaled, the game engine will make it into an image with a power of two width and height closest to that of the original. This means that the original image will be squashed or stretched to fit into the new space. This could result in undesirable distortions in the texture. If the image is resized, the original could be cut off or extra blank space added around the edges in order to make it fit into a power of two texture. Either way, the result could be something that you do not want, as it may misalign your UV mapping.

◁ Unity Specifics
Textures
Unity will accept non-power of two images as textures, but it will rescale them. It accepts widths and heights of 2, 4, 8, 16, 32, 64, 128, 256, 512, 1024, or 2048 pixels. The majority of image file formats are accepted including PSD, TIFF, JPG, TGA, PNG, GIF, BMP, IFF, and PICT. A multilayered PSD file created with Photoshop will appear flattened inside the Unity Editor, however, the layers will still be there and editable when reopened in Photoshop.

☺ Unity Hands On
Adding Textures to a Model

Step 1: Download *Chapter One/Texturing.zip* from the website, unzip, and open in Unity. In the Project, double-click on *texturedemo* to open the scene. The Scene will open with a shaded female model. In the Hierarchy, click on the little triangle next to the word Female to expose the entire mesh hierarchy. You will now see that the submeshes of eyes, face, hair, pants, shoes, and top are listed beneath the parent of Female as shown in Figure 1.34.

Step 2: In Project, select Create > Folder and call it Materials. Highlight the Materials folder and select Create > Material from the small drop-down menu. Rename the material to *top*.

Step 3: With *top* in Project highlighted, at the very top of the Inspector select the *Shader* drop-down list and click on *Standard*. The Inspector will reveal the properties of *Albedo, Metallic, Normal Map*, etc., as shown in Figure 1.35.

Step 4: The Main Color is a color added to the color of the texture. If you leave it as white it will have no effect. For now, leave it as white. In the texture box to the right of Base (RGB) click Select. From the image picker that pops up select the *female_top-1_green*. For the Normalmap, click on Select for the texture box and pick out *female_top-1_normal* by double-clicking on it. If the full name of the texture is not displayed beneath it, clicking once on the image will reveal the full name at the bottom of the picker, as shown in Figure 1.36.

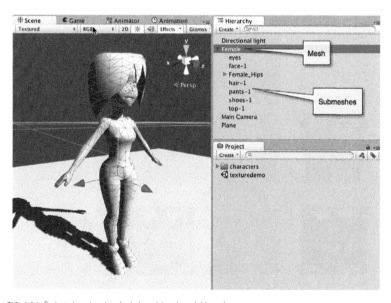

FIG 1.34 Project view showing shaded model and mesh hierarchy.

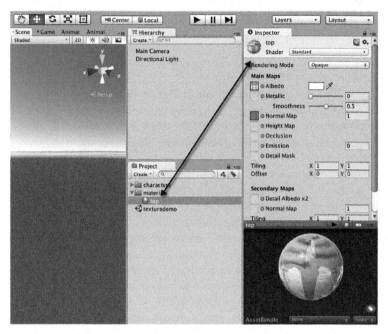

FIG 1.35 A Standard Shader opened in the Inspector.

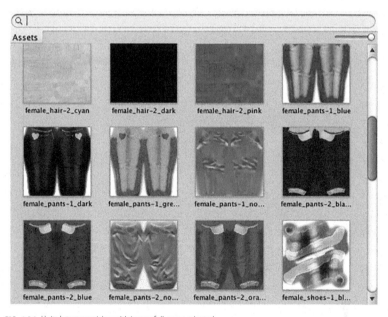

FIG 1.36 Unity's texture picker with image full name selected.

Step 5: Drag the *top* material from Project and drop it onto the *top* mesh in the Hierarchy. In the Scene and Game, the model will now appear with texturing on the top of the body.

Step 6: Repeat the process for the face, hair, pants, and shoes submeshes (not eyes), selecting appropriate Base (RGB) and Normalmaps from the texture picker.

Step 7: Create a new material for the eyes. In the Inspector, set the shader for this material to Legacy Shaders/Specular. Select an eye image for the Base (RGB) Gloss (A) texture. The *Specular Color* property for this shader sets the color that is reflected from the surface on any shiny parts. The shininess value changes the surface value from highly glossy to dull. Add the material to the eyes submesh and change the specular color and shininess values to see their effect.

Step 8: To give the ground plane a texture, open a browser window and search Google for *seamless grass texture*. Switch the search to *Images*. A seamless texture is one that neatly tiles both horizontally and vertically across a surface where the patterns meet exactly at the seams. Large areas such as terrains use seamless textures as it is less costly than one very large texture. From the search, locate a texture that is a power of two in size (and free to use), as shown in Figure 1.37. Download it to your desktop.

Step 9: Drag the image file from your desktop and drop it into the Project. Unity will load it for you automatically.

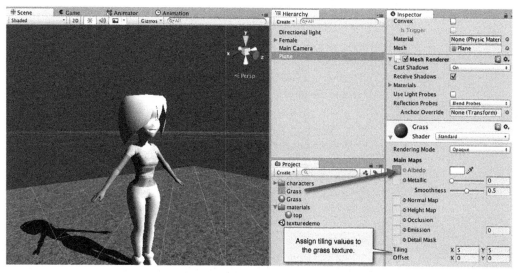

FIG 1.37 Grass material.

Step 10: Create a new material called grass. Leave the shader as Standard. Drag and drop the grass material onto the ground plane. Select Plane from the Hierarchy and find the grass material in the Inspector. Drag and drop the grass texture onto the Albedo in the Main Maps property, see Figure 1.37. Beneath Main Maps are Tiling values. These set the size and alignment of the texture on the surface. For example, setting Tiling's x to 5 will cause the texture to repeat five times across the surface. The bigger the tiling values, the smaller the tiles. Try setting the Tiling values to see the effect in the Scene.

1.6.2 Using Other People's Art Assets

Sometimes it is not worth your time recreating 3D models and textures when they are available on the web. For example, if it will cost you a week's worth of work to create a model that someone is selling on the web for $50, then it is worth purchasing if you can afford it. There are also many free 3D models available for use under a variety of licensing formats. Others are royalty free, which means that you pay for them once and then use them as many times as you like under the terms of the license.

There are many online websites for which you can freely sign up and download models for use in your own games. Some of the better ones include the following:

- Unity Asset Store: assetstore.unity.com
- TurboSquid: turbosquid.com
- HighEnd3D: www.highend3d.com
- Cubebrush: www.cubebrush.co

The model format used most widely and accepted in game engines is 3Ds. This was the original file format created by Autodesk's 3D Studio DOS release. This format can also be created and modified by Autodesk's 3D Studio Max, Maya, and Blender.

◁ Unity Specifics
3D models

Unity's native 3D model format is FBX. This can be created with Autodesk's 3D Studio Max. It will also import and use max files, but only if 3D Studio Max is installed on the same machine. The native files produced by Blender are also highly compatible and can be seamlessly added to projects as too can 3Ds formats. To add a model into your project simply drag and drop it, and any associated textures, into the Project.

◉ Unity Hands On
Adding a Model to a Unity Project

Step 1: Create an account on TurboSquid by visiting http://turbosquid. com and following the prompts.

Step 2: Search on TurboSquid for *car* or something else if you wish. Ensure that you set the filter to *3D Models* and sort by *Lower Prices* to have the free models appear first.

Step 3: Look through all the models and select one you like. Note that the file format type is listed beneath the image of the model. Look for a 3DS, FBX, or BLEND file. Download the file to your desktop.

Step 4: If the files are zipped, unzip them. Some files will be single mesh files such as a 3Ds; others may have textures with them. Three freely downloaded models and how they unzipped are shown in Figure 1.38: A pig model created with Blender and an asteroid and dinosaur.

Step 5: To import the models into Unity, select all the files associated with the model and drag and drop into the Project. If the model contains textures, ensure that you have the model file and the texture file in your selection. If the model and associated files are in a folder, drag the entire folder into Unity. The way they will appear is shown in Figure 1.39. Do not worry if you receive a couple of Unity error messages.

Step 6: Using free models is mostly a potluck as to the ones that will work in Unity. Sometimes they will be too big (Unity only allows 65,000 vertices per mesh), inside out, or just missing textures. If the model you get appears this way, go back and find another model.

◉ On the Website
A Model That Works

If you are having difficulty finding a model that works, one can be downloaded from the book website under *Chapter One/tyrannosaurus_ rex.zip.*

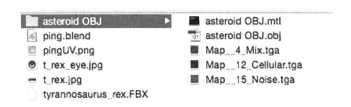

FIG 1.38 Example 3D model files.

FIG 1.39 A view of the project after importing three downloaded models.

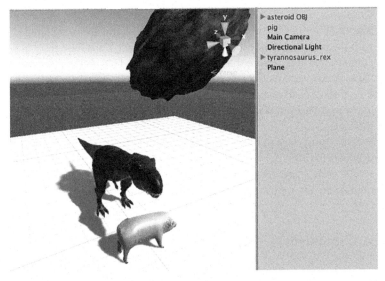

FIG 1.40 Models imported and viewed in Unity.

Step 7: Once the models are in the Project, find ones with a small cube icon next to them. Drag these into the Hierarchy or Scene to add them into the application. The three models shown in Figure 1.39 are imported into Unity as shown in Figure 1.40. In this case, the Asteroid model was too big, the pig model was okay, and the Tyrannosaurus Rex included a ground plane. Also note that the scaling for each mesh is different. This will be due to the scaling that the original modeler used.

Step 8: To resize the models, select them and use the Inspector to change their scale component. Alternatively, press the R key and use the resizing axes in the Scene. If you get a model without any texturing, but have an image for the texture, create your own material, select the texture for it, and apply the material to the mesh.

Step 9: Since Unity 2017, some models, such as FBX files, appear to lose their textures. To fix this: Select your model in the Assets folder. In the Inspector click on Materials then, if available, click on Extract Textures and extract them to a new folder called Materials. Don't worry if it looks like there's a problem with the mesh/materials—it's actually a shader problem.

Step 10: To fix the materials, select the model again and click on the Materials button in the Inspector and then Extract Materials into the Materials folder. You can now edit the shader component of any materials that aren't showing correctly, usually by changing the shader to Legacy Shader/Diffuse.

◁ Unity Specifics

Scaling

Another method of scaling is to resize the actual mesh as it is imported into Unity. You can do this by selecting the mesh in the Project Window and then in the Inspector setting the scale as shown in Figure 1.41.

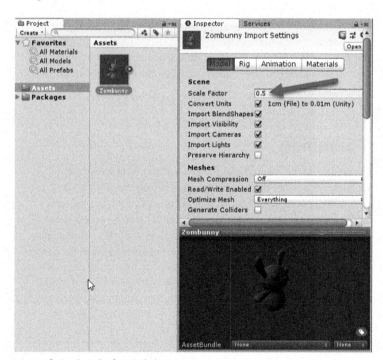

FIG 1.41 Setting the scaling factor in the Inspector.

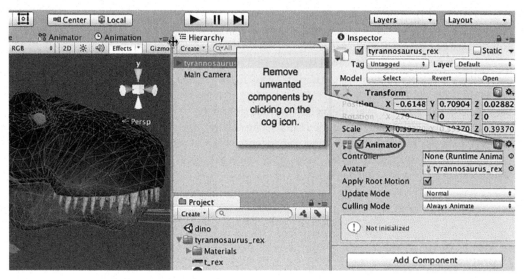

FIG 1.42 An unwanted Animator component attached to an imported model.

> ● **Note**
> *Watch out for Unwanted Animations*
> When an external model is brought into Unity, an Animator component will be added to it whether needed or not. To remove it, select the model in the Hierarchy and remove the Animator as shown in Figure 1.42. This component, if left on the model, can cause unwanted behavior in the game object on play.

1.7 Summary

Game art and game programming are two sides of the same coin. This chapter examined the complementary nature that both art and programming play and suggested that anyone can learn to program, and anyone can understand the logic behind art. While you may not become fluent in both art and programming, you will gain knowledge, and appreciation for both domains is important for working in the games industry. In addition, it is absolutely necessary for artists working in the area to appreciate the technical limitations placed on their artwork by game engines and computer hardware. Some simple planning ahead and modeling within the restrictions of a games platform can eliminate a lot of future time, money, and heartache.

CHAPTER 2

Real-World Mechanics

The player's primary logic operates within the known possibilities of physics. Keep in mind gravity, weight, mass, density, force, buoyancy, elasticity, etc. Use this as the starting point, but do not be limited by it.

Matt Allmer

2.1 Introduction

An understanding of motion and the driving forces thereof is crucial in understanding games. Most objects in games move. That is what makes them dynamic. Whether it be a two-dimensional (2D) character such as the original Mario or a fully-fledged three-dimensional (3D) character such as Geralt in *The Witcher 3*, they and their game environments are in constant motion.

To grasp the concept of motion, especially with respect to computer games, a development of foundation knowledge in vector mathematics is required. Vectors are used extensively in game development for describing not only positions, speed, acceleration, and direction but also within 3D models to specify UV texturing, lighting properties, and other special effects.

Before leaping into the use of vectors in games for defining motion, a crash course in essential vector mathematics for game environments is presented in the next section.

2.2 Principles of Vectors

In Chapter 1, a vector was introduced as a line with a length (magnitude) and a direction (indicated by an arrow). Vectors can be used to represent measurements such as displacement, velocity, and acceleration. In 2D, a vector has x and y coordinates. In 3D, it has x, y, and z coordinates. In pure mathematics, a vector is not a point in space, but a set of changing coordinate instructions. It can be likened to the instructions on a fictional pirate's treasure map; for example, take three steps to the west and seven steps to the south. As shown in Figure 2.1, the instructions three steps to the west could be interpreted as the vector (3,0), meaning move 3 in the positive x direction and nothing in the y direction. The instructions move seven steps to the south become the vector (0,−7), meaning move only 7 in a negative y direction.

To determine the final location, vector x and y values are added to the starting point x and y values. For example, in Figure 2.1, the pirate ship lands at (4,8), and moving (3,0) will place them at $(4 + 3, 8 + 0) = (7,8)$. Then moving (0,−7) will put them at $(7 + 0, 8 − 7) = (7,1)$. They can also take a shortcut by going directly in a straight line to the treasure. In this case, the two instruction vectors (3,0) and (0,−7) are added together and become (3,−7). By taking the starting location and adding this new vector, they will end up in the same location [i.e., $(4 + 3, 8 − 7) = (7,1)$].

To travel from the treasure back to the ship, the pirates can follow the same line but in the opposite direction. This is achieved by flipping the vector such

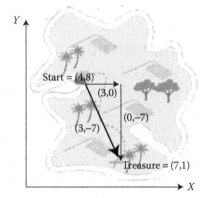

FIG 2.1 A pirate's treasure map illustrating the use of vectors.

that all coordinate values are multiplied by –1. In this case, to get back to the ship, they follow the vector (–3,7).

It might also be useful for the pirates to know how far the treasure is from the ship. The length of a vector, **v**, called its *magnitude* and written |**v**|, is found using the Pythagorean theorem:

$$|v| = \sqrt{v.x^2 + v.y^2}$$ (2.1)

For the pirates, it means that their journey is a length of 7.62 (kilometers, if the units being used are kilometers), that is, $\sqrt{3^2 + (-7)^2}$.

Sometimes it is necessary to scale a vector, so that it has a length equal to 1. The process of scaling the length is called *normalizing*, and the resultant vector, which still points in the same direction, is called a *unit vector*. To find the unit vector, each coordinate of the vector is divided by the vector's length. In the case of the pirate's journey, this would equate to (3/7.62,–7/7.62) = (0.39,–0.92). If the pirate takes 0.39 steps to the west and 0.92 steps to the south, he will end up a distance of 1 from his starting position, right on the original vector, as shown in Figure 2.2. As can be seen, the vectors (3,–7) and (0.39,–0.92) are parallel and the magnitude of (0.39,–0.92) is 1.

The unit vectors for north, south, east, and west as they would be overlaid on a map of the earth[*] are (0,1), (0,–1), (–1,0), and (1,0).

Two further important calculations can be performed with vectors. These are the *dot product* and the *cross product*. The use of these in computer graphics

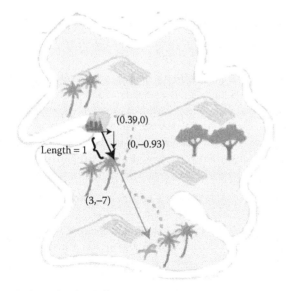

(0.39,0)

(0,–0.93)

Length = 1

(3,–7)

FIG 2.2 A normalized vector has a length of 1.

[*] This is only for a land map. For 3D coordinates there are no such equivalents.

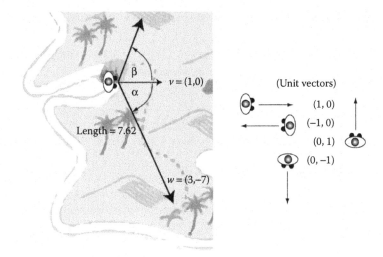

FIG 2.3 A pirate facing (1, 0) and the vector to the treasure.

and games programming will become overwhelmingly clear later. Among other things, the dot product can be used to calculate the angle between two vectors, and the cross product can be used to determine the direction.

The dot product is calculated by taking two vectors, **v** and **w**, and multiplying their respective coordinates together and then adding them. The dot product results in a single value. It can be calculated using the following equation:

$$v \cdot w = v_x \times w_x + v_y \times w_y \qquad (2.2)$$

Given the vectors **v** = (1,0) and **w** = (3,−7), the direction the pirate is facing and the direction to the treasure (shown in Figure 2.3), the dot product will be $1 \times 3 + 0 \times -7 = 3$.

But what does this mean? The most useful application of the dot product is working out the angle between two vectors. In a moment, we will work out the actual value of the angle, but for now, by just knowing the value of the dot product you can determine how the vectors sit in relation to each other. If the dot product is greater than zero, the vectors are less than 90° apart; if the dot product equals zero, then they are at right angles (perpendicular); and if the dot product is less than zero, then they are more than 90° apart.

To find out the exact angle the pirate must turn to face the treasure, the arccosine of the dot product of the unit vectors is calculated. The unit vector for (3,−7) is (0.39,−0.92) as already established and (1,0) is already a unit vector. This result for the angle between the vectors is therefore:

$= $ arcos[(1,0).(0.39,0.92)]
$= $ arcos[(1 × 0.39) + (0 × 0.92)]
$= $ arcos(0.39)
$= 67°$

You can always check the result of your calculation by looking at a plot of the vectors and measuring them with a protractor. In this case, by taking a visual estimate, the angle is larger than 45° and less than 90°; therefore, the calculation appears to be correct.

Now imagine the pirate is told to turn 67° and walk for 7.62 km to get to the treasure. Which way does he turn? The image in Figure 2.3 shows that a decision needs to be made as whether to turn to the right or the left.

In computer graphics, a positive value for an angle always indicates a counterclockwise turn. A counterclockwise turn in this case would have the pirate facing away from the treasure. When calculating the angle between vectors using the dot product, the angle is always positive. Therefore, you need another method to determine the turn direction. This is where the cross product comes into play.

The cross product of two vectors results in another vector. The resulting vector is perpendicular (at 90°) to both the initial vectors. This sounds odd working in 2D as a vector at right angles to two vectors in 2D would come right out of the page. For this reason, the cross product is only defined for 3D. The formula to work out the cross product is a little obtuse and requires further knowledge of vector mathematics, but we will try to make it as painless as possible.

The cross product of two vectors, v and w, denoted $v \times w$ is shown in the following equation:

$$v \times w = (v_y w_z - v_z w_y)(1,0,0) + (v_z w_x - v_x w_z)(0,1,0) + (v_x w_y - v_y w_x)(0,0,1) \quad (2.3)$$

The equation is defined in terms of standard 3D unit vectors. These vectors are three unit-length vectors oriented in the directions of the x, y, and z axes. If you examine Equation 2.3 you will notice that there are three parts added together. The first part determines the value of the x coordinate of the vector, as the unit vector $(1,0,0)$ only has a value for the x coordinate. The same occurs in the other two parts for the y and z coordinates.

To find the cross product of two 2D vectors, the vectors first need to be converted into 3D coordinates. This is as easy as adding a zero z value. For example, $v = (1,0)$ will become $v = (1,0,0)$ and $w = (0.39,-0.92)$ will become $w = (0.39,-0.92,0)$. The value of $v \times w$ would equate to $(0 \times 0 - 0 \times -0.92)(1,0,0) + (0 \times 0.39 - 1 \times 0)(0,1,0) + (1 \times -0.92 - 0 \times 0.39)(0,0,1) = 0(1,0,0) + 0(0,1,0) + -0.92(0,0,1) = (0,0,0) + (0,0,0) + (0,0,-0.92) = (0,0,-0.92)$. This vector only has a z coordinate, so is directed along the z axis. It is therefore coming out of the page.

An interesting thing to note about the cross product is that if the order of the equation is reversed, the resulting vector is different. $w \times v$ would equal $(0,0,0.92)$ (check this out!), which is a vector of the same length as the one produced by $v \times w$, but traveling in the exact opposite direction. This differs from the calculation of the dot product that yields the same answer no matter what the order of the vectors.

How does this help the pirate determine the direction in which to turn?

If he starts by facing in the direction of *v* and wishes to turn to face *w*, we can calculate *v* × *w*. If we examine Figure 2.3, we can see that *w* would be on the pirate's right and therefore would require a clockwise turn. We know from the previous example that a clockwise turn between two vectors produces a cross product result with a negative *z* value. The opposite is true for a counterclockwise turn. Therefore, we can say that if *z* is positive, it means a counterclockwise turn and if *z* is negative, a clockwise turn.

The pirate now knows to turn to his right 67° clockwise and travel 7.62 km in a straight line to reach the treasure.

This may all seem obvious by looking at the map. However, objects in a game environment that have no visual point of reference, such as artificially controlled bots or vehicles, require these very calculations in order to move around successfully in a virtual environment.

◁ **Unity Specifics**
Vectors
Every object in Unity has a number of vectors associated with it. A game object's transform component has three: position, rotation and scale. Figure 2.4 shows the layout of a typical game environment with a robot

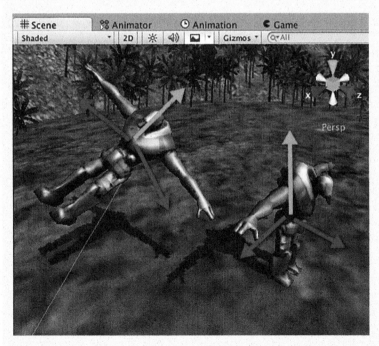

FIG 2.4 Vectors in the Unity 3D environment.

model as a game object. Usually in 3D, the *y* axis represents up, the *x* axis to the side, and the *z* axis forwards. Both the environment and all game objects have their own transforms. The axes are displayed in the Scene as red, green, and blue arrowed lines as shown in Figure 2.4. The *y*/up axis is green, the *x*/side axis is red and the *z*/forward axis is blue.

The environment has its own axes and the orientation is set by the way you change the scene around to look at different objects. In the Game, the orientation is dependent on the camera's orientation. Each game object has its own local orientation depicted by a set of axes appearing in the Scene when the object is selected. So while the *y* axis for the world may be vertical in a scene, it could be horizontal locally for an object that is lying down.

In Unity there are two vector classes: Vector2 and Vector3. A game object's position, rotation, and scale values are stored as Vector3. Vector2 is useful for storing 2D vector information.

A game object also has a vector for each of its *x*, *y*, and *z* axes: Vector3. left, Vector3.up, and Vector3.forward respectively. These are useful for moving an object along its axes without needing to know its orientation.

◉ On the Website
Vector2 and Vector3 Class Definitions
Detailed information about the Unity vector classes can be found in the Script Reference here:

http://unity3d.com/support/documentation/ScriptReference/Vector2.html
http://unity3d.com/support/documentation/ScriptReference/Vector3.html

2.3 Defining 2D and 3D Space

Whether it is in 2D or 3D space, the principles of vectors are applied in the same way. As we explored with vectors, the difference between a 2D coordinate and a 3D coordinate is just another value. In 3D game engines, such as Unity, 2D games are created by ignoring one of the axes. In the rocket ship application shown in Section 2.4, all game objects are positioned in the same plane, having a *y* position value initially set to 0. All movements thereafter only move and rotate the objects in *x* and *y*. This is the same principle as moving objects around on a flat tabletop. In the rocket ship game, the camera is positioned directly above the game objects and perspective is removed to give the illusion of a truly 2D world.

The camera in a game is a critical component, as it presents the action to the player. It is literally the lens through which the game world is perceived. Understanding how the camera moves and how to set what it looks at is essential knowledge.

2.3.1 Cameras

The camera in a game defines the visible area on the screen. In addition to defining the height and width of the view, the camera also sets the depth of what can be seen. The entire space visible by a camera is called the *view volume*. If an object is not inside the view volume, it is not drawn on the screen. The shape of the view volume can be set to orthographic or perspective. Both views are constructed from an eye position (representing the viewers' location), a near clipping plane, the screen, and a far clipping plane.

An orthographic camera projects all points of 3D objects between the clipping planes in parallel onto a screen plane, as shown in Figure 2.5. The screen plane is the view the player ends up seeing. The viewing volume of an orthographic camera is the shape of a rectangular prism.

A perspective camera projects all points of 3D objects between the clipping planes back to the eye, as shown in Figure 2.6. The near clipping plane becomes the screen. The viewing volume of a perspective camera is called the *frustum*, as it takes on the volume of a pyramid with the top cut off. The eye is located at the apex of the pyramid.

The result of using a perspective and orthographic camera on the same scene in Unity is illustrated in Figure 2.7. A perspective camera is used in Figure 2.7a. The way in which perspective projections best show depth is evident from the line of buildings getting smaller as they disappear into the distance. This is not the case for the orthographic camera shown in Figure 2.7b. Depth can only be determined by which objects are drawn in front. The buildings appear to be flattened with no size difference between buildings in the distance. Figure 2.7c and d illustrate the way in which the camera view volume is displayed in Unity's Editor Scene. If an object is not inside the view volume in the Scene, it will not appear on the screen in the Game.

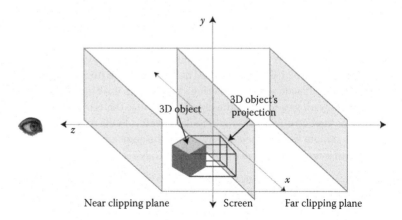

FIG 2.5 Orthographic projection.

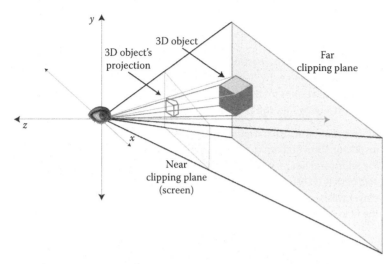

FIG 2.6 Perspective projection.

(a)

(b)

(c)

(d)

FIG 2.7 A 3D scene in Unity using (a) a perspective camera and (b) an orthographic camera. (c) The perspective camera's frustum as displayed in the Unity scene. (d) The orthographic camera's frustum as displayed in the Unity scene.

◁ **Unity Specifics**
Cameras

When you first create a new project in Unity, it will come with a Main Camera in the Hierarchy. Selecting a camera reveals the settings in the Inspector. Examples for the orthographic and perspective cameras are shown in Figure 2.8a and b, respectively.

While setting the camera values for the near and far planes in the Inspector, the resulting frustum can be watched in the Scene. To change the width and height of the viewing volume, for a perspective camera the *field of view* (FOV) is modified. The greater the field of view, the more the player will be able to see around their immediate area. To get a feel for the field of view hold your arms out to the side and look straight ahead as

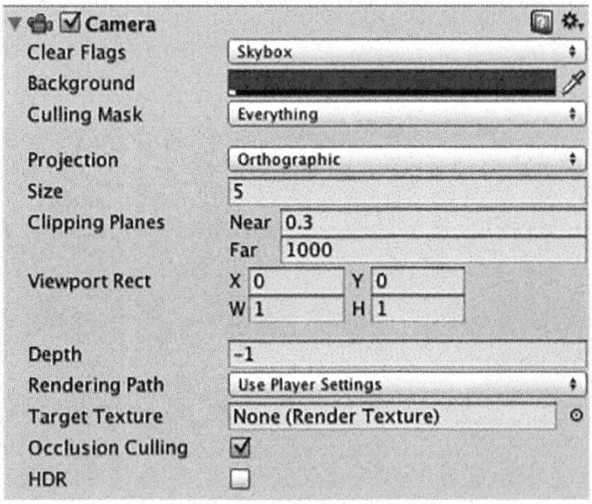

(a)

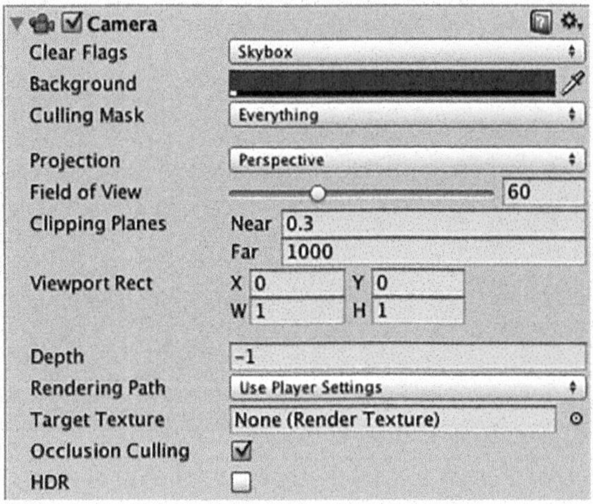

(b)

if to make a cross figure with your body. Slowly bring your arms around to your front until you can just see both hands out of the corners of your eyes (while looking straight ahead). When your hands come into your peripheral vision, the angle your arms make is your field of view. The average human forward facing field of view is close to 180 degrees while some birds are capable of almost 360 degrees.

The complementary field of view for the orthogonal camera in Unity is set by the size property.

FIG 2.8 Settings for the Unity camera. a) Orthographic Camera b) Perspective Camera.

◎ Unity Hands On
Getting Comfortable Behind the Camera
Step 1: Download *Chapter Two/CameraPlay.zip* from the website, unzip, and open in Unity. In the Project, double-click on *street* in the *Scenes* folder to open the scene. The Scene will appear with a row of medieval houses on a terrain.
Step 2: Modify the window tabs if necessary to enable viewing of the Game and Scene at the same time. Select Main Camera from the Hierarchy. Zoom in or out in the Scene so that the camera and its frustum are in full view. If you cannot find the camera, double-click on it in the Hierarchy to bring it into the center of the Scene.

◎ Note
To set the Game view camera to look at the environment from the same location set in the Scene, select the Main Camera in the Hierarchy and GameObject > Align with View from the main menu. This repositions the camera to be looking at the scene from your point of view.

To move independently around in the Scene, leaving the camera where it is, hold down the Q key and drag the mouse to pan and hold down the ALT key and drag the mouse to rotate.

Step 3: Locate the Camera component in the Inspector. Find the Field of View slider. Move the slider forward and back to change the viewing angle. Take note how the frustum is affected in the Scene and the resulting Game view.
Step 4: Set the Field of View to 60°. This is a popular setting for the FOV in many games. This setting is half the total viewing angle. In this case it gives you 120°.
Step 5: Change the Far clipping plane to 90°. Note that half of the background trees are missing in the Game. This is because they are now beyond the far plane and outside the frustum. The background color you see is set by the *Background* property in the camera settings.

Step 6: To watch the effect of changing the far plane distance continually, place the mouse over the word Far, hold down the right mouse button, and drag it left and right to decrease and increase the value in the Far box. This method can be used for changing the values of most properties in the Unity Editor.

Step 7: Now, do the same for the Near clipping plane and observe how the view in the Game is modified.

Step 8: Change the camera to Orthographic by changing the Projection property of the Camera component. Try modifying the size property to see how it affects the Game view.

Step 9: Change the camera back to a perspective projection. Set the FOV to 60° and the Near and Far planes to 1° and 200°, respectively.

Step 10: Create a sphere Game Object and position it at (620,15,715).

Step 11: Select GameObject > Camera from the main menu. Rename it to SphereCam. This camera will become the viewing camera automatically.

Step 12: Locate the Depth property in the SphereCam's Camera component. If this property is larger than the depth for the Main Camera, it will be the one that is drawn in the Game. Change the depth for both cameras so that the SphereCam's depth is −1 and the Main Camera's depth is 2°. The Main Camera will take control again.

Step 13: Set the SphereCam's position to (0,0,0).

Step 14: Drag and drop the SphereCam onto Sphere in the Hierarchy as shown in Figure 2.9.

Step 15: If you try to play the scene at this point, there will be an error reported saying "There are two audio listeners in the scene. Please ensure there is always exactly one audio listener in the scene." This is because there is an audio listener attached to all cameras by default. As with the *Highlander*, in the end there can be only one in your game. The audio listener is the component that listens for audio sources in the

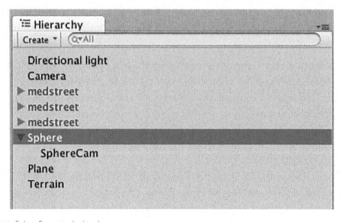

FIG 2.9 SphereCam attached to the scene.

game environment and ensures that they play at the right volume and in the correct speakers. To resolve the error, remove the audio listener from the SphereCam.

Step 16: Create a new C# file and call it *Orbit*. Enter the code in Listing 2.1.

Listing 2.1 Script to make a game object move in a circular path around its starting position

```
using System.Collections;
using System.Collections.Generic;
using UnityEngine;

public class Orbit : MonoBehaviour {

    float radius = 30;
    Vector3 startPosition;
    int speed = 3;

    void Start() {
        startPosition = transform.position;
    }

    void Update ()
    {
        transform.position = new Vector3(radius * Mathf.
            Sin(Time.fixedTime * speed) +
        startPosition.x,
        transform.position.y,
        radius * Mathf.Cos(Time.fixedTime * speed) +
        startPosition.z);
    }
}
```

Step 17: Attach the C# to the Sphere.

Step 18: Select SphereCam from Hierarchy such that the Camera Preview window opens in Scene.

Step 19: Ensure that you can see both Game and Scene views and press play.

Step 20: The camera preview for the SphereCam will display a moving scene as the Sphere moves about within the environment.

Step 21: Create a Plane and position and orient it as shown in Figure 2.10.

Step 22: In Project, select Create > Render Texture. Rename it to sphereCamView.

Step 23: Select SphereCam in the Hierarchy and in the Target Texture property of the Camera component, select and set sphereCamView. If you select sphereCamView from the Project, you will see the view captured by SphereCam on this new texture's surface in the Inspector.

Step 24: Drag and drop the sphereCamView render texture onto the new plane in the Scene. With the plane selected, change the shader for sphereCamView to Unlit/Texture.

FIG 2.10 Adding a new plane to the scene.

Step 25: Play to see the view from SphereCam play out on the big screen in your scene. This technique can be used in your games for surveillance cameras, minimaps, or reflections in mirrors or water.

While cameras can be used to create a number of different visual effects, they are also important for optimizing a game's performance. For example, the camera's view volume should not be considered a trivial setting. As mentioned previously, all objects inside the view volume get drawn to the screen. The more objects to be drawn, the slower the frames per second. Even objects behind other objects and not noticeably visible will be considered by the game engine as something to be drawn. So even though an object does not appear on the screen, if it is inside the camera's view volume it will be processed. Therefore, if you have a narrow back street scene in a European city where the player will never see beyond the immediate buildings, the camera's far plane can come forward to exclude other buildings that cannot be seen anyway.

Whether the camera is looking at an orthographic or a perspective view, the coordinate system within the game environment remains the same.

2.3.2 Local and World Coordinate Systems

There are two coordinate systems at work in game environments: local and world. The local system is relative to a single game object, and the world system specifies the orientation and coordinates for the entire world. It is like having a map for the local layout of a city versus the longitude and latitude system used for the entire earth.

A game object can move and rotate relative to its local coordinate system or the world. How it moves locally depends on the position of the origin, the (0,0,0) point, within the model. Figure 2.11a shows a 3D model in Blender with the origin situated at the tip of the head, and Figure 2.11b shows it in the center of the body. In Blender the default vertical axis is the z axis. The red and green lines in Figure 2.11a and b represent the x and y axes, respectively. When imported into Unity, the software automatically flips the z axis for you, making y the new vertical axis. As shown in Figure 2.11a and b, the origin of the model is carried across into Unity. When a model is selected, its origin is evident by the location of the translation handles used for moving the model around in the Scene. The location of the model's central point becomes an issue in Unity when positioning and rotating it. In Figure 2.11e, both models are placed in the world at (0,0,0) as set by the Inspector. As you can see, the models are placed in differing positions relative to their own central points. Figure 2.11f demonstrates how rotation is also affected by the model's origin. The model from Figure 2.11a rotates about the point in the center top of the head, whereas the model in Figure 2.11b rotates about its abdomen.

In Figure 2.12, the effect of rotations on local and world coordinate systems is illustrated. Any object at the world origin when rotated will be oriented in the same way around local and world axes. However, when the model is not at the world origin, a rotation in world coordinates will move as well as reorient the model. Local rotations are not affected by the model's location in the world.

2.3.3 Translation, Rotation, and Scaling

Three transformations can be performed on an object whether it be in 2D or 3D: translation, rotation, and scaling.

Translation refers to moving an object and is specified by a vector in the same way the pirate in Section 2.2 moved across the island. A translation occurs whenever the x, y, or z values of an object are modified. They can be modified all at once with a vector or one at a time. To move an object in the x direction by 5, the Unity C# is:

```
this.transform.Translate(5,0,0);
```

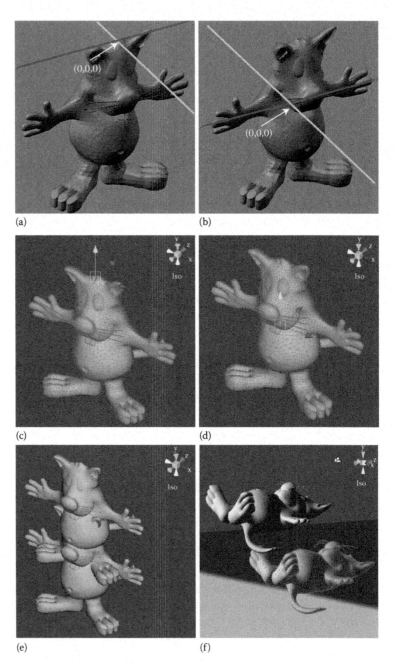

FIG 2.11 The effect of transformations based on local coordinates. (a) A model in Blender with the origin at the center top, (b) a model in Blender with the origin in the abdomen, (c) translation axes positioned in Unity for the model in (a), (d) translation axes positioned in Unity for the model in (b), (e) both models positioned at the world origin in a Unity scene, and (f) both models rotated 90° about their local *x* axes.

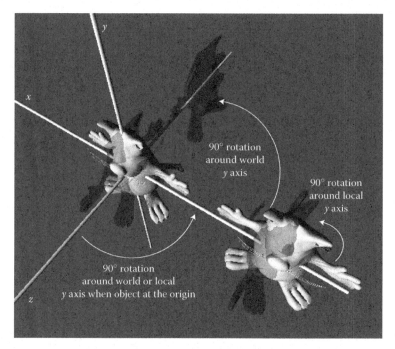

FIG 2.12 Local and world rotations affected by a model's position.

To move the object by 3 in the *x*, 5 in the *y*, and 8 in the *z*, in Unity C# it could be written as

```
this.transform.Translate(3,5,8);
```

Several examples of the Translate function are shown in Figure 2.13.

Rotation turns an object about a given axis by a specified number of degrees. An object can rotate about its *x*, *y*, or *z* axes or the world *x*, *y*, or *z* axes. Combined rotations are also possible. These cause an object to rotate around arbitrary axes defined by vector values. The Unity C# to rotate an object about 90° about the *y* axis is

```
this.transform.Rotate(Vector3.up, 90);
```

To rotate 90° around the *x* axis, the script is

```
this.transform.Rotate(Vector3.right, 90);
```

and to rotate 90° around the *z* axis, the script is

```
this.transform.Rotate(Vector3.forward, 90);
```

Some of these rotations are illustrated in Figure 2.14.

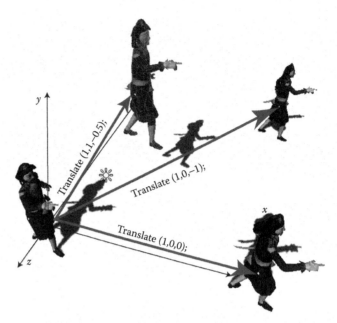

FIG 2.13 Using the translate function to modify the position of a game object.

FIG 2.14 Rotating a game object with the rotate function.

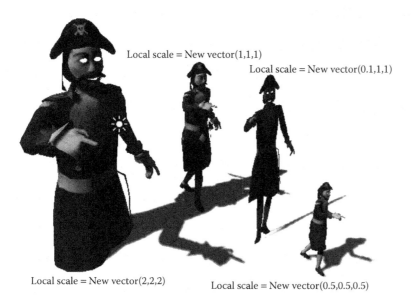

Local scale = New vector(1,1,1)

Local scale = New vector(0.1,1,1)

Local scale = New vector(2,2,2)

Local scale = New vector(0.5,0.5,0.5)

FIG 2.15 Scaling an object.

Finally, scaling changes the size of an object as shown in Figure 2.15. An object can be scaled along its *x*, *y*, or *z* axis. This can be achieved in C# at the same time using a vector, thus

```
this.transform.localScale = new Vector3(3,0.5,10);
```

Values for the scale are always multiplied against the original size of the object. Therefore, a scale of zero is illegal. If a negative scaling value is used, the object is flipped. For example, setting the *y* axis scale to −1 will turn the object upside down.

Taking some time to orient yourself with both 2D and 3D space is necessary to understanding how objects will move around within your game. Fortunately, Unity takes the hard mathematics and hides it behind many easy-to-use functions. However, when something goes wrong in your game, it's nice to have some idea where to start looking.

2.3.4 Polygons and Normals

Chapter 1 introduced polygons as the small shapes, usually triangles and sometimes squares, that make up 2D and 3D meshes (or models). A polygon in a mesh also represents a *plane*. A plane is a 3D object that has a width and height but no depth. It is completely flat and can be oriented in any direction, but not twisted.

The sides of planes are defined by straight edges between vertices. Each vertex has an associated point in space. In addition, planes only have one side. This means that they can only be seen when viewed from above. To see this, open Unity and create a plane game object. Rotate the plane around to the other side. It will become invisible, but it will still be there.

In order to define the visible side of a plane, it has an associated vector called a *normal*. This is not to be confused with normalization of a vector into a unit vector. A normal is a vector that is orthogonal (90°) to the plane as shown in Figure 2.16.

Knowing the normal to a plane is critical in determining how textures and lighting affect a model. It is the side the normal comes out of that is visible and therefore textured and lit. When a model is created in a 3D modeling package such as Blender, the normals are usually facing outward from the object. Figure 2.17 shows a model in Blender with the normals for each plane shown in blue.

The angle that a normal makes with any rays from light sources is used to calculate the lighting effect on the plane. Figure 2.18 illustrates the vectors and normal used in calculating the effect of light on a plane. The closer the normal becomes to being parallel with the vector to the light source, the brighter the plane will be drawn. This lighting model is called Lambert shading and is used in computer graphics for diffuse lighting.

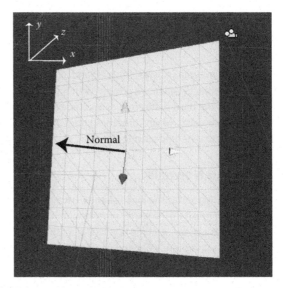

FIG 2.16 A plane and its normal.

FIG 2.17 A 3D model in Blender showing normals for each plane in blue. To turn this on, select the object and, in edit mode, click on Draw Normals in the mesh tools 1 panel.

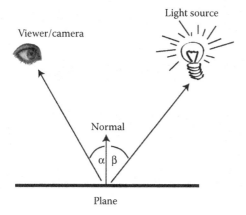

FIG 2.18 Vectors used in calculating the strength of lighting on a plane; a vector to the viewer, the normal and a vector to the light source.

⊙ Unity Hands On

Meshes and Normals

Step 1: Download *Chapter Two/PolyNormals.zip* from the website, unzip, and open.

Step 2: In the Scene, create two plane objects and place them side by side. Use GameObject > 3D Object > Plane to generate each new object.

Step 3: Add a directional light and rotate it, so the light is hitting the planes at about 30°.

Step 4: Take the *CrumbleMesh.cs* script and attach it to both planes.

Step 5: Select one of the planes in the Hierarchy, and tick the box next to *Recalculate Normals* of the *Crumble Mesh Script* component in the Inspector.

Step 6: Play. You will be able to see the planes deforming as shown in Figure 2.19.

Step 7: Examine the CrumpleMesh script in the editor. Although the code itself is complex for a beginner programmer, there are a few lines of significance to point out. First, the script uses a class called Perlin(). The complete code for this can be found in the Plugin folder in the Project. The specifics of this are not important at this time, but it is the cause of the smooth deformation movement of the planes. It is essentially a fractal algorithm for a random yet smooth movement. Each vertex of the plane's mesh is captured and translated using a value from the Perlin function.

```
Mesh mesh = GetComponent<MeshFilter>().mesh;
```

The line is the Unity method for getting the mesh of any object to which the script is attached. At the very bottom of the script is the option to

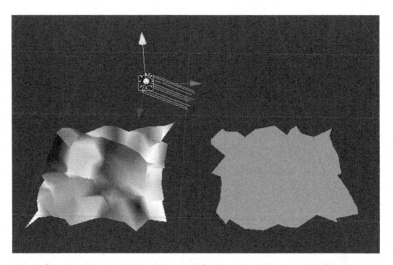

FIG 2.19 Two planes, a directional light, and a script to deform the surfaces. The plane on the left has its normal recalculated.

recalculate the normal. The script will do this when the tick box you selected before is ticked. This is the reason why one plane has updated shading and the other does not. The plane without the recalculated normal keeps the shading it started with on each polygon because, as far as the rendering system is concerned, the angle between the light source and the normal has remained unchanged. It is possible to move vertices around and leave the normals where they were. In this case, the original normals are no longer orthogonal with their polygons.

```
mesh.RecalculateNormals();
```

The line ensures that all normals are recalculated and made orthogonal to their polygons after the polygons' vertices are moved. In this case, recalculating the normal is essential to getting the correct lighting effect on the surface.

2.4 Two-Dimensional Games in a 3D Game Engine

Although 3D game engines are not often written to support 2D game creation, many developers use them for this purpose because (a) they are familiar with them, (b) they do not have to purchase software licenses for other development platforms, and (c) the engines provide support for multiple platforms and game types. As Unity added the feature to port from Android and iOS platforms in earlier versions, it became attractive to developers for the creation of 2D content. At the time, Unity was still strictly 3D and 2D had to be faked by ignoring one of the axes in the 3D world.

Now-a-days Unity supports 2D game creation by putting the camera into orthographic mode and looking straight down the *z* axis. This setup happens by default when a new project is created in 2D mode. The scene is still essentially 3D but all the action appears and operates in the *X-Y* plane.

○ **Unity Hands On**
A 2D Vector Based Space Shoot 'em Up
In this hands-on exercise we will create a simple 2D environment in which a rocket ship shoots at the earth. It will demonstrate how to program an object to automatically move around a target and shoot at it.

Step 1: Download *Chapter Two/Basic2DStarter.zip* from the website, unzip, and open in Unity. The new scene will have a Main Camera set to orthographic with a size of 5. Do not change these settings. In the Project you will see a couple of textures and materials. One is of the earth and one of a rocket ship.

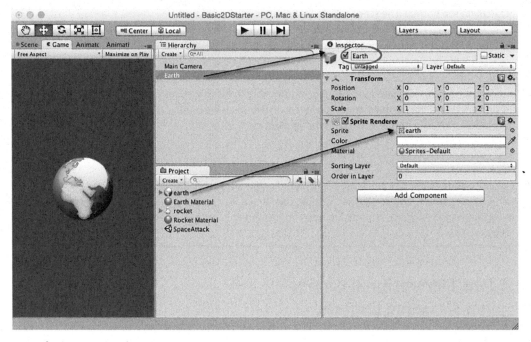

FIG 2.20 Creating a new sprite and assigning a texture.

Step 2: Add a new sprite to the Scene with GameObject > 2D Object > Sprite from the main menu. Call this new sprite "Earth." Select this sprite in the Hierarchy and drag and drop the earth texture from the project onto the sprite property of the Sprite Renderer as shown in Figure 2.20.

Step 3: Create another sprite in the same way as Step 2, name it "Rocket" and give it the rocket texture. The rocket will appear on top of the earth sprite. With the rocket selected in the Hierarchy, press the W key and then drag the rocket to one side, away from the earth in the Scene.

Step 4: Create a new C# Script in the Project. Recall the procedure to do this is to select the small drop-down Create menu in the Project window and select C#. Rename the file Attack.cs and enter the following code in Listing 2.2.

Listing 2.2 Script to make one game object face another

```
//Attack.cs
using System.Collections;
using System.Collections.Generic;
using UnityEngine;
```

```
public class Attack : MonoBehaviour {

    public GameObject target;
    public float turnSpeed = 5.0f;

    void LookAt2D(Vector3 targetPos)
    {
        Vector3 dir = targetPos - this.transform.
            position;
        float angle = Mathf.Atan2(dir.y, dir.x) * Mathf.
            Rad2Deg - 90;
        Quaternion q = Quaternion.AngleAxis(angle,
            Vector3.forward);
        this.transform.rotation = Quaternion.Slerp
            (transform.rotation, q,
            Time.deltaTime * turnSpeed);
    }

    void Update ()
    {
        LookAt2D(target.transform.position);
    }
}
```

The code in Listing 2.2 employs a function called LookAt2D(). This causes the object to which the code is attached to smoothly turn and look at the target object. Unity has a LookAt() function built in and works on 3D objects. It turns a game object such that the object's z axis is oriented toward the target. If you use this in the 2D environment the object in question will turn on its side and become invisible. In this case we want to turn the object such that its y axis faces the target. You will notice the code uses something called *quaternions*. These will be discussed in the next section.

In the angle calculation you will see a "−90" on the end of the calculation. This is assuming the game object travels in the direction of its y axis. If your object needs to move along the x axis instead, remove the "−90" from the calculation.

Attach the attack script to the rocket. Drag and drop the Earth sprite onto its exposed Target variable as shown in Figure 2.21.

Play. The rocket will turn slowly to face the earth. No matter where the rocket is placed in the Scene it will always turn to face the target. If you want to change the turn rate, adjust the exposed Turn Speed variable in the attack script.

Step 5: Now the rocket is turning toward the earth, we want to make it move forward. To do this is a matter of adding a single line into the code as shown in Listing 2.3.

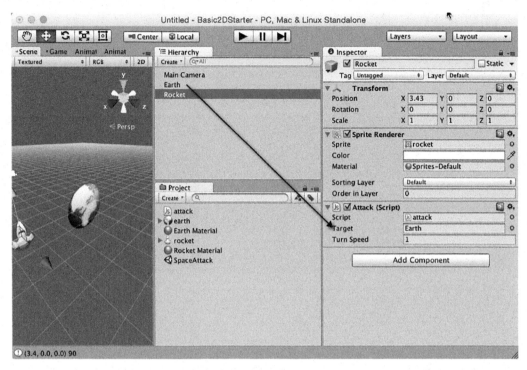

FIG 2.21 Attaching the code and assigning a target game object.

Listing 2.3 Script to make an object move toward its target

```
using System.Collections;
using System.Collections.Generic;
using UnityEngine;

public class Attack : MonoBehaviour {

    public GameObject target;
    public float turnSpeed = 5.0f;
    public float flightSpeed = 0.3f;

    void LookAt2D(Vector3 targetPos)
    {
        Vector3 dir = targetPos - this.transform.position;
        float angle = Mathf.Atan2(dir.y, dir.x) * Mathf.
            Rad2Deg - 90;
        Quaternion q = Quaternion.AngleAxis(angle,
            Vector3.forward);
        this.transform.rotation = Quaternion.Slerp
            transform.rotation, q,
            (Time.deltaTime * turnSpeed);
    }
```

```
    void Update ()
    {
        LookAt2D(target.transform.position);
        this.transform.Translate(Vector3.up *
            flightSpeed);
    }
}
```

Save and play. The rocket will fall into an orbit of the earth. This is because it is constantly turning toward it and moving forward. For a tighter orbit increase the Turn Rate speed.

Step 6: To make the rocket move away from the planet when it gets too close, we can test for the distance the rocket is from the planet and turn it back toward its starting position when it comes within a specific distance. To do this, modify your script to that in Listing 2.4.

Listing 2.4 Testing rocket's distance to planet

```
using System.Collections;
using System.Collections.Generic;
using UnityEngine;

public class Attack : MonoBehaviour {

    public GameObject target;
    public float turnSpeed = 5.0f;
    public float flightSpeed = 0.3f;

    float distanceToTarget;
    string state = "ATTACK";

    void LookAt2D(Vector3 targetPos)
    {
        Vector3 dir = targetPos - this.transform.position;
        float angle = Mathf.Atan2(dir.y, dir.x) * Mathf.
            Rad2Deg - 90;
        Quaternion q = Quaternion.AngleAxis(angle,
            Vector3.forward);
        this.transform.rotation = Quaternion.
            Slerp(transform.rotation, q, Time.deltaTime *
            turnSpeed);
    }

    void Update ()
    {
        distanceToTarget = (target.transform.position -
            this.transform.position).magnitude;
        if(distanceToTarget > 10)
```

```
    {
        state = "ATTACK";
    }
    else if (distanceToTarget < 2)
    {
        state = "RETREAT";
    }
    if(state == "ATTACK")
    {
        LookAt2D(target.transform.position);
        this.transform.Translate(Vector3.up *
            flightSpeed);
    }
    else
    {
        this.transform.Translate(Vector3.up *
            flightSpeed);
    }
}
}
```

Save and Play. When the rocket gets within a distance of 2 of the earth it will start retreating until it is further than a distance of 10 away and then it will start attacking again. At this stage you can play with the flightSpeed and turnSpeed values to get the behavior you desire from the rocket.

At this point is worth pausing for a discussion of quaternions, the mathematical construct at the heart of turning the rocket ship around.

2.4.1 Quaternions?

In 3D space there are three axes around which an object can rotate. These rotations are analogous with the rotational movements of an aircraft as shown in Figure 2.22 (a) a rotation about the x axis, (b) creates pitch, a rotation about the z axis, (c) creates roll, and a rotation about the y axis, (d) develops yaw.

The angles used to specify how far to rotate objects around these axes are called Euler angles. Euler angles are often used in 3D software and game engines because they are intuitive to use. For example, if someone asked you to rotate around your vertical axis by 180° you would know this meant to turn around and look in the opposite direction.

However, there is a fundamental flaw in using Euler angles for rotations in software that can cause unexpected rotational effects. These angles are applied one after the other and therefore have a mathematical

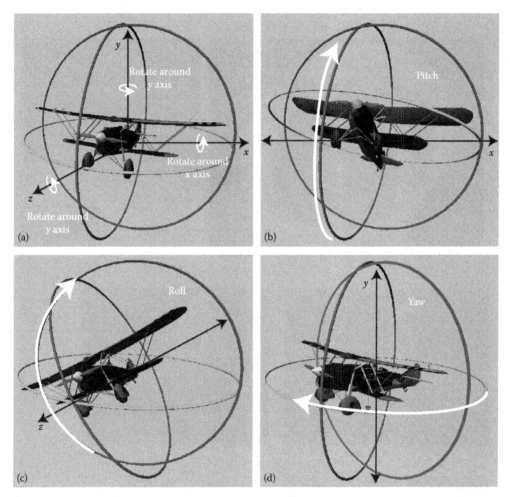

FIG 2.22 (a–d) Individual rotations about the *x*, *y*, and *z* axis in 3D space.

compounding effect. This consequence is seen in the mechanical devices used to stabilize aircraft, ships and spacecraft; the gyroscope.

A simple gyroscope is illustrated in Figure 2.23. It consists of three discs attached to the outer structure of a vehicle (in this example, a plane) and attached to each other at pivot points each representing rotations around the *x*, *y*, and *z* axes. These rotating discs are called gimbals. As the plane yaws, pitches, and rolls, the gyroscope responds to the forces with the rotating of the discs at their pivot points. The idea is that a plate attached to the central, third gimbal always remains upright. Navigational systems attached to the gyroscope monitor this plate to determine the orientation of the vehicle. For example, if the vehicle were on autopilot, the objective would be to keep it upright and level to the ground, and any change in the gyroscope's orientation assists with pitch, yaw, or roll corrections.

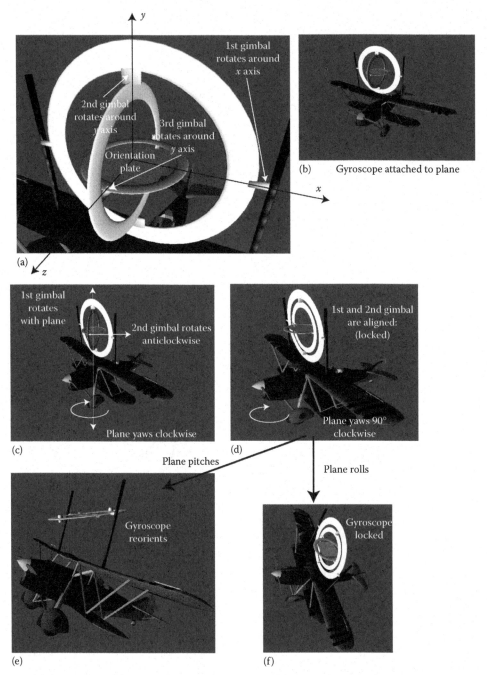

FIG 2.23 A simple gyroscope. (a) The gimbals and rotation points. (b) Attaching the gyroscope to a plane. (c) A clockwise yaw of the plane forces the first gimbal to move with it, as it is attached and has no freedom of movement in that direction, whereas the second gimbal is free to move in response in the opposite direction. (d) A 90° yaw will cause the first and second gimbals to align thereby entering a locked state. (e) After the first and second gimbals become locked, a pitch will retain the integrity of the third gimbal. (f) However, a roll can cause erratic behavior from gimbal 3.

A situation can occur in which two of the gimbals become aligned as shown in Figure 2.23d. This is called a gimbal lock. At this point, it can either be corrected with the right maneuver (e) or cause erratic behaviors. In Figure 2.23f, the third gimbal cannot rotate back such that the central plate is facing upward as its pivot points would not allow it. In some circumstances, alignment of the first and second gimbal can also cause the third gimbal to flip upside down, even if the vehicle itself is not upside down. When this occurs, the navigational system becomes very confused as it attempts to realign the vehicle.

While this is a simplistic examination of gimbals, the issue of gimbal lock is a reality. It is a mechanical reality that was experienced by the astronauts of the Apollo missions and it is a virtual reality when using Euler angles to rotation 3D objects. Just as the gyroscope compounds the rotations of the outer gimbal inward, multiplying x, y, and z angle rotations one after the other in software systems produces the same errors.

2.4.2 Quaternions to the Rescue

Quaternions are mathematical constructs that allow for rotations around the three axes to be calculated all at once in contrast to Euler angles that are calculated one after the other. A quaternion has an x, y, and z component as well as a rotation value.

In games using Euler angles, rotations can cause erratic orientations of objects. This is illustrated in Figure 2.24 where the rotations of two planes are compared.

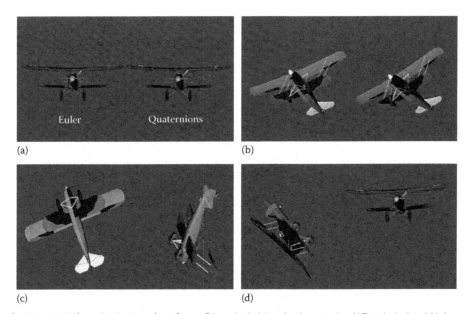

(a)   (b)

(c)   (d)

FIG 2.24 Two planes rotated 1° around each axis every frame. One uses Euler angle calculations, the other quaternions. (a) Planes begin aligned, (b) planes remain aligned at first, (c) once the x angle becomes 90° for the Euler plane, its rotations go off course with respect to the quaternion plane, (d) even further in the simulation.

Each plane is continually rotated around the x, y, and z axes by 1°. The plane on the left in Figure 2.24 is rotated using Euler angles and the other uses quaternions. The movement of the quaternion plane is smoother.

Quaternions are used throughout modern game engines, including Unity, as they do not suffer from gimbal lock.

⦾ For Research
Quaternions
If you are interested in the complex inner workings of quaternions check out *Visualizing Quaternions* by Andrew J. Hanson (2006, ISBN: 978-0120884001).

Although the rotation value for the transform component of game objects appears as Euler x, y, and z values in the Inspector, Unity uses quaternions for storing orientations. The most used quaternion functions are `LookRotation()`, `Angle()`, and `Slerp()`.

`LookRotation()` given a vector will calculate the equivalent quaternion to turn an object to look along the original vector. This means, `this.transform.rotation = Quaternion.LookRotation(target.position- this.transform.position);` achieves the same result as `this.transform.LookAt(target.transform.position)`.

The `Angle()` function calculates the angle between two rotations. It might be used to determine if an enemy is directly facing toward or away from the player.

`Slerp()` takes a starting rotation and an ending rotation and cuts it up into small arcs. It is extremely effective in making rotating objects change from one direction to another in a smooth motion. Originally, the previously created rocket ship was flipping back and forth as it changed direction. This occurs when the objects goes from the original facing direction to the goal facing direction in one frame. `Slerp()` breaks this rotation up, so small parts of it occur with each frame instead of all in one go.

Now you have a little understanding of quaternions we can continue with the 2D game. It contains two quaternion functions: `AngleAxis()` and `Slerp()`. `AngleAxis()` takes an angle and a vector, and rotates and object by the angle around the vector. It is being used to determine how to rotate the rocket, so it faces the earth. This value is required by the `Slerp()` function that uses the rotation speed and the time between the drawing of frames (`Time.deltaTime`) to carve up the complete turn angle into smaller pieces, making the rocket ship turn smoothly.

☺ Unity Hands On
Bullets and Explosions

Step 1: To create bullets that come from the rocket add a new quad to the Scene by selecting GameObject > 3D Object > Quad from the main menu. You will not be able to see it until a material is added.

Step 2: Create a new material in the Project by selecting Material from the drop-down Create menu. Set the main color of the material to red, its Shader to Sprites/Default, and rename it. Drag and drop the red material onto the new quad as shown in Figure 2.25.

Step 3: The bullet will need to be small therefore scale the square down to 0.1 for the x, y, and z scale values in the Inspector.

Step 4: Create a new C# file called MoveBullet.cs. Add the code in Listing 2.5. Attach this script to the bullet (called Quad in the Hierarchy).

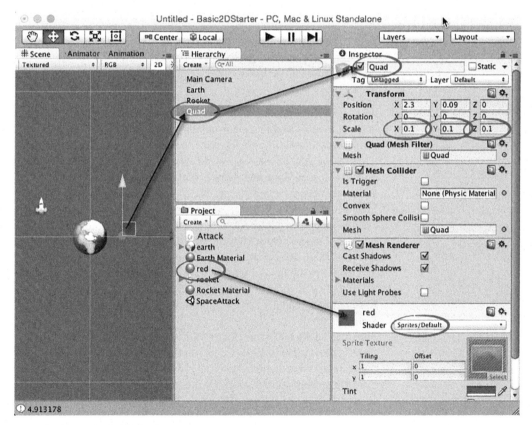

FIG 2.25 Creating a quad and coloring it red.

Listing 2.5 MoveBullet.cs

```
using System.Collections;
using System.Collections.Generic;
using UnityEngine;

public class MoveBullet : MonoBehaviour {

    float speed = 0.1f;

    void OnBecameInvisible()
    {
        Destroy(this.gameObject);
    }
    void Update ()
    {
        this.transform.Translate(Vector3.up * speed);
    }
}
```

Save and Play. The bullet will move up the screen along its up-axis and with it the *y*. If you wanted it to move sideways along the *x* you would change Vector3.up to Vector3.right.

The `OnBecameInvisible()` function ensures that the bullet gets destroyed by the game engine once it goes beyond the camera view. This will allow us to create many bullets and they will clean themselves up—meaning the game engine does not need to keep processing them if they move outside the game world. If you do not do this, you can end up with a million bullet game objects clogging up memory and eventually making your game crash.

Step 5: Next, select the bullet in the Hierarchy and remove the Mesh Collider by deleting the component in the Inspector. At the very bottom of the Inspector, click on the Add Component button. From this new menu select Physics 2D > Circle Collider 2D. This will add a 2D collider to the bullet object allowing us to detect its collisions in 2D space. If you zoom in on the bullet in the Scene you will be able to see the new collider as a circle around the red quad as shown in Figure 2.26.

Step 6: Drag the bullet from the Hierarchy and into the Project. This will create a new Prefab from the Quad. This bullet prefab can be used as a template to create multiple bullets at run time. They will all look the same, have the same properties, and have the same script attached. A prefab appears as a blue cube in the Project as shown in Figure 2.27.

Step 7: Select the bullet that remains in the Scene and delete it leaving only the prefab.

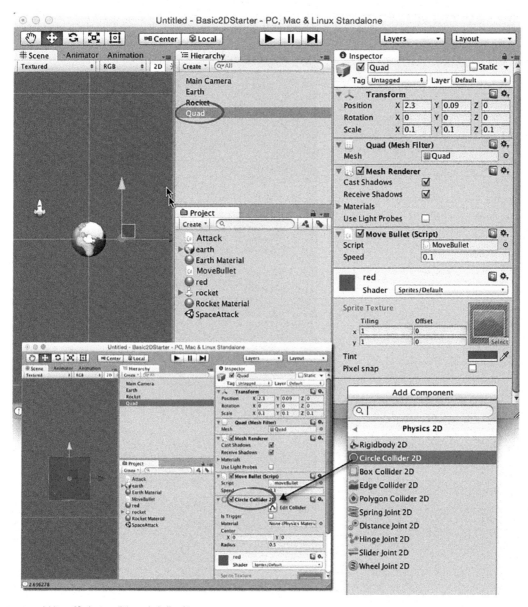

FIG 2.26 Adding a 2D physics collider to the bullet object.

Step 8: Return to the Attack.cs script. Open it in the editor. We will now add the bullet into here so the rocket shoots multiple copies of it. Modify the attack script as shown in Listing 2.6.

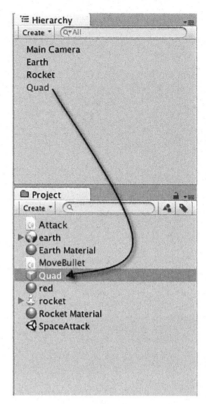

FIG 2.27 Creating a prefab.

Listing 2.6 Giving the script access to the bullet prefab

```
public class Attack : MonoBehaviour {

...
public float flightSpeed = 0.3f;

public GameObject bullet;

...

void Update ()
{
    Instantiate(bullet, this.transform.position, this.
    transform.rotation);
    distanceToTarget = (target.transform.position -
        this.transform.position).magnitude;
    if(distanceToTarget > 10)
    ...
}
```

The Instantiate function now included in update creates a copy of the bullet from the prefab we created, and places it in the game world at the position of the rocket and with the same rotation as the rocket. This means that when the script on the bullet runs and pushes it forward, it will push it forward in the direction of the rocket.

Before you can see this in action you need to drag and drop the bullet prefab from the Project and deposit it onto the exposed bullet variable on the rocket. This is shown in Figure 2.28.

Save and Play. Bullets will now come out of the rocket and proceed to move forward in the direction they were created, facing until they move off the screen. You will notice the bullets are running slower than the rocket and therefore fall behind it. To fix this, locate the bullet's speed in the moveBullet script and change it from 0.1 to 1.

Step 9: To make the rocket look like it is controlled by some half-intelligence, we should make it shoot only when it is likely to hit the target. Therefore, when it is facing away from the earth it should not be shooting at all. We do this again by calculating the angle between the rocket's facing direction and the direction to the target. If the angle is small, then the rocket should shoot. Modify the Attack.cs code as shown in Listing 2.7.

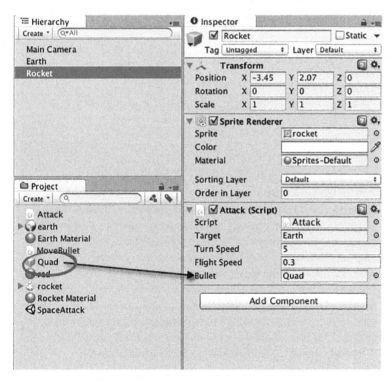

FIG 2.28 Assigning a prefab to be used by a script.

Listing 2.7 Controlling the shooting based on the rocket's facing direction

```
...
    void Update ()
    {
        //MOVE INSTANTIATE LINE FROM HERE TO BELOW
        distanceToTarget = (target.transform.position -
            this.transform.position).magnitude;
        if(distanceToTarget > 10)
        {
            state = "ATTACK";
        }
        else if (distanceToTarget < 2)
        {
            state = "RETREAT";
        }
        if(state == "ATTACK")
        {
            LookAt2D(target.transform.position);
            this.transform.Translate(Vector3.up *
                flightSpeed);
            Vector3 vectorToTarget = target.transform.
                position - this.transform.position;
            if(Vector3.Angle(vectorToTarget, this.
                transform.up) < 30)
            {
                Instantiate(bullet, this.transform.position,
                    this.transform.rotation);
            }
        }
        else
...
```

Save and Play. The rocket will now only instantiate bullets when there is 30° or less between the direction it is facing and the direction to the target. You can play around with the value of 30 as you so wish. If you use a smaller angle you might have to increase the rocket's turn rate so it can approach the target at the correct angle to trigger shooting.

Step 10: The final part of this hands-on will be to create small explosions when the bullets hit the target. The first step is to import a particle system. You will find one on the website with the starter files for this chapter called fireworks.unitypackage. To bring the file into Unity, select Assets > Import Package > Custom Package from the main menu. Locate the fireworks. unitypackage file and open it. It will create a new folder in the Project with a Fireworks prefab in Standard Assets > Particle Systems > Misc.

Step 11: To have the bullet detect when it has hit another collider we need to attach a Rigidbody to it. With the Quad prefab selected in the

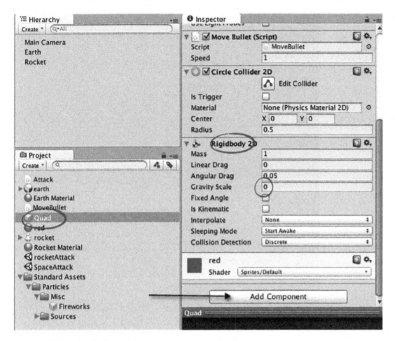

FIG 2.29 Adding a Rigidbody to an object.

Project, in the Inspector click the Add Component button and select
Physics2D > Rigidbody2D. A Rigidbody component will be added to the
Quad. Set its gravity value to 0 as shown in Figure 2.29.

Step 12: Next we need to add a collider to the Earth in order to detect
when the bullet has hit the Earth. With the Earth object selected in the
Hierarchy, in the Inspector click the Add Component button and select
Physics2D > Circle Collider 2D.

Step 13: Now modify the MoveBullet.cs script to include a Unity function
that detects collisions. When the bullet hits the earth, it will instantiate a
fireworks object. Make the changes shown in Listing 2.8.

Listing 2.8 Adding 2D collision detection function

```
using System.Collections;
using System.Collections.Generic;
using UnityEngine;

public class MoveBullet : MonoBehaviour {

    float speed = 0.1f;
    public GameObject explosion;

    void OnCollisionEnter2D(Collision2D collisionObj)
    {
```

```
            if (collisionObj.gameObject.name == "Earth")
            {
                Instantiate(explosion,this.transform.
                    position, this.transform.rotation);
                Destroy(this.gameObject);
            }
        }

        void OnBecameInvisible()
        {
            Destroy(this.gameObject);
        }

        void Update ()
        {
            this.transform.Translate(Vector3.up * speed);
        }
    }
```

Ensure the earth game object is called "Earth," with a capital "E" just like the one being tested for in the if statement in Listing 2.8 otherwise the explosion will not be instantiated.

Step 14: Before the explosion will work, you need to assign the fireworks prefab to the exposed explosion property of the MoveBullet.cs script. Locate the fireworks prefab in the Project and drag and drop it onto the explosion property as shown in Figure 2.30.

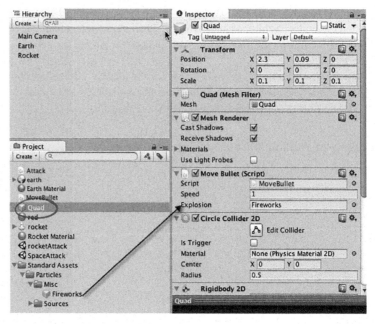

FIG 2.30 Assigning a prefab to be used by a script.

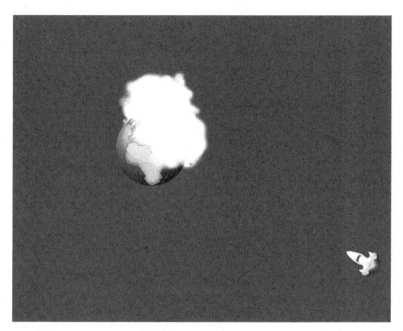

FIG 2.31 The game in play.

Step 15: Save and Play. Each time the rocket's bullets strike the earth it will instantiate a firework object as shsown in Figure 2.31.

2.5 The Laws of Physics

Game players bring their own experience of the real world to a game environment. They understand that gravity makes things drop, acceleration changes the speed of an object, and when an object hits another object, a reaction, such as bouncing or exploding, will occur based on the object's composition.

These expectations within game environments are essential to establishing the player's *suspension of disbelief*—a psychological state in which a player accepts the limitations of a medium in order to engage with the content. This can include anything from low-quality graphics to flying aliens. Anything that messes with the player's suspension of disbelief causes them to disengage and lose interest, like being woken from a dream. A big part of ensuring a game environment is making the virtual world act and react like the real one.

The laws of physics are a set of complex rules that describe the physical nature of the universe. Adhering to these rules when creating a game is key to creating a believable environment in which the player interacts. Sometimes the laws are bent to suit narrative; however, they essentially remain static throughout. For example, players in a modern warfare game, taking place on the earth, would expect gravity to react for their character as it does for them in the real world. In the case of science fiction, the effects of gravity may be altered to fit the story.

Physics is a fundamental element in games as it controls the way in which objects interact with the environment and how they move.

Although physics covers topics such as Einstein's theory of relativity and thermodynamics, the key ones used in game environments are Newton's three laws of motion and the law of gravity.

2.5.1 The Law of Gravity

Although it is a myth that an apple fell on Newton's head, he did devise his theory of gravity while watching an apple fall from a tree. In Newton's publication the *Principia*, the force of gravity is defined thus:

> *Every particle of matter in the universe attracts every other particle with a force that is directly proportional to the product of the masses of the particles and inversely proportional to the square of the distance between them.*

In short, this means the bigger an object, the more it attracts other objects and that this attraction gets stronger the closer it is. Kepler also used this law, a century later, to develop his laws of planetary motion.

In game environments, applying a downward velocity to an object simulates gravity. The *y* coordinate of the object's position is updated with each game loop to make it move in a downward direction. If you were to code this in Unity, the C# would look something like this:

```
transform.Translate(0,-1,0);
```

Unfortunately, the actual calculation for real gravity would be a little more complex than taking away one, as the effect of earth's gravity is a downward acceleration of 9.8 meters per second. This means that the downward speed of an object gets faster by 9.8 meters per second with each second. An object starting with a speed of 0 after 1 second will be moving at 9.8 meters per second, after 2 seconds it will be moving at 19.6 meters per second, and after 3 seconds it will be moving at 29.4 meters per second.

In addition, a game loop may not take exactly 1 second to execute. This will throw out any calculations you attempt with each loop update on a second by second basis.

Fortunately, game engines take care of all the mathematics and allow you to set just one gravity value for your environment. Let us take a look at how Unity does it.

◁ Unity Specifics
Gravity
From the main menu select Edit > Project Settings > Physics. The Physics properties will open in the Inspector as shown in Figure 2.32. The default setting is for a downward acceleration of 9.81 meters per second^2.

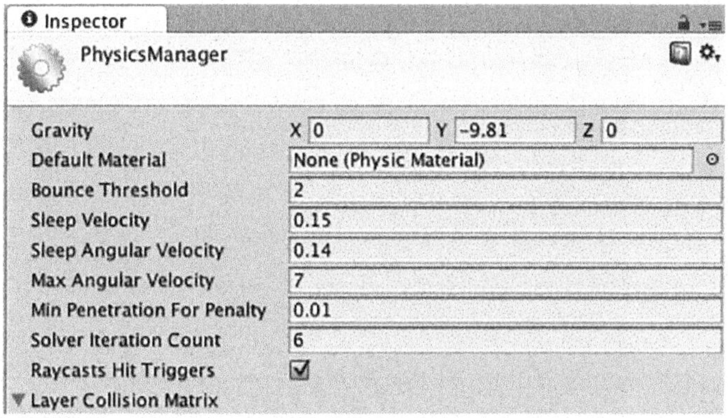

Inspector					
PhysicsManager					
Gravity	X	0	Y	-9.81	Z	0
Default Material	None (Physic Material)				⊙
Bounce Threshold	2				
Sleep Velocity	0.15				
Sleep Angular Velocity	0.14				
Max Angular Velocity	7				
Min Penetration For Penalty	0.01				
Solver Iteration Count	6				
Raycasts Hit Triggers	☑				
▼ Layer Collision Matrix					

As you can see, depending on your own game environment, gravity can be set in any direction including upwards and sideways.

FIG 2.32 Unity's physics properties.

◉ Unity Hands On
Applying Gravity
Step 1: Start Unity and create a new 3D project. Note, from now on, unless specified, all new projects should be created as 3D. Orient the Scene such that the y axis is pointing upward. Position the camera, so that it has the same view as shown in the Scene. To do this, select the camera from the Hierarchy and then from the main menu GameObject > Align with View.
Step 2: Add a sphere to the Scene and position it at the top of the camera view. With the sphere selected in the Hierarchy, click on the Add Component button in the Inspector. Navigate to add a Physics > Rigidbody. The result of this will be a new component added to the sphere in the Inspector, as shown in Figure 2.33. The Rigidbody component makes the sphere part of Unity's physics processing and as such gravity will be applied to it.
Step 3: Press play. The sphere will fall downward.

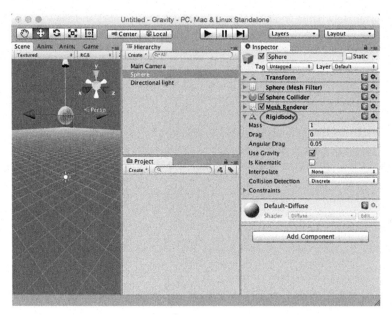

FIG 2.33 A Scene with a sphere that has a Rigidbody attached.

Step 4: Press stop and change the gravity via the main menu's Edit > Project Settings > Physics; in the Inspector click on Gravity to expand. You may want to set it to a positive y value or even have it go to the side with a change to the x. You choose.

Step 5: Press play to see the effect of the new gravity settings.

2.5.2 The First Law of Motion

Every body continues in its state of rest, or of uniform motion in a straight line, unless it is compelled to change that state by forces impressed upon it.

This means that an object will remain stationary and a moving object will keep moving in the same direction unless pushed or pulled. In the real world, a number of different forces act to move or slow objects. These include gravity and friction. In addition, objects colliding with each other will also act to change their movement.

⊙ **Unity Hands On**
Newton's First
Step 1: Create a new Unity Project. Ensure that the y axis is pointing up and position the Main Camera to the same view.
Step 2: Select GameObject >3D Object > Plane from the main menu. Resize the plane to twice its original size to create a large

ground area. You can do this by pressing the R key while the plane is selected, or changing the scale *x*, *y*, and *z* values in the Inspector to 2. Add a directional light. Add a grass or dirt seamless texture to the plane.

Step 3: Select GameObject > 3D Object > Cube from the main menu. Zoom in to center the cube in the Scene. Lift the cube so that it is slightly above the ground.

Step 4: With the cube selected in the Hierarchy, use the Add Component button in the Inspector to add a Physics > Rigidbody to it.

Step 5: Press play. The cube will fall until it hits the ground and stops. Although the plane does not have a Rigidbody attached, it does have a Collider. Select plane in the Hierarchy and look for the Mesh Collider in the Inspector. This collider is used by the physics system. Although the ground plane is not affected by the cube hitting it, the cube, because it has a Rigidbody, is stopped by the collider of the plane.

Step 6: Lift the cube higher above the plane. Add a Rigidbody to the plane. You may get an error after adding the Rigidbody to the plane. It will say something like "Computer mesh inertia tensor failed..." Ignore this for now—we will deal with it in a moment.

Step 7: Press play. Note that the plane and the cube both fall at the same rate.

Step 8: Select the plane from the Hierarchy and find its Rigidbody component in the Inspector. To add air friction, set the value of *Drag* to 10.

Step 9: Press play. The plane will fall away more slowly than the cube. When the cube hits the plane, the plane will speed up and possibly flip, depending on where you have placed the cube with respect to the plane.

Step 10: Remove the Rigidbody from the plane by selecting the small drop-down menu as shown in Figure 2.34.

Step 11: Select the cube in the Hierarchy, right-click on it, and select Duplicate as shown in Figure 2.35. Duplicating a GameObject after it has had components, such as a Rigidbody, attached to it will ensure that the duplicate has all the same attachments. Move the duplicate cube, which will be in the exact same location as the original. You can also duplicate with Ctrl+D (Windows) or Cmd+D (Mac).

Step 12: Continue duplicating and moving to build a stack of cubes as shown in Figure 2.36.

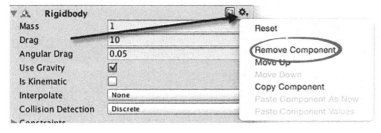

FIG 2.34 Removing a component from a game object.

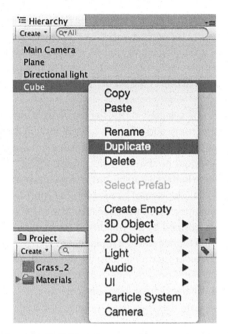

FIG 2.35 Duplicating a game object in the Inspector.

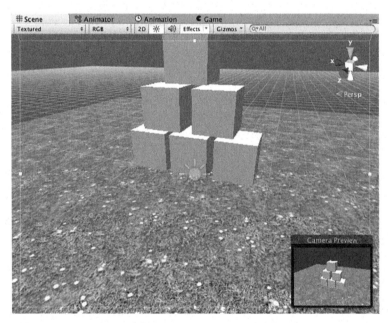

FIG 2.36 A stack of duplicated cubes, all with Rigidbodies.

Step 13: In the Project, create a new C# file and call it *fire*. Open it in the script editor and enter the code in Listing 2.9. Save the script and attach it to the Main Camera.

Listing 2.9 Script to create a sphere as a projectile on a left mouse click

```csharp
//Fire.cs

using System.Collections;
using System.Collections.Generic;
using UnityEngine;

public class Fire : MonoBehaviour {

    void Update ()
    {
        if(Input.GetButtonDown("Fire1"))
        {
            Ray ray = Camera.main.ScreenPointToRay
                (Input.mousePosition);
            GameObject sphere = GameObject.CreatePrimitive
                (PrimitiveType.Sphere);
            sphere.transform.position = ray.origin;
            sphere.AddComponent<Rigidbody>();
            sphere.GetComponent<Rigidbody>().AddForce
                (ray.direction * 1000);
        }
    }
}
```

Step 14: Save and play. A click in the Game will create a sphere at the click location and project it in the direction the camera is facing. Before a force is added to push the sphere, the `AddComponent()` function is used to add a Rigidbody component to the sphere as it is not attached by default. The `ScreenPointToRay()` takes the mouse click location and turns it into a vector (called a ray) that starts at the click location and continues in the direction the camera is facing. This direction is used as the push force on the sphere, propelling it forward.

Step 15: Gravity still affects the sphere. To see it in action, change the multiplier for the `AddForce()` function from 1000 to 100.

⊕ **Note**

Mesh Inertia Failure

From time to time when adding rigid bodies onto meshes you may get the error: Actor::updateMassFromShapes: Compute mesh inertia tensor failed for one of the actor's mesh shapes! Please change mesh geometry or supply a tensor manually! When this occurs, it means that you have tried to put a rigid body onto a mesh that has no depth and therefore no mass. A plane is so flat that it has literally 0 height; no volume, no mass. To fix this, remove the mesh collider that is on the object and replace it with something like a box or sphere collider.

2.5.3 The Second Law of Motion

The acceleration produced by a particular force acting on a body is directly proportional to the magnitude of the force and inversely proportional to the mass of the body.

This means that a larger force is required to move a heavier object. In addition, a heavier object with the same acceleration as a lighter object will cause more destruction when it hits something as the force will be greater. Imagine throwing a bowling ball and a tennis ball at a wall with the same acceleration. Which one is going to leave a bigger hole?

⊙ **Unity Hands On**
Newton's Second

Step 1: Begin by opening the Unity project from Section 2.5.2. Open the fire script and ensure that the `AddForce()` multiplier is set to 1000, for example, `AddForce(ray.direction * 1000)`.

Step 2: In the Hierarchy, select each cube in turn, locate the Rigidbody component in the Inspector, and set the *Mass* to 10.

Step 3: Press play. Note that the heavier cubes are now more difficult to knock over with the sphere.

Step 4: Edit *Fire.cs* to increase the mass of the sphere as shown in Listing 2.10. Save and play.

Listing 2.10 Script to change the mass of a Rigidbody

```
//Fire.cs

void Update ()
{
    if(Input.GetButtonDown("Fire1"))
    {
        ...
        sphere.AddComponent<Rigidbody>();
        sphere.GetComponent<Rigidbody>().mass = 10;
        sphere.GetComponent<Rigidbody>().AddForce(ray.
            direction * 1000);
    }
}
```

Step 5: Because the sphere has more mass, the added force has less effect. However, you may be able to get it to roll along the ground. The extra mass will be enough to knock over the cubes.

Step 6: Try setting the `AddForce()` multiplier to 10,000. Note that because the mass has increased 10-fold, the force required to move the sphere in the same way must also increase 10-fold.

2.5.4 The Third Law of Motion

To every action there is always opposed an equal reaction; or, the mutual actions of two bodies upon each other are always equal, and directed to contrary parts.

This can be rephrased to the well-known adage *for every action there is an equal and opposite reaction*. When a truck hits a car, energy from the movement of the truck is transferred to the car and it is propelled away from the truck. If a car hits another car of a similar size, some of the energy is transferred to the second car, whereas some goes back into the first car. If a car hits a brick wall, chances are most of the energy will go back into the car. This energy needs to go somewhere. In the case of cars, specially designed crumple zones absorb the energy. For a tennis ball, some of the energy is absorbed by the rubbery nature of the ball and the rest is used to propel the ball away. In other words, collisions occurring in the real world have an effect on the environment as well as the object.

The examples thus far examined in Unity see energy from an initial force transferred or totally absorbed by the objects. For a heavy sphere, cubes are knocked over easily, whereas a light sphere hits the cubes and drops straight to the ground. This rarely happens in the real world where things tend to *bounce*, to some degree. In Unity, adding a physics material to an object can simulate these extra effects.

◁ Unity Specifics
Physics Materials
In Unity, a physics material is created in the Project and then added to the object's Collider component. A physics material sets values for bounce and friction. The bounciness of an object can be set between 0 (no bounce) and 1 (full bounce) to simulate how much of a collision's force comes back to the object. For example, for a tennis ball, set bounce to 1. The friction value determines how well an object holds onto another surface when rubbed together. For example, rubber on concrete has a high friction value, whereas stone on ice has a low friction value. Friction is a force that slows down movement. Friction can be set to 0 (no friction) up to an infinite number (total friction).

☉ Unity Hands On
Newton's Third
Step 1: Create a new Unity project with a sloping plane and cube as shown in Figure 2.37. Attach a Rigidbody to the cube. Press play and watch the cube drop down until it hits the plane and then rolls the rest of the way. Try to rotate the cube such that one side is parallel to the plane as shown.

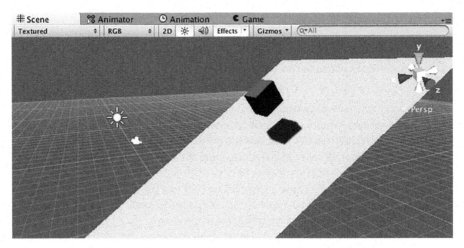

FIG 2.37 The initial scene required to demonstrate physics materials.

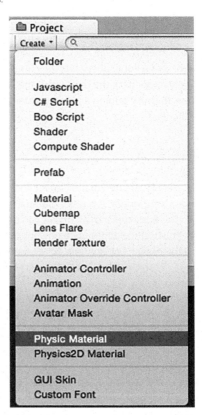

FIG 2.38 Creating physics material.

Step 2: To create physics material, in Project, select the Create menu and choose Physics Material, as shown in Figure 2.38. Rename the material box.

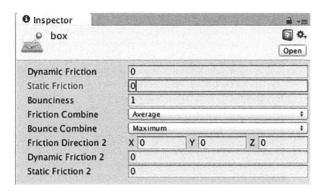

FIG 2.39   The Inspector view of physics material.

Step 3: Select the cube in the Hierarchy and locate its Box Collider in the Inspector. The first property will be Material. Click on the small circle to the very right of it and select the *box* physics material from the pop-up window. If you play the application at this point, there will be very little effect. Select box from the Project. The view of this physics material will appear in the Inspector as shown in Figure 2.39. Set the *Bounciness* value to 1. Press play to see the effect.

Step 4: To get a higher bounce, set the *Bounce Combine* value to *Maximum*. These combine values tell the physics engine how to work out the effect when two objects collide. When set to maximum it will apply the maximum bounce factor out of the two objects. If you set it to minimum the cube will not bounce, as the plane has no bounciness value.

Step 5: Now try setting *all* the box physics material values to 0 and the Friction Combine to minimum. Press play. With no bounce or friction, the box will fall to the plane and then slide down as if the surface was made of ice.

2.6 Physics and the Principles of Animation

In their 1981 book, *The Illusion of Life*, Disney animators Ollie Johnston and Frank Thomas introduced 12 rules to be applied when creating animated films. These are

> **Squash and stretch:** The deformation of objects in reaction to the laws of physics; for example, a tennis ball hitting a wall squashes on collision.
>
> **Anticipation:** Presenting short actions or hints to a viewer of what is about to happen; for example, a person about to jump in the air will bend their knees first.

Staging: Presenting an idea such that no mistake can be made as to what is happening; for example, viewing an angry person's face gives a better impression of their mood than the back of their head.

Straight-ahead action and pose to pose: These are animation drawing methods. Straight-ahead action refers to drawing out a scene frame by frame. Pose to pose refers to drawing key frames or key moments in a scene and filling in the gaps later.

Follow-through and overlapping action: This is the way in which momentum acts on a moving object to cause extra motion even after the initial force has stopped; for example, a baseball pitcher's arm does not stop moving the moment the ball leaves his hand. In addition, his legs and body also move in response to the action. Overlapping action occurs when secondary objects move with the main object.

Slow in and out: Natural movement in which there is a change in direction decelerates into the change and accelerates out; for example, a car turning a corner slows into the corner and accelerates out. A person jumping will slow into the impact with the ground and speed up as he pushes off the ground with his legs.

Arcs: Motion in animals and humans occurs along curved paths. This includes the rotation of limbs and the rise and fall of a body when walking. The same curved movement is also found in the trajectory of thrown objects.

Secondary actions: These animations support the principal animation. They give a scene more realism; for example, a person walking along the street would not just be moving his legs. His arms might swing, he may be talking, and his hair could be flowing with the breeze.

Timing: This refers to the speed of actions. It is essential for establishing mood and realism; for example, a fast-moving character will appear to be in a hurry, whereas a slow-moving character portrays lethargy or disinterest. For realism, the correct timing of actions with motion and sound is critical. Slow animated walking characters can look like they are slipping across the ground if their forward movement and leg cycles are not matched. A delay between an action and a sound, such as a bomb exploding and the associated sound effect, adds to suspension of disbelief.

Exaggeration: Perfect imitations of the real world in animation can appear dull and static. Often it is necessary to make things bigger, faster, and brighter to present them in an acceptable manner to a viewer. Overexaggeration is also used in the physical features of characters for the effects of physics; for example, in Warner Brothers' coyote and roadrunner films, when the coyote is about to fall from a great height, the time he spends in the air realizing his predicament is exaggerated far beyond what normal gravity would allow.

Solid drawing: This is the term given to an animator's ability to consider and draw a character with respect to anatomy, weight, balance, and shading in a 3D context. A character must have a presence in the environment, and being able to establish volume and weight in an animation is crucial to believing the character is actually in and part of the environment.

Appeal: This relates to an animator's ability to bring a character to life. It must be able to appeal to an audience through physical form, personality, and actions.

All but a couple of the preceding principles of animation can be conveyed in a game environment through the physics system. They are consequences of physics acting in the real world. We subconsciously see and experience them every day, albeit not with as much exaggeration as a game, and come to expect them in the virtual environment.

In the following hands-on sections, you will get a chance to see how these principles can be applied in your own games.

2.6.1 Squash and Stretch

2D Boy's two-dimensional adventure *World of Goo* features many moving balls of Goo. Each time Goo accelerates, it becomes elongated along the direction of movement, and it decelerates and squashes when it collides with another object. Such movement occurs in the real world and is explained by Newton's laws.

While game-based physics engines do allow for the creation of bouncy objects, typically they do not provide real-time squashing and stretching algorithms for the actual game object. The rigid body attached to a game object to simulate physics by very definition remains rigid even though its movement suggests otherwise. In most cases, it is too processor intensive in 3D environments to squash and stretch all objects, but just for fun this hands-on session will show you how to do it in Unity.

⚬ **Unity Hands On**
Squash and Stretch
Step 1: Download *Chapter Two/AnimPrinciples.zip* from the website, unzip, and open in Unity. In the Project, double-click on *squash* in the *Scenes* folder to open the scene. The warehouse scene from one of the Unity online resources will be visible.
Step 2: We want to be able to move around inside the warehouse and need to add a first person controller (FPC). Select Assets > Import Package from the main menu, and select the Characters (Figure 2.40).

⚬ **Note**
Locating Standard Assets
In some of the more recent installations of Unity, the Standard Assets have been missing or unable to be downloaded. You can get these from the Asset Store by searching for Standard Assets. Alternatively, the standard assets for V. 2018 are available with the resource files for this book.

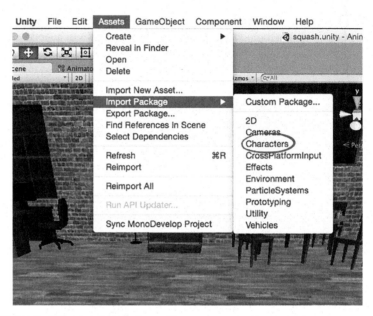

FIG 2.40 The Unity packages folder location on a Mac.

Step 3: Unity will decompress the package and then show you the files it is about to add to your project. Select all and click on Import. A folder called Standard Assets will appear in the Project. Inside this folder locate the RigidBodyFPSController and drag it into the Scene. A capsule-shaped object with a camera attached will show in the Scene, as illustrated in Figure 2.41.

Step 4: Delete Main Camera from the Hierarchy. There is already a camera attached to the FPC and the Main Camera is no longer needed.

Step 5: Play. The FPC will fall straight through the floor. Why? The warehouse mesh does not have any colliders and therefore there is nothing to stop the FPC falling. Each surface of the mesh requires a mesh collider to be added.

Step 6: In the Hierarchy, select wareHouseFBX and expand it by clicking on the small triangle to the left of its name. This model is made up of a number of meshes. They are called polySurface88, polySurface89, and so on. Select polySurface88, scroll to the bottom of the list, and SHIFT select polySurface 1518. With all the surfaces selected, click on Add Component > Physics > Mesh Collider. Each surface will have a mesh collider added to it using its own mesh shape. Quickly scan through the polySurface meshes individually and note the new Mesh Collider component added and that the Mesh property of this is set to its own mesh.

Step 7: Play. The FPC will fall and hit the floor.

Step 8: You will be able to move around with the arrow or WASD keys and jump with the spacebar. If the FPC falls through the floor it will be because it either starts slightly merged with the floor or the floor does not have a mesh collider. Move the FPC up a little and check the floor mesh for a collider and try again.

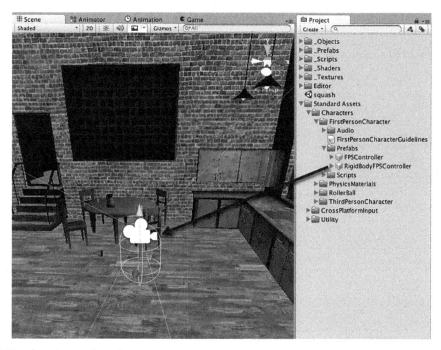

FIG 2.41   Adding a first person controller to a Scene.

Step 9: Create a Sphere. Set its scale to (0.5,0.5,0.5) and position it at (0,0,0).
Step 10: Add a Rigidbody to the Sphere by selecting it in the Hierarchy and choosing Add Component > Physics > Rigidbody.
Step 11: Create a C# file and call it *Blob*. Leave it empty.
Step 12: Attach *Blob.cs* to the Sphere.
Step 13: Rename the Sphere game object as bullet. Drag and drop it from the Hierarchy into the Project to create a prefab. Delete the bullet remaining in the Hierarchy.
Step 14: Create a C# file and call it *Fire*. Add the script from Listing 2.11.

Listing 2.11 Instantiating a game object and shooting it forward relative to the creator

```
//Fire.cs
using System.Collections;
using System.Collections.Generic;
using UnityEngine;

public class Fire : MonoBehaviour {

    public GameObject bulletObject;
    void Update ()
    {
```

```
if(Input.GetButtonDown("Fire1"))
{
    GameObject newBullet = Instantiate(bulletObject,
        this.transform.position + this.transform.
        forward*0.8f, this.transform.rotation);
    newBullet.GetComponent<Rigidbody>().AddForce
        (this.transform.forward * 500);
}
    }
}
```

Step 15: Save *Fire.cs* and attach it to the *Main Camera*, which is part of the FPC in the Hierarchy. Select the FPC Main Camera in the Hierarchy and drag and drop the bullet prefab from the Project onto the exposed bulletObject variable in the *Fire.cs* script as shown in Figure 2.42.

Step 16: Save and play. The left mouse button, called "Fire1" in the script, will instantiate copies of the bullet prefab and add a force with the same

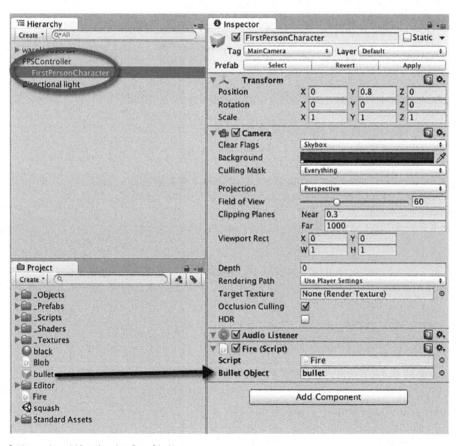

FIG 2.42   Setting a script variable to the value of a prefab object.

direction as the camera. To change the speed of the bullets, modify the force multiplier in *Fire.cs*.

◉ Note

If an object is moving too fast, Unity can sometimes miss the collision event and it will go through walls and floors. If this happens, try slowing the object down or making its collision component bigger. Also note that Unity will not register collisions between two complex mesh objects. If you have a mesh object that is not colliding, think of replacing its collider with a simple sphere or box collider. To do this, click on the object in the Hierarchy and select a new physics collider from the main menu.

Step 17: We are now going to create sticky bullets. Open the *Blob.cs* file. Enter the script from Listing 2.12.

Listing 2.12 Turn off an object's physics on a collision

```
//Blob.cs
using System.Collections;
using System.Collections.Generic;
using UnityEngine;

public class Blob : MonoBehaviour {

    void OnCollisionEnter(Collision collision)
    {
        if(collision.gameObject.name !=
            "RigidBodyFPSController")
        {
            GetComponent<Rigidbody>().isKinematic = true;
        }
    }

    // Use this for initialization
    void Start () {

    }
    // Update is called once per frame
    void Update () {

    }
}
```

Step 18: Save and play. You will have created sticky bullets that stop moving the instant they collide with something. The *is Kinematic* setting in the script will turn off physics effects on the object when it is set to true.

A test is performed to check if the object has hit the FPC before it turns off the physics. This is used to ensure that the bullets do not stick to the FPC.
Step 19: Finally, to make the bullet object squash when it hits the wall, modify your script to that in Listing 2.13.

Listing 2.13 Causing a squash effect by changing an object's scale

```
using System.Collections;
using System.Collections.Generic;
using UnityEngine;

public class Blob : MonoBehaviour {

    void OnCollisionEnter(Collision collision)
    {
        if(collision.gameObject.name !=
            "RigidBodyFPSController")
        {
            GetComponent<Rigidbody>().isKinematic = true;
            Destroy (this.GetComponent<Collider>());
            ContactPoint contact = collision.contacts[0];
            Quaternion rot = Quaternion.FromToRotation
                (Vector3.up, contact.normal);
            this.transform.position = contact.point +
                contact.normal*0.1f;
            this.transform.rotation = rot;
            this.transform.localScale = new Vector3(
                this.transform.localScale.x *
                collision.relativeVelocity. magnitude/5.0f,
                this.transform.localScale.y * 0.2f,
                this.transform.localScale.z *
                collision.relativeVelocity.magnitude/5.0f);
        }
    }
```

Step 20: Save and play. The code now destroys the collider component to stop the FPC from hitting the stationary bullets. If you take this line out you will notice that the bullets create barriers the FPC collides with. Data is taken from the collision and used to rotate the object just as the y axis is aligned with the normal of the point of contact. This means that when the y axis is scaled down, the object presses flat to the object it collided with. The x and z scales can then be resized based on the collision velocity to create a bigger *splat*.
Step 21: Create a shiny black material for the bullet prefab, and take a walk around the warehouse, leaving blobs everywhere. Note that funny

unaligned blobs will be caused by collisions with other complex meshes, such as chairs. This code works best with walls, floors, and other large flat areas.

● Note

You may have noticed that the spheres being created are dull and gray without any shading. This is because there is no light in the scene. The warehouse model itself has baked lighting. This is where the textures used are colored as though light is turned on when it is not. This process occurs back in the modeling package that created the model. If you want the spheres to have shading and appear more 3D, add a directional light to the scene.

2.6.2 Anticipation

A simple implementation of anticipation is seen in racing games. At the beginning of a race, a traffic light or countdown will display, giving the player a heads up to when the race is about to start. Another way to add anticipation is to have explosive devices with countdown timers. In *Splinter Cell*, for example, the lead character, Sam Fisher, may lay down explosive charges and then a countdown occurs before they explode.

● Unity Hands On
Anticipation

Step 1: Open the project from the last hands-on session or download and open *Chapter Two/AnimPrinciplesA.zip*. We are now going to make the sticky bullets into timed explosive devices.
Step 2: Download *Chapter Two/Explosion.unitypackage* and import into your project, Assets > Import Package > Custom Package.
Step 3: Open *Blob.cs* and modify the code to that in Listing 2.14.

Listing 2.14 Creating a timed explosion

```
//Blob.cs
public class Blob : MonoBehaviour {

    public GameObject exp;
    float timeToExplode = 5.0f;

    void Explosion()
    {
```

```
            Instantiate(exp, this.transform.position, this.
                transform.rotation); Destroy(this.gameObject,
                0.1f);
        }
        void OnCollisionEnter(Collision collision)
        {
            if(collision.gameObject.name !=
                "RigidBodyFPSController")
            {
                . . .
                this.transform.localScale = new Vector3(
                    this.transform.localScale.x *
                    collision.relativeVelocity. magnitude/5.0f,
                    this.transform.localScale.y * 0.2f,
                    this.transform.localScale.z *
                    collision.relativeVelocity.magnitude/5.0f);

                Invoke("Explosion", timeToExplode);
            }
        }
        . . .
```

Step 4: Click on the bullet prefab in the Project. Find the Explosion property of the blob script and set it to Explosion. You can find this by clicking on the little circle next to the property field or drag and drop this prefab from the Project. It can be found in Standard Assets > Misc.
Step 5: Save and play. Drop a sticky bullet somewhere and stand back and watch.

2.6.3 Follow-Through

Follow-through refers to actions occurring after and as a result of another action. For example, in racing games, a common follow-through is when one car clips another car and it goes spinning out of control. In most games where you have to blow something up, there is bound to be a follow-through action that removes obstacles from the player's game progression.

◉ Unity Hands On
Follow-Through
Step 1: Open the project from the last hands-on session or download and open *Chapter Two/AnimPrinciplesB.zip*. We are now going to add a door that can be blown up with the timed explosive devices. Create a cube and modify its scale, rotation, and position as necessary to have it fit one of the doorways in the warehouse as shown in Figure 2.43. Rename the cube "Door."
Step 2: Open *Blob.cs* and modify as shown in Listing 2.15.

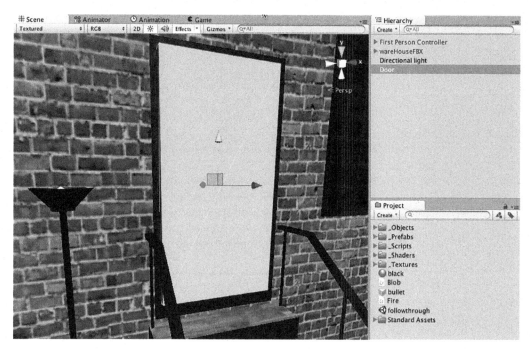

FIG 2.43 A cube used as a door.

Listing 2.15 Destroying another object in an explosion

```
//Blob.cs
public class Blob : MonoBehaviour {

    public GameObject exp;
    float timeToExplode = 5.0f;
    GameObject stuckOn;

    void Explosion()
    {
        Instantiate(exp, this.transform.position, this.
            transform.rotation);
        if(stuckOn && stuckOn.name == "Door")
        {
            Destroy(stuckOn);
        }

        Destroy(this.gameObject,0.1f);
    }

    void OnCollisionEnter(Collision collision)
    {
        if(collision.gameObject.name !=
```

```
        "RigidBodyFPSController")
    {
        stuckOn = collision.gameObject;
        GetComponent<Rigidbody>().isKinematic = true;
        Destroy (this.GetComponent<Collider>());
        ...
```

Step 3: Save and play. Position a sticky explosive on the door and watch as it gets destroyed.

Step 4: Create more cubes to fit in the other doorways. Ensure that they are named "Door" in the Hierarchy and any sticky explosive will destroy them. If you want to blow up anything the sticky bullet is stuck to, remove the if statement testing for just "Doors" (and the associated {})! Be careful though, you might fall through the floor if you destroy the wrong object.

2.6.4 Secondary Motion

Secondary motion brings the game environment to life. The simplest of movements can hint at a dynamic realistic environment with a life of its own. For example, a swaying tree or moving grass provides the illusion of a light breeze, while also suggesting to the player that these are living things. How often have you been for a walk in a forest that does not move around you? Even in a still warehouse environment there is the opportunity to add secondary motion to add extra atmosphere to the scene.

⍟ Unity Hands On
Secondary Motion

Step 1: Download the file *Chapter Two/AnimPrinciplesC.zip*. Unzip and open the Unity scene called follow-through. We are going to add some curtains and wind effects reminiscent of a deserted warehouse.

Step 2: In the Scene, move your point of view and the First Person Controller such that you are looking into the room that has the truck in it.

Step 3: Add a GameObject > 3D Object > Plane into the scene. Resize, rotate, and position it to fit the doorway into the room with the truck. For this example, the transform for the plane will be close to Position (5,2.5,–24.5), Rotation (0,0,90), and Scale (0.7,1,0.9).

Step 4: Using the Add Component button in the Inspector, add a Physics > Cloth component to the plane.

Step 5: Select the First Person Controller and use the Add Component button to add a Physics > Capsule Collider to it. Resize the capsule

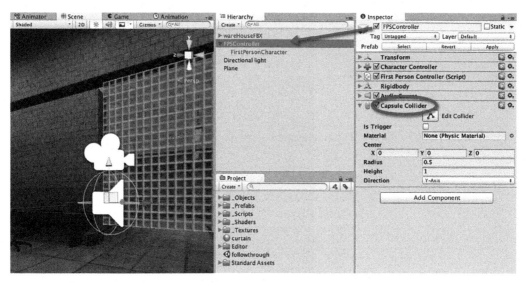

FIG 2.44 Adding a capsule collider to the character controller.

collider close to the same size as the collider already on the controller as shown in Figure 2.44. It will now have two colliders.

Cloth in Unity only responds to sphere and capsule colliders. As the First Person Controller has neither of these, one must be added.
Step 6: Next create a new material called curtain. Add one of the textures that is already in the Project to the material. One called innerWindow works well. Find a suitable one that looks like a curtain. Set the shader to Unlit/Transparent and adjust the properties to those shown in Figure 2.45.
Step 7: With the plane selected in the Hierarchy, drag the newly created curtain material onto its Skinned Mesh Renderer material.
Step 8. Remove the Cloth's Mesh Collider component.
Step 9: Then set the Cloth's capsule collider to the First Person Controller. Finally, to secure the cloth to the ceiling, select the Cloth's Edit Constraints button. A small editing window will pop up. The vertices of the plane in the Scene will become black dots. From the constraint window, select Paint and then click on each of the vertices along the top. They will turn green when selected and now act as immoveable points on the cloth. These steps are shown in Figure 2.46.

At the time of writing this activity there is a bug in Unity 2018/2019 with the Capsule Collider not working in both directions when used with a cloth. However, if you save your project and reopen it, it works just fine!

135

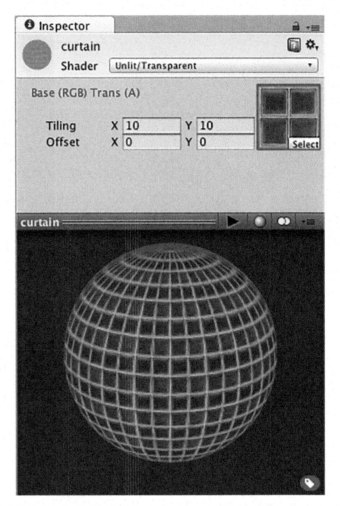

FIG 2.45 Creating a texture for the curtain.

Step 10: Save and Run. You will now be able to navigate through the curtain and it will react like cloth. Once inside the truck room, turn to look back at the cloth. It will not be visible because the normal for the plane is facing in the other direction. The easiest way to fix this is to duplicate the existing cloth and flip the new one around by 180°. A better solution would be using a custom shader, and this will be explained in the next activity.

◉ For Research
Interactive Cloth
For more information on the settings for cloth, check out http://docs.unity3d.com/Manual/class-Cloth.html.

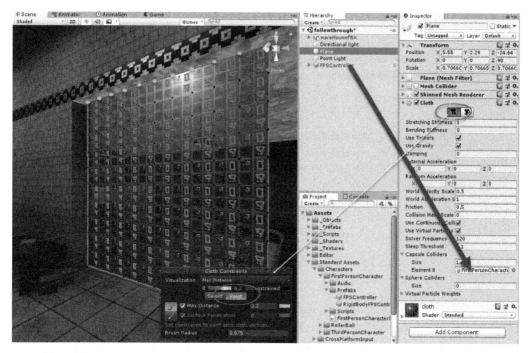

FIG 2.46 Full setup for an interactive cloth.

2.7 2D and 3D Tricks for Optimizing Game Space

The real world is a big place. The dream of many a game designer is to recreate the real world in all its detailed glory and vastness. Unfortunately, modeling everything down to the last nut and bolt and putting it into a game engine for real-time processing is not possible. However, many games do fake the vastness of the outside world very effectively, fooling the player into believing that the environment outside the game play area goes on forever.

A game requires a high frame rate to provide the player with a seamless game-playing experience. Between each frame, the computer must process all game object behaviors, sounds, physics, and player interactions. The number of game objects in view of the game has a large effect on the frame rate, as they must be processed and rendered. Therefore, when designing a game level or environment, it is critical to keep in mind how many things will need to be drawn in a scene and reduce this to an absolute minimum while keeping the quality high. Having said this, it might not necessarily be the number of objects in a scene that need to be reduced but a reconsideration of how they are treated and drawn.

This section explores some common ways for optimizing 3D game worlds.

2.7.1 Reducing Polygons

Each polygon, being the smallest part of a mesh, adds to the processing of a scene. On high-end gaming machines, the polycount must increase dramatically to affect the frame rate. However, on mobile devices, simply adding a couple hundred polygons can bring a game to a halt. Here are some methods to reduce the polycount.

2.7.1.1 Use Only What You Need

When creating a model for a game, consider the number of superfluous polygons in the mesh and reduce. For example, the default plane object created by Unity is essentially a square. If you only ever use it as a square, such as for objects in the rocket ship game, this object is inefficient as it has many polygons. A simple square plane only requires two triangular polygons. In this case, create a square plane in Blender and import it instead.

2.7.1.2 Backface Culling

As discovered earlier, Unity does not show the reverse side of surfaces. This is called *backface culling* and is a common technique in computer graphics for not drawing the reverse side of a polygon. In some cases, however, as with the curtain in the warehouse example, it may be necessary to draw both sides. In the hands-on session, we used two cloths, one for either side. This is an inefficient way as it immediately doubles the number of polygons used for the curtain. A better way is to turn backface culling off.

To do this in Unity requires the writing of a *shader*. A shader is a piece of code the game engine interprets as a texturing treatment for the surface of a polygon. When you set a material to *Diffuse* or *Transparent/Specular*, you are using a prewritten shader.

To write your own shader requires extensive knowledge of the shader language and complex computer graphics principles; however, numerous shaders are available on the Unity website for you to try, so here are the steps required to add a custom shader.

⊙ **Unity Hands On**

Loading a Custom Shader

Step 1: Open Unity and create a simple scene with plane or another object to test the shader. If you prefer, you could add this to the curtain in the warehouse application.

Step 2: In the Project, select Create > Shader > Unlit Shader. A new shader file will appear in the Project. Rename to BackfaceOn. Double-click to open this file.

Step 3: Add the line of code "Cull Off" under the Tags line, similar to the code in Listing 2.16.

Listing 2.16 A custom unity shader to remove backface culling

```
Shader "Unlit/BackfaceOn"
{
    Properties
    {
        _MainTex ("Texture", 2D) = "white" {}
    }
    SubShader
    {
        Tags { "RenderType"="Opaque" }
        Cull Off
        LOD 100

        Pass
        {
            CGPROGRAM
            #pragma vertex vert
            #pragma fragment frag
            // make fog work
            #pragma multi_compile_fog

            #include "UnityCG.cginc"

            struct appdata
            {
                float4 vertex : POSITION;
                float2 uv : TEXCOORD0;
            };

            struct v2f
            {
                float2 uv : TEXCOORD0;
                UNITY_FOG_COORDS(1)
                float4 vertex : SV_POSITION;
            };

            sampler2D _MainTex;
            float4 _MainTex_ST;

            v2f vert (appdata v)
            {
                v2f o;
                o.vertex = UnityObjectToClipPos(v.vertex);
                o.uv = TRANSFORM_TEX(v.uv, _MainTex);
                UNITY_TRANSFER_FOG(o,o.vertex);
                return o;
            }
```

```
            fixed4 frag (v2f i) : SV_Target
            {
                // sample the texture
                fixed4 col = tex2D(_MainTex, i.uv);
                // apply fog
                UNITY_APPLY_FOG(i.fogCoord, col);
                return col;
            }
        ENDCG
        }
    }
}
```

Step 4: Create a new material or select the Curtain material if using the warehouse example. In the shader drop-down selection box your new shader will be available as Unlit/*Backface On*. You can now use the material like any other.

2.7.1.3 Level of Detail
Level of detail (LOD) is a technique for providing multiple models and textures for a single object with reducing levels of detail. For example, you may have a high polycount, high-resolution textured model; a medium polycount, medium-resolution textured model; and a low polycount, low-resolution texture model for a single character. The model that gets drawn by the renderer will depend on the distance the camera is away from the character. If the character is close, the highest quality version is used. If the character is far in the distance, the lowest quality version is used.

This method not only mimics human vision-making objects in the distance less defined, but also allows for the drawing of more objects in a scene as the ones farther away take up less memory.

Note, since creating the next hands-on tutorial, Unity has added a new component to handle LODs. While the following tutorial will show you how to achieve LODs manually, you may also be interested in investigating https://docs.unity3d.com/Manual/class-LODGroup.html.

◉ Unity Hands On
Applying Level of Detail in Unity
Step 1: Download the file Chapter Five/LODHouse.zip from the website and open the **house** scene. In the scene you'll find a ground plane with a cobblestone texture and a pink house (called House_4 in the Hierarchy) as shown in Figure 2.47.

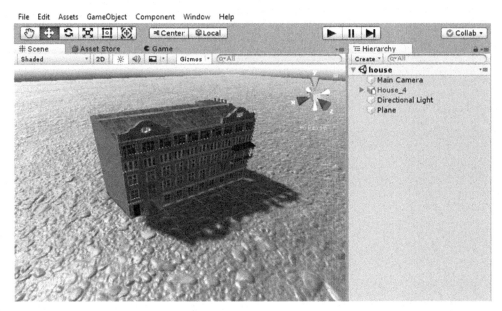

FIG 2.47 The house model placed on the ground plane in the Scene.

● Note

The House_4 model was kindly provided by Unity Asset Store artist *ChermandirKun*. Please show your appreciation by visiting his website for more excellent Unity assets at https://www.weblancer.net/users/ShprotZLO/portfolio/.

Step 2: Notice in the Hierarchy, House_4 has three children. These are the house at different levels of detail, though they are not yet in operation. To activate the levels of detail, select House_4 in the Hierarchy then in the Inspector add the LOD Group component as shown in Figure 2.48.

Step 3: With House_4 still selected, slide the camera icon in the Inspector as shown in Figure 2.49 left and right across the LOD Groups. These show the relative distances from the house that each different LOD model will display. As you slide the camera, you will notice the LOD that is activated in the scene, although we have not yet set up the specific models for each LOD so you won't see these changes yet.

Step 4: To setup the models that will appear for each LOD, drag and drop the appropriate child model from House_4 onto the differing LOD bands in the Inspector as shown in Figure 2.50.

Step 5: Now as you move the camera closer or further away from the house the different LOD models will display based on your distance from them until you are so far away the model is completely culled. Note you can also adjust the bands on the LOD colored percentage slider to modify the distances at which each LOD appears.

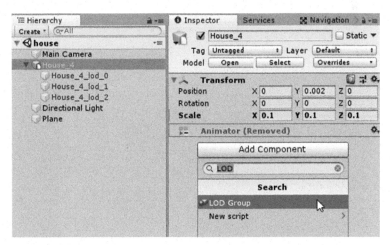

FIG 2.48 Adding a LOD Group to a model.

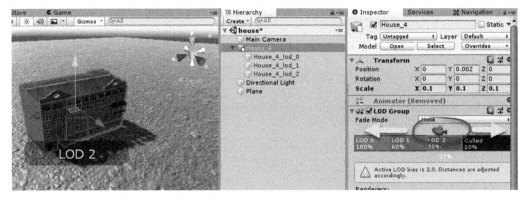

FIG 2.49 The LOD bands.

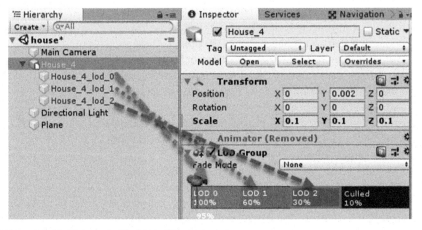

FIG 2.50 Assigning models with differing levels of detail to the LOD component.

2.7.2 Fog

Another very (very) handy trick in reducing the visual size of a game environment is fog. In the previous examples, when the FPC was at a far enough distance from the buildings they would slide behind the far plane of the camera or snap out of view because of the LOD. By adding fog, these other rather too obvious techniques can be hidden. A layer of fog can be added just before the far plane of the camera or the farthest distance of the LOD.

⊚ **Unity Hands On**

Fog

Step 1: Open the project from the last hands-on session.

Step 2: Select Window > Rendering > LightingSettings from the main menu. In the Lighting popup window select the Scene Tab and scroll near to the bottom to locate Fog.

Step 3: Tick the Fog box. Note that a gray fog covers the ground but not the sky in the Game.

Step 4: Play. Walk around the city. Buildings in the distance will be completely fogged out. As you move closer to a building the fog will lift.

Step 5: The thickness of the fog is modified in the Fog Density property of render settings. You will notice in the same place that you can change the color of the fog. The issue now faced is that the ground and buildings are fogged over, but the background color is not. This is a fact of life with using fog, as fog is only applied to game objects and not to the background. The best way to overcome this is to set the background color to the same color as the fog. This makes for a very convincing cloudy sky.

Step 6: Select the color picker for the fog and select a color. Note down the RGB and A values.

Step 7: In the Hierarchy, select the FirstPersonCharacter attached to the FPC. Change the background color of the Camera in the Inspector to the same color as the fog.

Step 8: Set the fog density to 0.005.

Step 9: Play. At this point it becomes a fine balance of testing if in the distance you can still see buildings disappearing instead of blurring into the fog. If so, try turning up the fog a little.

2.7.3 Textures

Fine-detailed, high-quality textures are the best defense against high polycounts. There is far more detail in a photorealistic image of a real-world item than could possibly fit into the polycount restrictions of any real-time game engine. Chapter 1 examined briefly the use of normal and specular maps to give extra texturing to game objects. Here we discuss two more popular tricks.

2.7.3.1 Moving Textures

When creating materials in Unity you may have seen properties for *x* and *y* offsets. These values are used to adjust the alignment and location of a texture on a polygon's surface. If these values are adjusted constantly with each game loop, the texture will appear animated. This is an effective way of creating an animation that does not involve modeling or extra polygons. It is often used in creating sky and water effects.

◉ **Unity Hands On**
Animated Textures
Step 1: Create a new Unity project.
Step 2: In the Scene add a plane.
Step 3: Create a new material and add it to the plane.
Step 4: Find a seamless texture of your choosing from the Web.
Step 5: Drag and drop the new texture into the Project.
Step 6: Add the texture to the material. It should appear on the surface of the plane.
Step 7: Create a new C# file called *Scrolling*. Add the code in Listing 2.16.

Listing 2.16 Scrolling a texture over the surface of an object

```
//Scrolling.cs
using UnityEngine;
using System.Collections;

public class scrolling : MonoBehaviour {
    Vector2 uvSpeed = new Vector2( 0.0f, -1.0f );
    Vector2 uvOffset = Vector2.zero;

    void LateUpdate()
    {
        uvOffset += ( uvSpeed * Time.deltaTime );
        this.GetComponent<Renderer>().materials[0].
        SetTextureOffset("_MainTex", uvOffset);
    }
}
```

Step 8: Attach the C# file to the plane.
Step 9: Play. The texture will move across the surface of the plane. To change the direction of the movement, modify the *x* and *y* values for the *uvSpeed* variable in the script. The `LateUpDate()` function is similar to

the Update() function in that it executes for an object every game loop. However, with `LateUpDate()` it occurs as the very last function called for an object so that it can take into consideration any related processing occurring in the same game loop.

Step 10: Open the project with the warehouse. Create a new C# file and enter the same code from Listing 2.16. Attach this script to polySurface437. This is the surface of the conveyor belt in the room where you placed the curtain. Play and watch the conveyor move!

2.7.3.2 Blob Shadows

Shadows give a scene an extra dimension of depth and add to visual realism. Generating shadows is processor intensive. Although shadows in game environments are covered in Chapter 7, a quick and easy method for generating processor light shadows called Blob Shadows is introduced here.

Usually the game rendering system calculates shadows based on the position and intensity of lights and the position of game objects. When many real-time shadows need to be calculated, such as those of moving objects like characters, it can slow the frame rate considerably. This is a big problem for games on mobile devices where such shadowing is not practical.

☺ Unity Hands On
Blob Shadows

Step 1: Download *Chapter Two/BlobShadows.zip* from the website, unzip, and open in Unity. In the Project, double-click on *blobshadowexamples* in the *Scenes* folder to open the scene. The Scene will appear with a character standing on a plane.

Step 2: Select Assets > Import Package and import the Effects Package from the book's resources or download and import from the Asset Store.

Step 3: Locate *Blob Shadow Projector* in the Effect > Projectors > Prefabs folder and drag and drop it onto the Male game object. A frustum object will appear under the Male model. This is the Blob Shadow Projector.

Step 4: Move the projector up until it is just above the top of the model's head. A black blob will appear on the ground. This is the blob shadow. The shadow is created using a material with the texture of the round black blob on it. When the projector intersects a plane, as it does here with the ground, the black texture is drawn inside the intersection area of the plane and the projector frustum.

Step 5: In its current state, the Male model is also inside the projector frustum and therefore the shadow is drawn on it too. To fix this, we place the model into another drawing layer. Select the Male object in the Hierarchy. In the Inspector at the very top to the right of Tag is a property called Layer. Click on the drop-down box next to Layer and select *Add Layer.*

Step 6: In the Tag Manager that opens in the Inspector, next to *User Layer 8*, type in *character*. This will create a new drawing layer called *character*.
Step 7: Select the Male object in the Hierarchy again. In the Inspector, set its Layer to character using the drop-down box.
Step 8: Select the Blob Shadow Projector in the Hierarchy. In the Inspector's Projector Component, set the *Ignore Layers* property to *character*. The projector will now ignore anything in the character layer, which in this case is the Male model, and draw the shadow object everywhere else it intersects. This is a very effective way to add convincing shadows to objects without adding too much processing overhead.

2.7.4 Billboards

Billboarding is a technique that uses planes to fake a lot of background scenery. A billboard is a plane usually having a partially transparent texture applied to give it the appearance of being a shape other than a square. Common uses for billboards are grass, clouds, and distant trees.

To give the illusion that the billboard is viewable from all angles, the plane orientates itself constantly so that it is always facing the player.

☮ Unity Hands On
Billboards
Step 1: Download the file *Chapter Two/Billboards.zip*. Unzip and open the Unity scene called grass. In it you will find a quad with a grass texture and a ground plane. The grass texture has transparency that allows you to see through the areas where there is no part of the grass image.
Step 2: Import the Character Controller asset package and drop a First Person Controller from it into the scene so you can walk around on Play.
Step 3: Create a new C# file called FaceCamera and attach it to the grass quad. Enter the code in Listing 2.17.

Listing 2.17 Script to create a billboard from a quad

```
//FaceCamera.cs
using System.Collections;
using System.Collections.Generic;
using UnityEngine;

public class FaceCamera : MonoBehaviour {

    // Use this for initialization
    void Start () {
    }
```

```
    // Update is called once per frame
    void Update () {
        //note the minus in here as a Unity Quad has its Z
            axis facing in the opposite
        //direction to its textured side.
        this.transform.LookAt(-Camera.main.transform.
            position);
    }
}
```

Save and Play. The billboard will have disappeared. Why?

If you take a look in the Scene, you will notice the quad is still there, but the grass is facing away from the player. The LookAt() function orients an object such that the blue forward-axis (z) faces the object in question. In this case, the image just happens to be on the opposite side as shown in Figure 2.51. This means we need to not only look at the camera with the quad but also rotate it by a full 180° around its up axis. To do this add:

```
    this.transform. Rotate(new Vector3(0,1,0),180);
```

as the last line inside the Update() function.

Now when you play, the grass will always face the player.

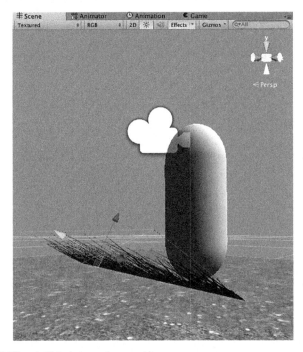

FIG 2.51 A billboard with the texture on the wrong side.

Step 4: To see the full effect, duplicate the quad, and place it around the scene multiple times. Play and walk around.

Step 5: When you walk over the top of the grass it will lay down flat. If the billboard were a tree you would not want this to happen. Rather, rotating around the *x* axis should be turned off. That way the object will stay vertical and only turn around its *y* axis. To allow for this, modify FaceCamera to the code in Listing 2.18.

Listing 2.18 Billboarding script that allows the *x* rotation to be turned off

```
using System.Collections;
using System.Collections.Generic;
using UnityEngine;

public class FaceCamera : MonoBehaviour {

    public bool stayUpright = true;
    // Use this for initialization
    void Start () {

    }

    // Update is called once per frame
    void Update () {
        this.transform.LookAt(-Camera.main.transform.
            position);
        if(stayUpright)
        this.transform.eulerAngles = new Vector3(0,
            this.transform.eulerAngles.y,
            this.transform.eulerAngles.z);
    }
}
```

Step 6: The grass will not bend over as the FPC approaches it. You can now turn this feature on and off using the tick box for StayUpright in the Inspector when FaceCamera.cs is attached to a game object.

More often than not, billboards are used on horizon lines and in the distance. Because they do not stand up under close scrutiny, you may want to use them en masse, but in areas of the game environment the player cannot quite reach.

2.8 Summary

This chapter covered a variety of techniques for replicating real-world mechanics in a game environment. These included movement with vectors and the physics system and optimization techniques that make the virtual world seem as extensive as the real world.

Most often satisfactory movement in a game environment can be achieved through knowledge of vector mathematics. Applying this first before jumping headlong into the physics system will optimize processing of the game environment. For example, in the rocket ship hands-on session, physics could have been employed to push the rocket ship around the planet. This would, however, have been overkill, as only a simple translation and slerping algorithm was required.

It is a common first-timer mistake when creating a game environment to make it detailed and vast without consideration for how game play will be affected as the frame rate drops. Few can understand how such top-quality AAA titles can run so fast with such intricate landscapes and mind-blowing special effects, and it is often the game engine that takes the blame. This is not the case, and this chapter has revealed some of the tricks employed by professionals to trick the player's perception of the environment.

CHAPTER 3

Animation Mechanics

Animation is about creating the illusion of life. And you can't create it if you don't have one.

Brad Bird

3.1 Introduction

Animation is the underlying mechanic on which the visual aspect of computer games is built. It is the illusion of movement created through the display of a rapid succession of images, each slightly different from the other, creating the impression of motion. Animation is possible because of biological phenomena involving the human eye.

Originally, the perception of motion was explained by a theory known as *persistence of vision*, which refers to the afterimage that appears on the retina for approximately 1/25 of a second. You will notice this effect after staring at something and then closing your eyes. A negative type of imprint will be apparent. This effect is exaggerated if you look at a high-contrast image such as the shadowed side of a tree with the sun shining through from the other side. It was initially thought that humans saw animation when the afterimage from one still shot merged with the next. Although persistence of vision is a term still used to explain our ability to see movement when there is none in film and cinema, the theory was discredited as the main explanation by German Gestalt psychologist Max Wertheimer in 1912. Rather he proposed that the perception of motion was a psychological phenomenon called *phi*. Phi, in short, is the way in which the human brain automatically fills in the gaps between the images we see and therefore creates a perception of seamless motion.

The traditional technique for producing animation was to hand draw each image, known as a *frame*, and display them one after the other. Early Disney cartoons were produced in this manner. In order to provide smooth motion, the frames need to be shown at 24 frames per second. These frames are shot in twos such that each still image is displayed on two frames of film. This means that 12 drawings are required for 1 second of film.

For modern computer games, frame rates between 30 and 100 are acceptable. Of course, if there were no motion on the screen, a frame rate of 1 would be adequate. The frame rate in a computer game will differ depending on the background processing that is occurring during any given game loop. Ironically, fast action-paced games with lots of moving objects need to run at a higher frame rate in order for the player to take all the action in, although all the extra processing would be taxing on the processor and could lead to low frame rates.

Animation in the very first computer games was the result of using vector graphics to draw an object on the screen, clearing the screen, and redrawing the object at a slightly different location and rotation. Essentially, each frame was being drawn on the fly by an algorithm—the reason being that the computers of this time did not have memory available for storing art assets created by others, not to mention the absence of digital paint programs to produce them. For very simplistic graphics, this worked effectively. The use of real-time drawing in one of the first computer games, *Spacewar!* (produced in 1962), is shown in Figure 3.1.

FIG 3.1 Spacewar!

When read-only memory was introduced to arcade games in 1974, it allowed for the storage of predrawn graphics along with the game's program. The game could then load the various graphical assets and integrate them into the animation on the screen. These two-dimensional bitmaps were first referred to as *sprites*.

3.2 Sprites

Loading a 2D image onto the screen and redrawing it along a path will create a simple animation. This very principle is illustrated in the rocket ship workshop from Chapter 2, in which the static rocket ship image is moved around the screen. The rocket ship and planet are sprites. In these examples, sprites are dealt with by placing a texture representing the graphic element over a plane game object. The plane is then moved around the screen to create an animation. Both the rocket ship and the planet each have its own materials representing the different images.

The more materials used in a game, the less efficiently it will run. This is closely related to the way in which the power of two images is processed. In the case of Unity, each material adds an extra load inside each game loop. This load is called a *draw call*. A draw call occurs when rendering commands are processed by the computer's graphics processor. Each material used equals one draw call. Therefore, if you have 100 materials, it will cost you 100 draw calls.

> ⚫ **For Research**
> *Rendering Statistics*
> For more details about rendering statistics in Unity see
> http://docs.unity3d.com/Manual/RenderingStatistics.html.

As the number of draw calls increases, the slower your game will run, although a great number of draw calls would be required to make any noticeable difference on a high-performance gaming machine. However, if you port your application to a mobile device, a dramatic effect on performance is seen after around 15 draw calls.

Materials are not the only things that will increase the number of draw calls. As the polycounts of the meshes in the game environment increase, so too will the draw calls. However, polycounts do not have a one-to-one relationship with performance as materials do. Therefore, it is essential to consider the way in which sprite materials are handled.

3.3 Texture Atlas

Considering that a single material made from a texture that is 512×512 will take the same number of draw calls as one that is 32×32, it seems a waste to use only a 32×32 texture. Therefore, if the 32×32 image were put into a 512×512 image, there would be plenty of space in that image for other small images.

Combining images into one texture is a common technique in games and is called a *texture atlas*.

In a texture atlas, each smaller image has its own set of pixel coordinates and a width and height. To create such an atlas, you can use a paint program such as Photoshop or GIMP to combine smaller images into a single larger one. Figure 3.2 shows an example texture map in GIMP. Each image is placed such that a bounding box around it does not overlap with any other image. This allows for easy extraction of single images from the texture map in the game engine. In this example, the bounding box for the small car starts at (0,0) pixels and ends at (40,40) pixels. GIMP is useful for creating texture atlases; the pixel location of the mouse cursor is shown in the lower left-hand corner of the window. This makes it easier to extract the bounding boxes for each image. In GIMP, however, (0,0) is in the upper left-hand corner of the image. If you were to use Adobe Illustrator, (0,0) is in the bottom-left corner. Keep this in mind when you are grabbing pixel coordinates. If your texture appears upside down, it could be because the y axis is inverted. This is not a problem, just something that needs to be taken into consideration in your game scripts.

The coordinates of the bounding box are then used to manipulate the UV values of a mesh such that only the pixels inside the bounding box appear on the mesh as its texture. This requires a thorough understanding of vertices and UVs.

While the vertices of a mesh can have any value in 2D or 3D space, UVs are always specified between 0 and 1.

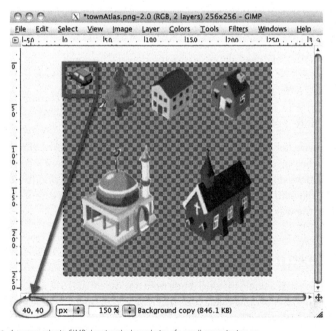

FIG 3.2 A texture atlas in GIMP showing the boundaries of a small car sprite image.

◎ Unity Hands On

Modifying Mesh UVs for Sprite mapping

Step 1: Download *Chapter Three/StaticSprites.zip* from the website. Unzip and open the project with Unity. Open the scene called spriteland. You will see a view of a 2D street scene.

Step 2: Locate the texture called townatlas in the Textures folder under Project. Click on the texture to reveal its properties in the Inspector. To use the image for sprite creation, set the Texture Type to Sprite 2D and UI as shown in Figure 3.3.

Step 3: Once the Texture Type is set beneath it, you will see a setting for Sprite Mode. Set this to Multiple.

Step 4: Still in the Inspector and looking at the settings for the townatlas image, click on the button Sprite Editor.

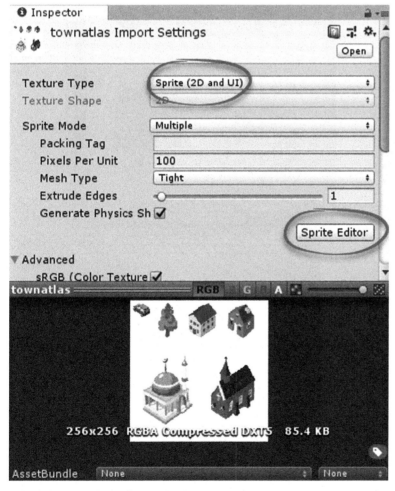

FIG 3.3 Inspector texture settings for creating a sprite.

Step 5: Drag the mouse over one of the smaller images, such as the house, to draw a square around it. This square defines the UV settings of the sprite. When you release the mouse, a sprite is created called townatlas_0 as shown in Figure 3.4.

Step 6: Drag the mouse around the tree to make another sprite. This will automatically be named townatlas_1.

Step 7: When you are finished defining the sprites, click on the Apply button at the top of the window and close it. In the Project, each sprite will appear as a child object of the texture. This is illustrated in Figure 3.5.

FIG 3.4 Creating individual sprites from a texture.

FIG 3.5 Sprites displayed as children of the texture to which they belong.

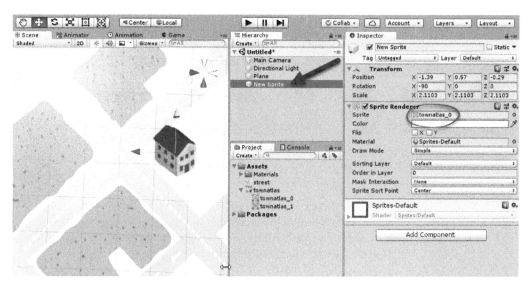

FIG 3.6 Putting the sprite texture onto an object in the scene.

Step 8: From the main menu, select Game Object > 2D Object > Sprite. A sprite object will be added to the Scene. You may have to move it forward on the z axis to see it as it could be behind the existing street scene quad. To place one of the sprites you just created on it as the texture, drag and drop the desired one onto the Sprite Renderer for the new sprite as shown in Figure 3.6.

If you ever go back to the Sprite Editor and adjust the UV settings for an individual sprite texture, it will be immediately reflected on any objects using that texture.

Step 9: Complete this exercise by setting UVs around each item in the townatlas and applying them to sprites in the scene.

3.4 Animated Sprites

Technically, any 2D image used as an object or character in a game is a sprite. However, the term is associated more often with a set of 2D animations representing specific movements of a game object. In this case, a sprite consists of a set of images that combine to animate specific gestures, such as walking, running, and jumping. The sprites are imported into a game engine and a code is used to control how the frames are presented in the game environment to give the illusion of character movement.

The animation images for a sprite are drawn based on the movement cycles originally developed for cartoon characters. Preston Blair, an acclaimed animator who worked for Disney, Warner Brothers, and Hanna-Barbera, published many illustrations demonstrating various character poses through a series of movement cycles.

FIG 3.7 Half of a walk cycle where the other half would be a reversal of the arm and leg positions.

The first of these cycles often referred to when teaching elementary animation is the *walk cycle* shown in Figure 3.7. Note the use of motion arcs for natural movement in the walk cycle here and the others by Preston Blair. The character rises and falls with each step.

Each of the images in Figure 3.7 becomes a single frame for the sprite. When these frames are cycled through in the game, it gives the illusion of a walking character.

◉ Unity Hands On
Creating a Texture Atlas with Code and Animated Sprite

Step 1: Create a new 2D Unity project.

Step 2: Download FBI_walk_cycle.png from the website. This is a freely available animated sprite sheet at opengameart.org created by FeralFantom. Add the texture to your Unity project.

Step 3: With the texture selected in the Project, set the Texture Type to Sprite 2D and UI, and set the Sprite Mode to Multiple.

Step 4: Click on the Sprite Editor button in the Inspector. At the top of the Sprite Editor window, set the editor to Splice then select Grid By Cell Size as shown in Figure 3.8. In the case of this sprite, each frame of the animation is 64 × 64. Use this as the pixel size for the grid. Click on the Slice Button when you are ready to create all the sprites and then click Apply.

Note that in order for this type of texture atlas UV mapping to work, each sprite has to be arranged in sequential and equal sized squares. This is typical of animated sprite sheets and something you should consider when making your own assets.

Step 5: Back in the project, the original texture will now have all the sprites shown as child objects. They will be named sequentially from FBI_walk_cycle_0 to FBI_walk_cycle_35.

Step 6: Take the Project tab and drag and drop it away from Unity to create a new window. Stretch it out horizontally and then right-click

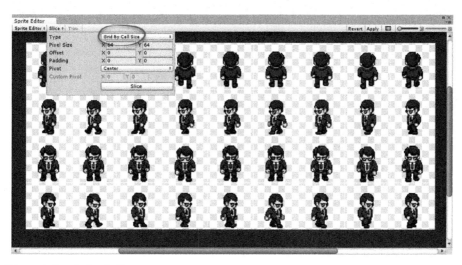

FIG 3.8 Slicing up a texture atlas for animation.

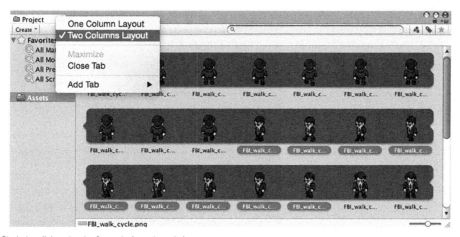

FIG 3.9 Displaying all the animation frames in the project window.

on the tab title and select Two Column Layout. Click the right icon on the sprite texture to expand; all the individual images will be visible as shown in Figure 3.9.

Step 7: Shift-select all the frames for the walking to the left animation in the Project. These are frames 9 through to 17. Drag them into the Hierarchy. On dropping them, Unity will ask for an animation name. Call this new animation as WalkingLeft. Click on Save.

FIG 3.10 A newly created animated sprite from single frames.

A new animation will be created in the scene complete with a Sprite Renderer and Animator as shown in Figure 3.10.

Press play and watch the animation play. The character will cycle through its walking to the left animation. You can make the character bigger by selecting it in the Scene, pressing the R key, and using the axes gizmos to drag out a new size.

Step 8: Download Chapter Three/background.png from the website. Add a new 3D Quad to the scene behind the character and put this new texture on it. Ensure the new texture is just a texture and not a sprite. Stretch the plane out to accommodate the texture. Move the background a quad away from the camera so the character is visible.

Step 9: Create a new C# Script named Scrolling.cs. Add the image scrolling code from Chapter 2, which is repeated here in Listing 3.1 for your convenience. Attach the C# to the new plane.

Listing 3.1 Code to scroll a texture over the surface of a mesh

```
//Scrolling.cs
using UnityEngine;
using System.Collections;

public class Scrolling : MonoBehaviour {
    public Vector2 uvSpeed = new Vector2(0.0f, -1.0f);
    public Vector2 uvOffset = Vector2.zero;

    void LateUpdate()
    {
        uvOffset += (uvSpeed * Time.deltaTime);
        this.GetComponent<Renderer>().materials[0].
            SetTextureOffset("_MainTex", uvOffset);
    }
}
```

Note that the background must be a 3D object, and the texture applied must be a basic texture, otherwise the code will not work. In other words, do not use sprites for this.

Step 10: With this new plane selected, in the Inspector change the UVSpeed to (−0.1,0).

Step 11: Play. The background will scroll making the character appear to walk along the street.

Step 12: To **move** the character itself with the arrow keys, create new C# script called Walk.cs, add the code in Listing 3.2 and attach it to the character's plane.

Listing 3.2 Code to scroll a texture over the surface of a mesh

```
//Walk.cs
using System.Collections;
using System.Collections.Generic;
using UnityEngine;

public class Walk : MonoBehaviour {

    public float speed = 0.1f;
    // Use this for initialization
    void Start () {

    }
```

```
// Update is called once per frame
void Update () {
    if(Input.GetKey("right"))
    {
        this.transform.Translate(speed,0,0);
    }

    if(Input.GetKey("left"))
    {
        this.transform.Translate(-speed,0,0);
    }
}
}
```

Step 13: Play. The arrow keys will move the sprite back and forth in front of the background. Remove the scrolling script from the background to get a better idea of how the character is moving.

Step 14: With the walking speed set to 0.1, the character appears to slide across the ground. This **is** a common error made by beginner animators when creating walk cycles and placing the character into an environment whether it be in 2D or 3D. The idea is to get the walk cycle speed to match with the motion speed so that each foot appears to be planted into the ground. For this character, a speed of about 0.04 works well. Try this out.

◉ **Note**

Making your own sprite frames

One of the easiest ways to create your own sprites, instead of drawing each frame by hand, is to use a software package that will do it for you. Adobe Flash has an export to image option that will allow you to create single frames from an animation and save them as a sequence of PNG files. *Anime Studio Pro* is a 2D animation software package that will take an image of a character and allow you to add your own bones (see Figure 3.11). You can then manipulate these bones to pose the character. After an animation has been created, *Anime Studio Pro* provides export features that will create a sequence of JPG or PNG files that can then be used on sprites in Unity.

◉ **On the Web**

Advanced Sprite Editor

Advanced use of the Unity Sprite Editor:
http://unity3d.com/learn/tutorials/modules/beginner/2d/sprite-editor
More Sprites: https://opengameart.org/
GIMP http://www.gimp.org

FIG 3.11 Manipulating character poses in Anime Studio Pro.

3.5 Baked 3D Animations

Calculating animations in real time through kinematics is a very processor-costly method for animating game characters. While this method can certainly produce spontaneous interactions with characters, far more artificially intelligent controls need to be programmed to make them feel real. If you examine game characters closely, you will notice that they repeat the same actions in exactly the same way over and over. This is because it is less effort on the part of the animation to make; for example, why use five different walk animations when just one will suffice? It does not add anything more to a game having characters that can select from different walking styles as they see fit.

If you stop to observe ancillary characters in the crowd such as those in *Assassin's Creed* or *Skyrim*, you will be able to spot their walk cycles and other repeated actions. Because the purpose of the game in these cases is not to eye the crowd, the same repeated walk cycle is not that important. You may also find a game hero who climbs a drainpipe in the same way as he climbs a rope. Reusing animations is just a trick to get better performance out of a game and a way to keep the development budget down. In the end, it is how these animations are used and how the game environment is designed around these limitations. For example, the animation for climbing a ladder could be used for scaling a building or a trellis if the objects are designed to have handholds and footholds in similar positions to a ladder.

When animations are fixed and not manipulated in real time by the program, they are called *baked*. This means that the entire animation sequence is calculated beforehand and that the program receives a set of model transformations for each frame.

Because the character modeler cannot possibly know at the time of animating how the player is going to direct and move the character, it is impossible to create a long strung out animation, for example, showing the character running up the road, jumping over a fence, and rolling through a window. If the player decides that the character should not jump over the fence but rather hop on the nearest motorbike, a single long animation will not allow for visualization. Instead, animations are broken into short action segments that can later be put together in any order to facilitate fluid animation. Such segments might include walk, run, and jump cycles. Depending on how the player wants the character to move, he or she can then run, jump, run, and walk—or walk, jump, jump, run, and walk seamlessly.

This means that each animation segment should start and end with the character in the same pose. When the next segment is added, there is no obvious gap in the sequence. As shown in Figure 3.12, the initial frame for the character's idle, run, walk, and shoot down animations has the character's feet and legs in exactly the same position. No matter what the sequence of actions, the full movement of the character will appear fluid. In a situation where the animation switches to the shoot down, the arms and shoulders will move away from the initial poses of the others. If this is a very small movement, and given the legs do not move, the change in pose will appear as a simple frame change in any other segment.

If a situation arises where the character needs to go from a walking to a crawling action, two in-between sequences are required to stitch the animations together: one for getting down and one for standing up.

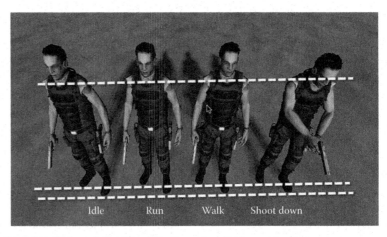

FIG 3.12 Starting frames for four different animations performed by the same character.

Sometimes a single animation is reused for its reverse action. For example, getting down is reused for the standing up, and walking forward is reused for walking backward. However, if you have a close look at both these examples, the results are usually very unconvincing and ruin the entire effect.

Baked animations can be made in software modeling and animation tools such as Autodesk's 3DS Max and Maya. The native format for animations in Unity is FBX, which can be created with both these applications. Once the FBX sequences have been imported into Unity, Script can be used to control how they play.

☺ Unity Hands On
Controlling Character Animation
Step 1: Download *Chapter Three/WalkingGranny.zip* from the website. Unzip and open the project in Unity. Open the scene called animations. In the Game, you will see a character called Sporty_Granny.

Note that in the Project > Granny folder, you will find a number of files named Sporty_Granny@*** where *** is an action such as idle or jump. Each one of these files is an FBX animation.
Step 2: Select the Sporty_Granny.fbx object in the Project as shown in Figure 3.13. In the Inspector, select the Rig tab and set the Animation

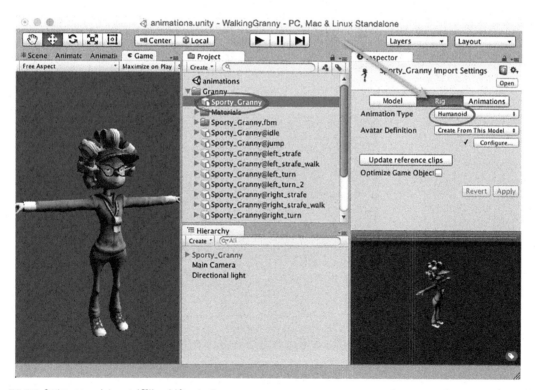

FIG 3.13 Setting up a newly imported FBX model for animating.

Type to Humanoid. Click on apply. If you now select the Sporty_Granny object in the Hierarchy, you will notice that the object has an Animator component attached. This component requires an Animator Controller. The Animator Controller will link all available animations to the model. You will need to do this for all the FBX files, shift select the remaining FBX files (i.e., Shorty_Granny@idle, etc.) and set the Animation Type to Humanoid and click Apply.

Step 3: In the Project, create a new Animator Controller as shown in Figure 3.14. Rename it Granny Controller. Having it selected in the Project window, you will see a small Open button appearing in the controller. Click on this to add the animations. The Animator window will open. It has a gridded background, and there will be a green round-cornered square with Any State written on it.

Step 4: With the Animator window open next to the Project, locate all the animation files and drag them from the Project into the Animator. The files you are looking for have a small blue "play" icon next to them. The first one you add will appear in orange. This will become the default animation for the model. The other animations will appear in gray. What you can expect to see during this process is illustrated in Figure 3.15.

Step 5: When you have finished dragging the animations to the controller, select the Sporty_Granny object in the Hierarchy. This is the model you can see in the scene. In the Inspector, the Animator component will be visible. Drag the newly created Granny Controller and drop it onto the Controller property of the animator as shown in Figure 3.16.

FIG 3.14 Creating a new animator controller in the project.

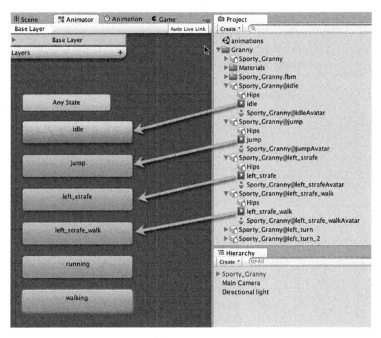

FIG 3.15 Adding individual models to an animator controller.

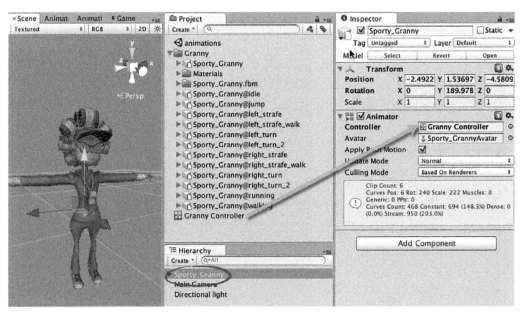

FIG 3.16 Attaching an animator controller to a model.

Save what you have done so far and press Play. The first animation you dragged into the animator (the one in orange) will play on the model. To change the default animation, return to the Granny_Controller editing window, right-click on one of the animations and set them to default. **Step 6:** Next we are going to control the movement and animations of Sporty_Granny with script. Begin by creating a new C# file named AnimControls. Into this file, type the code shown in Listing 3.3.

Listing 3.3 Script to control a model's movement and animation

```
//AnimControls.cs
using System.Collections;
using System.Collections.Generic;
using UnityEngine;

public class AnimControls : MonoBehaviour {

    Animator anim;
    float speed = 0.05f;
    float rotSpeed = 50.0f;

    // Use this for initialization
    void Start () {
        anim = gameObject.GetComponent<Animator>();
    }

    // Update is called once per frame
    void Update () {
        if(Input.GetKey("up"))
        {
            anim.Play("walking",0);
            this.transform.position += this.transform.
                forward * speed;
        }
        else if(Input.GetKey("down"))
        {
            anim.Play("walking",0);
            this.transform.position -= this.transform.
                forward * speed;
        }
        else if(Input.GetKeyUp("up") || Input.
            GetKeyUp("down"))
        {
            anim. Play("idle",0);
        }
    }
}
```

Attach this script file to the Sporty_Granny game object in the Hierarchy. When run, the script accesses the object's Animator and plays the "walking" animation when the up or down arrow keys are pressed.

The Play function takes two parameters. The first is the name of the animation. This must be written exactly as the animation is named in the Animator window (i.e., the word written on the orange or gray squares). The second, which in this case is 0, is the layer the animation is on. In the Animator window, you may have noticed all the animations went into the Base Layer. This is layer 0. We will use only layer 0, so always set the second parameter to this.

Play and use the arrow keys to move Sporty Granny around. She can only go forward and back at this stage.

Step 7: In moving the character in the previous step, you may have noticed the walk animation cycles once and then stops. The reason is that the animation is not set to loop. To fix this, select the animation you want to loop, in this case "walking," from the Project. In the Inspector, select the Animations tab and then tick the boxes for Loop Time and Loop Pose as shown in Figure 3.17. Ensure you scroll to the bottom of the Inspector and click on the Apply button.

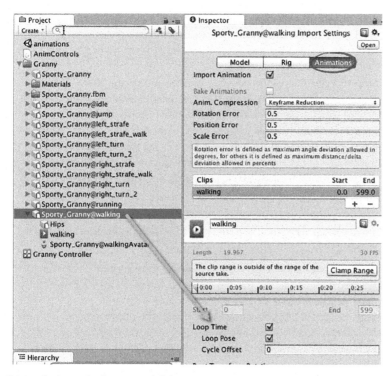

FIG 3.17 Setting an animation to automatically loop.

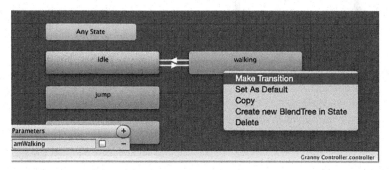

FIG 3.18 Adding transitions between animation states.

Step 8: Play again and try walking back and forth. The walk animation will now loop.

This is much better, but the animations still snap between idle and walk. To fix this, we need to create transitions in the Animator window.
Step 9: Double-click on the Granny Controller in the Project to open the Animator window. Bring the Idle and Walking animation boxes next to each other. Right-click on the Idle animation to bring up a menu with Make Transition as an option. Select this and then click on Walking. A white line with an arrow will link the two animations. Because we want to smoothly transition from Idle to Walking and back again, right-click on Walking and make a transition line from Walking to Idle. This process is illustrated in Figure 3.18. With these animations linked, you will be able to create smooth transitions from one to the other; however, to make this happen, you need to set up some variables.
Step 10: In the Animator window is a small box titled Parameters. Click on the + button and create a new Bool parameter called "amWalking." This value will now be used to control when the transitions between the animations occur.
Step 11: Select the arrow that points from Idle to Walking. It will become highlighted in blue. In the Inspector, you will see the details about this transition—untick Has Exit Time. At the bottom, in the Conditions area, you want to add the amWalking parameter as a condition and set its value to true as illustrated in Figure 3.19.

By adding this parameter, you are telling Unity that when the value of amWalking is set to true, it should play a transition animation from Idle to Walking.

You will want to do the exact same thing for the transition going from Walking back to Idle. But this time, add the parameter amWalking but make its value false.
Step 12: Transitions between animations do not just happen by themselves. You need to code them. In this case, both are determined by the value of amWalking; therefore, we set the value of amWalking to true or false in the code to control what the character does. Modify the Update function in AnimControls.cs to reflect that in Listing 3.4.

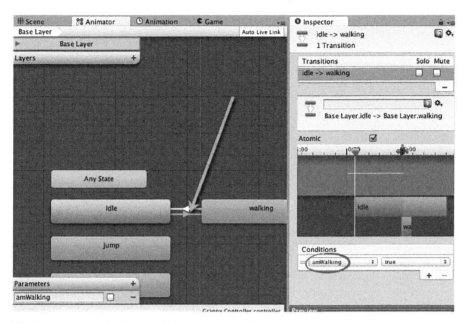

FIG 3.19 Adding a parameter to control animation transitions.

Listing 3.4 Updated AnimControls

```
//AnimControls.cs
using System.Collections;
using System.Collections.Generic;
using UnityEngine;

public class AnimControls : MonoBehaviour {

    Animator anim;
    float speed = 0.05f;
    float rotSpeed = 50.0f;

    // Use this for initialization
    void Start () {
        anim = gameObject.GetComponent<Animator>();
    }

    // Update is called once per frame
    void Update () {
        if(Input.GetKey("up"))
        {
            anim.SetBool("amWalking",true);
            this.transform.position += this.transform.
                forward * speed;
        }
```

```
    else if(Input.GetKey("down"))
    {
        anim.SetBool("amWalking",true);
        this.transform.position -= this.transform.
            forward * speed;
    }
    else if(Input.GetKeyUp("up") || Input.
        GetKeyUp("down"))
    {
        anim.SetBool("amWalking",false);
    }
  }
}
```

Step 13: Play. The character will now smoothly transition between animation states.

Step 14: To make the camera follow the character, in the Scene, move the view around until you look at the character from behind in a position slightly above as shown in Figure 3.20. With the camera selected in the Hierarchy, from the main menu select GameObject > Align With View. Once you have

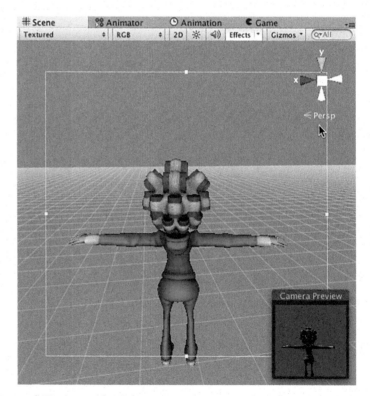

FIG 3.20 Position the camera for a third-person view.

the camera in a place you would like, drag and drop it in the Hierarchy onto the Sporty_Granny game object. The camera will become a child object of the model and follow it wherever it moves.

At this point, you might want to add in a ground plane, otherwise there will be nothing that Sporty_Granny is moving relative to and it will not appear as though she is going anywhere.

Step 15: To add turning to the character, the same format as the existing code is used to test for the left and right arrow keys. While turning, the model's transform is simply rotated. Modify AnimationControls.cs to add a couple of lines to the bottom of the Update function as shown in Listing 3.5.

Listing 3.5 Updated AnimControls

```
//AnimControls.cs
...
float rotSpeed = 50.0f;
...

// Update is called once per frame
void Update () {
    ...

    if(Input.GetKey("left"))
    {
        transform.Rotate(-Vector3.up * Time.deltaTime *
            rotSpeed);
    }
    else if(Input.GetKey("right"))
    {
        transform.Rotate(Vector3.up * Time.deltaTime *
            rotSpeed);
    }
}
```

Step 16: Play. The left and right arrows will turn Sporty_Granny. There are many other animations that come with the character. Try mapping these to keys in AnimationControls.cs for yourself.

For more detailed tutorials on Unity's Mecanim system, see the author's online video series at http://bit.ly/unityanimation and https://holistic3d.com/udemy/mastering-3d-animation/.

3.6 Biomechanics

Biomechanics is a field of study that examines the mechanical movement of biological systems such as humans, plants, and animals. It plays an important part in animation describing the way in which natural hierarchical systems such as the human skeleton move. The hierarchy for a skeleton begins at the skull and divides into a number of segments, including arms, legs, hands, and feet that connect to one another by joints. When higher-level joints—such as the shoulder—move, any connected lower level segments, such as the hand, move too. In contrast, when a lower level joint or segment moves, such as a finger, any higher-level segments, such as the skull, do not move. Aristotle first wrote about biomechanics in *De Motu Animalium* (*On the Movement of Animals*).

There are a number of ways in which a skeletal structure can be specified for animation. The Humanoid Animation Working Group (H-Anim; http://www. web3d.org/documents/specifications/19774/V1.0/index.html) is an international project with the goal of providing a standard profile for a humanoid skeleton so it can be used consistently across a number of applications. A partial view of the standard is illustrated in Figure 3.21. This makes the process of swapping characters in and out of games and virtual environments more streamlined. Imagine that you are able to take your favorite character from *Halo* and use it in *The Sims*. This of course would not work; however, if both games used the same rules from the H-Anim specification, it would work.

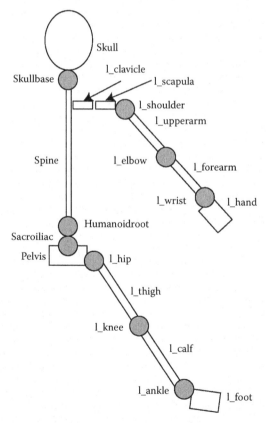

FIG 3.21 A partial view of the H-Anim project's specifications for a humanoid skeletal hierarchy showing minimal joints.

The premise behind H-Anim and any other skeletal representation is the connection of straight segments and rotatable joints. The way in which these structures move is analyzed by the applied mechanics discipline of kinematics.

Kinematics describes the motion of objects without consideration of the causes leading to the motion. It examines linear and rotational movement with respect to distance, direction, and velocity. These are the very same concepts developed in Chapter 2 through the examination of vector mathematics. Kinematics can be examined from two points of view: forward and inverse.

Forward kinematics calculates the final position of the end of an articulated object, given the angle and rotation of the joints and the length of the segments. To exemplify, forward kinematics can calculate the position of a character's hand, given the rotation and angles of joints and the length of the bone segments. The hand in this case is what is known in kinematics as the end effector. To solve such a problem, simple vector mathematics is employed. Each bone has a length and direction that are specified as a vector. Adding all the vectors together will give the final destination. As illustrated in Figure 3.22, if the shoulder is positioned at (10,10) with the humerus (upper arm bone) making a vector of (3,−3), the radius and ulna (lower arm bones) making a vector of (2,2), and the hand with a vector of (1,0), the final position of the finger tips will be at (16,9).

Inverse kinematics is used in games to ensure that characters connect with the environment. For example, in *The Sims*, when a character interacts with an object, the game must ensure that the character is standing in the correct position to pick the object up. Although the bending over and picking up an object are premade animations, the character still needs to be positioned in the correct location to perform a convincing connection with the object. For that reason, if a Sim is required to pick up a guitar, the character will walk over to the item first and position itself such that when the pickup animation plays, it looks as though the object is being picked up.

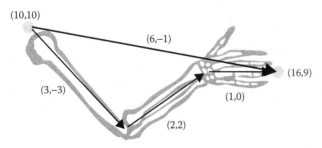

FIG 3.22 A forward kinematic example with an arm in 2D.

Inverse kinematics is somewhat more complex than forward kinematics. It performs the reverse operation of forward kinematics, asking what the angles of the joints must be to position the end effector at a specific location? For example, if the shoulder is at (10,10), how should the bones in the arm be positioned to place the hand at (16,9)? This is not as simple as it might first appear because, when you think about it, the joints in the arm can make a variety of angles, as shown in Figure 3.23.

Try it for yourself. Grab hold of a doorknob and keeping your shoulder at the same location in space, see how many different positions you can manipulate your arm into without removing your hand from the doorknob. These are just the movements for your arm, which consists of three basic joints and three principal segments. Imagine calculating the inverse kinematics for something with 10 or more joints.

Although we consider the shoulder as a single joint, for the purposes of inverse kinematics, it is actually three. If you hold your arm straight out to the side, you will be able to raise and lower it (like flapping to fly), move it from side to side (like waving past traffic), and also rotate it (as though your outreached hand is turning a knob). Each distinct movement is called a degree of freedom (DOF). Therefore, the shoulder has three DOFs: two DOFs that translate the attached segment and one that rotates it.

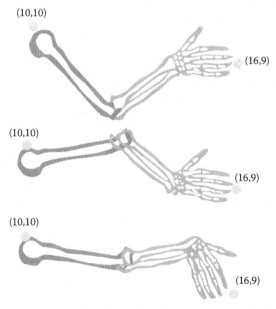

FIG 3.23 Three solutions to an inverse kinematic problem.

⚫ **For Research**
Inverse Kinematics
For further in-depth examination of inverse kinematic systems in Unity check out http://docs.unity3d.com/Manual/InverseKinematics.html.

3.7 Animation Management

In the preceding examples of 3D animations, character action sequences were split into segments. In the case of 2D sprites, only one sequence was given (walking); in the 3D examples, each action was contained in its own separate file.

It is not always the case that animations come to game developers in this way. If you were to download a fully animated character from a site such as TurboSquid, the character may come as a single file containing any number of animation sequences. In the case of 2D sprites, it is not uncommon to find all the action sequences for one character in a single texture atlas.

3.7.1 Single 2D Sprite Actions

As we have seen, a texture atlas is a convenient and optimizing way to keep sprites. More often than not, all the animations for a single character are kept in a texture atlas. This requires pixel management on the part of the programmer to ensure that the correct part of the texture is displayed at the right time. Figure 3.24 shows a texture atlas with several idle and walking animation frames. Although it is not strictly necessary to have the frames belonging to the same animation next to each other in the texture, it makes it monumentally easier to program if they are in sequence and packed together. It is also easier if each frame is of the same size. In the image shown, each frame is 32 × 64.

Individual animations are specified with a starting frame and a number of frames; for example, the walk left animation starts at frame 3 and is three frames in length. By knowing the fixed width for a frame, the exact pixel

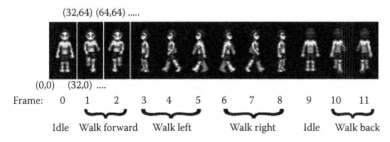

FIG 3.24 Joined frames for four separate animations. (Sprite art thanks to Dezire Soft).

value for the start of an animation sequence can be calculated. In this case, the walk left animation begins at frame 3, and therefore the starting *x* pixel location would be $3 \times 32 = 96$.

⬦ Unity Specifics
Sprite Dimensions

If the sprite atlas does not have power of 2 dimensions, Unity will squash and stretch it to make it so. This will produce an undesirable effect with the frame locations. To correct this, select the texture in the Project and in the Inspector set the Texture Type to Advanced and the Non Power of 2 to None.

⬭ Unity Hands On
Managing Animated Sprite Sequences

Step 1: Download *Chapter Three/SpriteManager.zip* from the website. Open the project in Unity and open the WalkingSprite scene. You will find a scene with four animated sprites in it. These sprites were created from a sprite sheet using a grid to cut the images up as was performed in a previous hands-on session.

Play. You will notice that all the sprites are shown and the animations are playing. Further investigation will reveal that all the sprites are positioned in the scene at exactly the same position.

Step 2: Create an empty game object in the Inspector and child all the sprites to it as shown in Figure 3.25. Rename the empty object TheProfessor. The position in space of the TheProfessor as long as each sprite is at position (0,0,0). This will ensure that, relative to TheProfessor, the sprites are at its origin.

Wherever we move TheProfessor, the sprites will now automatically follow.
Step 3: Create a new C# file called SpriteManagement.cs. Open SpriteManagement.cs in the script editor and add the code in Listing 3.6.

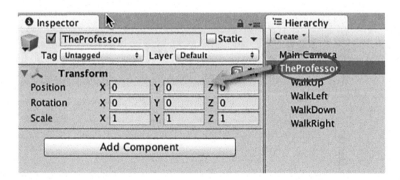

FIG 3.25 Adding sprite objects to an empty game object.

**Listing 3.6 Controlling the movement of
a sprite with the arrow keys**

```
//SpriteManagement.cs
using System.Collections;
using System.Collections.Generic;
using UnityEngine;

public class SpriteManagement : MonoBehaviour {

    float speed = 0.01f;

    // Update is called once per frame
    void Update () {

        if(Input.GetKey (KeyCode.UpArrow))
        {
            this.transform.Translate(0,speed,0);
        }
        else if(Input.GetKey (KeyCode.DownArrow))
        {
            this.transform.Translate(0,-speed,0);
        }
        else if(Input.GetKey (KeyCode.LeftArrow))
        {
            this.transform.Translate(-speed,0,0);
        }
        else if(Input.GetKey (KeyCode.RightArrow))
        {
            this.transform.Translate(speed,0,0);
        }
    }
}
```

Step 4: Attach the script to TheProfessor and Play. The sprite will be
moveable with the arrow keys. You will still see all sprites playing.
Step 5: Next we need to turn the sprites on and off depending on the
key being pressed. For example, if the up arrow is being pressed and the
character is moving up the screen, then that particular animated sprite
should be the only one visible. To achieve this, our code needs access
to each animation. We can put them into a simple array by modifying
SpriteManagement.cs as shown in Listing 3.7.

Listing 3.7 Creating an animation array

```
public class SpriteManagement : MonoBehaviour {

float speed = 0.01f;
public GameObject[] anims;

// Update is called once per frame
void Update () {
...
```

Save the code and return to the Inspector. You will find the new array visible in the script properties. As shown in Figure 3.26, set the array size to 4 and then drag and drop each sprite from the Hierarchy into a position in the array. The order the sprites appear in the array will matter to the way you program their appearance, therefore add them in the same order as shown in Figure 3.26.

Step 6: Now the script knows about the animated sprites, we can turn them on and off as needed. A simple function can be employed to turn off all the sprites which are then turned on as required. If no keys are being pressed, we should show the last frame of the sprite animation so the character just does not disappear. To achieve this, modify SpriteManagement.cs by adding the code shown in Listing 3.8.

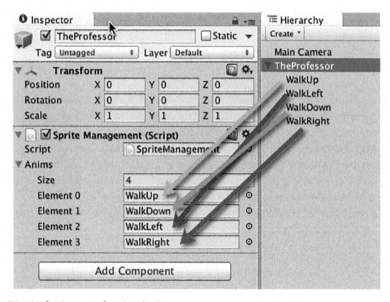

FIG 3.26 Creating an array for sprite animations.

Listing 3.8 Creating class structures for strong values

```
// Updated SpriteManagement.cs
using System.Collections;
using System.Collections.Generic;
using UnityEngine;

public class SpriteManagement: MonoBehaviour {

    float speed = 0.01f;
    public GameObject[] anims;
    int currentAnim = -1;

    // Use this for initialization
    void Start () {
        TurnAllAnimationsOff();
    }

    void TurnAllAnimationsOff()
    {
        foreach(GameObject i in anims)
        {
            i.SetActive(false);
        }
    }

    // Update is called once per frame
    void Update () {
        if(currentAnim != -1)
        //if there is a current animation set its speed
        //to 1
        anims[currentAnim].GetComponent<Animator>().speed
            = 1;

        if(Input.GetKey (KeyCode.UpArrow))
        {
            //before turning on this animation
            //turn off the previous if it is a different
            //one
            if(currentAnim != 0 && currentAnim != -1)
                anims[currentAnim].SetActive(false);

        //move the character
        this.transform.Translate(0,speed,0);

            //make the appropriate sprite active and
            //    start playing
            anims[0].SetActive(true);
```

```
            //update the number of the current animation
            currentAnim = 0;
        }
        else if(Input.GetKey (KeyCode.DownArrow))
        {
            if(currentAnim != 1 && currentAnim != -1)
            anims[currentAnim].SetActive(false);
            this.transform.Translate(0,-speed,0);
            anims[1].SetActive(true);
            currentAnim = 1;
        }
        else if(Input.GetKey (KeyCode.LeftArrow))
        {
            if(currentAnim != 2 && currentAnim != -1)
            anims[currentAnim].SetActive(false);
            this.transform. Translate(-speed,0,0);
            anims[2].SetActive(true);
            currentAnim = 2;
        }
        else if(Input.GetKey (KeyCode.RightArrow))
        {
            if(currentAnim != 3 && currentAnim != -1)
            anims[currentAnim].SetActive(false);
            this.transform. Translate(speed,0,0);
            anims[3].SetActive(true);
            currentAnim = 3;
        }
        else
        {
            //if there is no key being pressed, set the
            //current animation speed to 0
            //in other words, pause it.
            if(currentAnim != -1)
            anims[currentAnim].GetComponent<Animator>().
                speed = 0;
        }
    }
}
```

Save and Play. The character will now switch between animations as it moves around the screen. To add more animations, you would insert extra sprites into the array and then more if statements testing for key presses.

3.7.2 Single-Filed 3D Animations

Original 3D FPS games such as *Quake 3 Arena* (Q3A) use a single track of 3D animation that defines many separate animations in the same way as an animated sprite texture atlas. Animations for a character in Q3A, a Quakebot, for example, are played from specified frames—some are looped and some are not. To create a series of animations for a Quake character, a number of different animations need to be specified and then glued together. For example, the running animation might go from frame 30 to frame 45, and the swimming animation might go from frame 46 to frame 57.

Animations in Q3A must be set up in a specific order. The order and length of the animations are displayed in Table 3.1.

TABLE 3.1 Order and Frame Size of Animations used in Q3A[a]

Animation	Length (in frames)	Description
BOTH_DEATH1	~30	Full body animation
BOTH_DEAD1	~1	Death scenes and final
BOTH_DEATH2	~30	Death poses.
BOTH_DEAD2	~1	
BOTH_DEATH3	~30	
BOTH_DEAD3	~1	
Category: Upper Body		
TORSO_GESTURE	~45	e.g., taunting
TORSO_ATTACK	6*	Attack other player
TORSO_ATTACK2	6*	"
TORSO_DROP	5*	Drop arms as to change weapon
TORSO_RAISE	4*	Lift up new weapon
TORSO_STAND	1*	Idle pose for upper body
TORSO_STAND2	1*	"
Category: Lower Body		
LEGS_WALKCR	~10	Crouched while walking forward
LEGS_WALK	~15	Walking forward
LEGS_RUN	~12	Running forward
LEGS_BACK	~10	Back pedaling
LEGS_SWIM	~10	Swimming
LEGS_JUMP	~10	Jumping up forward
LEGS_LAND	~6	Landing after jump
LEGS_JUMPB	~10	Jumping up backwards
LEGS_LANDB	~6	Landing after backwards jump
LEGS_IDLE	~10	Idle pose for lower body
LEGS_IDLECR	~10	Crouched idle pose for lower body
LEGS_TURN	~8	Turning on the spot

[a] All animation lengths are approximations with the exception of those indicated by a * which need to be exact.

TABLE 3.2 A Partial Animation Configuration File

Animation	First Frame	Number of Frames	Times to Loop	Frames per Second
BOTH_DEATH1	0	30	0	25
BOTH_DEAD1	29	1	0	25
TORSO_GESTURE	90	40	0	15
TORSO_ATTACK	130	6	0	15

As shown in Table 3.1, upper and lower animations are separate with the exception of death scenes. Therefore, movement of the upper body is independent of the lower body. This allows for different animation effects by combining differing animation parts. However, this can be a slight problem when two unrelated animations are combined; for example, an upper TORSO_ATTACK combined with a LEGS_SWIM would look strange. Although this system of animation has the drawback of creating inappropriate movements, it does provide for an overall greater number of animations.

Because many of the animation sequences do not have a defined length, an animation configuration file needs to be generated for the Q3A game engine so that it can locate the correct animation progressions. The configuration file is called *animation.cfg* and is loaded into the Q3A engine with the appropriate model. The configuration file contains information on the first frame of the sequence, the length, in frames, of the sequence, the number of times to loop the animation, and how fast to play it. The file contains this information for each animation sequence in the order shown in Table 3.2.

A model is defined as three separate parts: head, torso, and legs. Each part of the model is linked internally by what is known as a tag. Tags control the locations at which the parts of the model are connected. Because each part is dealt with separately, the tags essentially join them together. There are three principal tags in a Q3A model: tag_head (which joins the head to the torso), tag_torso (which joins the upper body to the lower body), and tag_weapon (which provides a location to attach the weapon model). For games such as Q3A that allow players to modify and create their own character models, having a standard format such as this is crucial in ensuring that the models are animated and rendered consistently.

3.8 Secondary Animation

Secondary animation refers to movement that occurs as a result of primary animation. For example, when a character walks, in response to the movement, his hair might move and his muscles ripple. If a character shoots a weapon, you would expect a recoil action. Secondary animation is caused by the law of physics, which dictates that every action has an equal and opposite reaction. Without the extra animation, a character can appear static and unrealistic.

Depending on the level of secondary animation, it can be processor intensive and not feasible in a real-time game environment. The avatars used in *Quake 3 Arena* and *Unreal Tournament* are very simple, with tight-fitting clothing and close-cut hair. This is not because the artist could not be bothered or at the time did not have the technology to create highly realistic models—it is simply because animating all the extra elements with secondary animation was not feasible on the hardware available at the time these games were released. Even today, hair and cloth in 3D real-time environments are limited. A very nice example of the secondary animation of cloth can be seen in *Assassin's Creed*. The cloak and ropes of the main character move in response to the character's movements and the wind.

As hardware capabilities increase, so will the quantity and quality of secondary animation.

Other animations that could also be considered secondary to the main character are those that bring the environment to life, for example, trees swaying in the breeze, water running in a river, other characters walking down the street, or even the main character's own clothing, such as a cape.

◕ Unity Hands On
Adding Secondary Motion

In this exercise, we will add a cape to a model using the cloth component and a preexisting cape model.

Download the file *Chapter Three/SecondaryAnimation.zip*. Open the scene called secondaryAnim.

In the Project, you will find an asset called cape. Drag this into the scene next to the character and reposition to sit on the character's back. Make the cape a child of the Sporty_Granny > Hips > Spine > Spine1 > Spine2 > Neck object. This will ensure the cape is attached to the character and moves when it does.

With the cape selected in the Hierarchy, use the Add Component button in the Inspector to add a Physics > Cloth component. A new Skinned Mesh Renderer will also be added. If the old Mesh Renderer is still there, delete it. At this point, the cape will turn invisible. That is because the old renderer is gone. The new Skinned Mesh Renderer needs to know about the mesh it is drawing. Set its value to the cape's mesh as shown in Figure 3.27. You can do this by selecting the small round icon to the right of the property and then locating the cape's mesh in the window that pops open. Once assigned, the cape will reappear in the Scene.

With the cape selected, drag Sporty_Granny into the Cloth Capsule Collider as shown in Figure 3.28. This will cause the character's body to impact the movement of the cape.

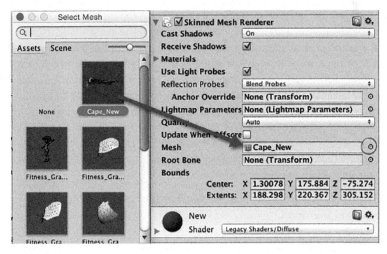

FIG 3.27 Assigning a mesh to a cloth's skinned mesh renderer.

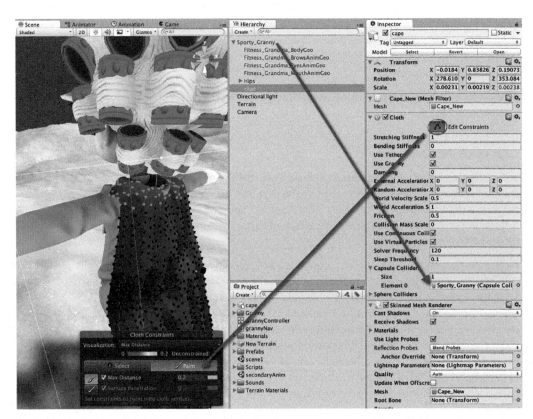

FIG 3.28 Setup for a character and cloth.

Next, select the Cloth's Edit Constraints button. From the window that opens, select Paint. The cloth's vertices will now be black dots. Use the mouse to paint over the vertices at the top of the cloth. They will turn green. These are the fixed vertices that will ensure the cloth remains pinned to the character.

Save and play. The character will be able to run around followed by a billowing cloth. If you find the cloth at an unnatural distance from the character, you may have to shrink the characters capsule collider.

3.9 Summary

This chapter examined 2D and 3D animation principles and techniques. As moving and animated objects are key elements in games, understanding how a game engine manages and manipulates these assets is a key to including them effectively in games.

Game Rules and Mechanics

But how can we speak of mere play, when we know that it is precisely play and play alone, which of all man's states and conditions is the one which makes him whole and unfolds both sides of his nature at once?

Friedrich von Schiller

4.1 Introduction

Games for recreational use are as old as known civilization. The oldest complete board game set thought to be the precursor of backgammon, the *Royal Game of Ur* (played with seven markers and three tetrahedral dice), dates back to 3000 BCE. Other such games include *Wei-qi*, otherwise known as *Go*, played in China as far back as 2000 BCE, and the Egyptian *Dogs and Jackals* (1800 BCE).

The underlying activity in games is *play*. Play can be found in all human cultures and most animal populations. At the most instinctual level, play provides teaching and learning opportunities. For example, young children

will play to assist them in practicing life skills. This is also evident in the animal kingdom through observing the young of cats, dogs, and other mammals; for example, puppies play fight with each other and practice pouncing on inanimate objects in preparation for the grown-up world. The key element of play is the cause-and-effect nature that reinforces certain behaviors. To practice is to attempt to get better at some skill set. Without feedback on one's actions, knowing how to improve is impossible.

When play becomes structured and when goals, rules, and actions are applied, they turn into games. In the playground, simple play involving chasing other children turns into a game of *Tag* or *Dodge Ball* when one child becomes "it" and the objective is to tag another child in order to make him or her "it."

These fundamental actions of human behavior found in the play and games of children are found at the very heart of computer games and make up the set of core game mechanics presented herein.

4.2 Game Mechanics

If play is the practice of core human "mechanical" behavior, then a game mechanic should define and constrain this behavior in a system with rules and rewards; for example, a child playing at stacking blocks will be learning how to position them correctly to build a stable tower. Once goals and/or restrictions are placed on the activity, it becomes a game; for example, build a stack of blocks to 1 meter or build a stack of blocks to 1 meter in 30 seconds. In this example, there is the play action (stacking), a goal (1 meter in 30 seconds), feedback (if the blocks are placed incorrectly they will fall over), and rules (use only these blocks).

The theme throughout this book plays on the word *mechanic* to refer to the actions taking place in games—from the internal workings of animation and programming to the interactions between the environment and the player. However, the term *game mechanic*, in game studies, is used to refer to designed game–player relationships that facilitate and define the game's challenges. Game mechanics are complex systems that include a set of possible player actions, motivations, goals, and feedback. Understanding that a game mechanic is much more than just an action and what other elements may be applied with that action opens up a plethora of almost infinite ideas for games by mixing and matching actions, goals, and rules. The cycle is illustrated in Figure 4.1. The player is presented with a challenge. To complete this challenge, they have tools they can use to perform actions and rules that define the scope of these actions. The tools include peripheral computing objects such as keyboards and game controllers, as well as virtual in-game tools such as vehicles, weapons, and keys. The rules dictate how the player can act in the environment. In a board game, rules are written in an instruction booklet and are monitored by players. In a computer game,

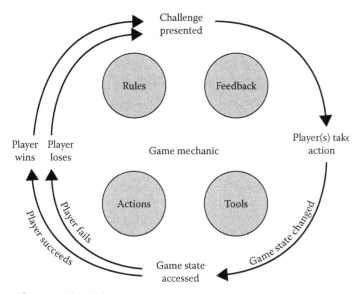

FIG 4.1 The game mechanic cycle.

the player is made aware of the rules, and the game's programming code ensures that the player follows them. The program also provides feedback to players based on their actions to assist them in learning how to better play the game and complete the challenge. Part of the feedback mechanism is to also inform players when they succeed or fail.

One of the developers of the original *Halo*, the game that launched Microsoft's Xbox, described the game as 5 minutes of fun over and over again. This first person shooter (FPS) game, in a visually rich 3D environment, employs numerous game mechanics that revolve around shooting and blowing things up. As a whole, the game is represented by the ultimate game mechanic that challenges the player to uncover the secrets of a ring-shaped planet named Halo while battling a variety of aliens. This umbrella mechanic is broken down into a number of smaller mechanics that see players performing the same tasks over and over again in order to complete their objectives, with the key mechanic being *kill or be killed*, typically found in FPS games. As such you could say that each of these tasks is a minigame in itself, although not as compelling to a player as automatons as they are put together and embedded within an engaging narrative. However, in order to understand how to design a game like *Halo*, it is necessary to examine the most fundamental part of game mechanics.

Consider the game of paper–rock–scissors, in which two players simultaneously count to three and then present their hands gesturing for rock, paper, or scissors. If one person has paper and the other has rock, paper wins because it can cover rock. If one person has scissors and the other has paper, scissors wins because scissors cut paper. If one person has rock and the other has scissors, rock wins because rock blunts scissors. If both players show the same gesture, the game is tied. One game of paper–rock–scissors completes one of the game mechanic cycles. The challenge is to show a hand gesture that is superior to your opponent on the count of three, the player action is to make a hand gesture, and the rules determine whose gesture wins.

This chapter introduces common generic game mechanic actions such as matching, sorting, searching, and hitting. Examples of how each of these is represented visually in a game and the programming that controls them are explained in depth. Common algorithms and data structures used for each mechanic will be worked through with the reader integrating the key art assets where appropriate.

4.3 Primary Mechanics

All primary game mechanics sit at the very heart of natural human behavior and ability. Humans have evolved to perform them instinctually. Abilities that have evolved over millions of years out of the need to survive now find themselves as repetitive actions in games. Why?

Humans are a pattern-seeking species. Our brains have evolved to deal with the plethora of sensations and information they deal with every day by symbolizing our knowledge internally. All decision-making activities therefore involve a prediction of risks and rewards, as we can never have enough time to do a rational atomic analysis of a situation. We are good at developing intuitive understandings of situations and internally develop our own understandings—whether right or wrong—by which we then make future decisions. So reliable have our brains become at being able to process information in this way that we receive neurochemical rewards of dopamine when we make sense out of complete chaos. For this reason we believe that we can see patterns where there are none. How often have you heard something like "that cloud looks like an elephant?" The greater the randomness and the more we make sense of it and have that judgment justified, the greater the neurochemical reward.

As Raph Koster points out in his book *A Theory of Fun for Game Design*, the thing that makes games fun is their ability to engage the human mind. They do this by presenting the brain with challenges that it is best designed to achieve. In short, this involves repetition and lots of pattern matching. The following sections outline many primary game action mechanics that all in some form require pattern matching and involve primitive human abilities. One or more of these actions can be found in all games.

4.3.1 Searching

Searching is a basic human cognitive process that involves perception and scanning of an environment. Whether one is searching for car keys, looking through a telephone directory, or trying to find a friend in a crowd, the process requires the human brain to take snapshots of the environment and scan it quickly for items matching their internal symbolization.

In computer games, this ability is leveraged to make the player look for a specific piece of information, item, location, or character in an environment. The objective of the player's search may be to find an item needed to proceed in the game—for example, a key to open a door, or to navigate a maze to get from one place to another.

Searching for the mineral resource titanium in an asteroid field in *EVE Online* is one primary mechanic employed in the game play. In order to begin making money to buy anything and progress in the game, mining minerals is the first action rookie players must learn. Part of the mining process is searching for minerals in mine fields and finding asteroids that have enough of the type you are looking for.

Looking for ammunition clips and medical packs has a long tradition in FPS games such as *Quake*. This action will either see a player who is low on firepower or health searching the game level madly for any of these items or trying to remember where he saw the last one and returning to that location. Often with this action, if the player does not need ammunition or health, the item cannot be picked up or used and therefore remains in the same location until it is needed.

4.3.2 Matching

Matching is an activity that is part of the searching process. For the human brain, identifying one object as being similar to another is a simple thing. To search for something is to be able to identify when the mental image you have of the thing you are looking for is the same as the thing you are looking at—that is, they match. Many day-to-day activities involve matching, such as finding a pair of socks and putting the right PIN into an ATM.

In a game, matching is used to get players to put one or more things together because they are smaller pieces of a whole, or are the same color or shape, or have other similar characteristics. This common action may find players putting together parts of a machine to make it work as a whole or placing the same colored items next to each other on a grid.

Guitar Hero uses matching superbly. The entire game is focused around the player's ability to match the guitar string on the screen with the button on the peripheral device. Not only must the player match the right note at the right time, but his rhythm of button pressing is also evaluated.

4.3.3 Sorting

Attempting to make order out of chaos is a common human behavior. People with very extreme cases of requiring everything to be in its place may suffer from obsessive-compulsive disorder. However, in many cases when things are sorted, life is much easier. When things are in order and when we can rely on them being in order, it lifts some of the cognitive load off doing other tasks. For example, if money is sorted correctly in a shop's till, it makes the task of giving a customer change easier. Imagine trying to do grocery shopping in a place where none of the items was sorted on the shelves.

Games use this sorting desire to motivate players to arrange two or more items according to their characteristics, such as size, color, species, age, or name. Sorting can also be employed in activities where performing tasks in order is necessary to complete a challenge.

For example, in the 2D puzzle game *Machinarium*, players must make their way through levels by having their character, a little robot, make machines work in certain orders to accomplish particular tasks. In one level, the robot must wire a circuit panel one way to perform the first task and then rewire it in another way to get the second one done. In *The Sims*, the player can sort the activities that their Sim must do in order to satisfy their most immediate needs.

At a simpler level, games such as *Bejeweled* use matching with sorting to get the player to sort through randomly placed colored jewels to sort like ones into lines.

4.3.4 Chancing

Chance devices such as die and the drawing of straws for purposes of sorting, selecting, and division are common among many cultures, and the practice is referenced in classical Greek literature as early as the Trojan War and beforehand in Egyptian artifacts.

Using chance in decision-making is referred to as risk. Research has shown that the types of risks people take today stem back to situations encountered by our ancestors, including competition with other individuals, competition with other cultures, mating, resource allocation, and environment. For example, chasing a bear away from one's food could pose certain risk, as would going to war with another tribe.

Chance in games is used to determine the probability of future outcomes. This is one of the oldest actions used in games involving the use of dice: rolling or coin tossing to determine an outcome based on chance. Without some element of probability in which players knew what the outcome of their actions would be before they did them, there would not be any need to take a risk. Research has shown that the greater the risk, the higher the neurochemical reward.

The most obvious and earliest use of probability in adventure games came when the board game of *Dungeons & Dragons* was computerized. The board game involves the rolling of dice to determine the character's ability levels, for example, how strong they are or how likely they are to shake off a magical spell. Probability also comes into play when characters face off against each other. If players knew for sure which character would win, there would be no enjoyment in a battle, nor reason for one. However, the game uses die rolls, which, in combination with their ability levels, are used to calculate success or failure. The computer game does the same thing. This mechanism has flowed through into almost all games to give an element of chance in situations and to make the outcome unknown.

4.3.5 Mixing

Mixing actions involves combining objects or actions to produce an outcome unachievable otherwise. In day-to-day life, people mix ingredients to make food, paint pigments to make new colors, and multitask actions to get jobs completed more quickly.

In computer games, actions can be combined to allow characters to perform tasks they could not do with single actions, for example, jumping while running to leap across a crevasse in the game world or combining multiple keystrokes to perform special moves such as those available to characters in the fighting game *Super Smash Brothers*.

Combining game objects to produce other game objects is also an example of mixing. For example, in *Doodle God*, players begin with the four elements (fire, wind, earth, and water) that they must combine in different combinations to discover other objects such as coal, turtles, and plasma. In *The Sims Medieval*, the wizard character has the ability to mix herbs and minerals to make potions.

4.3.6 Timing

Human society is run by time. Even before the advent of mechanical timekeeping devices, the earth's revolution around the sun meant humans were constantly on a time schedule.

The use of time in a computer game can be applied as a game mechanic. It could involve completing a task within an allotted time, timing an action, or waiting for some event to occur. This mechanism is used to instigate urgency in situations such as racing—whether it is against the clock or an opponent— or to generate anticipation when waiting for something to occur or forcing patience upon a player who has to wait for the game environment to change.

Time is an obvious mechanism in racing games. It is used in *Project Gotham*, for example, to determine how long it takes for a player to get around a track. This time is then converted into points. If the time is better than another set time, it may unlock another track or racing car.

In *EVE Online*, time is used to add respect to the long process of training one's character with new skills. In the only massively multiplayer role-playing game, players may fly larger and faster ships only when they have trained for long enough. Training tends to take many hours and sometimes days in real time. As the player's character can continue to train when the player is not logged in, it is also a clever mechanism to keep players attached to their character and to keep them logging back in to check on their progress and start new training regimes.

4.3.7 Progressing

Life is about progressing, whether it be growing from a baby to an adult, getting a university degree, or getting a job promotion. Humans, in general, experience stages in their lives that correlate with their age and achievements.

Games employ a progression scheme in which the player begins as a *noob* and progresses to the level of *expert* at the end. Along this journey, progression schemes are put in place that give players a feeling of achievement for their efforts. For example, in *EVE Online*, the longer you play the game, the higher the training level you can achieve. In *StarCraft*, the more you play, the more money you can make to spend on upgrading your equipment. In *The Sims*, one of the game goals is to progress the job of your Sim until it reaches its lifetime achievement.

Progression will occur naturally in any game as a player becomes more familiar and skilled at the game play. However, as can be seen from the preceding examples, it can also be built in as a reward system and a way to move the player through game levels or narrative.

4.3.8 Capturing

To capture is to take something that belongs to someone else through force or your own efforts. Throughout history there has been a long list of tribes capturing members of other tribes, armies capturing cities, and pirates taking ships.

Some games embed this mechanic as the primary objective of the game. For example, *Civilization* requires players to take over others cities and countries. The Dutch East India Company challenges players to take cities along the spice route in order to be able to build a more profitable trading company between European and East Asian cities.

Capturing can also be used in a game in a less literal sense. For example, it could involve knocking out another game character in order to steal his weapon or stealing a car to make a quick getaway.

4.3.9 Conquering

Similar to capturing is the action of conquering. Although capturing is more similar to stealing, conquering is about outdoing or annihilating the competition. Like capturing, human races have a long history of conquering.

For example, the Spanish conquered and wiped out the Aztec Empire in the region now known as Mexico beginning in August 1519 and declaring final victory on August 13, 1521.

Outdoing an opponent is a classic game play goal. For example, in *chess*, the aim is to get your opponent into checkmate while taking pieces along the way or make them surrender. In the online *StarCraft* one-on-one games, this too is the objective. In *Black & White*, the player who takes the part of a god must gather more loyal worshippers than the other gods in order to drive the other gods away and rule over an island.

Again, this mechanic need not be so literal. The conquering of another opponent in a game environment might mean you own a bigger house, have more money, or have a better car. This is the clichéd need to "outdo the Joneses" and can be a direct goal in the game environment or could evolve as an interpersonal consequence of players comparing their individual game play success and status with each other.

4.3.10 Avoidance

One key to human survival is the avoidance of disliked and harmful things. This includes not eating poisonous substances, not sitting on a fire, and getting out of the way of large moving objects.

Numerous games require the player to avoid items and situations that are harmful to their character. *Space Invaders* requires players to move their ship so that it does not get hit by alien fire, and FPS games require the player to avoid enemy fire. *Jojo's Fashion Show*, a game in which the player must dress models according to particular themes, even requires the player to avoid wearing the wrong clothes.

Instead of telling players what they can do, avoidance is all about showing them what they cannot do. The inability to avoid whatever it is they should be avoiding penalizes players through reduced points or health given the situation.

Avoidance places constraints on the actions of players such that they must keep in mind what they cannot do while trying to progress through the game environment.

4.3.11 Collecting

Collecting is another natural human behavior. At the extreme, someone who cannot control collecting items is classified as a *compulsive hoarder*. In a game environment, however, items are there to be collected for a purpose.

Some items can be collected and placed in an inventory to be used at a later time. When used, these might disappear or go back into the inventory. The collecting mechanic is often used with searching. In Disney's *Princesses* game, children are required to walk through the virtual kingdom searching for and collecting magical items to help the princesses.

Other collection activities can happen almost by mistake. In the 2D platformer versions of *Super Mario Bros.,* collecting coins, stars, and other items happens just as the player moves the character through the levels, as the items are unavoidable. They are not challenging to pick up, and the number found collected is a record of progression through the level rather than achievement.

The original *Doom* and *Wolfenstein 3D* games introduced the concept of collecting points for finding secret rooms, killing all the guards and/or monsters, and finding extra damage power-ups and the like. A count at the end of each level reveals how many have been found. A lack of finding them does not stop the player from progressing but can give some incentive to replay that level to find all the added extras.

● **For Research**

This by no means is an exhaustive list of game action mechanics. If you are interested in learning more, visit the links:

https://en.wikipedia.org/wiki/Game_mechanics
http://www.lostgarden.com/2006/10/what-are-game-mechanics.html
http://gamestudies.org/0802/articles/sicart

4.4 Developing with Some Simple Game Mechanics

This section revisits a number of the primary game action mechanics with some practical implementations in Unity. Note that more than one mechanic is required in order to make a playable game prototype or to make an interactive application slightly game like. For example, matching marbles of the same color is not a game. It is just matching. But matching as many marbles as you can, of the same color in 2 minutes, instantly provides the player with a challenge, a goal, and a reward.

4.4.1 Matching and Sorting

Matching is a simple yet compelling game mechanic that sees the player scanning a number of items to find ones that are similar. This mechanic occurs in games such as *Bejeweled*, in which the player swaps adjacent gemstones arranged in a grid to make horizontal or vertical sets of three or more of the same colored gem. When a line is created, it disappears from the grid and the player gets some points. The matching mechanic is found across a wide range of popular games such as *solitaire* where card suits are matched,

Monopoly in which property colors are matched, *memory* where images must be matched, and *Kinect* games, where body poses are matched.

Sorting is a game mechanic that is usually found with matching. It entails moving objects around to position them in a specific order or to match them. The game of memory does not including sorting, but solitaire does, as the player sorts through the deck of cards to arrange them into suits.

For either mechanic, there must be visual clues as to how the player should be sorting or matching game objects. For example, in *Dr. Mario 64*, the good doctor throws colored vitamins shaped like pills into a jar full of viruses. When four or more viruses and vitamins line up, they disappear. For this level of simplistic matching and sorting, iconic art is used throughout. For example, in *Dr. Mario 64*, the vitamin pills look like capsules and the viruses are small colored squares with sick and angry-looking faces.

It is important to engage the player in these games with logical icons. If items need to be matched or sorted, they should look similar in appearance or have very clear shared characteristics that make them part of a particular group. If leaving a player to guess what matches with what or what goes where is not the objective of your game, do not make it one.

◎ Unity Hands On
Matching and Sorting

In this hands-on session, you are going to create a game that involves matching and sorting. Balls of different colors will fall down the screen. At the bottom of the screen will be four different colored containers. The player will be required to use the mouse to sort the balls horizontally so they eventually land in the container that matches their color. Halfway down the screen, a bar will appear. The player will only be able to change the horizontal position of the balls while they are above the bar. Points are accrued for each correctly sorted ball.

Step 1: Download *Chapter Four/Matching.zip* from the website. Unzip and open the project in Unity. Open the scene called main game. Play it and you will see a Score area and a quit button. The quit button will take you back to the main menu where you can press the play button to get back to the main game screen. In the Scene, you will find four different colored boxes.

Step 2: Set the Y Scale value for each box to 0.5 as shown in Figure 4.2.

Step 3: Add a cube to the scene. Position it at (0,3,0) and give it a scale of (2,0.2,10) as shown in Figure 4.3. Tick the Is Trigger box of the Box Collider and set the z size to 10. The cube will appear as a white strip across the game with a large box collider. Ticking the Is Trigger box for the Box Collider will enable us to trigger an event when another object collides with it, however it will not cause any physics events. This will allow

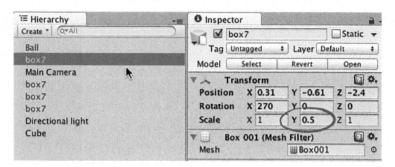

FIG 4.2 Resizing the boxes' y axes.

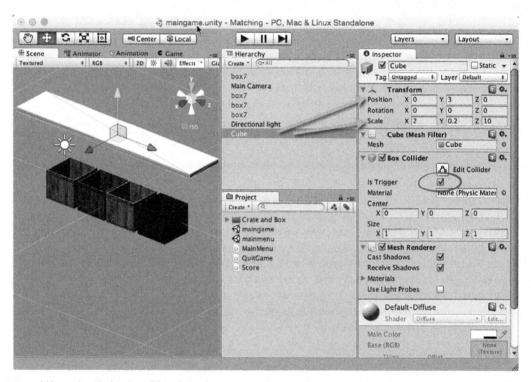

FIG 4.3 Adding a cube with a large box collider to the scene.

objects to fall through it, but we can programmatically detect when this is happening.

Step 4: Create a sphere. Position it at (0,0,0) and scale it to (0.5,0.5,0.5). Attach a Rigidbody and set the drag to 10. In the Rigidbody settings for Constraints tick the X value of Freeze Position. This will keep the sphere always at its initial X value (in this case 0) even after a physics event.

Step 5: Turn the sphere into a prefab object by dragging it from the Hierarchy into the Project. Rename the prefab "ball." Delete the original sphere object from the Hierarchy.

Step 6: Create a new C# file called DestroyWhenGone.cs. Enter the code shown in Listing 4.1.

Listing 4.1 Code to destroy an object when it moves out of the camera's view

```
//DestroyWhenGone.cs
using System.Collections;
using System.Collections.Generic;
using UnityEngine;

public class DestroyWhenGone : MonoBehaviour {

    void OnBecameInvisible()
    {
        Destroy(this.gameObject);
    }

    // Use this for initialization
    void Start () {
    }

    // Update is called once per frame
    void Update () {
    }
}
```

Step 7: Attach DestroyWhenGone to the ball prefab. This code will destroy the object when it goes outside the area visible on the screen because soon we will create code to continually spawn balls. When the balls move outside the screen, they will be outside the game play area. In this case they are no longer needed, and instead of the physics system constantly processing their location and the game engine performing any other behaviors with them, it makes more sense to just get rid of them completely.

Step 8: Create a new C# file called Spawn.cs. Enter the code shown in Listing 4.2.

Listing 4.2 Spawning objects at random intervals

```
//Spawn.cs
using System.Collections;
using System.Collections.Generic;
using UnityEngine;

public class Spawn : MonoBehaviour {

    public GameObject ball;
    public Material[] materialArray;
```

```
// Update is called once per frame
void Update () {
    if(Random.Range(0,200) < 1)
    {
        GameObject sphere = Instantiate(ball,
            new Vector3(0,5,0),
            Quaternion.identity);
    }
}
}
```

Step 9: Attach this script to the camera. With the camera selected in the Hierarchy, locate the script in the Inspector and set the value for ball to the ball prefab previously created. This process is illustrated in Figure 4.4.

Step 10: Play. At random intervals, a ball will be created and fall down the screen. When it goes out of view, it is destroyed. A ball is created according to a generated random number between 0 and 200. If this number is less than 1, a ball is instantiated. To increase the interval between balls, increase the upper range. To have them appear quicker, lower the upper range.

Step 11: To have the balls spawn at locations across the entire screen, modify the Spawn.cs code to that in Listing 4.3.

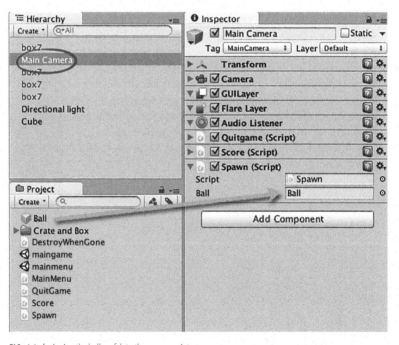

FIG 4.4 Assigning the ball prefab to the spawn script.

Listing 4.3 Setting a random value for the position of game objects

```
//Spawn.cs
// Update is called once per frame
void Update () {
    if(Random.Range(0,200) < 1)
    {
        Vector3 ballStartPosition =
            new Vector3(0,8,Random.Range(-4,4));
        GameObject sphere = Instantiate(ball,
            ballStartPosition, Quaternion.identity);
    }
}
```

Step 12: Play. As the starting X value for each ball is taken randomly from the range (−4, 4), the balls will appear across the width of the screen, as this is the range of Z values for the beakers. You may have placed your beakers at different distances depending on the screen resolution. In this case, increase or decrease the random range to suit. The starting Y position is set to 8. If this is not beyond the top of your screen, you may want to increase it a little. The balls should spawn just beyond the player's view.

Step 13: Play. The balls will fall and collide with the boxes. If you want the balls to fall faster, lower the drag value in the ball prefab. However, as the game play starts to take shape you will be glad they are falling slower.

Step 14: Modify Spawn.cs to that shown in Listing 4.4. This will add an array of materials to the script **so** each ball that is spawned can be assigned a random color. The shader for the material is changed to Diffuse as we will be using the existing transparent colored materials on the beakers but do not want the balls to be transparent.

Listing 4.4 Coloring a game object using an array of materials

```
//Spawn.cs
void Update () {
    if(Random.Range(0,200) < 1)
    {
        Vector3 ballStartPosition =
            new Vector3(0,8,Random.Range(-4,4));
        GameObject sphere = Instantiate(ball,
            ballStartPosition, Quaternion.identity);
```

```
            sphere.GetComponent<Renderer>().material =
                materialArray[Random.Range(0,material
                Array.Length)];
            sphere.GetComponent<Renderer>().material.shader =
                Shader.Find("Standard");
        }
    }
```

Step 15: With the main **camera** selected in the Hierarchy, locate the spawn script. Next to Material Array, click on the small triangle to expose the array values. Set the Size to 4. For each of the elements that appear, drag and drop the blue, green, red, and yellow materials into the locations as shown in Figure 4.5.

Step 16: Play. Each ball that **falls** will be assigned a random color. The colors are picked out of the array using the same Random.Range() function is used for the spawn timing.

Step 17: Select the ball **prefab** in the Project. At the very top of the Inspector, click on Tag. Select Add Tag from the popup menu. The Inspector will change to a different view. Select the triangle next to Tags at the very top of the Inspector and type ball into Element 0. Reselect the ball prefab in Project, click on Tag again and find the newly added ball tag in the popup menu. Select it. This process is illustrated in Figure 4.6.

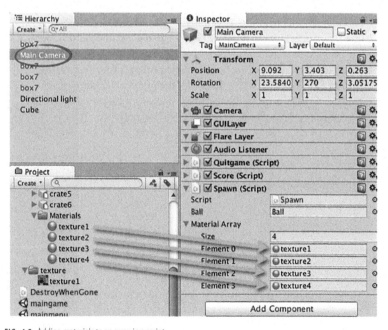

FIG 4.5 Adding materials to an array in a script.

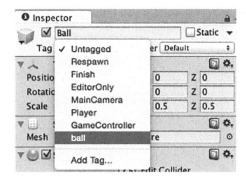

FIG 4.6 Adding a new tag.

The next step involves **moving** the balls with the mouse. The coding for this is not as simple as it might sound. Therefore, this hands-on session will be placed on hold to provide you with some essential background knowledge.

⊙ Note

The Screen and the World

Most games, especially those on a computer with mouse control, require calculations that transform the mouse position on the screen in 2D to game environment coordinates in 3D. This is necessary when you need to program for the player clicking on and interacting with objects in the 3D world. They are not actually clicking on the game world; they are in fact, clicking on an imaginary transparent flat plane through which the game is being viewed.

The screen coordinates are usually set with (0,0) in either the upper or lower left corner or exactly in the center. The mouse position is either counted in pixels or screen size proportions. For example, if the screen resolution was 640 pixels wide and 480 pixels high with (0,0) being in the lower left corner, the mouse coordinates when exactly in the center of the screen would be (320,240). When screen coordinates are proportional, values range from 0 to 1 in both the *x* and *y* directions no matter the resolution. For example, if (0,0) were in the top left corner, (1,1) would be in the lower right. The mouse position when the pointer is in the center of the screen would be (0.5,0.5).

If the different formats for the 2D screen space were not complicated enough, the 3D game world coordinates will be affected by rotation, perspective, or orthographic views and scaling. The nature of the problem is illustrated in Figure 4.7.

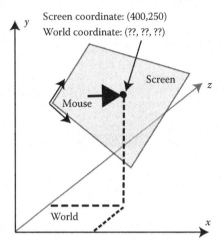

Screen coordinate: (400,250)
World coordinate: (??, ??, ??)

FIG 4.7 The difference between 2D screen coordinates and the 3D world.

◁ Unity Specifics

Screen, Viewport, and World Vectors

Unity, as with all 3D graphics systems, has three coordinate systems: one for the screen space, one for the viewport, and one for the world. The screen and viewport are 2D systems, and the world is 3D. The screen coordinates by default range from (0,0) to (screen width in pixels, screen height in pixels). The viewport coordinates are proportional going from (0,0) to (1,1) and the world coordinates are infinite. Having said that, the coordinates (−10,−50) in screen space and (−0.5,−1) in the viewport are legitimate. They just don't appear in the visible range of the camera, just like 3D coordinates outside the camera frustum.

Unity has a number of useful functions for converting all these coordinate systems among each other. They can all be found in the script reference by searching for "Camera." To try them out, create a new Unity Project with the script in Listing 4.5. Attach the script to the camera and the converted coordinates will be displayed in the console.

Listing 4.5 Code to convert the mouse position on the screen to viewport and world coordinates

```
//DisplayMousePos.cs
using System.Collections;
using System.Collections.Generic;
using UnityEngine;
```

```
public class DisplayMousePos : MonoBehaviour {

    // Use this for initialization
    void Start () {

    }

    // Update is called once per frame
    void Update () {
        Debug.Log("Screen to Viewport " +
            Camera.main.ScreenToViewportPoint(Input.
                mousePosition));
        Debug.Log("Screen to World " +
            Camera.main.ScreenToWorldPoint(Input.
                mousePosition));
    }
}
```

At first the coordinates may not change when you move the mouse over the screen. This will occur if the camera is in perspective mode and the near plane distance is very small. The reason being that the closer the near plane is to the camera the more the frustum becomes a pyramid with the screen space representing the apex. Therefore, the screen is almost a single point in 3D space and essentially you are moving the mouse around on this point as far as the 3D coordinate system is concerned. Changing the camera to orthographic will give a square view volume and provide more screen space area with respect to the 3D world. You can also move the near plane further away from camera if you want the mouse position changes to register.

There are also functions called ViewportToScreenPoint(), ViewportToWorldPoint(), WorldToScreenPoint() and WorldToViewportPoint().

◎ **Unity Hands On**
Matching and Sorting—Continued
Step 1: Create a new C# file called ClickNDrag and add the code in
Listing 4.6 and attach it to the ball prefab.

Listing 4.6 Creating a draggable object

```
//ClickNDrag.cs
using System.Collections;
using System.Collections.Generic;
using UnityEngine;

public class ClickNDrag : MonoBehaviour {

    GameObject focusObj = null;
    Vector3 lastMousePosition;
    Vector3 deltaMousePosition;
    float mouseSensitivity = 1000.0f;

    // Use this for initialization
    void Start () {

    }

    // Update is called once per frame
    void Update () {
        if(Input.GetButtonDown("Fire1"))
        {
            focusObj = null;
            //cast a ray
            Ray ray = Camera.main.ScreenPointToRay
            (Input.mousePosition);
            RaycastHit hit;

            //if the ray hits an object and that object
            //is a ball
            if(Physics.Raycast (ray, out hit, 100) &&
                hit.transform.gameObject.tag == "ball")
            {
                //take hold of it with the focusObj variable
                focusObj = hit.transform.gameObject;

                //remember the location of the mouse
                lastMousePosition = Input.mousePosition;
            }
        }
```

```
        //if the fire button is down
        if(focusObj && Input.GetButton("Fire1"))
        {
            //calculate how far the mouse has moved
            //across the screen
            deltaMousePosition = Input.
                mousePosition - lastMousePosition;

            //use this value to set the position of the
            //object
            focusObj.transform. Translate(0,0,
                deltaMousePosition.x/mouseSensitivity);

            //remember the location of the mouse
            lastMousePosition = Input.mousePosition;
        }

        //if the fire button is released
        if(focusObj && Input.GetButtonUp("Fire1"))
        {
            //forget about the object that was clicked on
            focusObj = null;
        }
    }
}
```

Step 2: Play. You will now be able to move the balls horizontally to line them up with the same colored boxes by clicking on them and dragging the mouse. To change the mouse sensitivity, modify the related variable at the top of the script.

Step 3: Next, the ability to move the ball once it has gone below the white line (fashioned from the cube added at the beginning) needs to be removed. The easiest way to do this is to change the ball's tag as it passes through the trigger collider of the cube. To achieve this, create a new C# file called StopBalls and add the code in Listing 4.7. Attach this script to the cube.

Listing 4.7 Script to register a collision on a triggering collider

```
//StopBalls.cs
using System.Collections;
using System.Collections.Generic;
using UnityEngine;

public class StopBalls : MonoBehaviour {

    void OnTriggerEnter (Collider obj)
    {
        obj.gameObject.tag = "Untagged";
    }
```

```
// Use this for initialization
void Start () {

}

// Update is called once per frame
void Update () {

}
}
```

Step 4: Play. When the balls go through the cube collider, it causes the `OnTriggerEnter()` function to run. When a collider is set to be a trigger only, it does not cause any collisions in the physics engine and therefore the `OnCollisionEnter()` and similar functions do not work. For each collision function, there is an equivalent set of trigger functions. When the balls are below the white line, they will no longer be movable by the mouse.

Step 5: To complete this game, we need to add a scoring mechanism. We will use a trigger collider at the entrance to each box to count the balls falling into them. Add four cubes to the Scene and resize and position them like lids on the top of each box as shown in Figure 4.8.

Step 6: For each cube, remove the Mesh Filter and Mesh Components, as we require only the Box Colliders. For each, ensure that the Is Trigger value is ticked.

Step 7: Create new C# called CountBalls and add the code shown in Listing 4.8.

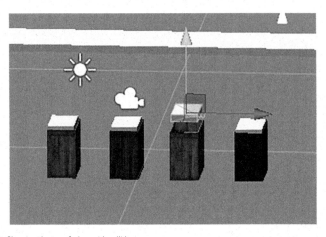

FIG 4.8 Plugging the top of a box with colliders.

Listing 4.8 Code to test the color of a game object against a variable value

```
//CountBalls.cs
using System.Collections;
using System.Collections.Generic;
using UnityEngine;

public class CountBalls : MonoBehaviour {

    public Material colorMatch;
    public int score = 0;
    void OnTriggerEnter (Collider obj)
    {
        if(obj.gameObject.GetComponent<Renderer>().
            material.color == colorMatch.color)
        {
            score += 1;
            //remove ball from game environment
            Destroy(obj.gameObject);
        }
    }

    // Use this for initialization
    void Start () {

    }

    // Update is called once per frame
    void Update () {

    }
}
```

Step 8: Attach CountBalls.cs to each of the cubes in the tops of the boxes.

Step 9: For each cube, select it in the Hierarchy and set the value of Color Match by dragging the corresponding material from the Project onto the script component.

Step 10: Because the code is attached to each cube, each cube will keep a tally of the correctly colored balls. These four values need to be added together to determine the total score. Create and open Score.cs and in the script editor add the code to in Listing 4.9. The `GetComponent()` function gains access to the CountBalls script that is attached to the sphere objects and pulls out the score by referring to the variable by name.

Listing 4.9 Gathering scores from each box for a single score

```csharp
//Score.cs
using System.Collections;
using System.Collections.Generic;
using UnityEngine;
using UnityEngine.SceneManagement;

public class Score : MonoBehaviour {

        public int score = 0;
        public GUIStyle scoreStyle;
        public GameObject[] scoringObjects;
        int maxBalls = 10;

        void OnGUI ()
        {
            score = 0;
            for(var i = 0; i < scoringObjects.Length; i++)
            {
            //extract the score from the object and tally
            score += scoringObjects[i].
                GetComponent<CountBalls>().score;
            }

            GUI.BeginGroup (new Rect (Screen.width - 85, 5,
                80, 80));
            GUI.Box (new Rect (0,0,80,60), "Score");
            GUI.Label (new Rect (0, 20, 80, 30), string.
                Format("{0:0}", score), scoreStyle);
            GUI.EndGroup ();
        }

        // Use this for initialization
        void Start () {
        }

        // Update is called once per frame
        void Update () {
        }
}
```

Step 11: Save and select the main camera in the Hierarchy. Locate the score script component in the Inspector and, at the very bottom set under ScoringObjects, set size to 4 and assign the values for the array of beaker spheres by dragging and dropping each one in place as shown in Figure 4.9.

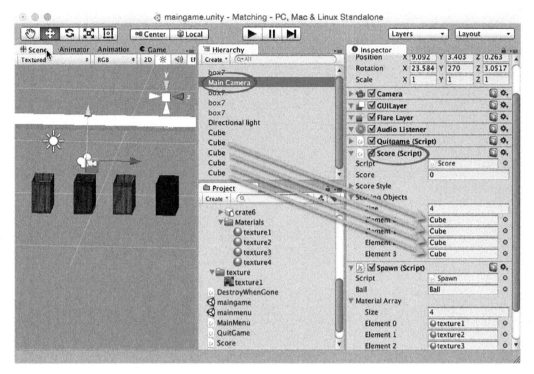

FIG 4.9 Adding game objects to an array in another script.

Step 12: Save and play. Your game now keeps score.

Step 13: Save the scene (File > Save Scene) and double-click on the mainmenu scene in the Project.

Step 14: Open MainMenu.cs in the script editor. This script is attached to the main camera and displays a small menu with a play button. Play to see that this appears on the screen. Click on the play button, and it will take you to the maingame scene. To swap scenes, the function `SceneManager.LoadScene()` is used. The name you give to this function is the name you gave the scene when it was saved. You cannot reference another scene, however, if it is not included in the build settings—the `LoadScene()` function will not be able to find it. To include a scene when the scene is open, select File > Build Settings from the main menu. The window that opens has an area at the top where all included scenes are listed. Press the Add Scene button to put the scene into the list. The scene at the top of the list is the one that will open first when your game is run as an application. Drag and drop the scenes in the list to change the order. The Build button at the bottom of the window is what you press to create a stand-alone application. This includes an APP for the Mac and an EXE for Windows. These are the files that you can then distribute to others for playing.

Step 15: Modify the code in MainMenu.cs to that in Listing 4.10.

Listing 4.10 Setting player preferences in code

```csharp
//MainMenu.cs
using System.Collections;
using System.Collections.Generic;
using UnityEngine;
using UnityEngine.SceneManagement;


public class MainMenu : MonoBehaviour {

    void OnGUI ()
    {
        // Make a group on the center of the screen
        GUI.BeginGroup (new Rect (Screen.width / 2 - 50,
            Screen.height / 2 - 60, 100, 120));
        // All rectangles are now adjusted to the group.
        // (0,0)
        // is the topleft corner of the group.

        // We'll make a box so you can see where the group
        // is on-screen.
        GUI.Box (new Rect (0,0,100,120), "Main Menu");
        if(GUI.Button (new Rect (10,30,85,30),
            "Play Level 1"))
        {
            PlayerPrefs.SetInt("Level", 1);
            SceneManager.LoadScene("maingame");
        }

        if(GUI.Button (new Rect (10,70,85,30),
        "Play Level 2"))
        {
            PlayerPrefs.SetInt("Level", 2);
            SceneManager.LoadScene("maingame");
        }


        // End the group we started above. This is very
        // important to remember!
        GUI.EndGroup ();
    }

    // Use this for initialization
    void Start () {

    }
```

```
    // Update is called once per frame
    void Update () {

    }
}
```

Step 16: The `PlayerPrefs.SetInt()` function allows a system level setting of a variable. In this case it is called Level and it is set to 1 or 2 depending on the button pressed. This makes the variable available to be picked up by the maingame scene when it opens. You can also use PlayerPrefs to store highest scores and other player details that can be used when the game is played the next time. To get the player's level preference before the game starts, open Spawn.cs and modify the code as shown in Listing 4.11.

Listing 4.11 A start function that loads the player preference and uses it to set the difficulty of the game

```
//Spawn.cs
...
// Use this for initialization
void Start () {
    int playerlevel = PlayerPrefs.GetInt("Level");
    if(playerlevel == 1)
    {
        GameObject.Find("Cutoff").transform.position = new
            Vector3(0,1,0);
    }
    else if(playerlevel == 2)
    {
        GameObject.Find("Cutoff").transform.position = new
            Vector3(0,3,0);
    }
}
...
```

Step 17: Before playing, check the white line cube you have used is called Cutoff in the Hierarchy. If it is not, change its name in the top of the Inspector. Play. The main menu buttons now set the level of difficulty that changes the height of the white line. The higher it is, the harder the game becomes.

Step 18: Finally, we want to add an end game scenario. To make it simple, we will have the game end after 10 balls have been caught. First create a new scene with File > New Scene. After the scene opens select File > Save Scene and call it gameover. A scene icon with this name will appear in the Project.

Step 19: Download from the website *Chapter Four/gameover.png* and add it to the Project.
Step 20: Create a new C# file called ShowScore.cs and add the code in Listing 4.12.

Listing 4.12 Displaying a game over screen with the score

```
//ShowScore.cs
using System.Collections;
using System.Collections.Generic;
using UnityEngine;
using UnityEngine.SceneManagement;

public class ShowScore : MonoBehaviour {
    public Texture2D goImage;

    void OnGUI ()
    {
        string scoreText = "You Scored" +
            PlayerPrefs.GetInt("LastScore");
        GUI.BeginGroup (new Rect (Screen.width / 2 - 100,
            Screen.height / 2 - 100, 200, 200));
        GUI.Box (new Rect (0,0,200,200), goImage);
        GUI.Label (new Rect (55, 15, 100, 30), scoreText);
        if(GUI.Button (new Rect (25,165,150,30), "Back to
            Menu"))
        {
            SceneManager.LoadScene("mainmenu");
        }
        GUI.EndGroup ();
    }

    // Use this for initialization
    void Start () {

    }
    // Update is called once per frame
    void Update () {

    }
}
```

Step 21: Attach ShowScore.cs to the Main Camera. Select the camera in the Hierarchy and locate the script in the Inspector. Drag and drop the gameover texture from the Project onto the goImage variable in the script component.
Step 22: Play to check if it displays correctly.

Step 23: From the main menu, select File > Build Settings and click on Add Current to add the gameover scene to the game build.

Step 24: Open Score.cs and change the code to check for a game over situation and to save the score before switching to the game over scene. This is given in Listing 4.13.

Listing 4.13 Code to compare the score to the max balls and end the game

```
void OnGUI {
...

    if(score >= maxBalls)
    {
        PlayerPrefs.SetInt("LastScore",score);
        SceneManager.LoadScene("gameover");
    }
}
```

Step 25: If you do not want to wait until you have caught 10 balls to check your handiwork, change the value of `maxBalls = 10` in Score.cs to a lower value.

Step 26: Open the mainmenu scene and test your game.

4.4.2 Shooting, Hitting, Bouncing, and Stacking

The shooting, hitting, bouncing, and stacking mechanics used in computer games are synonymous with similar mechanics that make real-world games with a ball so popular. In order to play, players must understand the laws of physics and how they can achieve their goals using the physical properties of the game environment to their best ability. For example, 10-pin bowling requires the player to toss a ball down an alleyway constructed of polished timber with gutters on each side in order to mow over as many pins as possible. Players must take into consideration the weight of the ball, the speed with which they throw, the angle at which they throw with respect to the length of the alley, and the mass of the pins. Players adapt succeeding attempts at knocking the pins over based on past performance. For example, if players find that they tend to always land the ball in the right gutter, they might decide to release it closer to the left or try to spin the ball in the opposite direction.

Many computer games implement these trial-and-error environmental impact practices. For example, the highly successful mobile game *Angry Birds* sees the player attempting to use a slingshot to hurl birds at stacked objects in order to knock them over. The Xbox Kinect game *Kinectimals* also presents the player with the same knock-over-the-stack minigames. Each time players take a shot at something, they gather feedback from their attempt based

217

on the number of items knocked over or the direction in which the ball (or bird) went and how fast they were flung. Players then use this knowledge to improve their next try.

Game engines, such as Unity, that include physics systems take much of the work out of creating these types of games, as developers can rely heavily on the physics calculations doing most of the work for them. For example, the old PC game *Gorillas* that saw gorillas throwing bananas across the screen in an attempt to hit each other using a variety of trajectories had to have the mathematics programmed directly into its base code. Today, the task is simpler because the player can just throw an object and let the physics system take care of the rest—well almost.

◑ Unity Hands On
Shooting
In this hands-on session, you will create a simple cannon to fire cannonballs at a stacked structure on the other side of a terrain.

Step 1: Download *Chapter Four/Shooting.zip* from the website. Unzip and open the project in Unity. Open the scene called *scorchedEarth*. In the game, you will see a terrain and a cannon.

Step 2: Create a new C# file called *Aim.cs*. Enter the code shown in Listing 4.14. This script provides rotation to a game object when the arrow keys are pressed. The rotation occurs around the object's position and axes at a rate proportional to *Time.deltaTime*, which is the time passed since the last frame update. This creates a nice smooth rotational movement.

Listing 4.14 Rotating a game object around its axes with the arrow keys

```
void Update () {
    if (Input.GetKey ("up")) //if up key is pressed
    {
        //rotate upward around the side axis
        this.transform.RotateAround
            (this.transform.position,this.transform.right,
                20 * Time.deltaTime);
    }
    if (Input.GetKey ("down"))
    {
        //rotate downward around the side axis
        this.transform.RotateAround
            (this.transform.position,this.transform.right,
                -20 * Time.deltaTime);
    }
```

```
    if (Input.GetKey ("right"))
    {
        this.transform.RotateAround
            (this.transform.position, this.transform.forward,
            -20 * Time.deltaTime);
    }
    if (Input.GetKey ("left"))
    {
        this.transform.RotateAround
            (this.transform.position,this.transform.forward,
            20 * Time.deltaTime);
    }
}
```

Step 3: Save and attach the script to the cannon2 object in the Hierarchy.
Step 4: Play. Use the arrow keys to rotate the cannon.
Step 5: Next we want the cannon to shoot when the mouse is clicked.
Create a new prefab from a sphere and add a Rigidbody to it. Name this
prefab cannonball.
Step 6: Change *Aim.cs* as shown in Listing 4.15 to add shooting capability.

Listing 4.15 Code to instantiate an object and shoot it from another game object

```
public class Aim : MonoBehaviour {

public GameObject cannonball;

    // Use this for initialization
    void Start () {

    }

    // Update is called once per frame
    void Update () {
        if (Input.GetKey ("up")) //if up key is pressed
        {
            //rotate upward around the side axis
            this.transform.RotateAround
                (this.transform.position,this.transform.
                    right, 20 * Time.deltaTime);
        }
        if (Input.GetKey ("down"))
        {
            //rotate downward around the side axis
            this.transform.RotateAround
```

```
            (this.transform.position,this.transform.
                right, -20 * Time.deltaTime);
    }
    if (Input.GetKey ("right"))
    {
        this.transform.RotateAround(this.transform.
            position, this.transform.forward, -20 *
            Time.deltaTime);
    }
    if (Input.GetKey ("left"))
    {
        this.transform.RotateAround
        (this.transform.position,this.transform.
            forward, 20 * Time.deltaTime);
    }

    if(Input.GetKeyUp ("space"))
    {
        GameObject cb = Instantiate(cannonball,
            this.transform.position,this.transform.
                rotation);
        cb. GetComponent<Rigidbody>().AddForce(this.
            transform.up * 10000);
    }
  }
}
```

Step 7: Save the code. Select Cannon in the Hierarchy; in the Inspector, set the aim script component's Cannonball variable to the prefab just created.

Step 8: Play. Press the space bar to shoot cannonballs from the cannon. Modify the value of 10000 in the *Aim.cs* script if you want to see the effects of adding more or less force to the balls.

Step 9: On the terrain opposite the cannon is a flat area. Create a cube and place it on the flat area. Ensure that you switch between top and side views to get it in the correct location. Coordinates near (1758,134,953) are good.

Step 10: Add a Rigidbody to the cube.

Step 11: Right-click on the cube in the Hierarchy and select Duplicate. Use the arrow keys in the Scene to move the duplicate cube next to the original.

Step 12: Continue this process to create your own castle of cubes. Copy and Paste will have the same effect as Duplicate and make the building process quicker.

Step 13: Play. Attempt to knock over the cubes with the cannonballs by changing the direction of the cannon. If the cannon seems too far away for you, drag and drop the cannon object onto the Main Camera in the Hierarchy. It will become attached to it. Move the camera to the desired location in the Scene. The cannon will move with it.

Step 14: To add some impact explosions, import the detonator package (*explosion.unitypackage*) used in Chapter 2.

Step 15: Create a C# file called *Explode.cs* and enter the code shown in Listing 4.16. This is the same code used for the flattening sphere bombs in Chapter 2 but with the flattening part removed.

Listing 4.16 Creating an explosion on impact

```
using System.Collections;
using System.Collections.Generic;
using UnityEngine;

public class Explode : MonoBehaviour {

    public GameObject explosion;
    public float explosionLife = 5.0f;
    Quaternion explosionDirection;
    Vector3 explosionLocation;

    void OnCollisionEnter(Collision collision)
    {
        GetComponent<Rigidbody>().isKinematic = true;
        Destroy (this.GetComponent<Collider>());
        ContactPoint contact = collision.contacts[0];
        explosionDirection = Quaternion.
            FromToRotation(Vector3.up, contact.normal);
        explosionLocation = contact.point;
        if(collision.gameObject.name != "Terrain")
        {
            Destroy(collision.gameObject,1);
        }
        Detonate();
        Destroy(this.gameObject);
    }

    void Detonate()
    {
        GameObject exp = Instantiate (explosion,
            explosionLocation,
            explosionDirection);
        Destroy(exp, explosionLife);
    }
}
```

Step 16: Save this code and attach it to the cannonball prefab.

Step 17: In the Standard Assets > Misc folder in the Project, select the Explosion prefab and drag and drop it onto the Explosion variable of the explode script attached to the cannonball.

Step 18: Play. The cannonballs will now explode when they impact.

Step 19: To allow the player to set the strength of the cannonball shot, we will add a meter. The shot strength will build up while the space is held down and the cannonball will be released when the space is released. Create a new C# file called *StrengthMeter.cs* and add the code in Listing 4.17.

Listing 4.17 Creating a visual meter for setting cannon strength

```
using System.Collections;
using System.Collections.Generic;
using UnityEngine;

public class StrengthMeter: MonoBehaviour {

    public static float shotStrength;
    void OnGUI ()
    {
        GUI.Box (new Rect (0,0,220,40), "Force");
        shotStrength = Slider (new Rect (10,20,200,30),
            shotStrength);
    }

    float Slider (Rect screenRect, float strength)
    {
        strength = GUI.HorizontalSlider (screenRect,
            strength, 0.0f, 1.0f);
        return strength;
    }
}
```

Step 20: Attach this new script to the Main Camera.

Step 21: Edit *Aim.cs* to reflect the changes shown in Listing 4.18. Ensure the new code for dealing with space bar press and releases replaces the old space bar down section.

Listing 4.18 Script to build up firing strength when space is down and to fire when space is released

```
void Update ()
{
    if (Input.GetKey ("up")) //if up key is pressed
    {
```

```
        //rotate upward around the side axis
        this.transform.RotateAround (this.transform.
            position, this.transform.right, 20 * Time.
            deltaTime);
    }
    ...
    if (Input.GetKey ("left"))
    {
        this.transform.RotateAround (this.transform.
            position, this.transform.forward, 20 * Time.
            deltaTime);
    }


    if(Input.GetKey("space"))
    {
        //each loop the space is down increase the strength
        StrengthMeter.shotStrength =
        StrengthMeter.shotStrength + 0.01f;
    }

    if(Input.GetKeyUp ("space"))
    {
        GameObject cball = Instantiate(cannonball,
            this.transform.position, this.transform.rotation);
        //use built up strength to influence the shot
        float strength = StrengthMeter.shotStrength * 10000;
        cball.GetComponent<Rigidbody>().AddForce(this.
            transform.up * strength);
        //set strength back to 0 after a shot
        StrengthMeter.shotStrength = 0;
    }
}
```

Step 22: Play. This time while firing, hold down the space bar to build up the strength and then release when you think it is enough. Slider bars used in the GUI only allow values between 0 and 1, which is why the final strength is multiplied with the maximum allowed strength in order to create a larger force for the cannon.

4.4.3 Racing

Racing involves one or more players attempting to get from one location to another in order to beat the clock or beat one another. Racing is a common sport found involving unaided human participants (in many Olympic events), motor vehicles (such as formula 1 or drag racing), and animals (including horses, dogs, and, on Australia Day in Australia, cockroaches!).

223

Many computer games include racing in a variety of forms. *Project Gotham* sees the players racing around the streets of the world's cities in production cars, *Grand Theft Auto* requires the player to race away from authorities or to locations, and *Kinect Sports* allows players to race in track and field events.

Racing need not involve people or vehicles moving around a track. Performing a task within a certain time is *racing against the clock*. In *The Sims*, for example, a player's Sims can be given packages to deliver downtown or tasks to perform within a specified time period. If the job gets done, the Sim is rewarded.

◎ Unity Hands On
Racing

In this hands-on session, you will create a simple racing game.

Step 1: Download *Chapter Four/Racing.zip* from the website. Unzip and open the project in Unity. Open the scene called *racing*. In the game, you will see a terrain and a car.

Step 2: Play. The car can be driven with the arrow keys. The Main Camera is attached to the car prefab such that when the car moves, the camera automatically moves too.

Step 3: Select the car prefab in the Hierarchy. Right-click on it and select Duplicate. Call the duplicate *Player2*. Select Player2 and in the Scene move it so the cars sit side by side.

Step 4: Select Player2 in the Hierarchy and delete the Car User Control Script in the Inspector. Also delete the Main Camera object attached to Player2. This is not needed as the original car already has a camera.

Step 5: Add a sphere to the Scene. Select it in the Hierarchy and delete the Sphere Collider component. Position the sphere in front of Player2, raised slightly above the ground. We are going to use a series of spheres as points to specify a path for Player2 to follow. This is a common technique used in games to direct the movement of nonplayer characters (NPCs). Each sphere acts as a waypoint.

Step 6: Number and duplicate the sphere; place the duplicate farther down the road as shown in Figure 4.10 (you may want to increment the sphere number). Each waypoint should be in line of sight of the other. As the NPC is traveling in a straight line between each waypoint, if they are on the other side of the terrain, the NPC will travel through the terrain mesh. This will not look real or be very fair to the human player.

Step 7: Continue duplicating and positioning spheres until the whole track is covered.

Step 8: Attach the script *Waypoints.cs* from the Project onto Player2. Select Player2 in the Hierarchy and locate the waypoint script in the Inspector. Add each sphere to the script under the Waypoints variable, as shown in Figure 4.11. Ensure that the spheres are added in the order you would like the Player2 car to move around the track, with the first sphere in front of the car being assigned to Element 0.

FIG 4.10 Adding and positioning waypoints.

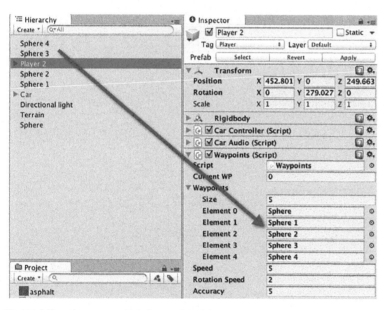

FIG 4.11 Adding spheres as waypoints to the waypoint script.

Step 9: Play. The NPC car will start moving off following the waypoints. In the Inspector you can change the speed, rotation speed, and accuracy values of the waypoint script to modify the car's behavior. When following a path and moving, sometimes objects do not land in the exact location of a waypoint. We need to give a *close enough is good enough* value. This is the value called *accuracy*. Rotation speed will cause the car to make tighter turns the higher the value.

Step 10: Now experiment with the speed of Player2 by racing against it.
Step 11: To create a finish line, add a cube to the scene. Resize it to stretch across the road. Remove its Mesh Filter and Mesh Renderer components. Leave the Box Collider and tick the Is Trigger box. The remaining box collider for the cube should be big enough to trigger an event when the NPC or player drives through it.
Step 13: Create a new C# file called *FinishLine.cs* and attach it to the new cube. Enter the code in Listing 4.19. This will cause a Game Over screen to pop open when either car collides with the cube.

Listing 4.19 Call a game over screen

```
//FinishLine.cs

using System.Collections;
using System.Collections.Generic;
using UnityEngine;

public class FinishLine : MonoBehaviour {

    string winner = "";
    Vector3 playerLocation;
    Vector3 npcLocation;

    void Start()
    {
        //remember location and orientation of both cars at
        //the start
        playerLocation = GameObject.Find("Car").transform.
            position;
        npcLocation = GameObject.Find("Player2").
            transform.position;
    }

    void OnTriggerEnter(Collider collision)
    {
        //if there is no winner yet
        if(winner == "")
        {
            //make this one the winner
            winner = collision.gameObject.name;
        }
    }
```

```
void OnGUI ()
{
    if(winner != "")
    {
        GUI.BeginGroup(new Rect(Screen.width/2-100,
            Screen.height/2-100,200,200));
        GUI.Box (new Rect (0,0,200,200), "Game Over");
        GUI.Label(new Rect (20,20,200,100), "Winner: "
        + winner);
    if(GUI.Button (new Rect (50,60,100,30),
    "Play Again"))
    {
        //reset the game
        winner = "";
        GameObject.Find("Car").transform.position =
            playerLocation;
        GameObject.Find("Player2").transform.position =
            npcLocation;
        (GameObject.Find("Player2").
            GetComponent("Waypoints")
            as Waypoints).currentWP = 0;
        }
        GUI.EndGroup ();
    }
    }
}
```

Step 14: The preceding script uses the name of the colliding object to display the winner on the screen. Currently, the elements of both the Car Prefab and Player2 are named the same. Select each Collider in the Hierarchy and give them different names in the Inspector.

Step 15: Play. But be ready for a quick restart when you click on Play Again.

We will leave this hands-on session at this point. When artificial intelligence is introduced later in the book, we will return to look at modifying the behavior of the NPC.

4.4.4 Avoidance and Collecting

Avoidance is a game action that involves players having to go out of their way not to interact with another game object or to make an effort not to perform some action. In the original *Donkey Kong*, the player had to get to the top of a set of scaffolding while avoiding rolling barrels. In all FPS games, the player has to avoid being shot. In *Snakes and Ladders*, the player must avoid landing on the head of a snake, and in *Minesweeper*, the player has to avoid mines.

Collecting is the opposite action to avoidance. The player must make all attempts to gather items. In *Super Mario Bros.*, players can collect coins and other items to improve their abilities and score. In *Dungeons & Dragons*, players collect magic potions and experience points and weapons. In *EVE Online*, players collect minerals.

Parts of these mechanisms are their visual cues. Items to be avoided should look like they should be avoided. For example, the lava flows in *Doom* obviously looked menacing and hot because they were red and bubbling. In nature, humans are attuned to the warnings of red colors. Red represents hot. Fire is hot, the sun is hot, and lava is hot. The game player already has a built-in instinct for avoidance. The same goes for sharp prickly objects. From cactus to underwater mines, the spikes relay a message of "keep away." As a game designer, if you can leverage human instinct and assume much about how someone will play your game, a lot of the work explaining how the game works is already done for you.

The same principle works for collecting. Why do you think so many games have little gold coins for the player to pick up?

☺ Unity Hands On
Avoiding and Collecting

In this hands-on session, you will create a simple scenario in which the player character must run around collecting chests to stay alive and also stay out of the way of dangerous obstacles.

Step 1: Download *Chapter Four/JoggingGranny.zip*. Open the scene called running. In it you will find Sporty_Granny, a chest, and a health bar. Play. Using the arrow keys, you will be able to move Sporty_Granny around.

Step 2: The first thing we will do is make the value on the health bar go down at a constant rate. To get the health to go back up, Sporty_Granny will have to run over the chest objects. Create a new C# file called Ginterface and at the code from Listing 4.20.

Listing 4.20 Code to decline the health bar

```
//Ginterface.cs
using System.Collections;
using System.Collections.Generic;
```

```
using UnityEngine;
using UnityEngine.UI;

public class Ginterface : MonoBehaviour {

    static public float gHealth = 100.0f;
    public Slider health;

    void Update ()
    {
        gHealth -= 0.1f;
        if(gHealth > 100) gHealth = 100;
        health.value = gHealth;
    }
}
```

Attach the new script to the Sporty_Granny game object. Locate the script in the Inspector and set the value of health to the Slider game object, which is a child object to Canvas from the Hierarchy as shown in Figure 4.12.

Notice that the gHealth variable has been made into a static. This will allow us to reference it from outside the script later. When gHealth changes, the slider value is updated to reflect the character's current health.

Step 3: To have a death animation play when the health reaches zero, modify the Update() function in GrannyWalker.cs as shown in Listing 4.21 by adding a small snippet of code to the very top of the function.

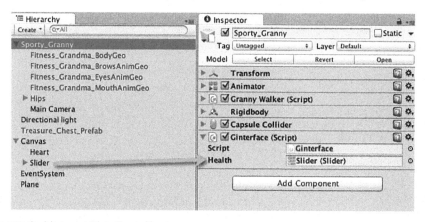

FIG 4.12 Connecting the slider to a script that will control its value.

Listing 4.21 Triggering a death animation

```csharp
//GrannyWalker.cs
using System.Collections;
using System.Collections.Generic;
using UnityEngine;

public class GrannyWalker : MonoBehaviour {

    Animator anim;
    float speed = 0.1f;

    void Start ()
    {
        anim = gameObject.GetComponent<Animator>();
    }

    void Update ()
    {
        if(Ginterface.gHealth <= 0)
        {
            anim.SetTrigger("dead");
            return;
        }

        if(Input.GetKey("left"))
        {
            this.transform.Rotate(Vector3.up, -3);
        }
        else if(Input.GetKey("right"))
        {
            this.transform.Rotate(Vector3.up, 3);
        }
        else if(Input.GetKey("up"))
        {
            anim.SetBool("running",true);
            this.transform.position += this.transform.
                forward * speed;
        }
        else if(Input.GetKey("down"))
        {
            anim.SetBool("running",true);
            this.transform.position -= this.transform.
                forward * speed;
        }
        else if(Input.GetKeyUp("up") || Input.
            GetKeyUp("down"))
        {
            anim.SetBool("running",false);
        }
    }
}
```

Step 4: We will now create a script to react when the character runs over a chest. Create a new C# file called Pickup.cs and add the code in Listing 4.22. Attach the code to the Treasure_Chest_Prefab in the Hierarchy.

Listing 4.22 Code to increase health bar

```
//Pickup.cs
using System.Collections;
using System.Collections.Generic;
using UnityEngine;

public class Pickup : MonoBehaviour {

    void OnTriggerEnter(Collider other)
    {
        if(other.gameObject.name == "Sporty_Granny")
        {
            Ginterface.gHealth += 50;
            this.GetComponent<AudioSource>().Play();
            Destroy(this.gameObject, 1);
        }
    }
}
```

Step 5: Before playing you will need to set the collider on the chest to be a trigger otherwise the script you have just written will not fire (Figure 4.13).

Play. When the character runs over the chest, its health will improve by 20 points, a sound will play and after a second, the chest will disappear. The reason the Destroy() function has a 1 in it is to tell Unity to destroy

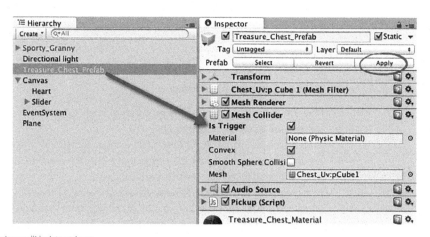

FIG 4.13 Turning a collider into a trigger.

the object after a second. You can remove the 1 to have the chest be destroyed immediately, but if you do this, the sound will not play. This is because the sound object is attached to the chest. Destroying the chest destroys the sound—even if it is playing. This is not ideal, so let us fix it.
Step 6: Create an empty game object in the Hierarchy and attach an AudioSource to it. Set the clip for the AudioSource to the yeah.mp3 from the Project's Sound folder. Turn off PlayOnAwake in the AudioSource. Call the new game object PickupSound. This is illustrated in Figure 4.14.

Remove the AudioSource attached to the Treasure_Chest_Prefab and apply the changes.
Step 7: To make the new sound play, modify the code in Pickup.cs to that in Listing 4.23.

Listing 4.23 Code to increase health and play sound

```
//Pickup.cs
using System.Collections;
using System.Collections.Generic;
using UnityEngine;

public class Pickup : MonoBehaviour {

    void OnTriggerEnter(Collider other)
    {
        if(other.gameObject.name == "Sporty_Granny")
        {
            Ginterface.gHealth += 50;
            GameObject.Find("PickupSound").
                GetComponent<AudioSource>().Play();
            Destroy(this.gameObject);
        }
    }
}
```

Note the 1 is gone from the Destroy() function. This will cause the chest to disappear immediately.

Play. When Sporty_Granny runs over a chest it will immediately disappear but the sound will continue to play.
Step 8: Now, we could drop a heap of the chests manually all over the ground plane, or we could write a script that will do it for us. The script is a better option in this case. With it, we can place as many chests as we like randomly all over the place. To begin, create a new C# called DropChests.cs and add the code shown in Listing 4.24. Attach this code to the ground plane and set the exposed variable for chestObj to the Treasure_Chest_Prefab that is in the Project (not the one in the Hierarchy) as shown in Figure 4.15.

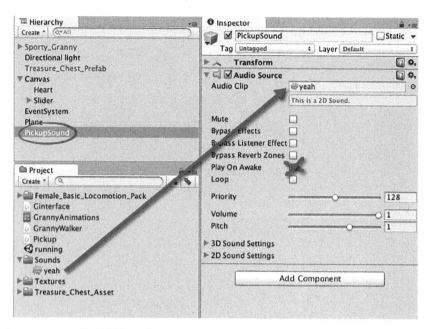

FIG 4.14 Creating a separate game object to hold an audio source.

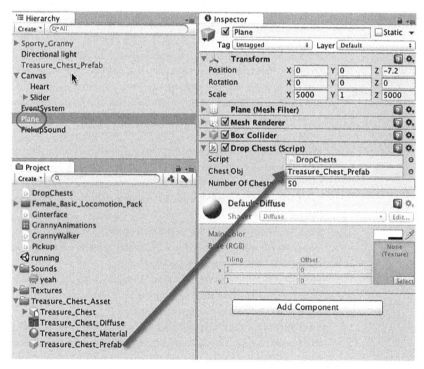

FIG 4.15 Adding a script to create many pickup items.

Listing 4.24 Code to randomly drop chests on the ground plane

```
//DropChests.cs
using System.Collections;
using System.Collections.Generic;
using UnityEngine;

public class DropChests : MonoBehaviour {

    public GameObject chestObj;
    public int numberOfChests = 50;

    void Start ()
    {
        for(int i = 0; i < numberOfChests; i++)
        {
            Vector3 pos = new Vector3(Random.
                Range(-100,100),
            0.14f, Random. Range(-100,100));
            Instantiate(chestObj, pos, Quaternion.identity);
        }
    }
}
```

Step 9: Next we will add some obstacles for Sporty_Granny to avoid. From the main menu select Assets > Import Package > Custom Package and bring in the effects package supplied with the book resources or Import the Standard Assets package from the Asset Store to access particle systems. Import all of the items when the next window pops open.

Step 10: Locate the object called Fire in the Project. It is inside the Standard Assets > ParticleSystem > Prefabs FireComplex. Drag it into the Hierarchy or Scene. You will see a fire effect appear. Uncheck the Particle System Destroyer Script, this will stop the fire from being destroyed after the set time.

Step 11: Add a Box Collider to the Fire object and resize it to 4 × 4 × 4 as shown in Figure 4.16. Make the collider a trigger. Ensure you click on Apply to save the changes to the prefab.

Step 12: Create a new C# file called FireHit.cs. Add the code shown in Listing 4.25. Attach to the Fire object in the Hierarchy and then click on apply to save the changes to the prefab.

Step 13: Play. If the character walks into the fire, the health will start to decline. It will continue to decrease until the character walks out. Duplicate the fire object around the map to create an avoidance object or modify the DropChests script to also include the fire object.

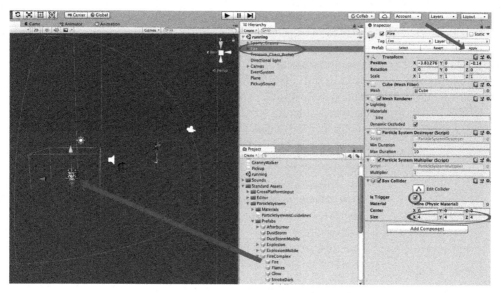

FIG 4.16 Adding a particle system to the scene with a trigger box collider.

Listing 4.25 A script to decrease the player health while they remain inside a collider

```
//FireHit.cs
using System.Collections;
using System.Collections.Generic;
using UnityEngine;

public class FireHit : MonoBehaviour {

    void OnTriggerStay(Collider other)
    {
        if(other.gameObject.name == "Sporty_Granny")
        {
            Ginterface.gHealth -= 2;
        }
    }
}
```

4.4.5 Searching

Searching is a common human activity. Whether it is for food (in combination with collecting—hunting and gathering), car keys, or Russian ultranationalists in *Tom Clancy's Ghost Recon*, the human brain is attuned to quickly examining environments and looking for icons and patterns. Naturally, the searching mechanism goes hand in hand with matching.

235

The ways in which searching is implemented as a game mechanic are as varied as game genre. In *Doom*, the player has to find colored keys to unlock the same colored security doors; in *Full Throttle*, the player must locate and use objects to help him in his quest to find a murderer in a cross-country road trip; and in *Manhunter: New York*, the player is entrusted with the task of hunting down resistance fighters. Searching can be performed by moving the mouse around a scene to find and pick up objects. This is the mechanism employed in the original *Myst*. It can also involve moving the main character around a game level, such as looking for medkits in *Quake*.

⊙ **Unity Hands On**
A HUD Radar for Searching
In this hands-on session, we are going to create a game environment with a number of items scattered over a large map that players must seek out. To assist them on their quest, a heads-up display (HUD) radar system will be deployed to give them some basic location details for the items.

Step 1: Download *Chapter Four/RadarSearching.zip* from the website. Open the project with Unity. Open the *hudRadar* scene.
Step 2: Create a new C# file named *Radar.cs* and add the code given in Listing 4.26.

Listing 4.26 Creating a HUD radar to track game objects with the tag orb

```
//Radar.cs
using System.Collections;
using System.Collections.Generic;
using UnityEngine;

public class Radar : MonoBehaviour {

    public Texture orbspot;
    public Transform playerPos;
    float mapScale = 0.5f;
    float radarSpotX;
    float radarSpotY;
    float radarWidth = 100f;
    float radarHeight = 100f;

    void OnGUI ()
    {
        GUI.BeginGroup (new Rect (10, Screen.
            height-radarHeight-10,
            radarWidth, radarHeight));
```

```
        GUI.Box (new Rect (0, 0, radarWidth, radarHeight),
            "Radar");
        DrawSpotsForOrbs();
        GUI.EndGroup();
    }


    void DrawRadarBlip(GameObject go, Texture spotTexture)
    {
        Vector3 gameObjPos = go.transform.position;
        //find distance between object and player
        float dist = Vector3.Distance(playerPos.position,
            gameObjPos);
        //find the horizontal distances along the
        //x and z between player and object
        float dx = playerPos.position.x - gameObjPos.x;
        float dz = playerPos.position.z - gameObjPos.z;
        //determine the angle of rotation between the
        //direction the player is facing and the location
        //of the object
        float deltay = Mathf.Atan2(dx, dz) *
        Mathf.Rad2Deg-270-playerPos.eulerAngles.y;

        //orient the object on the radar according to the
        //direction the player is facing
        radarSpotX = dist * Mathf. Cos(deltay * Mathf.
            Deg2Rad) * mapScale;
        radarSpotY = dist * Mathf. Sin(deltay * Mathf.
            Deg2Rad) * mapScale;
        //draw a spot on the radar
        GUI.DrawTexture(new Rect(radarWidth/2.0f + radar
            SpotX, radarHeight/2.0f + radarSpotY, 2, 2),
        spotTexture);
    }


    void DrawSpotsForOrbs()
    {
        GameObject[] gos;
        //look for all objects with a tag of orb
        gos = GameObject.FindGameObjectsWithTag("orb");
        double distance = Mathf.Infinity;
        Vector3 position = transform.position;
        foreach(GameObject go in gos)
        {
            DrawRadarBlip(go,orbspot);
        }
    }
}
```

Step 3: Attach the script to the Main Camera, which is a child object of the Granny game object.

Step 4: In order to draw radar blips on the HUD, you will need to create a texture. This need only be a very small texture of a single color as it will take up only one pixel on the screen. Create a PNG image that is 8 × 8 pixels and color it red. Call the file *spot.png* and add it to the Project.

Step 5: Select Main Camera in the Hierarchy and locate the Radar script in the Inspector. Drag and drop the spot texture from the Project for the value of *Orbspot*. Drag and drop Sporty_Granny object from the Hierarchy onto the Player Pos value for the Radar script. This will be used as the center and orientation for the radar.

Step 6: Play. The radar HUD will appear on the screen without any red blips.

Step 7: Locate the OrbPrefab in the Project. Select it in the Inspector view and create and assign the tag "orb" to it. The radar script will require the orb to be tagged in this way so it can find all the orbs in the Hierarchy. Drag and drop as many orbs as you like onto the terrain in the Scene at any location you like. Put some orbs near the player.

Step 8: Play. The radar will be populated with red spots indicating the location of the orbs. As the player turns and moves, the radar will reorient to show objects in the forward-facing direction at the top of the radar screen.

Step 9: The radar will not encompass the entire map. Orbs will only come into view as the player moves within a certain distance of them. To fit more of the environment map onto the radar, change the value of *mapScale* at the top of *Radar.cs* to a smaller value. If you want less of the environment map visible, make the value larger.

4.5 Rewards and Penalties

Let's face it: we play games for the rewards—whether they be in the form of points, unlocked levels, kudos, virtual clothing, virtual food, virtual health, more votes, more friends, or more money. It is the rewards that provide players with the motivation to perform any of the actions listed in this chapter. In some texts, rewards are listed as a mechanic themselves; however, they are really the motivation or reason for performing the mechanic in the first place.

Rewards are not just given at the end of the game, but rather throughout the game to influence the player's behavior. Rewards teach the player how to play and how to play better by providing continued feedback from the game environment. Sometimes this feedback can also be perceived negatively by the player as a penalty for incorrect game play.

Feedback can be both positive or negative and involves the addition or subtraction of something to/from the game environment. Feedback can be

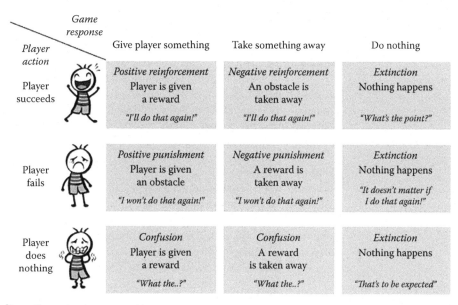

FIG 4.17 Player action versus game response matrix.

given for the player's actions to indicate success or failure. Together, action without feedback and feedback without action make six distinct categories, as shown in Figure 4.17.

With the exception of *confusion*, these classifications come from the domain of behavior management called *operant conditioning*. They are applicable in games, as operant conditioning is a behavioral management technique used for teaching the most relevant behaviors to participants under voluntary circumstances; that is, people wanting to be conditioned are open to behavior management techniques that will teach them to behave in the most appropriate way to succeed. These techniques include the following.

● Quick Reference

Player Action/Response Matrix

Positive Reinforcement

This is a situation in which positive behavior is followed by positive consequences. For example, when the player successfully completes a challenge, they are rewarded with something that influences their future game play progress in a good way. This could be in the form of gaining new powers or abilities, getting money to spend in the game environment to better their status, or simply getting points. This type of reward keeps the player motivated to continue playing for more reward.

Negative Reinforcement

This occurs when positive behavior is followed by the elimination of negative consequences. For example, if a player is in harm's way and can do something to get out of the situation, the removal of the continued harm is a reward. Such a situation will happen when a player being fired upon in a FPS stops being fired upon when they take cover. This reinforces to the player that hiding and ducking is a desirable behavior to keep their character alive.

Positive Punishment

This occurs when negative behavior is followed by the addition of a negative consequence. In a game, this is a situation in which a handicap is placed on the player's progress after they have done something wrong or performed inadequately. This type of punishment occurs in *The Sims* when the player makes their Sim eat rotten food. The Sim gets sick and is then in a bad mood for an allocated period of time.

Negative Punishment

This is the condition where negative behavior is followed by the removal of positive consequences. It is like taking away a child's toy when they are naughty. In the multiplayer version of the original *Halo* in sniper mode, the more frequently a player gets killed, the longer before their character will spawn again. In this example, the negative punishment is the taking away of the game world.

Extinction

This occurs when neither positive nor negative behavior attracts any feedback. This could happen when a player shoots at a tree or picks up a rock and tosses it in the ocean. As far as the game environment and the player's progress through the game is concerned, the action performed requires no feedback as it neither interrupts nor enhances the gameplay.

Confusion

Confusion is not a technique in operant conditioning. In fact, it has the exact opposite affect as it provides feedback when no action has occurred. When this occurs in a game the player becomes confused as to the reason behind any reward or penalty.

There is a fine line in game play between reinforcement and punishment. For example, in the *Black & White* series where the player is essentially a god, he can pick up and throw rocks at villages. In the real world, morally, this would be considered negative behavior and something that should be punishable. However, in the case of *Black & White*, the player is rewarded with more faith and worshipping from the villagers. This game play should be considered in the positive reinforcement category because it reinforces the behavior in the player that the game designer wanted. Punishment in a game is therefore a feedback mechanism that should stop the player from doing something for which the game was not designed. One example comes from *Colin McRae Rally*, a rally driving simulation game. If a player goes off the road or drives in the wrong direction for too long, the game resets the player's position on the road. It stops the player from performing that behavior and also slows down his time.

Some rewards and penalties inherently exist in a game environment without the need for onscreen advice or information. In the case of 3D environments, designers can force players in certain directions by physically restricting their access to out-of-bound areas of a level map. For example, the map levels in *Halo* may seem infinitely large; however, although the player can move freely around the map by foot or vehicle, the terrain and physics system prevents him from going to parts of the map that do not exist. Any attempt to walk or drive up steep mountain edges just results in the player sliding down the side.

When using feedback to mold a player's behavior, the effectiveness of the feedback will be increased and decreased according to a variety of factors.

● Quick Reference
Player Feedback

Saturation
The more a player is rewarded with or receives the same feedback, the less they will be motivated by it. For example, if a player receives a gold star for some activity, the highest award for a particular game, the less likely they will be motivated to try it again. Of course, in order for this strategy to be effective, the game must be sufficiently difficult that the first time they play they are more likely to get a bronze star and get better with time.

Immediacy
The time between the player's action and the feedback is critical. Rewarding a player minutes after they've performed a task successfully will make it difficult for the player to attribute the reward with the action. It's like punishing a puppy an hour after it has chewed up your shoe. There is no association. Haptic feedback mechanisms in games such as vibrating controllers would not make sense if the actions in the game didn't meet exactly with the vibrations. The same applies to sound effects.

Consistency

The feedback given to a player needs to align with their beliefs about the environment and how consistently it reacts to their interaction. In an FPS, a player would expect to get killed 100% of the time they step on a land mine. However, if this does not turn out to be the case, and instead they only die 20% of the time, the feedback will not become an effective way to curb player behavior.

Cost versus Benefit

Players will evaluate the effort they need to spend on an action based on the reward. This fits with *the greater the risk the greater the reward* philosophy. The evaluation will differ from person to person based on their attitudes toward risk aversion. For example, in *EVE Online*, mining and trading in the more dangerous zones of the universe can make greater amounts of money. Because there is a bigger chance a pirate will blow up your ship in these areas, the designer has to provide extra incentive for the player to go there in the first place.

4.6 Summary

This chapter examined how games *play* the human brain by providing it with the tasks for which the brain was designed. These fundamental game interaction patterns are known as game mechanics. An understanding of what makes these mechanics so compelling and how they can be made manifest in a game environment is critical to designing a playable game. It is these very primary mechanics that define what the player does when engaged in playing your game. For example, in defining *Bejeweled*, one could say it is a game where the player sorts and matches jewels. It is laughable how obviously simple these mechanics are when you think about it, but it takes some ingenuity to put them together in the right context to make a truly exceptional game to stand for all time.

Reference

Koster, R. (2013). *Theory of Fun for Game Design*. "O'Reilly Media," Scottsdale, Arizona.

CHAPTER 5

Character Mechanics

We are builders of our own characters. We have different positions, spheres, capacities, privileges, different work to do in the world, different temporal fabrics to raise; but we are all alike in this—all are architects of fate.

John Fothergill Waterhouse Ware

5.1 Introduction

It seems appropriate to have a chapter about Artificial Intelligence (AI) that follows one on elementary game mechanics, as these are the very same mechanics that drive the AI domain. In the field, researchers and developers create algorithms that can search, sort, and match their way through tasks as complex as pattern matching in face and voice recognition systems, and reasoning and decision-making in expert systems and vehicle control. It makes sense that algorithms used for making artificial brains are modeled on the same ones that compel fundamental human behavior and make game playing so much fun.

Of all the forms and applications of AI, games use a very small subset, the majority of which is to develop the behavior of nonplayer characters (NPCs). AI is used primarily for decision-making in NPCs to allow them to find their way around maps and interact intelligently with other players. Occasionally, novel uses such as machine learning are employed to create characters that can learn from the game environment and the player, such as the creatures in *Black & White*.

Artificial intelligence algorithms require a lot of computational processing. In the past, after all the animation and special effects were placed in a game, only about 10% of the computer's processing capabilities remained for AI. This has stunted the development of AI in games for quite a while. However, with advances in technology, more and more AI is creeping in.

Some examples of AI in games include the following:

- *F.E.A.R*: A first person shooter (FPS) in which the player must outsmart supernatural beings. It uses planning algorithms that allow characters to use the game environment in a smart way, such as hiding behind objects or tipping them over. Squad tactics are also used to present formidable enemies that can lay down suppression fire and perform flanking maneuvers.
- *Halo*: An FPS in which the player must explore an extraterrestrial environment while holding back aliens. The aliens can duck for cover and employ suppression fire and grenades. Group tactics also cause enemy troops to retreat when their leader is killed.
- *The Sims*: A god view game in which the player controls a household of virtual people called Sims. This game introduced the concept of smart objects that allowed inanimate objects in the environment to provide information to the characters on how they should be used. The Sims themselves are driven by a series of basic desires that tell them when they are hungry, bored, tired, and so on.
- *Black & White*: This god view game has the player in the role of an actual god overseeing villages of little people while trying to dominate the villages of other gods. The player is given a creature in the form of a gigantic animal such as a tiger. This creature is programmed with an AI technique called belief–desire–intention, which makes the character act based on what it might need or want at any particular time.

AI is a theoretically intensive field grounded in applied mathematics, numerical computing, and psychology. This chapter provides but a scrap of what the domain has to offer games. It is a gentle introduction designed to give you an appreciation for the field and to fuel your desire to experiment with its use in your own games.

5.2 Line of Sight

The simplest method for programming an NPC to follow the player and thus provide it with modest believable behavior is using the *line of sight*. Put simply, the NPC sees the player, turns to face the player, and travels in a straight line forward until it reaches the player. This straightforward approach can make the player feel under attack and that the NPC is a threat and has bad intentions. In fact, the NPC has no intentions whatsoever. It is just a computer algorithm. This illustrates how the simplest of programming feats can create a believable character. Although you will examine numerous techniques in this chapter to program *intelligence*, sometimes complex AI systems are not required just to achieve the behavior you want in your artificial characters.

In an open game environment, the easiest way to determine if an NPC has seen the player is to use simple vector calculations. As shown in Figure 5.1, a field of vision is defined for an NPC based on the direction it is facing, its position, visible range, and the angle of its vision (α).

If a player is inside this range, the NPC can be said to have detected the presence of the player (see player 1); if not, the player is still hidden (as is the case with player 2). The problem is very similar to that in Chapter 1, where vectors were being calculated for the pirate to follow to the treasure. Instead of treasure, the goal location is a moving player. The NPC detects the player within its field of vision using the vector between its position and the players. This is calculated as

```
direction = player.position - NPC.position;
```

The magnitude (length) of the direction vector represents the distance the player is from the NPC. If the angle between the facing vector and direction vector is less than the angle of vision and if the magnitude of the direction vector is less than the visible range, then the player will be detected by the NPC.

The next workshop will demonstrate this in Unity.

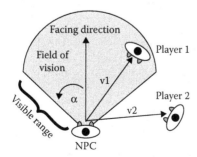

FIG 5.1 Vectors between an NPC and players used to determine line of sight.

◎ Unity Hands On

Line of Sight AI

Step 1: Download *Chapter Five/ChasingAI.zip* from the website. Open the chasingAI scene. In it, you will find a large room with a wizard.

Step 2: Open LineOfSight.cs with the script editor and add the code shown in Listing 5.1.

Listing 5.1 Basic line of sight script

```
using System.Collections;
using System.Collections.Generic;
using UnityEngine;

public class LineOfSight : MonoBehaviour {

    public Transform target; //the enemy
    public Transform head;
    float seeRange = 12.0f; //maximum attack distance -
    //will attack if closer than
    //this to the enemy
    float shootRange = 8.0f;
    float keepDistance = 2.0f; //closest distance to get
    //to enemy
    float rotationSpeed = 4.0f;
    float speed = 0.1f;
    ParticleSystem magicParticles;

    Animator anim;
    GameObject magic;

    void Start()
    {
        anim = gameObject.GetComponent<Animator>();
        magic = GameObject.Find("Magic");
        magicParticles = magic.
            GetComponent<ParticleSystem>();
        magicParticles.Stop();
    }

    void TurnOnMagic()
    {
        magicParticles.Play();
    }

    void TurnOffMagic()
    {
        magicParticles.Stop();
    }
```

```
void Update ()
{
    if(anim.GetCurrentAnimatorClipInfo(0)[0].clip.
        name == "Standing_Walk_Forward")
    speed = 0.1f;
    else
    speed = 0.0f;

    if (CanSeeTarget ())
    {
        if(CanShoot())
        {
            anim.SetBool("isWalking",false);
            anim.SetBool("isAttacking",true);
            Shoot();
        }
        else
        {
            anim.SetBool("isWalking",true);
            anim.SetBool("isAttacking",false);
            Pursue();
        }
    }
    else
    {
        anim.SetBool("isWalking",false);
        anim.SetBool("isAttacking",false);
        //stand around
    }
}

bool CanSeeTarget ()
{
if (Vector3.Distance(head.position, target.position)
    > seeRange)
    return false;

return true;
}

bool CanShoot()
{
    if (Vector3.Distance(head.position, target.
        position) > shootRange)
    return false;

    return true;
}
```

```
void Pursue()
{
    Vector3 position = target.position;
    Vector3 direction = position - head.position;
    direction.y = 0;
        // Rotate towards the target
    head.rotation = Quaternion.Slerp (head.rotation,
        Quaternion.LookRotation(direction),
        rotationSpeed * Time.deltaTime);
    transform.eulerAngles = new Vector3(0,transform.
        eulerAngles.y, 0);
        // Move the character
    if(direction.magnitude > keepDistance)
    {
        direction = direction.normalized * speed;
        transform.position += direction;
    }
}

void Shoot()
{
    Vector3 position = target.position;
    Vector3 direction = position - head.position;
    direction.y = 0;
    // Rotate towards the target
    transform.rotation = Quaternion.Slerp(transform.
        rotation, Quaternion.LookRotation(direction),
        rotationSpeed * Time.deltaTime);
    transform.eulerAngles = new Vector3(0, transform.
        eulerAngles.y, 0);
}
}
```

Step 3: Locate the LineOfSight script in the Inspector attached to the Gatrillian object in the Hierarchy. Drag and drop the RigidBody FPS Controller from the Hierarchy onto the exposed *Target* variable. This sets the object that the NPC will consider its enemy.

Step 4: Drag and drop the Gatrillian > Head object in the Hierarchy onto the exposed *Head* variable. You will find the Head object under Gatrillian > mixamorig:Hips > mixamorig:Spine > :Spine1 > :Spine2 > :Neck. This is used to determine the forward-facing direction of the wizard.

Step 5: Play. The CanSeeTarget() and CanShoot() functions use the variables seeRange and shootRange, respectively, to determine when the player is close enough to pursue and close enough to shoot. If you run away from the NPC backward as fast as possible, you will notice the point at which it gives up chasing you.

Step 6: The current code does not take into consideration the direction that the NPC is facing. If you approach it from behind, it will still sense your presence when you are close enough. For it to use a field of vision angle, modify the AI script as shown in Listing 5.2.

Listing 5.2 Restricting the field of vision of an NPC to an area in front of it

```
using System.Collections;
using System.Collections.Generic;
using UnityEngine;

public class LineOfSight : MonoBehaviour {

    public Transform target; //the enemy
    public Transform head;
    float seeRange = 12.0f; //maximum attack distance -
    //will attack if closer than
    //this to the enemy
    float shootRange = 8.0f;
    float keepDistance = 2.0f; //closest distance to get to
    //enemy
    float rotationSpeed = 4.0f;
    float sightAngle = 60f;
    float speed = 0.1f;
    Animator anim;
    GameObject magic;
    ParticleSystem magicParticles;

    void Start()
    ...

    bool CanSeeTarget ()
    {
        Vector3 directionToTarget = target.position -
            head.position;
        float angle = Vector3.Angle(directionToTarget,
            head.forward);

        if (Vector3.Distance(head.position, target.
            position) > seeRange || angle > sightAngle)
            return false;

        return true;
    }
    ...
```

Step 7: Play. You will now be able to sneak up behind the NPC without it noticing you.

5.3 Graph Theory

It would be impossible to begin talking about the ins and outs of AI without a brief background in graph theory. Almost all AI techniques used in games rely on the programmers having an understanding of graphs. A graph in this context refers to a collection of nodes and edges. Nodes are represented graphically as circles, and edges are the lines that connect them. A graph can be visualized as nodes representing locations and edges as paths connecting them. A graph can be undirected, which means that the paths between nodes can be traversed in both directions or directed, in which case the paths are one way. Think of this as the difference between two-way streets and one-way streets. Graphs are drawn with nodes represented as circles and edges as lines as shown in Figure 5.2. Nodes and edges can be drawn where nodes represent coordinates such as those on a flight plan or as symbolic states where the physical location in the graph is meaningless. For example, the state diagram in Figure 5.2 could be drawn with nodes in any position and any distance from one another. Some directed graphs allow bidirectional traversal from one node to another in the same way as undirected graphs. However, if

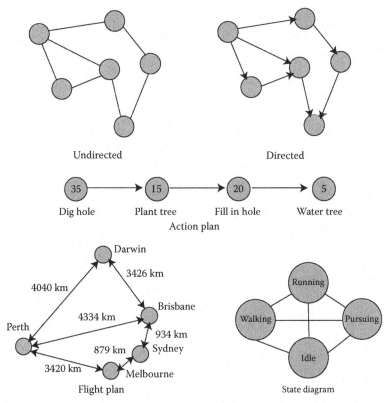

FIG 5.2 Undirected and directed graph representations and some examples.

arrows are already being used in a directed graph to show some one-way-only paths, they should also appear on bidirectional edges for consistency.

Both nodes and edges can have associated values. These values could be the distance between nodes, such as those representing distances in the flight plan of Figure 5.2, or the time it takes to complete an action, such as nodes in the action plan of Figure 5.2.

The ways in which graphs are useful in games AI will become evident as we progress through the chapter.

5.4 Waypoints

The concept of waypoints was introduced in Chapter 4 as a means of marking a route on a map that NPCs can follow. In the workshop, we developed a very simple algorithm to cycle through the waypoints and have an NPC follow them continuously.

A waypoint is simply a remembered location on a map. Waypoints are placed in a circuit over the map's surface and are connected by straight-line paths. Paths and waypoints are connected in such a way that an NPC moving along the paths is assured not to collide with any fixed obstacles. Waypoints and their connecting paths create a graph. Moving from one waypoint to another waypoint along a path requires an algorithm to search through and find all the nodes and how they are connected to each other. An example maze and a set of waypoints are illustrated as a graph in Figure 5.3. The graph does not necessarily need to reflect the physical layout of the maze when drawn. This example shows only which nodes connect to other nodes, not the location of the nodes or the distances between them.

In the graph of Figure 5.3, an NPC wanting to move from waypoint A to waypoint L could not simply plot a straight line between the two waypoints as they are not connected directly by an edge. The NPC then has the choice of navigating from waypoint A to waypoint L with the following sequences: A, M, J, K, L or A, B, C, D, E, F, I, J, K, L or A, M, I, J, K, L. The second sequence is obviously longer than the others, although all are legitimate paths. So how do you determine the best path from one waypoint to another?

Usually you will want an NPC to move from one waypoint to another via the shortest path. Often the meaning of shortest refers to the Euclidian distance between points, but not always. In real-time strategy (RTS) games where maps are divided up into grids of differing terrain, the shortest path from one point to another may not be based on the actual distance, but on the time taken to traverse each location; for example, the shortest Euclidean distance from point C2 to point A2 of Figure 5.4 will take an NPC through a river. Moving through the river may take the NPC twice as long as if it were to go the longer distance across the bridge. The definition of

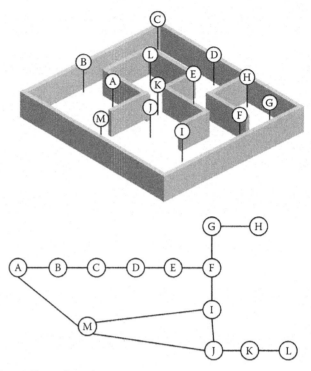

FIG 5.3 A maze with a set of waypoints.

shortest is therefore left up to a matter of utility. The term *utility* originates in classical game theory, and it refers to the preferences of game players. If time is more important to an NPC than distance, then the NPC will place a higher utility on time, thus avoiding the river. Utility values can be represented on a graph as weights on the edges, as shown in Figure 5.4. In this example, to travel from waypoint C2 to A2 directly via B2 will cost the NPC $3 + 3 = 6$ points. Assuming a high number means less desirable, we might attribute these weights with travel time and say this route will take the NPC 6 hours. Further examination of the graph shows that it will only cost 4 hours to travel from waypoint C2 to A2 via points C1, B1, and A1.

In order to implement waypoints effectively in a game, there needs to be an efficient way to search through them to find the most appropriate paths.

5.4.1 Searching through Waypoints

There are several methods for finding the shortest path from one node to another in a graph. These include algorithms such as breadth-first search (BFS) and depth-first search (DFS).

The BFS takes the given starting node and examines all adjacent nodes. Nodes that are adjacent to a starting node are the ones that are connected directly to the starting node by an edge. In turn, from each of the adjacent

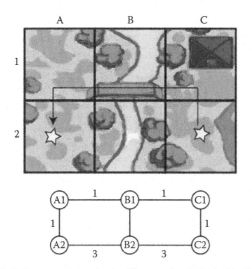

FIG 5.4 An example tiled strategy game map showing different terrain and a graph with utilities.

nodes, nodes adjacent to these are examined. This process continues until the end node is found or the search for adjacent nodes has been exhausted. The algorithm can be written as Listing 5.3.

Listing 5.3 A breadth-first search algorithm

```
1.  Let i = 1;
2.  Label starting node as i.
3.  Find all unlabeled nodes adjacent to at least one node
    with label i. If there are no adjacent nodes, stop
    because we have run out of nodes. If the ending node is
    found, stop because we have found a path.
4.  Label all nodes found in step 3 with i + 1.
5.  Let i = i + 1, go to step 3.
```

This algorithm will always find the shortest path (Euclidean distance) from the start to the end vertices, assuming that each vertex is the same distance apart. For example, in a maze game where the environment is represented by a grid of squares of equal size, each square represents a node for the purposes of the algorithm. As shown in Figure 5.5, the starting square is labeled with a 1. Radiating out from this square, all adjacent squares are labeled with a 2. All squares adjacent to the 2 squares not already labeled with a 1 or a 2 are labeled with a 3. This process continues until the destination square is found. This can be quite a long way of searching, as almost all squares in the grid will be examined. This algorithm can be modified to take into consideration other costs, such as terrain type and traversal times, in addition to or instead of distance by keeping track of all possible paths to the destination and adding up the costs. The path with the least cost can then be selected.

FIG 5.5 Environment map for a maze with path found using BFS.

The DFS is simpler than the BFS and hence less effective. Instead of radiating out from the starting node, this algorithm simply follows one adjacent node to the next until it reaches the end of a path. Recursion works well for this algorithm and can be written as Listing 5.4.

Listing 5.4 A depth-first search algorithm

```
DFS(a, vertex)
1.  Let i = a;
2.  Label node as i
3.  For each adjacent node, n, to i, if n is labeled skip
    it, if n is the end node then stop the search, else if
    n is not labeled run this algorithm with DFS(a + 1, n).
```

An implementation of this algorithm is shown in Figure 5.6. Note that the algorithm does not find the shortest path to the destination, just a path. The success of finding the destination in a reasonable time is left to the luck

FIG 5.6 Environment map for a maze with path found using DFS.

of which adjacent node is selected first. In Figure 5.6, nodes are selected in a counterclockwise order, beginning with the one immediately above the current node. If a clockwise order had been chosen, the path would be different. Of course, this algorithm could also be modified to perform an exhaustive search to find all paths to the destination; by finding the path with a minimum cost the best could be selected. However, it is an ineffective way of finding the shortest path.

The most popular algorithm used in games for searching graphs, is called A* (pronounced A-Star). What makes A* more efficient than BFS or DFS is that instead of picking the next adjacent node blindly, the algorithm looks for one that appears to be the most promising. From the starting node, the projected cost of all adjacent nodes is calculated, and the best node is chosen to be the next on the path. From this next node, the same calculations occur again, and the next best node is chosen. This algorithm ensures that all the best nodes are examined first. If one path of nodes does not work out, the algorithm can return to the next best in line and continue the search down a different path.

The algorithm determines the projected cost of taking paths based on the cost of getting to the next node and an estimate of getting from that node to the goal. The estimation is performed by a heuristic function. The term *heuristic* seems to be one of those funny words in AI that is difficult to define. Allen Newell first defined it in 1963 as a computation that performs the opposite function to that of an algorithm. A more useful definition of its meaning is given by Russell and Norvig in *Artificial Intelligence: A Modern Approach* published in 1995. They define a heuristic as any technique that can be used to improve the average performance of solving a problem that may not necessarily improve the worst performance. In the case of path finding, if the heuristic offers a perfect prediction—that is, if it can calculate the cost from the current node to the destination accurately—then the best path will be found. However, in reality, the heuristic is very rarely perfect and can offer only an approximation.

◎ Unity Hands On
Pathfinding with A*

Step 1: Download *Chapter Five/Waypoints.zip* from the website. Open the project and the scene *patrolling*. Programming the A* algorithm is beyond the scope of this book and has therefore been provided with this project. If you are interested in the code, it can be found in the Project in the Plugins folder.

Step 2: Locate the robot model in the Robot Artwork > FBX folder in the Project. Drag the model into the Scene as shown in Figure 5.7. For the terrain and building models already in the scene, the robot will need to be scaled by 400 to match. If the textures are missing, find the material called *robot-robot1*, which is on the *roothandle* submesh of the robot; set it to *the Standard Shader*; and add the appropriate textures. The texture

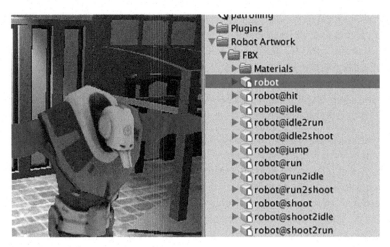

FIG 5.7 A robot model added to the scene and scaled by 400.

files will be in the Project. The model may also have a cube on its head. Make this invisible by finding the *headhandle* subobject of the robot in the Hierarchy and unticking its Mesh Renderer.

Step 3: Waypoints can be added to the scene in the same way as they were in Chapter 3. Any GameObject can act as a waypoint. Create nine spheres and arrange them in a circuit around the building. Add a 10th sphere out the front and an 11th sphere in the driveway as shown in Figure 5.8. Name the spheres as Sphere1, Sphere2, and so on.

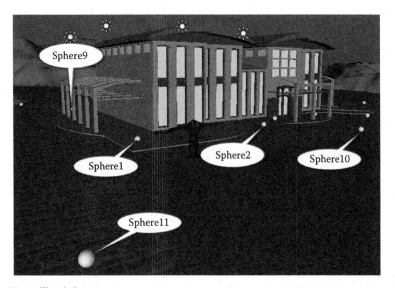

FIG 5.8 Waypoint layout.

Step 4: Create a new C# file called *Patrol* and open it in the script editor.
Add the code shown in Listing 5.5.

Listing 5.5 Initializing waypoints in a graph object

```
using System.Collections;
using System.Collections.Generic;
using UnityEngine;

public class Patrol : MonoBehaviour {

    public GameObject[] waypoints;
    Graph graph = new Graph();
    int currentWP = 0;
    GameObject currentNode;

    int speed = 8;
    int rotationSpeed = 5;
    float accuracy = 1.0f;

    // Use this for initialization
    void Start () {
        if(waypoints.Length > 0)
        {
            // add all the waypoints to the graph
            for(int i = 0; i < waypoints.Length; i++)
            {
                graph.AddNode(waypoints[i], true, true);
            }

            //create edges between the waypoints
            graph.AddEdge(waypoints[0], waypoints[1]);
            graph.AddEdge(waypoints[1], waypoints[2]);
            graph.AddEdge(waypoints[2], waypoints[3]);
            graph.AddEdge(waypoints[3], waypoints[4]);
            graph.AddEdge(waypoints[4], waypoints[5]);
            graph.AddEdge(waypoints[5], waypoints[6]);
            graph.AddEdge(waypoints[6], waypoints[7]);
            graph.AddEdge(waypoints[7], waypoints[8]);
            graph.AddEdge(waypoints[8], waypoints[0]);

        }
        currentNode = waypoints[0];
    }

    // Update is called once per frame
    void Update () {
        graph.debugDraw();
    }
}
```

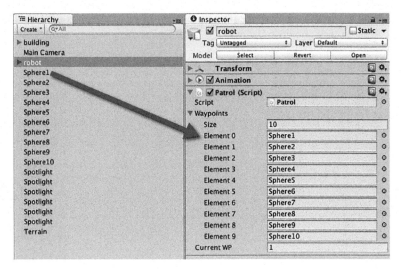

FIG 5.9 Adding waypoints to the *Patrol* script.

Step 5: Attach the *Patrol* script to the *robot* in the Hierarchy. Add the waypoints in order to the Waypoints array of the Patrol script as shown in Figure 5.9.

Step 6: Play. While playing, switch to the Scene. The code in the Update function will draw lines along the edges. The blue tip indicates the direction of the path. If you have all the waypoints collected correctly, there should be a circuit around the building.

Step 7: To get the robot guard to patrol around the building, modify the patrol code as shown in Listing 5.6.

Listing 5.6 Ordering a guard to traverse waypoints

```
public GameObject[] waypoints;
...
    void OnGUI ()
    {
        GUI.Box (new Rect (10,10,100,90), "Guard's
            Orders");
        if (GUI.Button (new Rect (20,65,80,20), "Patrol"))
        {
            graph.AStar(waypoints[0], waypoints[8]);

            this.GetComponent<Animation>().Play("run");
            this.GetComponent<Animation>()["run"].wrapMode
                = WrapMode.Loop;
        }
    }
```

```
...
    void Update () {
        graph.debugDraw();
        //if there is no path or at the end don't do
        //anything
        if(graph.getPathLength() == 0 || currentWP ==
            graph.getPathLength())
        {
            this.GetComponent<Animation>().Play("idle");
            return;
        }

        //the node we are closest to at this moment
        currentNode = graph.getPathPoint(currentWP);

        //if we are close enough to the current waypoint
        //move to next
        if(Vector3.Distance(
            graph.getPathPoint(currentWP).transform.
                position,transform.position) < accuracy)
        {
            currentWP++;
        }
        //if we are not at the end of the path
        if(currentWP < graph.getPathLength())
        {
            //keep on movin'
            Vector3 direction =
                graph.getPathPoint(currentWP).transform.
                    position - transform.position;
            transform.rotation = Quaternion.
                Slerp(transform.rotation, Quaternion.
                LookRotation(direction), rotationSpeed *
                Time.deltaTime);
            transform.Translate(0, 0, Time.deltaTime *
                speed);
        }
    }
```

Step 8: Play. When the Patrol button is pressed, the A* algorithm will calculate a path between the first and last waypoint, and the guard will start running around it.

◉ Note

The character in this instance will move between the position of waypoints. If you have placed your spheres on the ground the character will sink into the ground as it is aiming its (0,0,0) position, which is in the center of the model, to the (0,0,0) of the sphere. To make the character appear to be moving on the terrain, move the spheres up to the right height. You can do this collectively by selecting all spheres in the Hierarchy by holding down shift while clicking on them and then dragging them up in the Scene.

In addition, if a character ever gets to a waypoint and starts circling it unexpectedly, it will be the accuracy setting. You may have it set to small and if the character can never get close enough to a waypoint, it will just keep trying. In this case, set the accuracy value to something higher.

Step 9: Using the A* algorithm to calculate a circuit is a little bit of overkill, as a circuit can be performed simply using the code from Chapter 3. So now we will put it through its paces by adding some more button commands to get the character to move about the building. Modify the patrol code to that in Listing 5.7.

Listing 5.7 Testing A* pathfinding by giving movement comments to a character

```
...
void OnGUI ()
{
    GUI.Box (new Rect (10,10,100,90), "Guard's Orders");
    if (GUI.Button (new Rect (20,65,80,20), "Front Door"))
    {
        graph.AStar(currentNode, waypoints[0]);
        currentWP = 0;

        this.GetComponent<Animation>().Play("run");
        this.GetComponent<Animation>()["run"].wrapMode =
            WrapMode.Loop;
    }
    if (GUI.Button (new Rect (20,90,80,20), "Driveway"))
    {
        graph.AStar(currentNode, waypoints[9]);
        currentWP = 0;

        this.GetComponent<Animation>().Play("run");
        this.GetComponent<Animation>()["run"].wrapMode =
            WrapMode.Loop;
    }
```

```
    if (GUI.Button (new Rect (20,115,80,20), "Front"))
    {
        graph.AStar(currentNode, waypoints[1]);
        currentWP = 0;

        this.GetComponent<Animation>().Play("run");
        this.GetComponent<Animation>()["run"].wrapMode =
            WrapMode.Loop;
    }
}

// Use this for initialization
void Start () {
    if(waypoints.Length > 0)
    {
        // add all the waypoints to the graph
        for(int i = 0; i < waypoints.Length; i++)
        {
            graph.AddNode(waypoints[i], true, true);
        }

        //create edges between the waypoints
        graph.AddEdge(waypoints[0], waypoints[1]);
        graph.AddEdge(waypoints[1], waypoints[2]);
        graph.AddEdge(waypoints[2], waypoints[3]);
        graph.AddEdge(waypoints[3], waypoints[4]);
        graph.AddEdge(waypoints[4], waypoints[5]);
        graph.AddEdge(waypoints[5], waypoints[6]);
        graph.AddEdge(waypoints[6], waypoints[7]);
        graph.AddEdge(waypoints[7], waypoints[8]);
        graph.AddEdge(waypoints[8], waypoints[0]);

        //and back the other way
        graph.AddEdge(waypoints[1], waypoints[0]);
        graph.AddEdge(waypoints[2], waypoints[1]);
        graph.AddEdge(waypoints[3], waypoints[2]);
        graph.AddEdge(waypoints[4], waypoints[3]);
        graph.AddEdge(waypoints[5], waypoints[4]);
        graph.AddEdge(waypoints[6], waypoints[5]);
        graph.AddEdge(waypoints[7], waypoints[6]);
        graph.AddEdge(waypoints[8], waypoints[7]);
        graph.AddEdge(waypoints[0], waypoints[8]);

        //create edges to extra to waypoints
        graph.AddEdge(waypoints[0], waypoints[8]);
        graph.AddEdge(waypoints[0], waypoints[9]);
        graph.AddEdge(waypoints[9], waypoints[9]);
        graph.AddEdge(waypoints[5], waypoints[8]);
        //and back again
```

```
        graph.AddEdge(waypoints[8], waypoints[0]);
        graph.AddEdge(waypoints[9], waypoints[0]);
        graph.AddEdge(waypoints[9], waypoints[9]);
        graph.AddEdge(waypoints[8], waypoints[5]);

    }
    currentNode = waypoints[0];
}
```

Step 10: The preceding code adds extra paths between the original circuit waypoints to point back the other way. This makes it possible to travel in any direction between points. Extra paths are also added between points in the driveway and out the front of the building. Play and switch to the Scene to see the red lines connecting the points (illustrated in Figure 5.10).

A new variable called currentNode has also been added to keep track of the waypoint the character last visited. This enables the algorithm to plot out paths based on the character's current position to the destination node.

FIG 5.10 Debug lines showing paths in a waypoint graph.

◉ Note

Optimizing Code

In the preceding code there are an awful lot of calls to GetComponent(). This can be quite heavy, processing wise. Instead you should declare a variable at the top of the code, then call GetComponent only once in the Start(), like this:

```
Animation anim;

void Start()
{
    anim=this.GetComponent<Animation>();
}
```

Then whenever you want to gain access to the animation anywhere else in the code you simply write:

```
anim.Play("run");
```

This waypoint system is used in the next section after the development of a self-motivated character is explained. However before we get to that we will examine another A* using mechanism that is built into Unity, the Navigation Mesh or NavMesh.

◉ Unity Hands On

Setting up and using a NavMesh

Step 1: Download the *Chapter Five/NavmeshStationStarter.zip* and open it up in Unity.

Step 2: Align the view in the Scene window to look something similar to Figure 5.11.

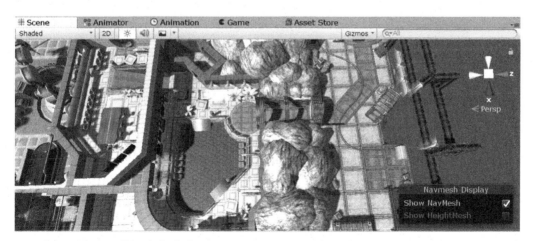

FIG 5.11 Suggested alignment of Scene window for this exercise.

Step 3: Select the Main Camera in the Hierarchy. Then from the main menu, select GameObject > Align With View from the menu so that your camera is looking down when you press play.

Step 4: Create two new materials, red and blue, for the different agents so that we can tell them apart.

Step 5: Make sure you have the Navigation window open in your project. To do this, from the main menu select Window > AI > Navigation.

Step 6: Hold down the Shift key and select an area similar to Figure 5.12 for the agents to navigate.

Step 7: With your chosen area selected, in the Inspector, click on the Static drop-down list and select Navigation Static as shown in Figure 5.13.

Step 8: Next select the Navigation tab as shown in Figure 5.14 and its Bake tab and then click on the Bake button.

You should end up with something like Figure 5.15 where the navigable area turns blue.

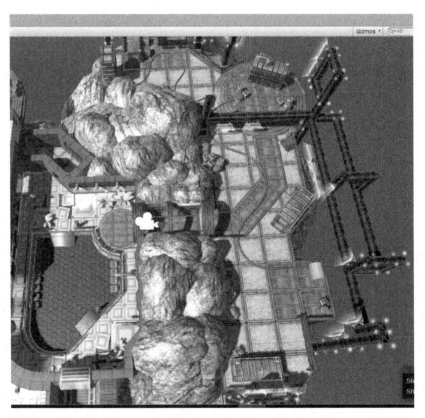

FIG 5.12 Area to select for agent navigation.

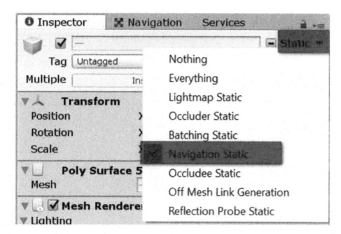

FIG 5.13 Setting mesh areas to navigation static.

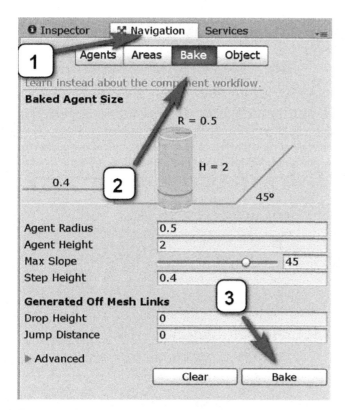

FIG 5.14 The navigation tab.

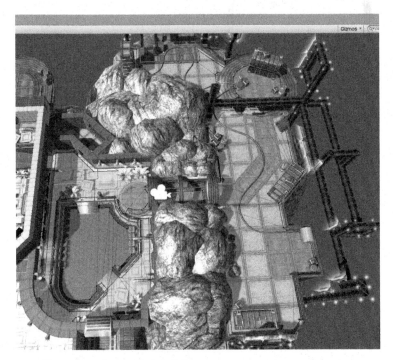

FIG 5.15 The appearance of a navigable area in the Scene.

Step 9: Make sure nothing is selected in the hierarchy. Right click in it and select 3D Object/Capsule. Rename the capsule RedAgent. Create a red material and add it to the capsule. Place it somewhere over to the right in the open. With the RedAgent still selected, press the Tag drop-down list in the Inspector and then Add Tag as shown in Figure 5.16.

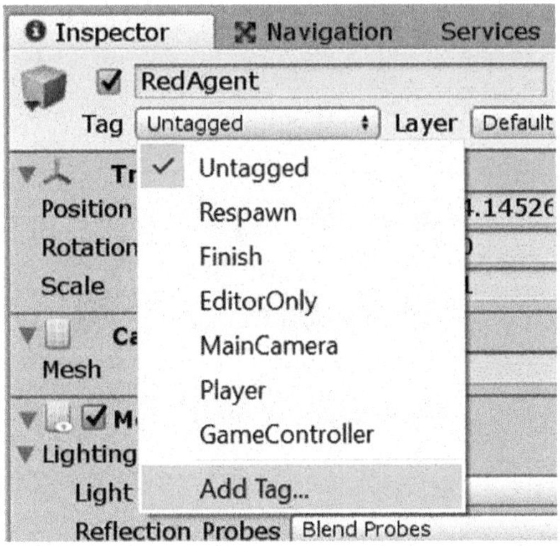

FIG 5.16 Creating and adding a tag.

Under Tags (List is Empty). Select the plus button and enter "ai" and hit save. Again, select the RedAgent in the hierarchy and the Tags dropdown list where you can now select "ai" as a tag.

Step 10: Create a new C# Script named *AIControl.cs* and enter the code in Listing 5.8.

Listing 5.8 AI controller code

```
using System.Collections;
using System.Collections.Generic;
using UnityEngine;
using UnityEngine.AI;

public class AIControl : MonoBehaviour {

    public NavMeshAgent agent;

    // Use this for initialization
    void Start () {
        agent = this.GetComponent<NavMeshAgent>();
    }
}
```

Step 11: Save the script and, back in Unity, add an empty object to the Hierarchy called AgentManager. Create a second C# script named *AgentManager.cs* and add the code in Listing 5.9.

Listing 5.9 Agent management code

```
using System.Collections;
using System.Collections.Generic;
using UnityEngine;

public class AgentManager : MonoBehaviour {

    GameObject[] agents;

    // Use this for initialization
    void Start () {
        agents = GameObject.FindGameObjectsWithTag("ai");
    }

    // Update is called once per frame
    void Update () {
        if (Input.GetMouseButtonDown(0)) {
            RaycastHit hit;
```

```
if(Physics.Raycast(Camera.main.
    ScreenPointToRay(Input.mousePosition), out
    hit, 100)) {
    foreach(GameObject a in agents) {
        a.GetComponent<AIControl>().agent.
            SetDestination(hit.point);
    }
}
}
}
}
```

Step 12: Again, save your code and head back into Unity.

Step 13: With the RedAgent selected, head over to the Inspector and scroll down to the bottom and select Add Component. Enter *Nav Mesh Agent* in the search box and click to select. When you press play, you will now be able to click anywhere on the previously baked area and your agent should now walk to the chosen spot. It does this using A* to calculate the path from one location to another using the NavMesh as a reference of points for where it is allowed to travel.

Step 14: You can adjust the agent's speed in the Inspector in the Nav Mesh Agent component section you added. Set it to about 10 as shown in Figure 5.17.

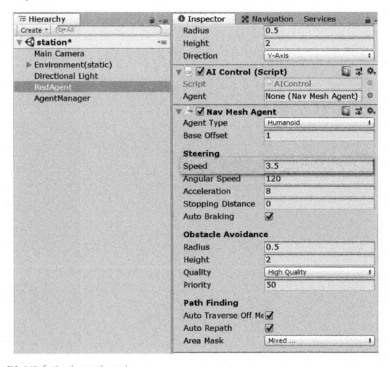

FIG 5.17 Setting the agent's speed.

FIG 5.18 Multiple NavMesh agents moving across a mesh.

Step 15: Select the RedAgent in the Hierarchy and press CTRL + D several times to make several duplicates. They will all occupy the same world space until you hit play and tell them to move as demonstrated in Figure 5.18.

5.5 Finite State Machines

The most popular form of AI in games and NPCs is *nondeterministic automata*, or what are more commonly known as *finite state machines* (FSM). An FSM can be represented by a directed graph (digraph), where the nodes symbolize states and the directed connecting edges correspond to state transitions. States represent an NPC's current behavior or state of mind. Formally, an FSM consists of a set of states, *S*, and a set of state transitions, *T*. For example, an FSM might be defined as $S = \{WANDER, ATTACK, PURSUE\}$ and $T = \{out\ of\ sight, sighted, out\ of\ range, in\ range, dead\}$ as shown in Table 5.1.

In short, the state transitions define how to get from one state to another. For example, in Table 5.1, if the NPC is in state WANDER and it sights its opponent,

TABLE 5.1 State Transition for a FSM

	Transitions (*opponent is...*)				
State	**Out of Sight**	**Sighted**	**Out of Range**	**In Range**	**Dead**
WANDER	*WANDER*	*PURSUE*	—	—	—
PURSUE	*WANDER*	—	*PURSUE*	*ATTACK*	—
ATTACK	—	—	*PURSUE*	*ATTACK*	*WANDER*

then the state transitions to PURSUE. The state is used to determine elements of the NPC's behavior; for example, when the NPC is in the ATTACK state, the appropriate attacking animation should be used.

Programming an FSM is a case of providing an NPC with a *state* value that represents its current behavior. Each state is accompanied by an *event* value representing the status of that state. The event tells us if the NPC has just entered that state, has been in the state for a while, or is exiting the state. Keeping track of this is critical for coordinating NPC movements around the environment and its animations. The FSM runs each game loop; therefore, knowing where the NPC is within a state is important for updating its status, the status of other game characters, and the environment.

For example, consider a Sim whose state changes to "take bath." Before it can take a bath, it needs to make its way to the bathroom, run the bath, get undressed, and hop in the bath. This would happen on entering the state. The state would then enter update mode where the Sim is sitting in the bath washing itself, singing, blowing bubbles, and so on. Once the Sim is clean, the state transitions to the exit phase in which it gets out of the bath and redresses. In pseudocode, the code might look something like that in Listing 5.8.

Listing 5.8 Code for simple FSM

```
void FSM()
{
    if(state == "BATH")
    {
        if (event == "ENTER")
        {
            walkToBath();
            runBath();
            getUndressed();
            hopInBath();
            event = "UPDATE";
        }
        else if (event == UPDATE)
        {
            while(!clean)
            {
                wash();
            }
            event = "EXIT";
        }
        else if (event == "EXIT")
        {
            getOutOfBath();
```

```
            getDressed();
            state = "IDLE";
            event = "ENTER";
        }
    }
}
```

The FSM works by entering a state and then transitioning from enter, through update, to exit. At the end of each event, the event is updated such that during the next loop the FSM runs, the code goes into the next event. On exiting a state, the state value is changed to something else and the event is set to enter.

◉ Unity Hands On
Implementing an FSM
In this workshop, you will learn how to implement an FSM in conjunction with a waypoint system and the A* algorithm to program a guard character that patrols a warehouse and pursues intruders.

Step 1: Download *Chapter Five/FSM.zip* from the website and open the scene warehousePatrol. In the Scene you will see the warehouse model, the robot from the last workshop, and a waypoint system of spheres.
Step 2: Create a new tag named *waypoint* and set it for the tag of each sphere.
Step 3: Create a new C# file called *Patrol.cs* and open with the script editor. Enter the code in Listing 5.9 and attach it to the robot.

Listing 5.9 Setting up a waypoint system with automatic waypoint collection

```
using System.Collections;
using System.Collections.Generic;
using UnityEngine;

public class Patrol : MonoBehaviour {

    Graph graph = new Graph();
    int currentWP = 0;
    GameObject currentNode;
    int speed = 8;
    int rotationSpeed = 5;
    float accuracy = 1;

    void CreateBiPath(string a, string b)
    {
        GameObject w1 = GameObject.Find(a);
        GameObject w2 = GameObject.Find(b);
```

```
            if(w1 && w2) //if both objects exist
            {
                //create edges between the waypoints
                //in both directions
                graph.AddEdge(w1, w2);
                graph.AddEdge(w2, w1);
            }

        }
        // Use this for initialization
        void Start () {
            GameObject[] gos;
            gos = GameObject.FindGameObjectsWithTag
                ("waypoint");
            foreach (GameObject go in gos)
            {
                graph.AddNode(go, true, true);
            }
            CreateBiPath("Sphere3","Sphere2");
            CreateBiPath("Sphere2","Sphere1");
            CreateBiPath("Sphere1","Sphere4");
            CreateBiPath("Sphere3","Sphere4");
            CreateBiPath("Sphere4","Sphere5");
            CreateBiPath("Sphere5","Sphere6");
            CreateBiPath("Sphere6","Sphere7");
            CreateBiPath("Sphere7","Sphere8");
            CreateBiPath("Sphere8","Sphere9");
            CreateBiPath("Sphere9","Sphere10");
            CreateBiPath("Sphere10","Sphere11");
            CreateBiPath("Sphere11","Sphere12");
            CreateBiPath("Sphere12","Sphere13");
            CreateBiPath("Sphere13","Sphere14");
            CreateBiPath("Sphere14","Sphere15");
            CreateBiPath("Sphere15","Sphere17");

            currentNode = GameObject.Find("Sphere2");
        }

        // Update is called once per frame
        void Update () {
            graph.debugDraw();
        }
    }
```

Step 4: Play. Go into the Scene view and have a look at the paths that have been created. In this code, a function has been written to help take away part of the laborious job of programming how points connect by creating bidirectional paths. This code also populates the waypoint graph automatically by looking for all the spheres that were tagged with *waypoint* in the Start() function.

Step 5: Locate Sphere2 and place the guard model near it as it has been set as the initial value for currentNode and will be used as the starting location of guard. Alternatively, you could add code such as this. transform.position = currentNode.transform.position to the end of the Start() function to have the code place the model.
Step 6: Modify the Patrol script to that in Listing 5.10.

Listing 5.10 Adding an FSM function

```
using System.Collections;
using System.Collections.Generic;
using UnityEngine;

public class Patrol : MonoBehaviour {

    Graph graph = new Graph();
    ...
    string state = "idle";
    string event = "enter";
    GameObject goalLocation;

    void CreateBiPath(a: String, b: String)
    {
            ...
    }
    void Start ()
    {
            ...
    }

    void FSM()
    {
        Vector3 direction;
        Vector3 position;

        if(state == "patrol")
        {
            if(prevState != state)
            {
                print("patrol "+ currentNode.name);
                graph.AStar(currentNode, goalLocation);
                graph.printPath();
                currentWP = 0;

                this.GetComponent<Animation>().Play("run");
                this.GetComponent<Animation>()["run"].
                wrapMode = WrapMode.Loop;
```

```
            eventname = "update";
            prevState = state;
        }
        else if (eventname == "update")
        {
            if(graph.getPathLength() == 0 ||
                currentWP == graph.getPathLength())
            {
                state = "idle";
                eventname = "enter";
                return;
            }

            //the node we are closest to at this moment
            currentNode = graph.getPathPoint(currentWP);

            if(Vector3.Distance(graph.getPathPoint
                (currentWP).transform.position,
                transform.position) < accuracy)
            {
                currentWP++;
            }

            //if we are not at the end of the path
            if(currentWP < graph.getPathLength())
            {
                //keep on movin'
                direction =
                graph.getPathPoint(currentWP).
                    transform.position -
                    transform.position;
                transform.rotation = Quaternion.
                    Slerp(transform.rotation,
                    Quaternion. LookRotation(direction),
                    rotationSpeed * Time.deltaTime);
                transform.Translate(0, 0,
                    Time.deltaTime * speed);
            }

        }
        else if (eventname == "exit")
        {

        }
    }
    else if(state == "attack")
    {
        if(prevState != state)
        {
```

```
            this.GetComponent<Animation>().
                CrossFade("shoot");
            this.GetComponent<Animation>()["shoot"].
                wrapMode = WrapMode.Loop;
            eventname = "update";
        }
        else if(eventname == "update")
        {
            position = target.position;
            direction = position - transform.position;
            direction.y = 0;
            // Rotate towards the target
            transform.rotation = Quaternion.
                Slerp(transform.rotation,Quaternion.
                LookRotation(direction),
            rotationSpeed * Time.deltaTime);
            transform.position = new Vector3(
                transform.position.x,
                target.position.y + heightOffset,
                transform.position.z);
        }

    }
    else if(state == "pursue")
    {
        if(prevState != state)
        {
            this.GetComponent<Animation>().
                CrossFade("run");
            this.GetComponent<Animation>()["run"].
                wrapMode = WrapMode.Loop;
            eventname = "update";
        }
        else if(eventname == "update")
        {
            direction = target.position - transform.
                position;
            direction.y = 0;
            // Rotate towards the target
            transform.rotation = Quaternion.Slerp(
                transform.rotation, Quaternion.
                LookRotation(direction), rotationSpeed
                * Time.deltaTime);

            // Move the character
            if(direction.magnitude > keepDistance)
            {
                transform. Translate(0, 0, Time.
                    deltaTime * speed);
            }
```

```
                    transform.position = new Vector3(transform.
                        position.x, target.position.y +
                        heightOffset, transform.position.z);
                }


            }
            else if(state == "idle")
            {

                this.GetComponent<Animation>().Play("idle");
                eventname = "update";
                prevState = state;

                if(eventname == "update")
                {

                    //just remain idle
                    if(Random.Range(0,10) < 5)
                    {
                        state = "patrol";
                        eventname = "enter";

                        if(currentNode == GameObject.
                            Find("Sphere17"))
                        goalLocation = GameObject.
                            Find("Sphere2");
                        else
                        goalLocation = GameObject.
                            Find("Sphere17");
                    }
                }
            }
        }
    void Update()
        {
            //draw the paths in the scene view of the editor
            //while playing
            graph.debugDraw();
            FSM();
        }
    }
```

Step 7: Play. With the 1 in 1000 chance of the guard going into patrol mode, if you watch it for a while, it will start moving from its current location to the last waypoint. When it gets there, it will go into idle mode again, until after another 1 in 1000 chances, it will start to patrol back in the other direction. Note that, as with the waypoints in the previous workshop, the spheres may need to be moved up so that the guard model does not sink into the floor.

Step 8: Select Assets > Import Package > Custom Package from the main menu and add the First Person Controller package available with the book's resources or downloadable from the Asset Store.

Step 9: Drag the First Person Controller prefab from the Project into the Hierarchy. Delete the existing main camera, as the First Person Controller has its own camera.

Step 10: Move the First Person Controller into the same room as the guard, so you can watch it moving.

Step 11: In the Hierarchy, shift-select all the *polySurface* submeshes of the warehouse model and select Components > Physics > Mesh Collider to add colliders to the warehouse. Without the colliders, the First Person Controller will fall through the floor.

Step 12: Play. You will now be able to watch the guard patrolling from the first person view.

Step 13: The guard model will seem dark, as there is no directional light—so add one to the scene.

Step 14: Next we are going to add code to make the guard shoot and chase the player. To do this, add pursue and attack states as shown in Listing 5.11.

Listing 5.11 Adding an FSM function and extending with more states

```
using System.Collections;
using System.Collections.Generic;
using UnityEngine;

public class Patrol : MonoBehaviour {

    Graph graph = new Graph();
    int currentWP = 0;
    GameObject currentNode;
    int speed = 8;
    int rotationSpeed = 5;
    float accuracy = 1;

    string prevState = "";
    string state = "idle";
    string eventname = "enter";
    GameObject goalLocation;

    public Transform target;
    float seeRange = 10;
    float shootRange = 5;
    float keepDistance = 1;
    float heightOffset = 0.3f;

    void CreateBiPath(string a, string b)
    {
```

```
        GameObject w1 = GameObject.Find(a);
        GameObject w2 = GameObject.Find(b);

        if(w1 && w2) //if both objects exist
        {
            //create edges between the waypoints
            //in both directions
            graph.AddEdge(w1, w2);
            graph.AddEdge(w2, w1);
        }

    }

    bool CanSeeTarget ()
    {
        if (Vector3.Distance(transform.position, target.
            position) > seeRange)
        return false;
        return true;
    }

    bool CanShootTarget()
    {
        if(!CanSeeTarget()) return false;
        if (Vector3.Distance(transform.position, target.
            position) > shootRange)
        return false;
        return true;
    }
    // Use this for initialization
    void Start () {
        GameObject[] gos;
        gos = GameObject.FindGameObjectsWithTag("waypoint");

        foreach (GameObject go in gos)
        {
            graph.AddNode(go, true, true);
        }

        CreateBiPath("Sphere3","Sphere2");
        CreateBiPath("Sphere2","Sphere1");
        CreateBiPath("Sphere1","Sphere4");
        CreateBiPath("Sphere3","Sphere4");
        CreateBiPath("Sphere4","Sphere5");
        CreateBiPath("Sphere5","Sphere6");
        CreateBiPath("Sphere6","Sphere7");
        CreateBiPath("Sphere7","Sphere8");
        CreateBiPath("Sphere8","Sphere9");
        CreateBiPath("Sphere9","Sphere10");
```

```
    CreateBiPath("Sphere10","Sphere11");
    CreateBiPath("Sphere11","Sphere12");
    CreateBiPath("Sphere12","Sphere13");
    CreateBiPath("Sphere13","Sphere14");
    CreateBiPath("Sphere14","Sphere15");
    CreateBiPath("Sphere15","Sphere17");

    currentNode = GameObject.Find("Sphere2");
}

void FSM()
{
    Vector3 direction;
    Vector3 position;

    if(state == "patrol")
    {
        if(prevState != state)
        {
            print("patrol " + currentNode.name);
            graph.AStar(currentNode, goalLocation);
            graph.printPath();
            currentWP = 0;

            this.GetComponent<Animation>().
                Play("run");
            this.GetComponent<Animation>()["run"].
                wrapMode = WrapMode.Loop;
            eventname = "update";
            prevState = state;
        }
        else if (eventname == "update")
        {
            if(graph.getPathLength() == 0 ||
                currentWP == graph.getPathLength())
            {
                state = "idle";
                eventname = "enter";
                return;
            }

            //the node we are closest to at this moment
            currentNode = graph.
                getPathPoint(currentWP);

            if(Vector3.Distance(graph.getPathPoint
                (currentWP).transform.position,
                transform.position) < accuracy)
```

```
            {
                currentWP++;
            }

            //if we are not at the end of the path
            if(currentWP < graph.getPathLength())
            {
                //keep on movin'
                direction =
                graph.getPathPoint(currentWP).transform.
                    position - transform.position;
            transform.rotation = Quaternion. Slerp
                (transform.rotation, Quaternion.
                LookRotation(direction), rotationSpeed
                * Time.deltaTime);
            transform.Translate(0, 0, Time.deltaTime *
                speed);
            }

        }
        else if (eventname == "exit")
        {

        }
    }
    else if(state == "attack")
    {
        if(prevState != state)
        {
            this.GetComponent<Animation>().
                CrossFade("shoot");
            this.GetComponent<Animation>()["shoot"].
                wrapMode = WrapMode. Loop;
            eventname = "update";
        }
        else if(eventname == "update")
        {
            position = target.position;
            direction = position - transform.position;
            direction.y = 0;
            // Rotate towards the target
            transform.rotation = Quaternion.
                Slerp(transform.rotation, Quaternion.
                LookRotation(direction), rotationSpeed *
                Time.deltaTime);
            transform.position = new Vector3(transform.
                position.x, target.position.y +
                heightOffset, transform.position.z);
        }
    }
```

```
    else if(state == "pursue")
    {
        if(prevState != state)
        {
            this.GetComponent<Animation>().
                CrossFade("run");
            this.GetComponent<Animation>()["run"].
                wrapMode = WrapMode.Loop;
            eventname = "update";
        }
        else if(eventname == "update")
        {
            direction = target.position - transform.
                position;
            direction.y = 0;
            // Rotate towards the target
            transform.rotation = Quaternion.
                Slerp(transform.rotation,
            Quaternion.LookRotation(direction),
                rotationSpeed * Time.deltaTime);

            // Move the character
            if(direction.magnitude > keepDistance)
            {
                transform.Translate(0, 0, Time.
                    deltaTime * speed);
            }
            transform.position = new Vector3(transform.
                position.x, target.position.y +
                heightOffset, transform.position.z);
        }

    }
    else if(state == "idle")
    {
        print("play idle");
        this.GetComponent<Animation>().Play("idle");
        eventname = "update";
        prevState = state;

        if(eventname == "update")
        {

            //just remain idle
            if(Random.Range(0,10) < 5)
            {
                state = "patrol";
                eventname = "enter";
```

```
                    if(currentNode == GameObject.
                        Find("Sphere17"))
                    goalLocation = GameObject.
                        Find("Sphere2");
                    else
                    goalLocation = GameObject.
                        Find("Sphere17");
                }
            }
        }
    }

    // Update is called once per frame
    void Update () {
        graph.debugDraw();
        if(CanShootTarget())
        {
            prevState = state;
            state = "attack";
        }
        else if(CanSeeTarget())
        {
            prevState = state;
            state = "pursue";
        }
        else if(state != "patrol")
        {
            prevState = state;
            state = "idle";
        }

        FSM();
    }
}
```

Step 15: The preceding code now controls the shooting and pursuing actions of the guard. Setting the state's event to enter has also been replaced. If the NPC's previous state was different from the current state, it runs the original event = "enter" code—the same as initializing a state. The distance the NPC shoots and pursues is controlled by variables at the top of the code. Before playing, locate the patrol script attached to the robot model in the Hierarchy and set the *target* variable to the *First Person Controller* as shown in Figure 5.19.

When the NPC is pursuing and attacking the player, its position is made relative to the player. Because the model sizes of the player

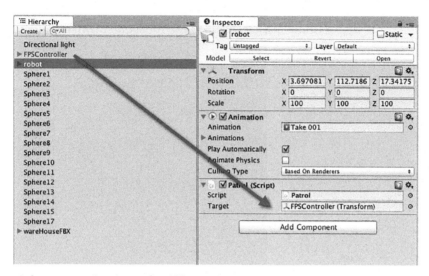

FIG 5.19 Setting the first-person controller as the target for an NPC.

and the robot mesh are different, and the center points differ with respect to their *y* position, without some kind of height offset for the robot, it will either sink into the ground or float above it. This is the same issue the NPC has when following the waypoints and the reason why spheres are lifted above the ground. To fix this, the *heightOffset* variable has been added.

To get the best offset value, usually the game needs to be played a number of times, and the NPC needs to be observed. If you know the exact height of the model's mesh and its center position, it could be calculated.

Step 16: Play. The guard will chase and shoot at the player, but move up the stairs into another room and see what happens. The guard will follow the player but take shortcuts through the walls of the warehouse.

Step 17: This presents another problem to solve. We could make the NPC stick to the waypoints and paths while trying to follow the player, but what if the player goes to a place where there are no waypoints? You could also spend a lot of time placing waypoints all over the map as a solution. However, a simpler solution is to place temporary waypoints down on the map that draw out the path the player is walking and have the NPC follow them instead. This is another common technique used in games called *breadcrumb pathfinding*. To develop a simple breadcrumb script, create a new C# file called *breadcrumbs.cs* and add the code in Listing 5.12.

Step 18: Attach this script to the FPCController.

Listing 5.12 Recording player movement with breadcrumbs

```
using System.Collections;
using System.Collections.Generic;
using UnityEngine;

public class breadcrumbs: MonoBehaviour {

    public ArrayList crumbs = new ArrayList();
    Vector3 lastPos;

    public void RemoveBreadCrumb()
    {
        Destroy(crumbs[0] as GameObject);
        crumbs.RemoveAt(0);
    }

    void Update ()
    {
        if(lastPos != this.transform.position)
        {
            GameObject bc = GameObject.
                CreatePrimitive(PrimitiveType.Sphere);
            bc.transform.position = this.transform.
                position;
            Destroy(bc.GetComponent<Collider>());
            bc.transform.localScale = new
                Vector3(0.5f,0.5f,0.5f);
            bc. GetComponent<Renderer>().material.color =
                Color.green;
            crumbs.Add(bc);
        }
        lastPos = this.transform.position;

        if(crumbs.Count > 100)
        {
            RemoveBreadCrumb();
        }
    }
}
```

Step 19: Play. Walk backward and look at the green spheres being added to the map. These are your breadcrumbs. They mark the last 100 locations your First Person Controller was on the map. Of course, in a real game you would not see these, but they are added here for illustrative purposes.

Step 20: To get the NPC to follow these breadcrumbs when it is in pursuit, modify the patrol script as shown in Listing 5.13.

Listing 5.13 Adding breadcrumb following code to the NPC

```
...
else if(state == "pursue")
{
if(prevState != state)
{
    this.GetComponent<Animation>().CrossFade("run");
    this.GetComponent<Animation>()["run"].wrapMode
        = WrapMode.Loop;
    eventname = "update";
}
else if(eventname == "update")
{
    position = (target.gameObject.GetComponent
        <breadcrumbs>().crumbs[0] as
        GameObject).transform.position;
    if(Vector3.Distance(position, this.transform.position)
        < 2)
    {
        target.gameObject.GetComponent<breadcrumbs>().
        RemoveBreadCrumb();
    }

    direction = target.position - transform.position;
    direction.y = 0;
    ...
```

Step 21: Play. When the NPC is in pursuit of the player, it will follow the breadcrumb trail. As it reaches a breadcrumb, it deletes it from the player's breadcrumb array.

Step 22: Last but not least, we want the NPC to continue patrolling when the player manages to move beyond its range. To do this, we need to set the state to idle and also find the NPC its closest waypoint. That way the A* algorithm can work to set the NPC back on its patrol path. To do this, modify the patrol script to that in Listing 5.14.

Listing 5.14 Finding the closest waypoint to set NPC back to patrol

```
using System.Collections;
using System.Collections.Generic;
using UnityEngine;

public class patrol: MonoBehaviour {

    Graph graph = new Graph();
```

```
int currentWP = 0;
GameObject currentNode;
int speed = 8;
int rotationSpeed = 5;
float accuracy = 1;

string prevState = "";
string state = "idle";
string eventname = "enter";
GameObject goalLocation;

public Transform target;
float seeRange = 10;
float shootRange = 5;
float keepDistance = 1;
float heightOffset = 0.3f;

void CreateBiPath(string a, string b)
{
    GameObject w1 = GameObject.Find(a);
    GameObject w2 = GameObject.Find(b);

    if(w1 && w2) //if both objects exist
    {
        //create edges between the waypoints
        //in both directions
        graph.AddEdge(w1, w2);
        graph.AddEdge(w2, w1);
    }

}

bool CanSeeTarget ()
{
    if (Vector3.Distance(transform.position, target.
        position) > seeRange)
    return false;
    return true;
}

bool CanShootTarget()
{
    if(!CanSeeTarget()) return false;
    if (Vector3.Distance(transform.position, target.
        position) > shootRange)
    return false;
    return true;
}
```

```
// Use this for initialization
void Start () {
    GameObject[] gos;
    gos = GameObject.FindGameObjectsWithTag("waypoint");

    foreach (GameObject go in gos)
    {
        graph.AddNode(go, true, true);
    }

    CreateBiPath("Sphere3","Sphere2");
    CreateBiPath("Sphere2","Sphere1");
    CreateBiPath("Sphere1","Sphere4");
    CreateBiPath("Sphere3","Sphere4");
    CreateBiPath("Sphere4","Sphere5");
    CreateBiPath("Sphere5","Sphere6");
    CreateBiPath("Sphere6","Sphere7");
    CreateBiPath("Sphere7","Sphere8");
    CreateBiPath("Sphere8","Sphere9");
    CreateBiPath("Sphere9","Sphere10");
    CreateBiPath("Sphere10","Sphere11");
    CreateBiPath("Sphere11","Sphere12");
    CreateBiPath("Sphere12","Sphere13");
    CreateBiPath("Sphere13","Sphere14");
    CreateBiPath("Sphere14","Sphere15");
    CreateBiPath("Sphere15","Sphere17");

    currentNode = GameObject.Find("Sphere2");
}

GameObject findClosestWP()
{
    GameObject[] gos;
    gos = GameObject.FindGameObjectsWithTag("waypoint");
    GameObject closest = gos[0];

    foreach (GameObject go in gos)
    {
        if(Vector3.Distance(closest.transform.position,
                this.transform.position) >
          Vector3.Distance(go.transform.position,
                this.transform.position))
        {
            closest = go;
        }
    }
    return closest;
}
```

```
void FSM()
{
    Vector3 direction;
    Vector3 position;

    if(state == "patrol")
    {
        if(prevState != state)
        {
            print("patrol "+ currentNode.name);
            graph.AStar(currentNode, goalLocation);
            graph.printPath();
            currentWP = 0;

            this.GetComponent<Animation>().Play("run");
            this.GetComponent<Animation>()["run"].
                wrapMode = WrapMode.Loop;
            eventname = "update";
            prevState = state;
        }
        else if (eventname == "update")
        {
            if(graph.getPathLength() == 0 || currentWP
                == graph.getPathLength())
            {
                state = "idle";
                eventname = "enter";
                return;
            }

            //the node we are closest to at this moment
            currentNode = graph.getPathPoint(currentWP);

            if(Vector3.Distance(graph.
                zetPathPoint(currentWP). transform.
                position, transform.position) <
                accuracy)
            {
                currentWP++;
            }

            //if we are not at the end of the path
            if(currentWP < graph.getPathLength())
            {
                //keep on movin'
                direction =
                    graph.getPathPoint(currentWP).
                        transform.position - transform.
                        position;
```

```
                transform.rotation = Quaternion.
                    Slerp(transform.rotation,
                    Quaternion.LookRotation(direction),
                    rotationSpeed * Time.deltaTime);
                transform.Translate(0, 0, Time.
                    deltaTime * speed);
            }

        }
        else if (eventname == "exit")
        {

        }
    }
    else if(state == "attack")
    {
        if(prevState != state)
        {
            this.GetComponent<Animation>().
                CrossFade("shoot");
            this.GetComponent<Animation>()["shoot"].
                wrapMode = WrapMode.Loop;
            eventname = "update";
        }
        else if(eventname == "update")
        {
            position = target.position;
            direction = position - transform.position;
            direction.y = 0;
            // Rotate towards the target
            transform.rotation = Quaternion.
                Slerp(transform.rotation, Quaternion.
                LookRotation(direction), rotationSpeed *
                Time.deltaTime);
            transform.position = new Vector3(transform.
                position.x, target.position.y +
                heightOffset, transform.position.z);
        }

    }
    else if(state == "pursue")
    {
        if(prevState != state)
        {
        this.GetComponent<Animation>().
          CrossFade("run");
```

```
        this.GetComponent<Animation>()["run"].wrapMode
          = WrapMode.Loop;
                eventname = "update";
        }
        else if(eventname == "update")
        {
            position = (target.gameObject.
                GetComponent<breadcrumbs>().crumbs[0]
                as GameObject).transform.position;
            if(Vector3.Distance(position, this.
                transform.position) < 2)
            {
                    target.gameObject.
                    GetComponent<breadcrumbs>().
                    RemoveBreadCrumb();
            }

            direction = target.position - transform.
                position;
            direction.y = 0;
            // Rotate towards the target transform.
                rotation = Quaternion.Slerp(transform.
                rotation, Quaternion.
                LookRotation(direction), rotationSpeed
                * Time.deltaTime);

            // Move the character
            if(direction.magnitude > keepDistance)
            {
                transform.Translate(0, 0, Time.
                    deltaTime * speed);
            }
            transform.position = new Vector3(transform.
                position.x, target.position.y +
                heightOffset, transform.position.z);

        }

    }
    else if(state == "idle")
    {
        print("play idle");
        this.GetComponent<Animation>().Play("idle");
        eventname = "update";
```

```
            prevState = state;

            if(eventname == "update")
            {
                //just remain idle
                if(Random.Range(0,10) < 5)
                {
                    state = "patrol";
                    eventname = "enter";
                    currentNode = findClosestWP();
                    if(currentNode == GameObject.
                        Find("Sphere17"))
                    goalLocation =
                    GameObject.Find("Sphere2");
                    else
                    goalLocation = GameObject.
                        Find("Sphere17");
                }
            }


        }
    }
    // Update is called once per frame
    void Update () {
        graph.debugDraw();
        if(CanShootTarget())
        {
            prevState = state;
            state = "attack";
        }
        else if(CanSeeTarget())
        {
            prevState = state;
            state = "pursue";
        }
        else if(state != "patrol")
        {
            prevState = state;
            state = "idle";
        }

        FSM();
    }
}
```

Step 23: Play. If you can manage to outrun the NPC, you will find that it
goes into idle mode and then resumes its patrolling path.

> ⦿ **Note**
>
> *More On Optimization*
>
> We previously discussed how too many `GetComponent()` calls can affect performance of your code, and hopefully you noticed where these would be modified in the code presented in this section. Another call that is performance heavy when used all the time is `GameObject.Find()`. This is being called in this case as:
>
> ```
> GameObject.Find("Shield");
> ```
>
> This occurs repetitively in the `OnCollisionEnter()` method. Instead you could declare a global variable to hold it and perform a single find in the `Start()` as be previously did for the animation `GetComponent()` thus:
>
> ```
> GameObject theShield;
>
> void Start()
> {
>     theShield = GameObject.Find("shield");
> }
> ```

5.6 Flocking

When you observe the movement of crowds or groups of animals, their motions appear aligned and coordinated; for example, a flock of birds flying across the sky appears synchronized, staying together as a group, moving toward a common goal, and yet not all following the exact same path.

Applying flocking principles to NPCs in a game can add extra realism to the environment as secondary animations. If the game is set in a jungle setting, having a flock of birds fly across the sky looks far better than random birds flying in random directions.

In 1986, Craig Reynolds developed an unparalleled simple algorithm for producing flocking behavior in groups of computer characters. Through the application of three rules, Reynolds developed coordinated motions such as that seen in flocks of birds and schools of fish. The rules are applied to each individual character in a group with the result of very convincing flocking behavior. These rules (illustrated in Figure 5.20) include the following:

1. Moving toward the average position of the group
2. Aligning with the average heading of the group
3. Avoid crowding other group members

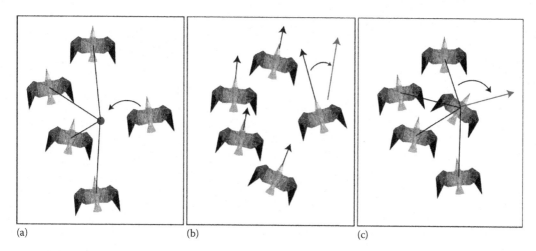

(a)   (b)   (c)

FIG 5.20 Flocking rules: (a) Move towards average group position, (b) align heading with average group heading, (c) avoid others.

Flocking creates a moving group with no actual leader. The rules can be increased to take into consideration moving toward a goal position or the effect of wind. These rules are used to create a flock of birds in the following workshop.

○ Unity Hands On

Flocking

Step 1: Download *Chapter Five/flockStarter.unitypackage* from the website and open the *testFlock* scene. Play. You will see a radar showing the position of seagulls created with the globalFlock script attached to the camera. To move the camera, use the arrow keys. This will allow you to look at parts of the flock. Currently the seagulls do not move. In the globalFlock script, 100 seagulls are being created. If you want more, change the value where it currently states 100. If your computer starts to slow down, you may need to reduce the flock size.

Step 2: Open the flock script and add the code in Listing 5.15.

Listing 5.15 Starting the flock code

```
using System.Collections;
using System.Collections.Generic;
using UnityEngine;

public class Flock: MonoBehaviour {
    float speed = 0.001f;
    float rotationSpeed = 5.0f;
    Vector3 averageHeading;
    Vector3 averagePosition;

    float neighbourDistance = 2.0f;
```

```
void Start()
{
    speed = Random.Range(0.1f, 1f);
}

void Update()
{
    transform.Translate(0, 0, Time.deltaTime
        * speed);
}
}
```

Step 3: Note the flock script is attached to the *SeagullPrefab* in the Project.
Step 4: Play. Each seagull will have a random speed setting and will be flying in a straight line. You can use the arrow keys to follow the birds.
Step 5: Let us apply the first flocking rule to the population. Modify the flock script as shown in Listing 5.16.

Listing 5.16 Script to make seagulls move to the average location of their neighbors

```
float speed = 0.001f;
...
void Update()
{
    if (Random. Range(0, 5) < 1)
        ApplyRules();

    transform.Translate(0, 0, Time.deltaTime
        * speed);
}
void ApplyRules()
{
    GameObject[] gos;
    gos = GameObject.FindGameObjectsWithTag("Seagull");
    Vector3 vcentre = Vector3.zero;
    Vector3 vavoid = Vector3.zero;
    float gSpeed = 0;
    float dist = 0;
    int groupSize = 0;

    foreach (GameObject go in gos)
    {
        if (go != this.gameObject)
        {
            dist = Vector3.Distance(go.transform.
                position, this.transform.position);
```

```
            if (dist <= neighbourDistance)
            {
                vcentre += go.transform.position;
                groupSize++;
            }
        }
    }
}
if (groupSize != 0)
{
    vcentre = vcentre / groupSize;

    var direction = vcentre - transform.position;
    if (direction != Vector3.zero)
        transform.rotation = Quaternion.
        Slerp(transform.rotation,
            Quaternion. LookRotation(direction),
            rotationSpeed * Time.deltaTime);
    }
}
```

Step 6: Play. Small flocks will form in the population. In the script, Random. Range is used to apply the rules about one in five game loops. This ensures that not all the birds have the rules that run each game loop. If this happens, the application runs very slowly and gets slower the more birds you have. Note that the average position is also only determined for neighboring birds, not the whole population. This is determined by the neighbourDistance variable. If you make this value larger, you will get one big flock.

Step 7: Currently, because the birds have random speeds, birds will eventually break away from their flocks because they cannot keep up or are going too fast. To keep them together, the second rule is applied. Birds in the flock match the average speed. To achieve this, modify the flock script to that in Listing 5.17.

Listing 5.17 Applying an average speed to a flock

```
void ApplyRules()
{
    ...
    foreach (GameObject go in gos)
    {
        if (go != this.gameObject)
        {
            dist = Vector3.Distance(go.transform.
                position, this.transform.position);
            if (dist <= neighbourDistance)
            {
                vcentre += go.transform.position;
```

295

```
                    groupSize++;
                    gSpeed = gSpeed + go.
                        GetComponent<Flock>().speed;
                }
            }
        }

        if (groupSize != 0)
        {
            vcentre = vcentre / groupSize;
            speed = gSpeed / groupSize;

            ...

        }
    }
```

Step 8: Play. Averaging of the speed will help keep the formed flocks together.

Step 9: Finally, adding the third rule will enable the birds to keep out of each other's way. Before changing the code, observe the current flocking movement. Once a bird is flying in a circular pattern within the flock, it stays with that pattern. Now change the flock script to that in Listing 5.18.

Listing 5.18 Adding avoiding behavior to flocking script

```
void ApplyRules()
    {
        ...

        foreach (GameObject go in gos)
        {
            if (go != this.gameObject)
            {
                dist = Vector3.Distance(go.transform.
                    position, this.transform.position);
                if (dist <= neighbourDistance)
                {
                    vcentre += go.transform.position;
                    groupSize++;
                    if(dist < 0.5)
                    {
                        vavoid = vavoid + (this.transform.
                            position - go.transform.
                            position);
                    }
                    gSpeed = gSpeed + go.
                        GetComponent<Flock>().speed;
                }
```

```
            }
        }

        if (groupSize != 0)
        {
            vcentre = vcentre / groupSize;
            speed = gSpeed / groupSize;
            Vector3 direction = (vcentre + vavoid) -
                transform.position;
            ...
        }
    }
}
```

Step 10: Play. Take a close look at the birds' behavior. You will notice that they now dart out of the way in a similar movement to what is observed in real flocking birds.

So far, the flocks created are reminiscent of crows or vultures circling in the sky around their next meal. This could be used for a dramatic effect in a game to point out the position of something sinister in the game environment. More often than not, flocks used for ambience tend to be traveling across the scene. To achieve this type of flocking, more rules can be added.
Step 11: To make the birds move across an endless sky, we can add a *wind* value. This is a vector indicating the direction of travel. Modify the flock script to that in Listing 5.19.

Listing 5.19 Directing flock to fly in a set direction

```
void ApplyRules()
    {
        ...
        Vector3 vavoid = Vector3.zero;
        float gSpeed = 0;
        Vector3 wind = new Vector3(1,0,1);
        float dist = 0;
        int groupSize = 0;

        ...

        if (groupSize != 0)
        {
            vcentre = vcentre / groupSize + wind;
            speed = gSpeed / groupSize;

            Vector3 direction = (vcentre + vavoid) -
                transform.position;
            ...
        }
    }
```

Step 12: Play. The added wind vector will cause the birds to fly along the same course. The birds will still flock together, but instead of circling they will form close-streamed groups.

Step 13: If you want the birds to fly across the screen to a particular location, a goal position can also be added to the rules. Modify the flock script to that in Listing 5.20.

Listing 5.20 Directing flock to fly to a specific location

```
//Flock.cs ---------
using System.Collections;
using System.Collections.Generic;
using UnityEngine;

public class Flock : MonoBehaviour {

    float speed = 0.001f;
    float rotationSpeed = 5.0f;
    Vector3 averageHeading;
    Vector3 averagePosition;

    float neighbourDistance = 2.0f;

    void Start()
    {
        speed = Random.Range(0.1f,1f);
    }

    void Update ()
    {
        if(Random.Range(0,5) < 1)
        ApplyRules();
        transform.Translate(0, 0, Time.deltaTime
            * speed);
    }

    void ApplyRules()
    {
        GameObject[] gos;
        gos = GameObject.FindGameObjectsWithTag("Seagull");

        Vector3 vcentre = Vector3.zero;
        Vector3 vavoid = Vector3.zero;
        float gSpeed = 0;

        Vector3 wind = new Vector3(1,0,1);
        Vector3 goalPos = globalFlock.goalPos;
```

```
        float dist = 0;

        int groupSize = 0;
        foreach (GameObject go in gos)
        {
            if(go != this.gameObject)
            {
                dist = Vector3.Distance(go.transform.
                    position, this.transform.position);
                if(dist <= neighbourDistance)
                {
                    vcentre += go.transform.position;
                    groupSize++;

                    if(dist < 0.5f)
                    {
                        vavoid = vavoid + (this.transform.
                            position - go.transform.
                            position);
                    }

                    gSpeed = gSpeed + go.
                        GetComponent<flock>().speed;
                }
            }
        }

        if(groupSize != 0)
        {
            vcentre = vcentre/groupSize + wind + (goalPos -
                this.transform.position);
            speed = gSpeed/groupSize;

            var direction = (vcentre + vavoid) - transform.
                position;
            if(direction != Vector3.zero)
            transform.rotation = Quaternion.
                Slerp(transform.rotation, Quaternion.
                LookRotation(direction), rotationSpeed
                * Time.deltaTime);

        }
    }
}

//globalFlock.cs -----------
using System.Collections;
using System.Collections.Generic;
using UnityEngine;
```

```
public class globalFlock: MonoBehaviour {

    public GameObject gull;

    static public Vector3 goalPos;

    void Start()
    {
        //create seagulls
        for(int i = 0; i < 100; i++)
        {
            Vector3 pos = new
            Vector3(Random.Range(-10,10),0,Random.
                Range(-10,10));
            Instantiate(gull, pos, Quaternion.identity);
        }

        goalPos = new Vector3(0,0,0);
    }

    void Update ()
    {
        if(Random.Range(0,10000) < 50)
        {
            goalPos = new
            Vector3(Random.Range(-1.0f,1.0f),0,
                Random.Range(-1.0f,1.0f));
        }

    }
}
```

Step 14: Play. The birds will form into groups flying toward a single goal location.

These flocking rules have been used in movies to create flocking characters. They were used in *Batman Returns* to create realistic swarms of bats and in *The Lion King* for a herd of wildebeest.

The rules can also be modified in games to develop intelligent group enemy behavior and optimize processing speeds. For example, in the workshop that introduced breadcrumb path finding, if there were hundreds of enemies, having them all process the breadcrumbs could prove computationally costly. Furthermore, if each one even had to run the A* algorithm, it could certainly slow down the performance. However, if just one *leader* followed the breadcrumbs, the rest could flock and follow that leader.

5.7 Decision Trees

Decision trees are hierarchical graphs that structure complex Boolean functions and use them to reason about situations. A decision tree is constructed from a set of properties that describe the situation being reasoned about. Each node in the tree represents a single Boolean decision along a path of decision that leads to the terminal or *leaf* nodes of the tree.

A decision tree is constructed from a list of previously made decisions. These could be from experts, other players, or AI game experience. They are used in *Black & White* to determine the behavior of the creature. For example, a decision tree based on how tasty the creature finds an object determines what it will eat. How tasty it finds an object is gathered from past experience where the creature was made to eat an object by the player.

To illustrate the creation of a decision tree for an NPC, we will examine some sample data on decisions made about eating certain items in the environment. The decision we want to make is a yes or no about eating given the characteristics or *attributes* about the eating situation. Table 5.2 displays some past eating examples.

Given the attributes of a situation (hungry, food, and taste), a decision tree can be built that reflects whether the food in question should be eaten. As you can see from the aforementioned data, it is not easy to construct a Boolean expression to make a decision about eating. For example, sometimes it does matter if the NPC is hungry and other times it does not; sometimes it matters if the food is tasty and sometimes it does not.

TABLE 5.2 Examples for Making an Eating Decision[a]

Example	Attributes			Eat?
	Hungry	**Food**	**Taste**	
1	Yes	Rock	0	No
2	Yes	Grass	0	Yes
3	Yes	Tree	2	Yes
4	Yes	Cow	2	Yes
5	No	Cow	2	Yes
6	No	Grass	2	Yes
7	No	Rock	1	No
8	No	Tree	0	No
9	Yes	Tree	0	Yes
10	Yes	Grass	1	Yes

[a] The values for the attribute taste are 0 for awful, 1 for okay, and 2 for tasty.

To construct a decision tree from some given data, each attribute must be examined to determine which one is the most influential. To do this, we examine which attributes split the final decision most evenly. Table 5.3 is a count of the influences of the given attributes.

To decide which attribute splits the eat decision, we look for examples where an attribute's value definitively determines if Eat is yes or no. In this case, when Food equals Rock, every instance of Eat is no. This means that we could confidently write a Boolean expression such as

```
if food = rock
then eat = no
```

without having to consider any of the other attributes. The total number of exclusive 0s counted in a column determines the attribute with the best split. By exclusive we mean that the value of the attribute must be 0 in one column and greater than 0 in another. If both columns were 0, then the value would have no effect at all over the decision. In the cases of Rock, Grass, and Cow, the final value for Eat is already known, and thus these values can be used to create instant leaf nodes off the root node as shown in Figure 5.21.

TABLE 5.3 Attribute Influence Over the Final Eating Decision

Attribute	Eat = Yes	Eat = No	Total Influences
Hungry			
Yes	5	1	
No	2	2	
Total Exclusive 0's	0	0	0
Food			
Rock	0	2	
Grass	3	0	
Tree	2	1	
Cow	2	0	
Total Exclusive 0's	1	2	3
Taste			
0	2	2	
1	1	1	
2	4	0	
Total Exclusive 0's	0	1	1

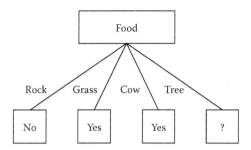

FIG 5.21 Partial decision tree for data from Table 5.3.

However, in the case of Tree, the decision is unclear, as sometimes Eat is yes and sometimes it is no.

To find the next best splitting attribute, outcome decisions involving the Tree value are combined with the remaining attributes to give the values shown in Table 5.4.

In this case, the second-best attribute is Hungry. Hungry can now be added to the decision tree under the Tree node to give the graph shown in Figure 5.22. Note that the yes and no choices for Hungry provide definitive answers for Eat, and therefore the nodes do not need to be classified further with any other attributes. The decision tree in Figure 5.22 is the complete decision tree for data from Table 5.2. You could say in this case that the taste of the food is irrelevant.

A famous algorithm used for creating decision trees from examples (and that was used in *Black & White*) is ID3, developed by computer scientist J. R. Quinlan in 1979.

TABLE 5.4 Attribute Influence Over the Final Eating Decision with Food = Tree

Attribute	Eat = Yes	Eat = No	Total Influences
Food = Tree and Hungry			
Yes	2	0	
No	0	1	
Total Exclusive 0's	1	1	2
Food = Tree and Taste			
0	1	1	
1	0	0	
2	1	0	
Total Exclusive 0's	0	1	1

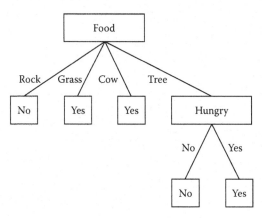

FIG 5.22 Complete decision tree for eating objects.

☺ Unity Hands On
Decision Trees

In this workshop, we create a very simple decision tree for an RTS AI game opponent that will decide on its strategy based on the map layout. The decision being made is about whether or not to give priority to mining for minerals and gas instead of building defenses or attacking the enemy. Based on the amounts of nearby minerals and gases, the ease of entry by which the enemy can access the base, and the overall distance to the enemy, a table with all combinations of the values for each decision variable (the attributes) is drawn up. Data for decision-making are shown in Table 5.5.

In this case, data are fictitious; however, they could be gathered from other human players or experience from previous games.

Step 1: Download *Chapter Five/DecisionTrees.zip* from the website and open the *decisionTree* scene in Unity. Play to see the decision tree constructed from data in Table 5.5. This tree is illustrated in Figure 5.23. Note that the full code for decision tree construction using the ID3 algorithm is contained in the Plugins > ID3.cs file in the Project. The original code can be found at http://codeproject.com/KB/recipes/id3. aspx. Data have been changed to reflect the values in Table 5.5. Although we are not focusing on C# in this book, the complexities of most AI algorithms lend themselves to being written in a more robust language than C#. The objective here is not to teach you C# but rather to point out parts of the code you could experiment with changing should you want to create your own decision tree.
Step 2: Open *ID3.cs* in the script editor. Scroll to the very bottom of the code to find the `createDataTable()` function.

TABLE 5.5 Data for RTS AI Build Decisions

	Number Mineral Resources Nearby	Number of Gas Resources	Easy Enemy Access to Base	Distance to Enemy	Give Priority to Mining
1	Low	High	No	Far	Yes
4	Low	High	Yes	Far	Yes
7	Low	Low	No	Far	No
10	Low	Low	Yes	Far	No
13	High	High	No	Far	Yes
16	High	High	Yes	Far	Yes
19	High	Low	No	Far	Yes
22	High	Low	Yes	Far	Yes
25	Low	High	No	Close	Yes
28	Low	High	Yes	Close	No
31	Low	Low	No	Close	No
34	Low	Low	Yes	Close	No
37	High	High	No	Close	Yes
40	High	High	Yes	Close	Yes
43	High	Low	No	Close	Yes
46	High	Low	Yes	Close	No

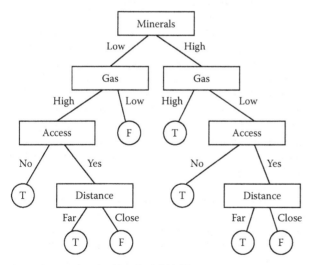

FIG 5.23 A tree graph produced from data in Table 5.5.

Unity demo output

Step 3: First the attributes are defined, and for each of these there is a set of values. Data are then laid out in a table. The name of each column is the attribute name followed by a final decision column, in this case named *strategy*. Following this, each row from the data is added to the table. If you want to create your own decision tree, you can add as many attribute columns as you wish by following the same coding format. Just ensure that there is an associated column for each item in the data. The last column, denoting a decision, is a Boolean value.

Decision trees provide a simple and compact representation of complex Boolean functions. Once constructed, a decision tree can also be decomposed into a set of rules. The beauty of the decision tree is that the Boolean functions are learned from a set of complex data that could take some time for a programmer to deconstruct manually into rules. In addition, a decision tree can be updated as the program runs to incorporate newly learned information that may enhance the NPC's behavior.

5.8 Fuzzy Logic

Fuzzy logic provides a way to make a decision based on vague, ambiguous, inaccurate, and incomplete information. For example, properties such as temperature, height, and speed are often described with terms such as *too hot*, *very tall*, or *really slow*, respectively. On a daily basis, we use these terms to make decisions with the unspoken agreement as to the interpretation of such vague statements. If you order a hot coffee, for example, you and the barista have an idea for a range of temperatures that are considered hot (for coffee).

Computers, however, understand only exact values. When you set the temperature in an oven to cook a pie, you give it an exact temperature—you cannot tell it you want the pie just *hot*. There is, however, a type of computational logic system that interprets vague terminology by managing the underlying exactness of the computer. It is called fuzzy logic. It is based on the concept that properties can be described on a sliding scale.

Fuzzy logic works by applying the theory of sets to describe the range of values that exist in vague terminologies. Classical set theory from mathematics provides a way of specifying whether some entity is a member of a set or not. For example, given the temperatures $a = 36$ and $b = 34$ and the set called *Hot*, which includes all numerical values greater than 35, we could say that *a* is a member of the set *Hot* and *b* is not.

Classical set theory draws lines between categories to produce distinct true and false answers; for example, *b* = *Hot* would equate to false. Fuzzy logic blurs the borderlines between sets (or makes them fuzzy!). Instead of a value being a member of a set, fuzzy set theory allows for a degree of membership.

To illustrate this, Figure 5.24 conceptualizes the difference between classical and fuzzy sets—the difference being that values in fuzzy sets overlap. In this example, the lower ranges of warm values are also members of the cold set. Values in fuzzy sets are given a *degree of membership* value that allows them to be partially in one set and partially in another. For example, the temperature value 34 could be 20% in the cold set and 80% in the warm set.

A fuzzy rule can be written as

```
if x is A
then y is B
```

where *x* and *y*, known as *linguistic variables*, represent the characteristics being measured (temperature, speed, height, etc.) and *A* and *B*, known as *linguistic values*, are the fuzzy categories (hot, fast, tall, etc.). A fuzzy rule can also include *AND* and *OR* statements similar to those in Boolean algebra. The following are examples of fuzzy rules:

```
if      temperature is hot
or      UV_index is high
then    sunburn is likely
if      temperature is warm
and     humidity is low
then    drying_time will be quick
```

Given a set of fuzzy rules and a number of inputs, an output value can be deduced using fuzzy inferencing. There are two common ways to inference based on fuzzy rules: Mamdani style and Sugeno style, both named after

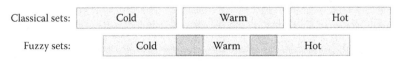

FIG 5.24 Classical sets have distinct boundaries. Fuzzy sets do not.

their creators. The Mamdani style is widely accepted for capturing human knowledge and uses a more intuitive form of expressing rules.

The Mamdani style consists of four steps: fuzzification, rule evaluation, aggregation, and defuzzification. Consider the following rules by which an NPC may operate:

Rule 1:	if	health is good
	and	shield is adequate
	then	mood is happy
Rule 2:	if	health is bad
	or	shield is moderate
	then	mood is indifferent
Rule 3:	if	health is bad
	and	shield is inadequate
	then	mood is angry

Fuzzification takes inputs in the form of discrete values for the NPC's health and shield strength and fuzzifies them. To fuzzify them, we simply pass them through the respective fuzzy sets and obtain their degrees of membership.

Rule evaluation involves substituting the degrees of membership into the rules given. For example, if the value for *health is good* was 17% and the value for *shield is adequate* was 25%, Rule 1 would become:

if 17% and 25% then mood is (17%) happy

Only the part of the rule in the *if statement* (shown in bold) has the fuzzy values substituted. If the values are connected by an AND, the smallest degree of membership is assigned to the *then* part. If the values are connected by an OR, the larger degree of membership is assigned. Assuming *health is bad* is 50% and *shield is moderate* is 25%, Rule 2 would become:

if 50% or 25% then mood is (50%) indifferent

These values are then used to *clip* the fuzzy sets for happy and indifferent pertaining to mood. In brief, 17% of the happy set and 50% of the indifferent set are merged to create a new fuzzy set as shown in Figure 5.25. This is the third step of Rule Aggregation.

The final step is defuzzification. This takes the final aggregated fuzzy set and converts it into a single value that will be the fuzzy output. The final fuzzy set contains the value; all that is needed is to extract it. The simplest method for doing this is called the *centroid* technique, which finds the mathematical center of gravity of the set. This involves multiplying all the values in the set

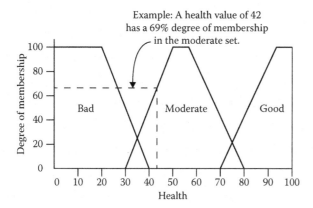

Example: A health value of 42 has a 69% degree of membership in the moderate set.

FIG 5.25 Merged fuzzy sets.

with their degree of membership, adding them together, and dividing by the sum of all the degrees of membership in the set. This gives a percentage value, in this case, pertaining to the *mood* value. For example, the result might be a 40% mood that would result in the mood being *indifferent*.

Developing a fuzzy logic engine requires a great deal of understanding in programming and mathematics. There is certainly not enough room in this chapter to provide a full example. Therefore, the next workshop uses an Open Source fuzzy logic engine called DotFuzzy written in C#.

◑ Unity Hands On
Fuzzy Logic

This hands-on session uses the DotFuzzy engine to create behavior rules for an NPC. The NPC's health and shield strength will be used to calculate its mood. Depending on its mood, it will decide to chase, attack, or ignore the player who is able to shoot at it.

Step 1: Download *Chapter Five/FuzzyLogic.zip* from the website and open the fuzzyAI scene. Play. You can walk around the scene and shoot spheres from the large gun being held by the player. In the middle of the environment, you will find a robot. This robot has similar code to that used in the Line of Sight workshop; however, it will not attack you. The robot's health and shield strengths are displayed on the screen. If you shoot at the robot with the left mouse button, its health and shield strength will go down. If you leave the robot alone, it will recover after some time.

The DotFuzzy engine has been loaded and is in the Project Plugins folder.
Step 2: Open the FuzzyBrain C# file with the script editor. The linguistic variables for the engine are defined at the top. Add the code as shown in Listing 5.21. Note, towards the bottom of the code are a number of rules containing IF, THEN, AND, and OR. The code between the double quotes should be entered as a single line without the line returns.

Listing 5.21 Implementing a fuzzy logic engine in Unity

(Includes C# code for all files necessary to make it work)

```csharp
//AI.cs
using System.Collections;
using System.Collections.Generic;
using UnityEngine;

public class AI : MonoBehaviour {

    public Transform target;      //the enemy
    float seeRange = 100.0f; //maximum attack distance ?
                                  //will attack if closer
                                  //than
                                  //this to the enemy
    float shootRange = 20.0f;
    float keepDistance = 20.0f;   //closest distance to
                                  //get to enemy
    float safeDistance = 200.0f;
    float rotationSpeed = 5.0f;
    float sightAngle = 30f;
    float speed = 0.01f;
    string state = "PATROL";

    void Start()
    {
        Patrol();
        this.GetComponent<Animation>()["shoot"].wrapMode =
            WrapMode.Loop;
        this.GetComponent<Animation>()["run"].wrapMode =
            WrapMode.Loop;
        this.GetComponent<Animation>()["idle"].wrapMode =
            WrapMode.Loop;
    }

    void Update ()
    {
        this.GetComponent<fuzzyBrain>().UpdateStatus();

        if(this.GetComponent<fuzzyBrain>().moodValue < 20)
        {
            state = "RUNAWAY";
            GetComponent<Animation>().CrossFade("run");
            speed = 0.20f;
            RunAway();
            return;
        }
```

```
    if (CanSeeTarget ())
    {
        if(this.GetComponent<fuzzyBrain>().moodValue <
            50)
        {
            state = "SHOOTING";
            GetComponent<Animation>().
                CrossFade("shoot");
            speed = 0.00f;
            Shoot();
        }
        else if (this. GetComponent<fuzzyBrain>().
            moodValue < 80)
        {
            state = "PURSUE";
            GetComponent<Animation>().CrossFade("run");
            speed = 0.08f;
            Pursue();
        }
    }
    else
    {
        state = "PATROL";
        if (!GetComponent<Animation>().
            IsPlaying("idle"))
        {
            GetComponent<Animation>().Play ("idle");
            speed = 0.00f;
        }
        Patrol();
    }

}

void Patrol ()
{
    //stand around
}

bool CanSeeTarget ()
{
    var directionToTarget = target.position -
        transform.position;
    if (Vector3.Distance(transform.position, target.
        position) > seeRange)
    return false;

    return true;
}
```

```
bool CanShoot()
{
    if (Vector3.Distance(transform.position, target.
        position) > shootRange)
    return false;

    return true;
}

void Pursue()
{
    var position = target.position;
    var direction = position - transform.position;
    direction.y = 0;

    // Rotate towards the target
        transform.rotation =
        Quaternion.Slerp(transform.rotation,
        Quaternion.LookRotation(direction),
        rotationSpeed * Time.deltaTime);

    transform.eulerAngles = new Vector3(0, transform.
        eulerAngles.y, 0);

    // Move the character
    if(direction.magnitude > keepDistance)
    {
        direction = direction.normalized * speed;
        transform.position += direction;
    }
    else
    {
        GetComponent<Animation>().Play ("idle");
        speed = 0.00f;
    }
}

void RunAway()
{
    var position = target.position;
    var direction = transform.position - position;
    direction.y = 0;

    // Rotate away from the target
        transform.rotation = Quaternion.Slerp
        (transform.rotation, Quaternion.
        LookRotation(direction), rotationSpeed * Time.
        deltaTime);
```

```
        transform.eulerAngles = new Vector3(0, transform.
            eulerAngles.y, 0);

        // Move away the character
        if(direction.magnitude < safeDistance)
        {
            direction = direction.normalized * speed;
            transform.position += direction;
        }
        else
        {
            GetComponent<Animation>().Play ("idle");
            speed = 0.00f;
        }
    }

    void Shoot()
    {
        var position = target.position;
        var direction = position - transform.position;
        direction.y = 0;

        // Rotate towards the target
        transform.rotation = Quaternion.Slerp(transform.
            rotation, Quaternion.LookRotation(direction),
            rotationSpeed * Time.deltaTime);
        transform.eulerAngles = new Vector3(0,
            transform.eulerAngles.y, 0);
    }
}

//FuzzyBrain.cs
using System.Collections;
using System.Collections.Generic;
using UnityEngine;
using DotFuzzy;

public class FuzzyBrain : MonoBehaviour {

    public float moodValue = 100;
    public GameObject explode;

    LinguisticVariable health;
    LinguisticVariable shield;
    LinguisticVariable mood;
    FuzzyEngine fuzzyEngine;
```

```
public int botHealth = 100;
public int botShield = 100;

int updateTime = 2; //seconds
int lastUpdate = 0;

void OnCollisionEnter(Collision obj)
{
    GameObject e = Instantiate(explode, this.
        transform.position,Quaternion.identity);
    Destroy(e.gameObject,2);
    Destroy(obj.collider.gameObject);
    botShield -= 10;
    botHealth -= (int) (10 + (100 - botShield)/5.0f);

    if(botHealth < 0) botHealth = 0;
    if(botShield < 0) botShield = 0;

    health.InputValue = botHealth;
    shield.InputValue = botShield;

    //set alpha color of shield relative to shield
        strength
    GameObject.Find("Shield").GetComponent<Renderer>().
        material.color = new
        Color(1,0,0,botShield/200.0f);

}

public void UpdateStatus()
{
    if(botHealth == 100 && botShield == 100) return;
        //don't bother updating
    if(botHealth > 100) botHealth = 100;
    if(botShield > 100) botShield = 100;

    if(Time.fixedTime > lastUpdate + updateTime)
    {
        if(botHealth < 100)
        botHealth += 5;
        if(botShield < 100)
        botShield += 10;

        GameObject.Find("Shield").
            GetComponent<Renderer>().material.color
            = new Color(1,0,0,botShield/200.0f);
```

```
            health.InputValue = botHealth;
            shield.InputValue = botShield;
            moodValue = (float) fuzzyEngine. Defuzzify();
            lastUpdate = (int) Time.fixedTime;
        }
    }

    void Start()
    {
        health = new LinguisticVariable("Health");
        health.MembershipFunctionCollection.Add
            (new MembershipFunction("Bad", 0, 0, 20, 40));
        health.MembershipFunctionCollection. Add
            (new MembershipFunction("Moderate", 30,
            50, 60, 80));
        health.MembershipFunctionCollection.Add(new
            MembershipFunction("Good", 70, 90, 100, 100));
        shield = new LinguisticVariable("Shield");
        shield.MembershipFunctionCollection.Add(new
            MembershipFunction("Low", 0, 0, 10, 50));
        shield.MembershipFunctionCollection.Add(new
            MembershipFunction("Medium", 20, 50, 60, 80));
        shield. MembershipFunctionCollection.Add(new
            MembershipFunction("High", 40, 80, 100, 100));
        mood = new LinguisticVariable("Mood");
        mood.MembershipFunctionCollection.Add(new
            MembershipFunction("Angry", 0, 0, 20, 40));
        mood.MembershipFunctionCollection.Add(new Membership
            Function("Indifferent", 30, 50,50, 80));
        mood.MembershipFunctionCollection.Add(new
            MembershipFunction("Happy", 60, 90, 100, 100));
        fuzzyEngine = new FuzzyEngine();
        fuzzyEngine.LinguisticVariableCollection.
            Add(health);
        fuzzyEngine.LinguisticVariableCollection.
            Add(shield);
        fuzzyEngine.LinguisticVariableCollection.
            Add(mood);
        fuzzyEngine.Consequent = "Mood";
        fuzzyEngine.FuzzyRuleCollection.Add(new
            FuzzyRule("IF (Health IS Good) AND (Shield IS
            High) THEN Mood IS Happy"));
        fuzzyEngine. FuzzyRuleCollection.
            Add(new FuzzyRule("IF (Health IS Bad) OR
            (Shield IS Low) THEN Mood IS Angry"));
```

```
        fuzzyEngine. FuzzyRuleCollection.
            Add(new FuzzyRule("IF (Health IS Moderate) AND
            (Shield IS High) THEN Mood IS Indifferent"));
        fuzzyEngine. FuzzyRuleCollection.Add(new
            FuzzyRule("IF (Health IS Moderate) OR (Shield
            IS Medium) THEN Mood IS Indifferent"));
        fuzzyEngine.FuzzyRuleCollection.Add(new
            FuzzyRule("IF (Health IS Bad)AND (Shield IS
            High) THEN Mood IS Indifferent"));
    }
}
//Ginterface.cs
using System.Collections;
using System.Collections.Generic;
using UnityEngine;

public class Ginterface : MonoBehaviour {

    public GUIStyle myStyle;

    void OnGUI()
    {
        GUI.Label(new Rect(10,10,800,50),"Health "+
        this.GetComponent<fuzzyBrain>().botHealth
            + "Shield "+ this. GetComponent<fuzzyBrain>().
            botShield, myStyle);
    }

    void Update () {
}
}
```

Step 3: Note in *FuzzyBrain.cs* how the fuzzy rules are written out in an English-type manner. This allows you to write out your own fuzzy rules to suit the purposes of your NPC. Using fuzzy rules creates NPCs that are less predictable, as not even the programmer can be sure what they will do under specific conditions.

Step 4: Play. When you shoot at the robot, it will ignore you until its health and shield strength become reasonably low. When it is almost dead, it will run away and wait for its strength to return. The robot model does not have a death animation, and therefore when its health and shield reach 0, they stay at zero. You will not be able to kill it.

This workshop has provided a brief overview of including fuzzy logic in a game environment. It demonstrates how to link the DotFuzzy engine into Unity. From this point, you will be able to create your own rules and define fuzzy behaviors for other NPCs.

5.9 Genetic Algorithms

Evolutionary computing examines intelligence through environmental adaptation and survival. It attempts to simulate the process of natural evolution by implementing concepts such as selection, reproduction, and mutation. In short, it endeavors to replicate the genetic process involved in biological evolution computationally.

Genetics, or the study of heredity, concentrates on the transmission of traits from parents to offspring. It not only examines how physical characteristics such as hair and eye color are passed to the next generation, but it also observes the transmission of behavioral traits such as temperament and intelligence. All cells in all living beings, with the exception of some viruses, store these traits in *chromosomes*. Chromosomes are strands of deoxyribonucleic acid (DNA) molecules present in the nuclei of the cells. A chromosome is divided up into a number of subparts called *genes*. Genes are encoded with specific traits such as hair color, height, and intellect. Each specific gene (such as that for blood type) is located in the same location on associated chromosomes in other beings of the same species. Small variations in a gene are called *alleles*. An allele will flavor a gene to create a slight variation of a specific characteristic. A gene that specifies the blood group A in different people may present as an allele for A+ and in another person as an allele for A−. Chromosomes come in pairs, and each cell in the human body contains 23 of these pairs (46 chromosomes total) with the exception of sperm and ova, which only contain half as much. The first 22 pairs of human chromosomes are the same for both males and females, and the 23rd pair determines a person's sex. At conception, when a sperm and ova meet, each containing half of its parent's chromosomes, a new organism is created. The meeting chromosomes merge to create new pairs. There are 8,388,608 possible combinations of the 23 pairs of chromosomes with 70,368,744,000,000 gene combinations.

Evolutionary computing simulates the combining of chromosomes through reproduction to produce offspring. Each gene in a digital chromosome represents a binary value or basic functional process. A population is created with anywhere between 100 and many thousands of individual organisms, where each individual is usually represented by a single chromosome. The number of genes in the organism will depend on its application. The population is put through its paces in a testing environment in which the organism must perform. At the end of the test, each organism is evaluated on how well it performed. The level of performance is measured by a fitness test. This test might be based on how fast the organism completed a certain task, how many weapons it has accumulated, or how many human players it has defeated in a game. The test can be whatever the programmer deems is the best judgment of a fit organism. Once the test is complete, the failures get killed off and the best organisms remain.

These organisms are then bred to create new organisms, which make up a new second-generation population. Once breeding is complete, first-generation organisms are discarded, and the new generation is put through its paces before being tested and bred. The process continues until an optimal population has been bred.

A chromosome in a genetic algorithm is represented by a string of numbers. Each chromosome is divided into a number of genes made up of one or more of the numbers. The numbers are usually binary; however, they need not be restricted to such.

> ◉ **Note**
> *Creating Genetic Algorithms*
> The steps involved in a genetic algorithm are:
>
> *Create a population and determine the fitness*
> A genetic algorithm begins by specifying the length of a chromosome and the size of the population. A 4-bit chromosome would look like 1100. Each individual in the population is given a random 4-bit sequence. The population is then allocated some task. How each individual performs determines their fitness. For example, if the task is to walk away from a starting location, then the individuals who walk the furthest are the fittest.
>
> *Mate the fittest individuals*
> The population is sorted according to fitness and the top proportions of the group are mated. This involves crossing their chromosomes to create new individuals. The process of crossover involves slicing the chromosomes and mixing and matching. For example, the parents with chromosomes 0011 and 1100 with their chromosomes sliced half way will produce offspring with chromosomes 0000 and 1111.
>
> In nature a rare event occurs in breeding called mutation. Here, an apparent random gene change occurs. This may lead to improved fitness or, unfortunately, a dramatically handicapped offspring. In evolutionary computing, mutation can reintroduce possibly advantageous gene sequences that may have been lost through population culling.

Introducing new randomly generated chromosomes into the population or taking new offspring and randomly flipping a gene or two can achieve mutation. For example, an individual with a chromosome 0101 could be mutated by flipping the third gene. This would result in 0111.

Introducing the new population

The final step is to introduce the new population to the task at hand. Before this occurs, the previous population is killed off. Once the new population's fitness has been determined, they are again sorted and mated.

The process is a cycle that continues creating and testing new populations until the fitness values converge at an optimal value. You can tell when this has occurred as there will be very little change in the fitness values from population to population.

An example of a working genetic algorithm can be found in the Unity project available from the website as a download from *Chapter Five/ GeneticAlgorithms.zip*. In this project, NPCs are programmed to navigate a maze based on genetic algorithms. Each generation has 60 seconds to explore as much of the maze as possible. The ones that explore the most are bred for the next generation.

Each NPC does not know what the maze looks like. It has only information on its current surrounding area. This information is coded into a binary sequence. From the NPC's location, what is to the left, front, and right of it are recorded. Take, for example, the layout in Figure 5.26. To the left is a wall, to the front is a wall, and to the right is free space. This is coded with a 1 for a wall and a 0 for a space. In this example, the code would be 110 (wall to left, wall in front, and space to right).

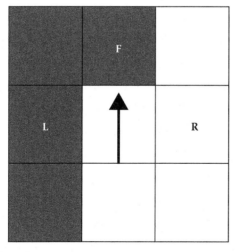

FIG 5.26 An example maze layout.

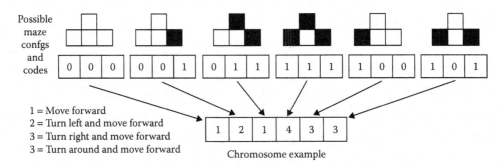

Possible maze configs and codes

1 = Move forward
2 = Turn left and move forward
3 = Turn right and move forward
3 = Turn around and move forward

Chromosome example

FIG 5.27 All possible maze configurations and an example of NPC DNA string.

The NPC has four actions available to it: move forward, turn left and move forward, turn right and move forward, and turn around and move forward. These are coded into the NPC's chromosome as 1, 2, 3, and 4 for each action, respectively.

Returning to the maze layout, at any position the NPC could be faced with one of six layouts. These are as follows:

1. [0,0,0], no walls
2. [0,0,1], a wall to the right
3. [0,1,1], walls to the front and right
4. [1,1,1], walls left, front, and right
5. [1,0,0], a wall to the left
6. [1,0,1], walls to the left and right

For each possible maze configuration, the NPC has an associated action. In this case, the NPC's DNA is six chromosomes long. An example is shown in Figure 5.27.

In Figure 5.28, if the NPC encounters a wall to the right only, its associated action is 2, meaning turn left and move forward. In the case of a wall to the front and right, the action tells the NPC to move forward. This is obviously a bad choice, but nonetheless, the NPC has nothing to go on but the actions provided in its DNA. The fewer times an NPC's DNA leads it into a wall, the farther it will get exploring the maze.

In the beginning, 100 NPCs are created each with random DNA setting. The NPCs are allowed to explore the maze. The ones that get the farthest will have DNA sequences that allow them to move farther. These are the ones kept for breeding. Now and then mutations are thrown in to create DNA sequences that may not occur from the natural selection process. Results from 10 generations of this program are shown in Figure 5.28. Feel free to download the code and play around with it for yourself.

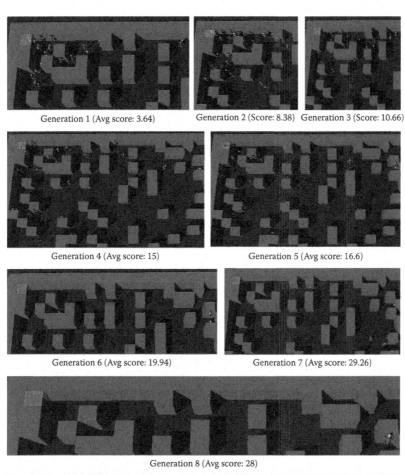

Generation 1 (Avg score: 3.64)   Generation 2 (Score: 8.38)   Generation 3 (Score: 10.66)

Generation 4 (Avg score: 15)   Generation 5 (Avg score: 16.6)

Generation 6 (Avg score: 19.94)   Generation 7 (Avg score: 29.26)

Generation 8 (Avg score: 28)

Generation 9 (Avg score: 27.25)

Generation 10 (Avg score: 28)

FIG 5.28   A maze exploring genetic algorithm over 100 generations.

5.10 Cellular Automata

Many strategy and simulation games are played out on a grid. The best example is *SimCity*. The AI running beneath *SimCity* is cellular automata. In short, cellular automata are a grid of cells with associated values, where each value is updated constantly by the value in neighboring cells. *SimCity* uses this mechanism to decide what happens in associated cells based on what the player is doing. For example, if the player puts a nuclear power plant in a particular location, any mansions in surrounding cells become worthless, and soon the occupants will move out. Cells between an apartment block and the bus stop will affect the distance the occupants must travel to work and also the occupancy rate. Such a simple AI mechanic can create some complex-looking relationships.

One of the most famous cellular automata is the *Game of Life* developed by the researcher John Conway in 1970. It is an infinite 2D grid of cells. Each cell can be in one of two states: dead or alive. The state of the cell is based on

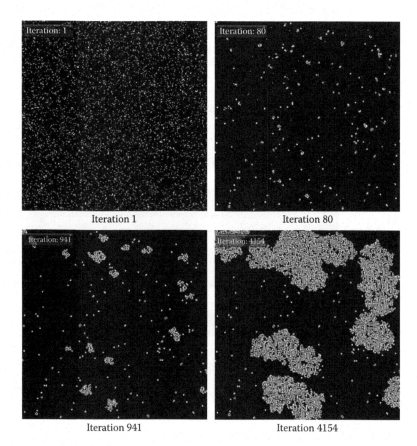

Iteration 1   Iteration 80

Iteration 941   Iteration 4154

FIG 5.29 The *Game of Life*.

the states of its closest eight neighbors. Each update, the status of the cell is calculated using four rules. These are as follows:

1. If the cell is alive but has less than two alive neighbors, it dies.
2. If the cell is alive and has two or three alive neighbors, it remains alive.
3. If the cell is alive but has more than three alive neighbors, it dies.
4. If the cell is dead but has exactly three alive neighbors, it becomes alive.

In the same way that the simple flocking rules create complex behaviors, so too does the *Game of Life*. An example run of the *Game of Life* is shown in Figure 5.29. The Unity project for this can be downloaded from *Chapter Five/ CellularAutomata.zip*.

5.11 Summary

This chapter has given a broad but brief introduction to some of the AI techniques used in games. There are numerous other AI techniques, such as neural networks and Bayesian networks, that have not been covered. Many of the topics are complex mathematically; if you require a deeper understanding of the domain, there are many good books available dedicated to the topic.

● On the Web
If you are interested in checking out some more uses of AI in games, I highly recommend these websites:

* http://aigamedev.com/
* http://www.aiwisdom.com/

I also have an online course dedicated to game character AI for which readers of this book can get a special discount with the coupon link:

* https://www.udemy.com/artificial-intelligence-in-unity/?
  couponCode=H3DGAMEDEVBOOK

For now, though, it is hoped that you have come to appreciate the beauty of AI in the examples contained in this chapter and opened up a new realm of possibilities for implementation of these mechanics in your own games.

CHAPTER 6

Player Mechanics

You have to learn the rules of the game. And then you have to play better than anyone else.

Albert Einstein

6.1 Introduction

We have already examined numerous ways for the player to interact with the game environment. One of the easiest methods is to let the physics engine do all the work for determining how the player's avatar collides and moves game objects. Before physics engines, this was probably one of the more difficult and laborious jobs in programming the player mechanics.

Players require feedback from the game in order to determine their status and progress. This could be in the form of a heads-up display (HUD) that informs them of their health, money, enemy location, and much more. One of the first classic HUDs that comes to mind is that from *Wolfenstein*. The bottom of the screen shows the player's health, the weapon they are carrying, the weapons they have in their possession, and a comical image of the player's face. The face changes from a determined *bring-it-on* expression through various phases until it becomes bloody and exhausted. The facial expression is synchronized with the player's health value, giving a visual representation to a numerical value.

A visual representation of the player's status is a common way to relay information from the game to the player. For example, hovering the mouse over a unit in *StarCraft* presents a small health bar from which the player can immediately determine the viability of the unit. Instead of giving the player a health value, the visual health bar gives an almost fuzzy representation of the unit's status. It can also change from green to red when the unit's health becomes critical.

The player's status bar can be as simple as a health bar or more complex such as the dials used in *Crysis* and *Halo*. These dials allow for more complex information to be relayed to the player than just a health value. For example, in both aforementioned games, the dials provide health and shield information. A nice addition to these advanced interfaces was introduced in the original *Splinter Cell*, with a meter showing how visible the player's avatar was in the environment based on its position in the shadows.

There are all sorts of numeric values stored in the game code for keeping track of the player's status. This chapter examines some of the ways of making these values accessible and user-friendly for the player.

6.2 Game Structure

It is common in software development to design flowcharts that outline the structure of software. Flowcharts can be created at many differing levels depending on the level of detail required. For example, one flowchart can show the menu and scene structure illustrating the menu items and where they go when a player selects them. At another level, a flowchart can specify how the player interacts with the environment and what happens to him when he performs different actions.

Flowcharts assist in the formalization of ideas about the game and help communicate these ideas among game development team members. If you are the sole developer, a flowchart can outline the game structure and support your design process, ensuring that all menu selections go somewhere and the player is able to get from each game screen to another. You would not want a player to enter a particular section of the game and then not have any way to get back!

Although there are all manner of standards used to create flowcharts, they are often made up of square and diamond shapes connected by arrows. The squares contain information or screen mockups, and the diamonds represent decisions that allow the program flow to change based on the player's choices. The arrows indicate the path the player will take to get from one screen to another. A flowchart can take any form that meets your needs (Figure 6.1).

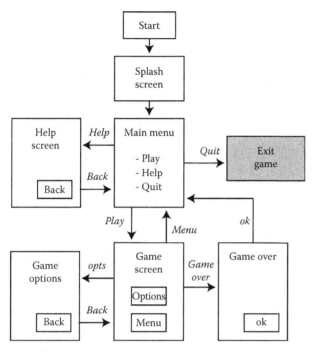

FIG 6.1 An example flowchart.

More often than not, once you have decided on the basic game and mocked up some prototypes, chances are you would not yet have created or thought about the main menu, splash screen, game over screen, and so on. This is when it is best to create a flowchart to ensure that you have thought about all the game elements and possible situations that could be encountered by the player.

◁ Unity Specifics
Graphical User Interface Objects
Unity has an extensive built-in set of graphical user interface (GUI) objects. You will have already experienced a number of them in previous workshops. They appear in the OnGUI() functions. These are the original way of creating a user interface and still come in handy if you want to quickly create some buttons or text boxes. This system—now called the Immediate Mode GUI (IMGUI)—is a useful set of tools, especially if you want to develop your own custom Inspector editors or windows inside the Unity Editor. For more information on this see: https://docs.unity3d. com/Manual/GUIScriptingGuide.html.

The newer UI system is more intuitive to use, as it is a drag and drop system supported by settable properties in the Inspector. We are about to cover some of these, but for more information see: https://docs. unity3d.com/Manual/UISystem.html.

⊙ **Unity Hands On**

Application Structure

In this workshop, you will learn how to turn a flowchart such as the one in the previous section into a skeleton for a game. Each box with menu options in the flowchart becomes a scene in Unity, and the scenes are linked to each other with buttons.

Step 1: Open Unity and create a new project.

Step 2: The first screen a player sees is the splash screen. This usually contains some artwork with the name of the game and/or your company logo. Unity takes care of this initial scene for you. All you need to do is supply the artwork as a single image file. If you are building for PC or Mac, Unity supplies the player with a dialog box for setting screen resolution and other preferences. For other platforms, the start-up will be different. For example, for the iOS and Android applications, the dialog box does not appear, just the splash screen. If you are using Unity Indie, your splash image is replaced with the Unity logo.

Step 3: Using Photoshop or a drawing package of your choosing, create a quick splash image. Make it 256 × 256 in size.

Step 4: Drag the image into the Project in Unity.

Step 5: Select File > Build Settings from the main menu.

Step 6: On the Build Settings window, click on the Player Settings button at the very bottom of the screen. These settings will appear in the Inspector as shown in Figure 6.2. In this part of the Inspector, you can also give your application an icon image.

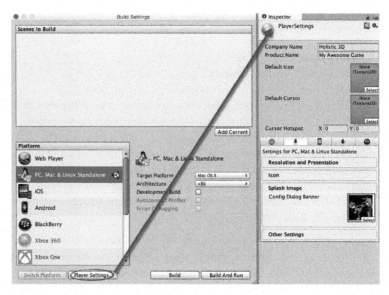

FIG 6.2 The Unity Build Settings and Player Settings.

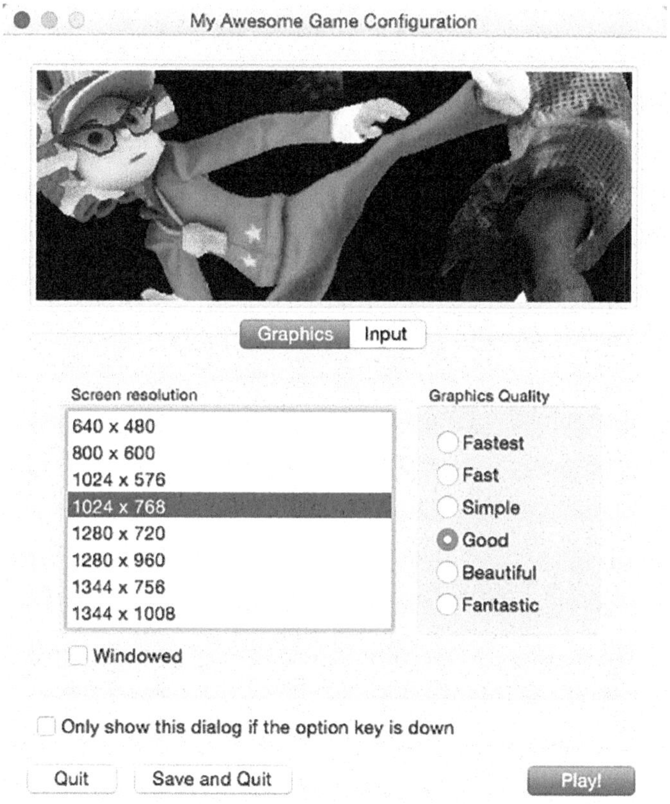

FIG 6.3 The default Unity game start-up dialog box.

Step 7: The Build Settings window also allows you to change the target platform; for now, we are building for Mac or PC. Click on Build and Run. Give the application a name and location when asked. When the application runs, you will see a dialog box with your splash image such as the one in Figure 6.3.

This dialog box can be turned off in the Player Settings of the Inspector under Resolution and Presentation > Display Resolution Dialog.

Step 8: You have already experienced the use of scenes in Unity, but you have not created your own and linked them yet. So, to begin, let us make the current scene the main menu. Although there is nothing in the scene, save it with File > Save Scene As and call it mainmenu. This scene name will appear in the Project.

Step 9: In the Hierarchy, create a new UI Canvas as demonstrated in Figure 6.4.

Step 10: The new canvas object is where a GUI is created using the tools available in Unity 4.6 onwards. These supersede the OnGUI() method, although it is still useful. To move into the design view for the canvas,

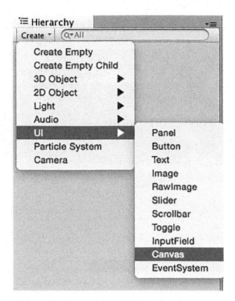

FIG 6.4 Creating a new 2D Canvas in the game to hold a GUI.

select it in the Hierarchy, click on the 2D view in the Scene, and with the mouse over the Scene window, press the F key. The outline of the canvas will show with blue dots in the corners, as shown in Figure 6.5. Setting the canvas's Render Mode to Screen Space—Overlay (as also shown in Figure 6.5) will ensure that the canvas resizes automatically to whatever the game screen size. This is extremely useful for mobile game development.

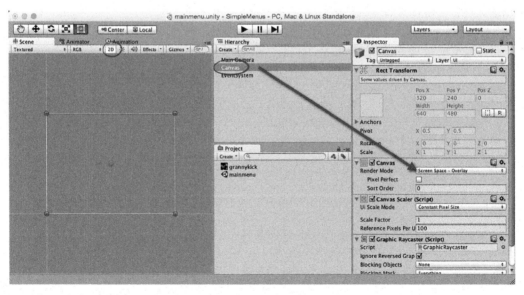

FIG 6.5 Viewing the Canvas in 2D.

Step 11: Right-click on the Canvas in the Hierarchy. From the drop-down list select UI > Text. A text element will be created and childed to the Canvas. All GUI items that display with the Canvas need to be children of it to ensure correct alignment.

Step 12: Change the properties for the new text item. Set the text to "Main Menu" and change the font size and color to your own liking. You can access the properties by selecting the Text object in the Hierarchy and working with the properties revealed in the Inspector.

Step 13: Next, add three buttons to the GUI using the same method. Right-click on Canvas and then UI > Button. Each button has an attached Text element. You can edit this to change the words written on the button. Name them Play, Help, and Quit.

Step 14: In the Scene, you are able to change the size of the buttons and other GUI items and move them around. For each, you will see an anchor diagram in the top left of their Inspector view. This allows you to anchor a GUI item in place. Then, when the screen size changes, the GUI item will adjust automatically. By default, GUI items are anchored to the center middle. However, if you wanted one to stay attached to the top right corner, you could set this by clicking on the anchor square and changing the settings. All GUI items are shown in Figure 6.6.

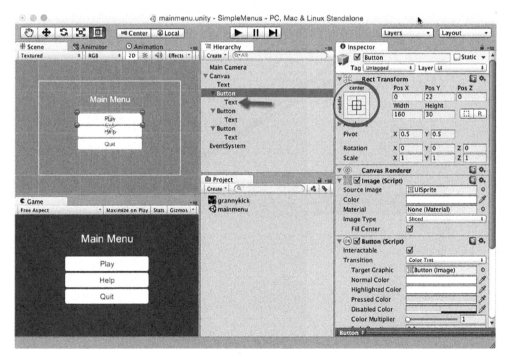

FIG 6.6 Creating GUI items on a Canvas.

Step 15: Before we can program the Play button to switch to another scene, the scene needs to be created. Save the current scene and then create a new one from the main menu with File > New Scene. For now, pretend this empty scene is your game. Put something in the scene such as a sphere so you will know when it had loaded from the previous menu screen.

Step 16: Save the scene and call it game. Now open up the build settings and add both scenes into the Scenes In Build box. You can do this by dragging and dropping each scene file from the Project into the Build Settings dialog as shown in Figure 6.7. The first scene in the list will be the opening scene for your game. It is therefore essential that this scene be the main menu. The order of the other scenes is inconsequential. Close the Build Settings window when you are done.

Step 17: Double-click on the mainmenu scene to return to your menu of buttons.

Step 18: Create a new C# file and name it MenuController. Add the code shown in Listing 6.1. Save the script and attach the file to the Main Camera in the Hierarchy. The GoToGame() method when run will load the game scene.

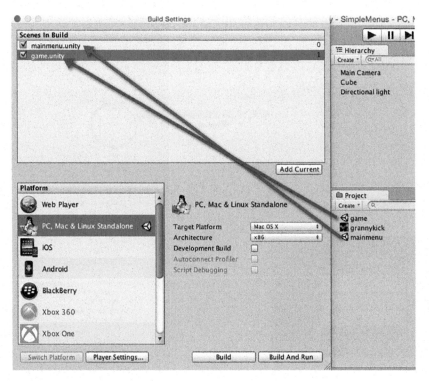

FIG 6.7 Adding Scenes to the Game Build.

Listing 6.1 Script to switch to another scene

```
using System.Collections;
using System.Collections.Generic;
using UnityEngine;
using UnityEngine.SceneManagement;

public class MenuController : MonoBehaviour {

    public void GoToGame()
    {
        SceneManager.LoadScene("game");
    }
}
```

Step 19: To connect the Play button in the menu to the GoToGame() function, select the Button with the Play text in the Hierarchy. In the Inspector view, there will be an area where you can setup OnClick() responses as shown in Figure 6.8.

Set the object of the OnClick() to the Main Camera and then find the attached script and its GoToGame() function in the drop-down box in the OnClick() section.

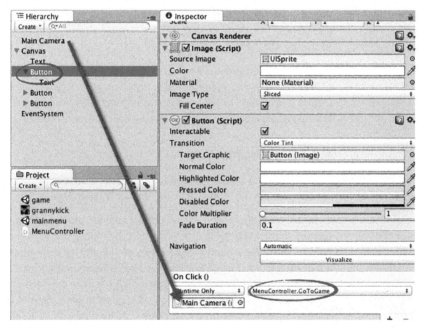

FIG 6.8 Linking a function in a script to a button.

Just above this section in the Inspector, you will see color options. These can be set to have the button change colors for when the mouse hovers or clicks on it.

Save and run. Clicking the Play button in the main menu will now take you to your game scene.

6.3 Principles of Game Interface Design

For the most part, HUDs are displayed as 2D screen overlays whether the game is 2D or 3D. Sometimes extra essential information is displayed directly on or near a character in the game environment. For example, in *Dead Space*, a third person space game, the player's health and air values are displayed as colored bars and circles directly on the avatar's space suit.

The best-designed HUDs are ones that show the most amount of information without cluttering the screen or distracting the player from the game itself. A great majority of HUDs are designed with critical information across the bottom of the screen, modeled after the original *Wolfenstein 3D* and *Doom* HUDs. Extra information such as a radar appears on the left-hand side.

So where do you start when designing an interface? How do those people who design good game interfaces know how to do it? It is the same as for animation. As there are principles of animation, so too are there principles for interface design. The research domain known as *graphical user-interface design* has, for as many years as there have been computer screens, endeavored to analyze the interactions between human and computer and to classify and categorize best practices.

Sections 6.3.1 through 6.3.9 build on an examination of the principles of user interface design presented at http://en.wikibooks.org/wiki/GUI_Design_Principles. For our purposes, this general list relating to all software applications is reworked to focus on best practice for computer games.

6.3.1 User Profiling

Before designing a HUD, you need to know for whom you are designing. You should consider the player's existing skills and experience, goals, and needs.

If you are creating a serious game, chances are the players will be non-gamers. In this case, the interface needs to be ultra-intuitive to the point of holding the player's hand through every step in the initial game play. If you are developing an Xbox game that is a sequel to an existing franchise—*Assassin's Creed VII*, for example—you would keep the interface similar to the other versions, as you might expect a great deal of the players to be hard-core gamers who have grown up playing the previous six versions.

The objective of the game will also be central to your design considerations. The player's goals and needs should be clearly visible. For example, in *The Sims*, the character's needs, such as sleep and food, are clearly displayed in the bottom center of the screen, as ensuring that these needs are satisfied is the main objective of the game. If the player is on a mission, these mission objectives need to be visible in addition to how close the player is to achieving them.

For example, in *Majesty 2*, a role-playing game in which the player is the ruler of the land, a single mission is split into subgoals displayed as a list in the bottom left corner of the screen. As these goals are achieved, the subgoals are visibly checked off.

6.3.2 Metaphor

As we have already established, the human brain loves to work with patterns. Metaphors are the perfect example of how we love to liken one thing to another and how we make sense of new imagery from our experiences. The perfect example of this with respect to game mechanics and interfaces is the *play button* first appearing on original analogue sound-playing devices. The little triangle with its right-facing apex is a universally understood icon—so much so that it is used in games to indicate *play* with the meaning of either starting the game or, if in the game, unpausing it to make the game time run forward. Play and its counterparts (stop, pause, rewind, and fast forward) appear in all manner of games from *Project Gotham* to *SimCity*, and *The Sims*. This recognition of well-known icons extends to other imagery in your interface. For example, a small floppy disk is often used to represent *Save* (although nowadays younger players will not have even seen a real one).

Two popular metaphors that have arisen purely within the game domain are the *space bar* for jump and holding down the *shift key* to run. Although they are not visual metaphors, they are still part of the user interface and clearly illustrate how metaphors can be leveraged. Any seasoned desktop computing gamer will expect that these exist in any new first-person shooter (FPS) game without even reading the manual.

Metaphors also extend to any menu systems in the game. Because the Mac OS and Windows 3.1 moved to the menu strip across the top of applications, all desktop users, even gamers, expect to find *save* and *open* functionality under the *File* menu option.

Colors are also metaphoric. The use of the correct color immediately conveys messages to the player without words or other imagery: for example, red represents something bad, such as an error, low health, or danger; yellow represents a warning or caution that is needed; and green is good. Although the interpretation of some colors is culturally dependent, these three colors are consistent globally—thanks to the UNESCO Vienna Convention on Road Signs and Signals that defines the traffic light colors worldwide.

Your use of color in a game interface can represent the state of a player, object, or character. It also assists in the differentiation of game elements; for example, enemy characters may have different colored uniforms. Color-coding will also group items, making it easier for the player to distinguish among them. An obvious example of this is *Bejeweled* in which the player must match jewels. The jewels not only have the same shape but also have the same color.

Although designing an extremely new and unique interface may seem appealing, if you do not stick with well-used and well-known metaphors, you will just end up frustrating the player. The interface is not something you want to have get in the players' way and stop them from your ultimate objective—having them play the game! Navigating the interface should not be the game.

6.3.3 Feature Exposure

Unless you are developing a very simple game, displaying all player options, statuses, and inventory items on the screen at the same time is impossible. However, such information and commands should not be buried to the point that it becomes frustrating to find. Remember, the interface is not the game.

Another common metaphor linked to feature exposure is the *ESC key*. Many FPS games have this linked to the display of the main menu, making feature exposure one key press away.

In games that have toolbars that are commonly used, they always appear on the screen such as in *StarCraft*, *SimCity*, *Civilization*, and the majority of other city building or strategy/simulation games where the player must access the toolbar constantly. However, sometimes not all features can be exposed at the top toolbar level, as there may be too many and the interface would be overcomplicated. In this case, the toolbar is given a hierarchical structure in which, if one option is clicked, it opens up a second lot of options. For example, in *StarCraft*, selecting the build option for a space construction vehicle opens up a submenu for categories of buildings, being normal or advanced, and these provide a further submenu of the exact buildings that are available.

How you decide to expose information and options to the player should be based on what the player needs to know and do, followed by various depths of what the player may want to know and do. What the player needs to know and do will be directly related to the objectives of the game. For example, the primary objective in all FPS games is *not to die*, and therefore you will always find a health indicator present on the screen.

The following game interface elements should be considered for exposure depth:

> Primary player data, including health, money, armor level, current remaining ammunition, and current weapon, should always appear on the screen.

Primary player actions, including building, moving units, pickup item, drop item, and swap guns, should always appear on the screen.

The toolbar (if any) should always appear on the screen. It may have a rollout feature that extends it into a bigger toolbar.

The main menu should be one click, key press, or button press away. In some cases, it can appear inconspicuously across the top of the game window as a fully exposed feature.

Submenu items should be one click, key press, or button press away from their associated main menu item.

Dialog boxes are only for displaying or gathering information as it becomes available or is required. They involve textual exchange with the player and are best kept hidden until required.

The help screen should be accessible directly from the main screen via the use of a metaphoric button with a "?" or one click away from the main menu.

6.3.4 Coherence

Elements of your interface design should fit together both functionally and visually. For example, submenu colors and fonts should fit with the main menu colors and fonts. In addition, the game interface should match the functionality of the platform for which it has been built. For example, Xbox *Kinect* games all allow the players to stand up straight with their left arm out at 45° to call up the main menu.

Artwork, borders, colors and fonts of toolbars, menus, buttons, and other interface items should follow a common theme. For example, *The Sims* interface is instantly recognizable by its blue-on-blue color theme with round-edged windows.

Functionality should be coherent, in that the same commands in different areas of the game perform the same actions. If you can click an X in the top right of a window to close it, all windows should allow for it. Any buttons that do the same thing should be named the same. For example, another metaphoric example in interfaces is the "Ok" button. If you are using an "Ok" button, do not change the capitalization on some occurrences such that it is "Ok" in one window and "OK" in another and do not change it to be "Yes" somewhere else.

An example of bad coherence in game interface design is exposed by Marcus Andrews in his Gamasutra article *Game UI Discoveries: What Players Want* (http://gamasutra.com/view/feature/4286/game_ui_discoveries_ what_players_php). *Far Cry 2* has a very elegant and embedded interface. Player status and information are built into displays in the 3D environment. For example, a radar system is built into the player's weapon, the player's hand can be revealed holding a compass, and bullets can be dug out of the player's arm as he recovers (all in 3D). Where the coherence fails is in the 2D messages that appear on the screen to give player status updates.

While the 3D part of *Far Cry 2* nicely immerses players into the 3D environment where, for a while, they are brought back to the reality that they are looking through a 2D screen, it is not practical for all elements.

While we are on the subject of 2D versus 3D, it has been cool in the past to create 3D menus. In reality, these just do not add anything. They become difficult to read and skew any images placed on the surface.

6.3.5 State Visualization

For players, being able to see their status clearly is paramount, which is why player health for FPS games is the largest item shown in the screen, money is always visible in RTS, and the player's position and lap times are highlighted on the screen in racing games.

In addition to primary information, the interface should act like other software interfaces in that it shows players their current choice. For example, if they have selected a particular building in an RTS, its information is shown somewhere on the screen, including its name, units it can produce, its health, and other functions. In addition, the selected item is accompanied by a highlighted square around it or it changes color to indicate that it is currently selected.

For functionality that is in the game, but not necessarily available at the time, grayed out images or buttons should be used. These can be accompanied by a comment about why they are grayed out to assist the player. For example, in *EVE Online*, players may not be able to buy a particular ship because they do not have the training to fly it. In such a case, ways to acquire the relevant training are given to the player.

6.3.6 Shortcuts

Learning keyboard shortcuts is synonymous with learning what the buttons on a game controller control. These shortcuts allow players to get to regularly used functionality or to information embedded in the menu system or toolbar and usually require some clicking action to achieve. Players will use shortcuts to perform game actions more quickly.

In regular software applications, shortcut keystrokes reflect their name and location in the menu system; for example, in Windows, ALT + F opens the File menu and CTRL + S saves the current document.

If possible, shortcuts should meet with any metaphors already in the space: for example, ESC for the main menu.

6.3.7 Layout

The display of the player interface on the screen should follow graphic design principles. This assists the player develop a spatial sense of the layout, which enhances his performance. Things to consider in your design include the presentation of key information in prominent locations, using sizing and contrast to distinguish elements, grouping related actions and data, and using fixed locations for certain types of information and actions. In addition, the layout should be well organized. Graphic designers use a grid system of evenly spaced horizontal and vertical lines to group and align related components.

This key principle is known as CRAP (contrast, repetition, alignment, and proximity). Contrast makes some elements more dominant than others and more important items that are easier to find on the screen. Repetition refers to the repeated use of design elements, such as using the same font, sizing, and colors. This creates unity and consistency, making the interface appear whole. Alignment connects the elements and creates a visual flow for the eye to follow. Proximity refers to grouping similar and related elements of the interface in the same place on the screen.

Furthermore, to add with alignment, the screen is ruled into equal-sized parts with smaller gutters dividing each area. How many sections you need on the screen is entirely up to you. If the smallest area holds your smallest screen object, then larger objects can span multiple areas.

An example screen layout illustrating the CRAP rule with ruled sections is shown in Figure 6.9. Contrast is achieved through the use of a white and gray color scheme. It is sometimes difficult in FPS environments to display information on the screen without a background color, as the text can get lost in the 3D scene behind it. In this case, a partially transparent gray is used to define the edge of the HUD and also give more definition to the white text. Never use black text on a HUD without a background, as it is almost impossible to see. Buttons and textboxes also have contrast between the fill color and the outline. In addition, contrast is used in the weapon selection area to distinguish between the current weapon and other weapon choices. Repetition occurs in the reuse of the same font for all the text, the same color for items, the shape of items, and the graphical bar used to represent the health and armor strength. Alignment is achieved through the use of ruled lines. These lines make it clear where things are placed on the screen, taking away any guesswork. The text and input boxes on the Options window are also aligned. Textboxes should all be the same size and text labels left aligned to meet the box. In other designs, you may find the text label above the box. Finally, proximity is achieved by grouping related elements. Information important to the player—that being their health and armor strength—is positioned together with weapon selection nearby.

FIG 6.9 An example HUD for an FPS.

6.3.8 Focus

The HUD displays the player status and other information, but should also draw the eye to any critical changes made to the interface. Color changes and animations work best for attracting the player's attention. The interface in Figure 6.9 uses global colors for danger, caution, and good to represent the player's health and armor strength. In addition, red is used to display spent ammunition cartridges. As the player's health becomes critical, the health value or bar could blink on and off to further attract the attention of the player.

A blatant way to attract the player's attention is to present a pop-up window, which stops him from playing. A well-known example of this is the Xbox's "Saving. Do not turn off your console" warning.

6.3.9 Help

It goes without saying that a game should present the user with help on how to play. In her book *The Art of Human Computer Interface Design*, Brenda Laurel lists five basic help needs an interface should be able to provide the user: goal oriented, descriptive, procedural, interpretive, and navigational.

⬤ **Note**

Addressing Player Needs

With respect to a game, you should attempt to fulfill these needs (in order) translate to the following player questions:

1. What is the goal of this game? What is my immediate goal? What should I be doing right now?
   The goal of the game should be immediately clear from the beginning. Most games provide a backstory video clip while others have tutorial levels that step the player through the game. For example, Halo provides a video scene explaining some of the game goals up to the point when Master Chief is first thrown from the helicopter, whereas SimCity holds the player's hand through a step-by-step tutorial.

2. What are these options and what do they do?
   Not all icons you use in the HUD will be metaphor related and therefore the player may not know what will happen if they click on certain buttons in a toolbar. To assist the player, most games, especially RTS that have numerous toolbars and even layered toolbars, include mouse-over tooltips. They don't appear straight away, but are timed for when the player hovers too long over a button or some element of the game environment.

Some tutorials ease players into options by making them available one at a time after each is explained and used. In other games, making new options and game actions available is part of the game. In *Alice Greenfingers*, a market gardening game, the player starts out only being able to dig, plant seeds, water, and pick the crop. As the player gains more experience, they are given more types of seeds to plant and different farming implements to use. Each time one is introduced, it is explained.

3. How do I perform certain actions in the game?
   Answering this with your interface requires some intuition and mind reading on the part of your game. If it is a very complex environment, it could be impossible to know what the player wants to achieve. In a puzzle game however, where there are limited options on what the player's next move will be, by monitoring the player's progress, the game can provide hints on the next best move. In the iPad game *Fishdom*, the player can raise money to put fish in a virtual aquarium by playing a *Bejeweled* type puzzle game. When the player stops interacting with the puzzle game, after a short period, they are presented with the next best move.

4. Why did that happen?

The feedback mechanisms within the game environment should always endeavor to explain anything that has occurred in the game environment. This can occur passively—for example, if a player steps on a mine and gets blown up resulting in their health value going down, it is obvious what happened. On the other hand, if the player's status changes without any environmental feedback or visual clues, more active explanations are required. For example, in the RTS kingdom building game, *Stronghold*, the player's economic status is linked to the population of the kingdom. If people leave the kingdom, something not necessarily observed by the player, they start to lose money. As villages start to leave, the game displays information on the screen informing the player their population is dropping and they need to act fast to increase it again. The game also gives hints on how this might be achieved.

SimCity also does this through the team of virtual mayoral advisers. On first starting a city, Mr. Neil Fairbanks pops up asking the player if they want some help. Later in the game, as pollution or power become issues, other advisers come along to help. Rather than anticipating what the player is trying to do, they give advice on the state of the player's city.

5. Where am I?

This question needs to be answered on two levels. First, the player might be lost in the game environment itself or they might be lost in the toolbar or menu system. To address the first, mini-maps, compasses, or zooming in and out capability can be added to the game to assist the player to navigate. Sometimes the actual navigation can be the goal of the game, in which case, this type of help should not be supplied.

For the latter, menu and toolbar navigational aids are rare in games. Unlike software such as Microsoft Word or Adobe Photoshop, where the help search will provide a set of instructions and illustrations as to where to locate certain commands and actions, games do not tend to do this. At least, not in the game environment itself. This type of information is usually supplied in the paper manual accompanying the physical purchase of the game or in digital format online. While this type of information is not part of the HUD or game interface, it is indeed something that should be considered as ancillary information to accompany your game.

6.4 Inventories

Inventories are a game mechanic that span numerous game genres. Basically, they are a list of items that players have in their possession. In *The Sims*, each Sim has an inventory of items such as books, food, and other objects they can take with them to different locations. If a Sim is required to deliver a parcel, it is added to their inventory. When they arrive at the parcel's destination, it is removed. In *Splinter Cell*, the player's character Sam Fisher carries quite an arsenal around with him.

Inventories can be a fixed size, allowing only a finite number of items or infinite items. In the *Dungeons & Dragons* classic title *Eye of the Beholder*, characters could carry only several items. In order to take on another item, the player had to decide which item to discard to make way for the new one. This inventory size restriction adds a new mechanic all of its own, where players must prefer the items they have. In *Doom*, the player can have up to six weapons (each switchable with the keys 2–7 on the keyboard), whereas in *Halo*, if Master Chief picks up a weapon, the current weapon is thrown away (with the exception that sometimes he can brandish a gun in each hand).

One example of a very complex inventory is the one that players have in *EVE Online*. Players can have many ships, minerals, ship parts, and blueprints in their possession—and these all are not in the same location. Minerals and parts can be on ships and ships can be docked on different planets. It is quite a feat of logistics to manage the location of items and ships to facilitate the most efficient game play.

In the following workshop, you will create a *Doom*-like scenario with a user interface and fixed-size inventory in which the player collects colored keys to open doors of the same color.

⊙ Unity Hands On
A Pickup Inventory System
In this hands-on exercise, you will create a simple inventory system that keeps track of items picked up by a character. The focal object for managing inventories is an array data structure coded to manage the items.

Step 1: Download and open *Chapter Six/Inventory.zip*. Open the file in Unity and open the scene called moonwalking. Play. Astrodude (a Unity character) is standing in the middle of a moonscape and you can control him with the arrow keys.

Step 2: In the Prefab folder inside Project, you will find a series of prefabs of different cartoon food types. Take these prefabs and scatter them around the terrain where Astrodude will be able to pick them up. Be sure to add multiples of the same type.

Step 3: We will now add a GUI to the screen that will display the items as they are picked up. In the Hierarchy, create a Panel (Create > UI > Panel).

A panel covering the entire screen will be created, and you will notice in the Hierarchy that it has been automatically parented to a Canvas.
Step 4: Switch the Scene to 2D view and then focus on the Panel by having it selected in the Hierarchy and with the mouse over the Scene press the F key. To begin, the Panel will be as big as the Canvas. Drag it to a smaller size and then set its anchor point to the center bottom of the Canvas as shown in Figure 6.10.

This panel will be the holder of the inventory display. Each time Astrodude picks up an item and icon representing that object will be added to the panel.
Step 5: Next, with the Panel selected in the Hierarchy, add a Grid Layout Group to the Panel using the Add Component button (Layout > Grid Layout Group). This will cause the panel to automatically arrange children display objects in a grid arrangement. Set the Child Alignment on the Grid Layout Group to Middle Center, the Cell Size to 25 × 25, and the Spacing to 10 × 10. The Cell Size will be the pixel dimensions of each icon in the inventory. You might like to adjust this and make it bigger if you find that the icons are too small for your liking.

The cell size will dictate the size of the child objects, and the alignment will start images accumulating in the panel from the center.
Step 6: Right-click on the Panel in the Hierarchy and add a UI > Image. A white image 25 × 25 (the size taken from the Grid Layout) will appear

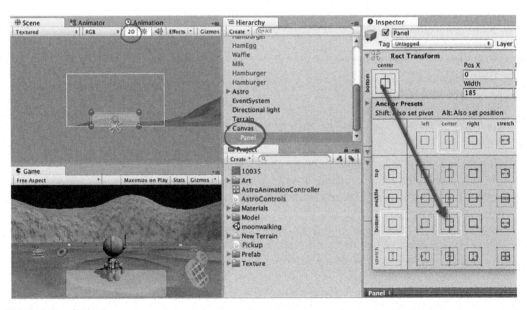

FIG 6.10 Adding a Panel to the screen.

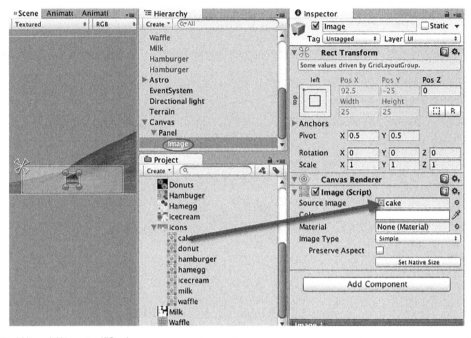

FIG 6.11 Adding a child image to a UI Panel.

in the panel situation in the center. Set this image's Source Image to the cake icon in the Project, as shown in Figure 6.11. Change the name of the image to CakeImage.

Notice how the image is automatically centered on the panel.
Step 7: With the CakeImage selected, press CTRL+D (Windows) or CMD+D (Mac) to create a duplicate image. Notice how the Panel automatically makes room for the new image. Rename this duplicate image to DonutImage and change its source to the Donut sprite.
Step 8: Repeat the previous step until you have an image in the panel for each of the food items that Astrodude will be able to pick up. When you add the sixth one, it will not fit, and the panel will relocate it beneath the rest.

Once all the images have been added (seven in total), you can click on the Panel in the Hierarchy and then in the Scene adjust its size so that the seven images fit nicely within as shown in Figure 6.12.
Step 9: So we can create these icons on the fly each time Astrodude walks over an item, the images need to be made into prefabs. One by one, drag CakeImage, DonutImage, and the rest into the Project until you have seven prefabs. Then delete the originals from the Panel in the Hierarchy.
Step 10: Now, we need a script to control the picking up of items and placing them into the inventory. Create a new C# file called Pickup and add the code shown in Listing 6.2.

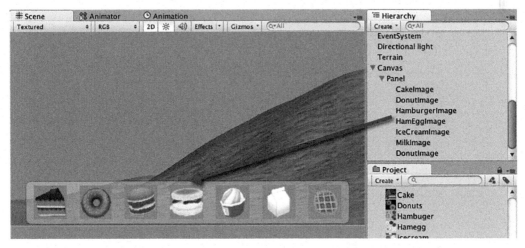

FIG 6.12 All possible inventory images displayed in the panel.

Listing 6.2 Picking up a collided with object

```
using System.Collections;
using System.Collections.Generic;
using UnityEngine;

public class Pickup : MonoBehaviour {

    public GameObject inventoryPanel;
    public GameObject[] inventoryIcons;

    private int count = 0;

    void OnCollisionEnter(Collision collision)
    {
        if(count >= 7) return;

        GameObject i;
        if(collision.gameObject.tag == "cake")
        {
            i = Instantiate(inventoryIcons[0]);
            i.transform.SetParent(inventoryPanel.
                transform);
            count++;
            Destroy(collision.gameObject);
        }
        else if(collision.gameObject.tag == "donut")
        {
            i = Instantiate(inventoryIcons[1]);
```

```
            i.transform.SetParent(inventoryPanel.transform);
            count++;
            Destroy(collision.gameObject);
        }
        else if(collision.gameObject.tag == "hamburger")
        {
            i = Instantiate(inventoryIcons[2]);
            i.transform.SetParent(inventoryPanel.transform);
            count++;
            Destroy(collision.gameObject);
        }
        else if(collision.gameObject.tag == "hamegg")
        {
            i = Instantiate(inventoryIcons[3]);
            i.transform.SetParent(inventoryPanel.
                transform);
            count++;
            Destroy(collision.gameObject);
        }
         else if(collision.gameObject.tag == "icecream")
         {
            i = Instantiate(inventoryIcons[4]);
            i.transform.SetParent(inventoryPanel.
                transform);
            count++;
            Destroy(collision.gameObject);
        }
        else if(collision.gameObject.tag == "milk")
        {
            i = Instantiate(inventoryIcons[5]);
            i.transform.SetParent(inventoryPanel.
                transform);
            count++;
            Destroy(collision.gameObject);
        }
        else if(collision.gameObject.tag == "waffle")
        {
            i = Instantiate(inventoryIcons[6]);
            i.transform.SetParent(inventoryPanel.
                transform);
            count++;
            Destroy(collision.gameObject);
        }
    }

}
```

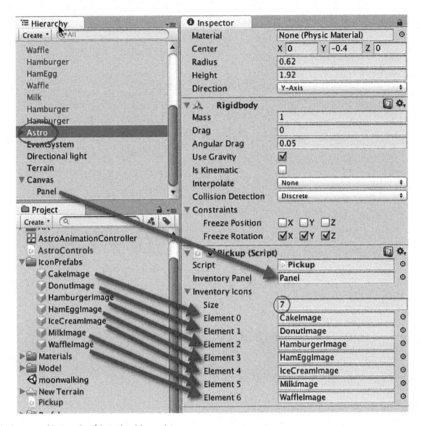

FIG 6.13 Assigning game objects and prefabs to the pickup script.

Attach this code to Astrodude. Select Astrodude in the Hierarchy and locate the attached script in the Inspector. Set the Inventory Panel variable to the Panel object in the Hierarchy and the Inventory Icons to the prefab images you previously made as shown in Figure 6.13. The order does matter, as the code uses the order to determine which icon to show.

Once you have added all the necessary components to the script, play. Take Astrodude for a walk and pick up some items. Once you hit seven, the code will prevent Astrodude picking anything else up.

Step 11: To remove items from the Inventory, we will set up a method for clicking on the icon to destroy it. First create a new C# file called DestroyOnClick. Add the code from Listing 6.3.

Listing 6.3 A destroy function to be called from button presses

```
using System.Collections;
using System.Collections.Generic;
using UnityEngine;
```

```
public class DestroyOnClick : MonoBehaviour {

    public void DestroyMeNow()
    {
        Destroy(this.gameObject);
    }
}
```

Save the script and attach a copy of it to all of the image prefabs created earlier.

Step 12: Working through each of the image prefabs, one-by-one, add a new button component to each. This can be done by clicking on Add Component > UI > Button.

Step 13: For each image prefab, set the button's OnClick() to the DestroyOnClick.destroyMeNow() function, making sure that you use the script attached to that particular object as shown in Figure 6.14.

Play. You will be able to remove items from the inventory by clicking on them.

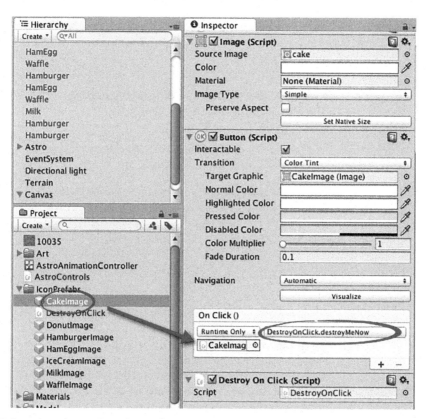

FIG 6.14 Assigning a script to a button to destroy the same object.

Or so it will seem. The items will disappear from the panel but the value of count in the pickup script will remain at seven.

Step 14: To decrease the count of inventory items when an item is removed, changes in both the pickup and DestroyOnClick scripts should be made as shown in Listing 6.4 and 6.5, respectively.

Listing 6.4 Making the inventory counter into a global static in Pickup.cs

```
public class Pickup : MonoBehaviour {

    public GameObject inventoryPanel;
    public GameObject[] inventoryIcons;

    private int count = 0;

    public void DropItem(string itemtag)
    {
        count--;
    }

    void OnCollisionEnter(Collision collision)
    }
...
```

Listing 6.5 Destroying an item and decreasing the global counter in DestroyOnClick.cs

```
...
public class DestroyOnClick : MonoBehaviour {
    public void DestroyMeNow()
    {
        GameObjectastro = GameObject.Find("Astro");
        astro.GetComponent<Pickup>().DropItem(this.
            gameObject.tag);
        DestroyImmediate(this.gameObject,true);
    }
}
```

Play. You will now be able to run around and pick up and drop items from the inventory.

Step 15: Currently, when an item is dropped from the inventory, it does not respawn back into the world. For this to occur, the pickup script needs access to the prefabs for each of the food items. When they are placed into an array in the same manner as the inventory images, the prefabs can be easily accessed and used to make new 3D objects each time one is dropped.

To achieve this, modify the pickup script to that shown in Listing 6.6.

Listing 6.6 Updating the Pickup script to drop 3D items back into the game environment

```
public class Pickup : MonoBehaviour {

    public GameObject inventoryPanel;
    public GameObject[] inventoryIcons;

    public GameObject[] pickUpObjects;

    private int count = 0;

    public void DropItem(string itemtag)
    {
        count--;
        Vector3 pos = this.transform.position +
        this.transform.forward*3;
            pos.y = 0.23f;
            if(itemtag == "cake")
                Instantiate(pickUpObjects[0],
                pos,
                Quaternion.identity);
            else if(itemtag == "donut")
                Instantiate(pickUpObjects[1],
                pos,
                Quaternion.identity);
            else if(itemtag == "hamburger")
                Instantiate(pickUpObjects[2],
                pos,
                Quaternion.identity);
            else if(itemtag == "hamegg")
                Instantiate(pickUpObjects[3],
                pos,
                Quaternion.identity);
            else if(itemtag == "icecream")
                Instantiate(pickUpObjects[4],
                pos,
                Quaternion.identity);
            else if(itemtag == "milk")
                Instantiate(pickUpObjects[5],
                pos,
                Quaternion.identity);
```

```
        else if(itemtag == "waffle")
            Instantiate(pickUpObjects[6],
            pos,
            Quaternion.identity);
    }

    void OnCollisionEnter(Collision collision)
    {
        if(count >= 7) return;
...
```

Save the script.

Step 16: The new pickup script uses the game object tag to identify the 3D model that needs to be instantiated back into the world. This tag comes from the inventory image. Thus far, these images do not have tags associated with them. Work through them now to assign them tags that correspond with their image, as shown in Figure 6.15.

Step 17: Next, select Astrodude in the Hierarchy and locate the pickup script in the Inspector. It will now have a Pick Up Objects array that needs filling with the prefabs of the 3D items. Change the size of this array to seven and then drag and drop the item prefabs from the Project in the

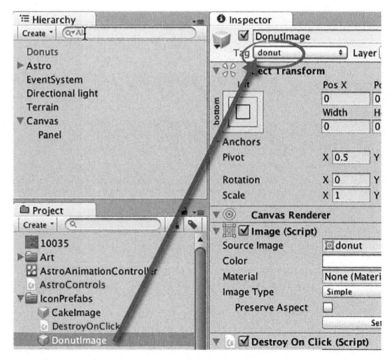

FIG 6.15 Tagging each of the inventory images to associate them with a corresponding 3D object.

352

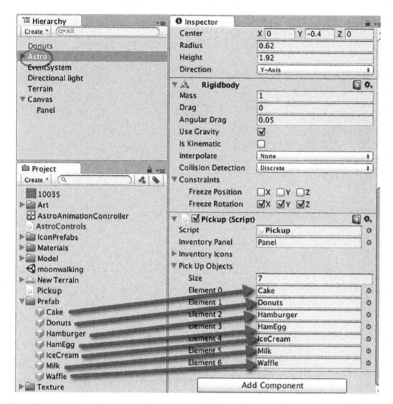

FIG 6.16 Assigning 3D prefabs to the pickup script.

same order as the inventory images were placed in the Inventory Icons array. Note, Pick Up Objects should be filled with the 3D prefabs, not the inventory images, as shown in Figure 6.16.

Play. Astrodude will pick up items, and you can then drop them back into the game world by clicking on them in the inventory.

Step 18: Some inventory systems allow stackable items. This is where a single icon shows with an item count for multiple pickups of the same thing. To achieve this in our inventory system, each item icon first requires a text component.

To do this, drag one of each of the item icon prefabs back onto the Panel so you can see one of each in the Scene and Game views. Beginning with the first item image, right-click on it in the Hierarchy and from the drop-down box select UI > Text. A new Text object will become a child of the image.

Set the text of the new Text object to "1" and align it to the right and bottom as shown in Figure 6.17. You might also like to change the color of the text to white to make it a little more visible. Adjust the position of the Text object to position the text as you would like it to appear relative to the icon image.

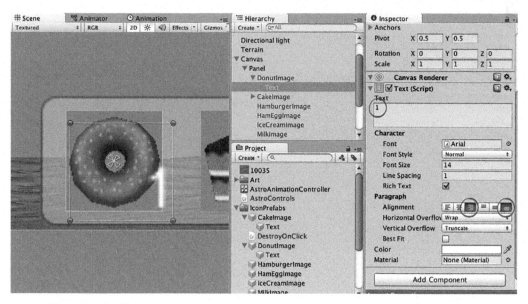

FIG 6.17 Adding an item count to the inventory icons.

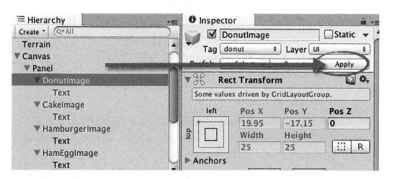

FIG 6.18 Be sure to click Apply when changing the properties of a prefab.

Step 19: Repeat this step for all the inventory icon images now in the panel. When you are finished, ensure that you apply the changes for each image with the Apply button in the Inspector as shown in Figure 6.18.

Step 20: With all changes made to the inventory image prefabs, you can delete them all from the Hierarchy.

Step 21: The next step is to update the Pickup and DestroyOnClick scripts to handle stackable items. When an item is first picked up, we can check if it exists in the inventory. If it does, we increase the count. When an item gets clicked on for removal, we check if there is more than one in the inventory. If there is, the count is decreased but the icon remains visible. Modify the Pickup and DestroyOnClick scripts as shown in Listing 6.7 and 6.8, respectively.

Listing 6.7 Updating the pickup script to stack inventory items

```
import UnityEngine.UI;
...
void OnCollisionEnter(Collision collision)
{
    //if(count >= 7) return; DELETE THIS LINE
    //look through children for existing icon
    foreach(Transform child in inventoryPanel.transform)
    {
        //if item already in inventory
        if(child.gameObject.tag == collision.gameObject.
            tag)
        {
            child.Find("Text").GetComponent<Text>().text =
                "" + (int.Parse(child.Find("Text").
                    GetComponent<Text>().text) + 1);

            Destroy(collision.gameObject);
            return;
        }
    }


    GameObject i;
    if(collision.gameObject.tag == "cake")
    {
...
```

**Listing 6.8 Updating the DestroyOnClick
script to remove items one by one**

```
import UnityEngine.UI;
...
public class DestroyOnClick : MonoBehaviour {
    public void DestroyMeNow()
    {
        GameObject astro = GameObject.Find("Astro");
        astro.GetComponent<Pickup>().DropItem(this.
            gameObject.tag);
        Text t = this.gameObject.transform.Find("Text").
            GetComponent<Text>();
        if(int.Parse(t.text) > 1)
```

```
            {
                t.text = "" + (int.Parse(t.text) - 1);
            }
            else
            {
                DestroyImmediate(this.gameObject,true);
            }
        }
    }
```

Save and Play. You will be able to pick up items and, if they are the same, the count will increase. When an item is clicked on in the Panel to be removed, the count will go down.

Step 22: The last thing we will implement in this hands-on is an inventory contents checking system. Many games use this mechanic to allow the player to perform certain tasks if a particular item is in their inventory. Let us begin by adding a large red cube to the Scene. Name it CubeOfDeath and give it a tag of cubeofdeath (in lowercase) as shown in Figure 6.19.

We will program the cube to kill Astrodude if he walks into it. However, if he has a donut in his inventory, he will be immune to its devastating effects.

Step 23: Open the Pickup script and modify the code as shown in Listing 6.9. Note that it is a matter of adding a couple of lines to the beginning of the OnCollisionEnter() function.

Listing 6.9 Triggering a death animation on running into the CubeOfDeath

```
...
void OnCollisionEnter(Collision collision)
{
if(collision.gameObject.tag == "cubeofdeath")
{
    this.gameObject.GetComponent<Animator>().
        SetTrigger("dead");
}

foreach(Transform child in inventoryPanel.transform)
{
...
```

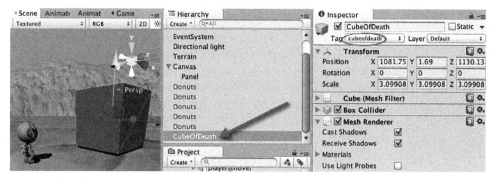

FIG 6.19 Adding the CubeOfDeath to the scene.

Save and Play. Walk Astrodude into the red cube and the death animation should play.

Step 24: Next we need to check through the inventory items before declaring death. If there is a donut, Astrodude will be safe. Modify the pickup code to do this as per Listing 6.10.

Listing 6.10 Providing Astrodude with immunity if a donut is in the inventory

```
...
void OnCollisionEnter(Collision collision)
{
    if(collision.gameObject.tag == "cubeofdeath")
    {
        foreach(Transform child in inventoryPanel.
            transform)
        {
            if(child.gameObject.tag == "donut")
            {
                //astro is safe
                return;
            }
        }
        this.gameObject.GetComponent<Animator>().
            SetTrigger("dead");
    }

    foreach(Transform child in inventoryPanel.transform)
    {
...
```

Save and Play. Astrodude will now be immune to the effects of the cube if there is a donut in the inventory.

6.5 Teleportation

Teleportation is a player mechanic often used to move the player's character very quickly to different locations in a map. It can happen explicitly via actual teleportation devices placed in a game environment, such as in *Quake*, which make it obvious that the player's location has changed, or inexplicitly when teleportation is the developer's trick for loading another game level or another part of a map. Inexplicit teleportation can occur when very large game environments need to be divided up into workable chunks the computer's processor can handle. If you play the original *Halo*, you will experience this transition. When the player reaches the physical boundary of a game mesh, a shimmer falls over the screen and the next part of the map is loaded. The same type of teleportation can occur when a character reaches the exterior door of a building and the game needs to load the inside map of the building so the player can enter it and continue playing.

Both types of teleportation are examined in the next workshop.

6.5.1 Implicit Teleports

◉ **Unity Hands On**

Teleportation

Step 1: Download *Chapter Six/teleport.zip* from the website. Open the project in which you will find two scenes inside a folder called *_Scenes*, one called *outside* and the other *sewerScene*. The one with the sewer model is an original project downloaded from the Unity website. The other is a simple terrain. Open the *outside* scene.

Step 2: Play. You will have control over a first-person character and be able to move around on a terrain in which there is a large factory and a door with a light above it.

Step 3: Add a cube game object to the scene. Transform, rotate, and scale the cube until it sits neatly in front of the factory door, as shown in Figure 6.20.

Step 4: Select the cube in the Hierarchy, and in the Inspector turn off the Mesh Renderer and check the IsTrigger for its box collider. This will make the cube invisible and leave just the collider as a trigger.

Step 5: Create a new tag called *toSewer* and set this as the tag for the cube.

Step 6: Create a new C# file named *Teleport*, add the script shown in Listing 6.11, and attach it to the First Person Controller (FPC).

Listing 6.11 Using a trigger event to teleport to another scene

```
using System.Collections;
using System.Collections.Generic;
using UnityEngine;
using UnityEngine.SceneManagement;

public class Teleport : MonoBehaviour {

    void OnTriggerEnter (Collider obj)
    {
        if(obj.gameObject.tag == "toSewer")
        {
            SceneManager.LoadScene("sewerScene");
        }
    }
}
```

Step 7: Select File > Build Settings from the main menu and add the *outside* and *sewerScene* scenes to the *Scenes in Build* box by dragging them from the Project.

Step 8: Play. Walk up to the factory door and you will be teleported into the sewer room. You could add any number of doors in this way to your game by giving each one its own tag and sending the player to a different scene using if statements in the `OnTriggerEnter()` function.

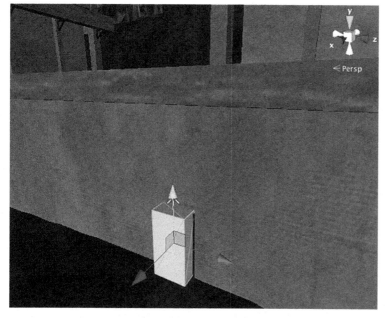

FIG 6.20 Positioning a cube in front of the factory door.

Step 9: To get back from the sewer room to the outside scene, you need to replicate the previous task. Double-click on sewerScene in the Project to open it. There is a first person controller in this scene too. Note that it is not the same first person controller as the outside scene and therefore does not have the teleport code attached.

Step 10: Create a cube like the previous one and place it in front of the door at the top of the sewer room. Tag it with *toOutside*.

Step 11: Create a C# file named *TeleportOutside* and add the code from Listing 6.11, except replace *toSewer* with *toOutside* and change the scene name from *sewerScene* to *outside*.

Step 12: Attach teleportOutside to the First Person Controller.

Step 13: Play. You will now be able to teleport back and forth between the outside scene and the inside scene.

6.5.2 Explicit Teleports

Explicitly transporting from one location to another in the same scene works in a similar way. Now we are going to create a set of particle systems that teleport the player from one location to another.

◉ Unity Hands On
Explicit Teleport

Step 1: Import the particles package from the main menu with Assets > Import Package > Custom Package and import the particles package that comes with the resources for this book or the equivalent Standard Assets package from the Asset Store. The particle prefabs will be loaded into the Standard Assets > ParticleSystems > Prefabs folder in the Project.

Step 2: Place a Smoke particle system on the ground near the door. Change the smoke's Start Color to green and set the Shader to Particles/Additive (Soft) as shown in Figure 6.21.

Remove the attached scripts Particle Systems Destroyer and Particle Systems Multiplier.

Step 3: Add a box collider to the particle system and resize to fit around the particles. Check the collider's IsTrigger checkbox.

Step 4: Rename the particle system in the Hierarchy to Smoke1.

Step 5: Duplicate Smoke1 and rename it as Smoke2.

Step 6: Place Smoke2 somewhere else in the game environment—for example, on the roof of the factory.

Step 7: Create a C# file named *TeleportTo* and add the code from Listing 6.12.

Listing 6.12 Script to reposition a colliding game object at the position of another game object

```
using System.Collections;
using System.Collections.Generic;
using UnityEngine;

public class TeleportTo : MonoBehaviour {

    public GameObject to;

    void OnTriggerEnter(Collider obj)
    {
        obj.gameObject.transform.position = to.transform.
            position + obj.gameObject.transform.forward*3;
    }
}
```

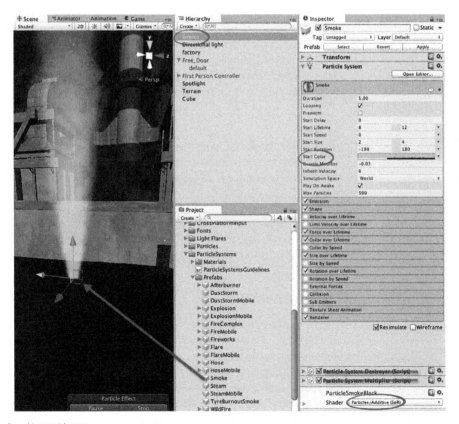

FIG 6.21 A smoking particle system.

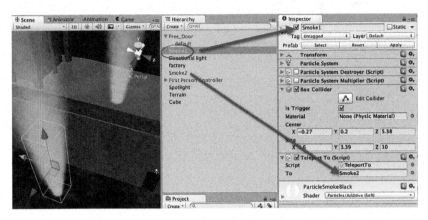

FIG 6.22 Setting up objects for teleportation.

Attach this script to Smoke1 and Smoke2. Any game object with a collider attached that enters Smoke1 will automatically be teleported to the position of Smoke2. This not only includes the player's character, but any game object that might be thrown into it. *Think portal.*

The position the player is transported to should be slightly outside the collider of the destination teleport, as otherwise the player will get stuck in an endless loop between transporters. This is why the *x* position has 1 added to it in Listing 6.12, although you could also modify the *z* position as needed. **Step 8:** Select Smoke1 in the Hierarchy, and in the Inspector set the *to* variable in the *TeleportTo* script to Smoke2 as shown in Figure 6.22.

● Note
If the player falls through the floor or ground plane after teleporting, it will be because the position they are teleporting to is below the ground plane. Always ensure the teleportation object sits above the ground plane it is meant to be on.

Step 9: Now do the same for Smoke2 except set its *to* variable to Smoke1.
Step 10: Play. You will be able to teleport back and forth via the smoke.

6.6 Summary

This chapter examined the parts of games impacting directly on players: user interface and interaction with the game environment. From a design point of view, user interfaces borrow many principles from the domain of graphic art. What looks good and how someone perceives visual elements in two dimensions have been studied and disseminated in art and visual communication long before computer games, and these realms hold much valuable knowledge that we can transform into digital interfaces.

CHAPTER 7

Environmental Mechanics

Environments are not just containers, but are processes that change the content totally.

Marshall McLuhan

7.1 Introduction

One of the most exciting tasks in creating art assets for a game is designing the game world. From molding mountains and placing trees on a terrain to designing a high-quality building interior, the task can seem enormous and daunting at first. But before diving into the design, sometimes it is a good idea to sit back and examine the way things are in the real world—how shadows fall on the ground, how natural vegetation grows, what clouds look like, and all the little details inside buildings from stains on the carpet to the emergency exit sign.

It's the items that are not missing that a player will not notice that will make your game environment more believable. For example, a hospital is not a series of corridors painted gray. There are so many little details, such as posters on the walls, rubbish bins, seating areas, and clocks on the wall that make the location feel like a hospital. One of the most difficult game environments for newbies to create is an outdoor landscape. At first trees can look clumped together and awkwardly positioned, mountains impossibly steep and oddly shaped, and there may be a lack of correct shading and shadows.

This chapter is primarily about observing how things are and applying the rules of nature and architecture to develop game environments. It begins by examining fundamental map design, followed by terrain design, using camera effects for professional-looking scene rendering, and finishes up with the creation of some simplistic but highly effective weather systems.

7.2 Map Design Fundamentals

Map design for game levels is a sizable area of discussion and rules, and opinions on the best approach differ between genre and game developers. In this section, numerous ideas have been gathered from single-player and multiplayer 3D environments. Many of these suggestions have been taken from online discussions of designers at Valve, Ubisoft, Bungie, and a variety of other blogs and postings.

7.2.1 Provide a Focal Point

In a vast map, it is a good idea to provide a focal point. This will act as the player's goal location. If the terrain is rather desolate, like the one shown in Figure 7.1, the player's eye will be drawn to the dominating tower. In addition, because there are no other structures or objects in the area, the player will have no choice but to go toward the tower.

In a rather busy map, a large focal object that can be seen from most places in the level will assist the player with orientation. In *Crysis*, the player is placed in a thick jungle environment with many ridges. A crumbling and trembling massive mountain is shown in the distance as the obvious goal destination. Although at times the player can become disorientated among the trees, the mountain is visible from many positions, guiding and beckoning the player toward it.

7.2.2 Guide and Restrict the Player's Movement

Although many game maps, whether they are outdoor terrains or inner-city streetscapes, may seem endless, they are not. They are designed cleverly to draw a player along a certain path and restrict access to parts of the map

FIG 7.1 A large map terrain with focal point.

that are not actually there. For example, racing games such as *Split Second* blatantly guide the player along a path—the racing circuit! The player cannot jump the barriers along the sides of the road and drive off into the distance because there is no distance. What can be seen in the distance are billboards and 3D objects with very low polycounts. As the player can never get anywhere near these objects, having them in high definition is a pointless waste of computer memory.

Terrain maps, such as those encountered in *Halo*, subtly guide the player along a path where the sides are defined by steep inclines, vast drops, or endless water.

Enemy and reward placement also push the player into moving in a certain direction. Players of first person shooter games know that they are moving toward their goal as the number of enemies increases. If there are nonplayer characters in a certain location, they are obviously guarding something important, and the player feels the need to investigate. Even in children's games, where there are no such gruesome enemies, placing power-ups or extra point pickups along the path will keep the player moving in the right direction.

FIG 7.2 A scene with barrels of different sizes.

7.2.3 Scaling

A recurring mistake that newbie map designers make is in the scaling and detail of an environment and the objects within it. While some people are naturally talented at being able to create realistic-looking scenes, others have to work at it. The most common error is to create a huge building, terrain, or city and place tiny little objects in it.

Do not be afraid to resize an original asset. Look at the real world and the proportions of objects within it. Figure 7.2 demonstrates the unnatural-looking proportions of the barrels (a) and how they are better matched to the size of the player's character (b). If there is a door in the scene, make sure it has correct proportions with respect to the player's character. The same goes for stairs, furniture, trees, cars, and anything else in the scene.

7.2.4 Detail

As they say, "the devil is in the details." With this in mind, the same observational prowess used for proportions should be applied to map details. Wherever you are, look around at the details that make the real world seem … well … real! Have a look at the way trees intersect with the ground. They do not just look as though they are sitting on top of a pole driven into the ground. The terrain at the base undulates from the tree's roots, the grass is higher near the base where the gardener could not fit the lawn mower, and there might be other interesting weeds or rocks scattered about. Even a pole that has been driven into the ground will eventually get taller grass growing at its base.

If you get a chance to look at a mountain or river view, take note of where the trees and grasses are positioned and the color of the dirt. Mountains have a tree line beyond which trees do not grow because it is too cold. At this point,

(a)   (b)

FIG 7.3 Two trees on a terrain (a) with no detail and (b) with detail.

you might find rockier ground and snow. Nearer the water, you will find taller reeds and grasses. There is a reason why nature looks the way it does, and if you want your maps and terrain to be convincing, you need to notice the little things.

Figure 7.3 contains a screen capture of two trees in a Unity scene: (a) just the tree added to a terrain and (b) the tree surrounded by detail with shadowing and other camera effects added. Note how the tree in Figure 7.3b is more convincingly part of the landscape than the one in Figure 7.3a. The idea is to strategically position objects and use special effects to remove the harsh boundary where one object meets another.

If you are creating a map based on a real-world landscape or building, go to that building. Sit and observe. Take photographs. If you are mapping the inside of a hospital, go and have a look at all the things in a hospital that make it look and feel like a hospital. The colors, charts on the walls, carts, exit signs, and markings on the floor, to name a few, are all symbolic things that will keep the player immersed in your game environment.

7.2.5 Map Layout

Physical map layout differs dramatically according to the restrictions of perspective, narrative, and genre. Sometimes the logical structure of the story and the game play paths from start to end match with the analytical structure of the game environment and sometimes they do not. For example, a game that is a simple *from start to end* consists of a linear story in which the player is moving through the story like an actor in a movie. Instead of being a key decision-maker, the player will have a very linear game map in which the player moves from some starting position to an ending position. The level may convince the player that he has some control over his destiny with smatterings of game play; however, in the end, the real options are that the player dies or moves on at each challenge. Other open-type simulations such as *SimCity* have an evolving narrative that in no way at all dictates the physical layout of the map.

With this in mind, we examine several game-level design structures and discuss how the player's journey through the story and the actual game world are related. While each of the ones presented illustrate a single game progression strategy, it is more the case for real games to use a hybrid of the ones presented to make for a more engaging player experience. Their generalization, illustrated in Figure 7.4, herein is for academic purposes only.

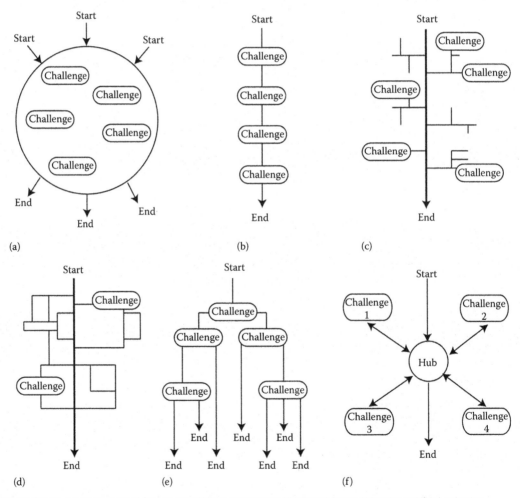

FIG 7.4 Game level design structures. (a) Open, (b) linear, (c) linear with sidetracks, (d) linear with circuits, (e) branches, and (f) hub and spokes.

7.2.5.1 Open

A truly open game map will have multiple starting positions and ending positions with numerous unordered challenges in between, as shown in Figure 7.4a. From a narrative point of view, *The Sims* is this type of game, as you can start with any character you like, end the game when you like, and take on whatever challenges take your fancy along the way. The game environment of *The Sims* is also quite open as to how players can decide on the look, personality, and goals of their avatars and the layout and furnishing of their houses. The city map, however, is not open. It is physically a network structure with fixed positions of housing blocks and city buildings.

Physically speaking, the *EVE Online* maps are open, with a variety of starting positions, numerous ways of traveling from one location to another, many unordered challenges, and multiple places to end/complete your journey. The players' choices in these types of games are vast. Of course, the game map is not one large infinite mesh, as it would be too big to process, but a series of minimaps cleverly linked together to give the impression of immeasurable universes.

7.2.5.2 Linear

Most games based around a story are linear; that is, they have a start, a journey, and an end (shown in Figure 7.4b). Players typically accompany their character, the hero, through a series of carefully crafted challenges to the end. The start is always the same, the journey is always the same, and the end is always the same. In terms of a map, it means a game environment in which there is only one path to travel to get from the starting position to the end. Along the way there may be puzzles, barriers, and enemies to battle, but the path is always the same.

To add some interest to the linear map, sidetracks (shown in Figure 7.4c) can be added that can take players down a dead-end path but provide extra bonuses or clues to aid in their progression along the main path. The danger here is that players could choose to skip an entire sidetrack unless encouraged to go down it because they have no other choice; for example, the main path might contain a locked door and the key is down a sidetrack.

Even more complexity is created when circuits (shown in Figure 7.4d) are added off the main path. These provide players with opportunities to bypass parts of the main path. They can also disorient players and send them back to the beginning. *Dungeons & Dragons* and other maze-type games are created with both circuits and sidetracks. These maze games align perfectly with the narrative and map structures, as it is the sidetracks and circuits that dictate the maze's physical layout.

Racing games are another example of a linear path with a circuit. The circuit takes the player from the start, around a track, and back to the start. The player's journey is one that evolves according to the player's racing skills;

however, in the end, the game remains linear, as the start position, end position, and goal always remain the same.

Any game that has a linear story line similar to that in books and movies will require a linear map to ensure that players play through the story and live out the full life of their character. If the physical map has sidetracks and circuits, players will require a motivational story to choose to explore them. This can be achieved by placing side rooms or corridors off the main path that reward players' exploration with extra ammunition, health, or other items that can assist their game progress.

7.2.5.3 Branching

A level with branching has the one starting position and multiple ending positions, as shown in Figure 7.4e. Narratively speaking, this means a story that starts in the same place but has multiple outcomes depending on the player's game choices. These are difficult narratives to write, as a new story needs to be written for each branch. In addition, extra branches require extra artwork with respect to map designs. While a fork in the road might not literally represent a branch, it could mean that the player travels to another map or enters through a one-way door into another world.

If branching is used in physical terms in a game map, it will mean that players can skip over a lot of game play and be content on their way to the end. On the other side, players can replay the game and take a different journey each time until they have explored all branches.

7.2.5.4 Spoke and Hub

Last but not least is the spoke and hub structure. This provides a progressive set of challenges by which the player must achieve challenge 1 to unlock challenge 2, complete challenge 2 to unlock challenge 3, and so forth. After each challenge, the player returns to the same central hub state. The single player path in *StarCraft II* is very similar to this, as the player is located on a spaceship representing his home base, but must leave this hub to take on challenges. After each challenge, the player, if successful, has accumulated money and points and can upgrade his armada, weapons, and troops before proceeding to new unlocked challenges.

This level design structure requires numerous maps or map areas in which the challenges take place. Because of the progressing unlocking nature of the design, the player will eventually explore and experience all the game play and maps, unlike in a branching scenario.

As mentioned previously, today's games are far more complex than the preceding level structures; however, they do include elements of one or more of those structures. What is important to keep in mind is that the game does not start with the game art or map levels. It must start with a conceptual design and story, as otherwise you might find yourself developing a lot of art assets that never see the light of day.

7.2.6 Other Considerations

7.2.6.1 Player Starting Position

How often have you loaded a game level and had your character looking at a wall or the ground? Cannot remember? Never? There is a reason why. The first thing players want to do when entering a game environment is to start the game. If they are facing a strange unexpected direction, they will have little idea where to go next. It might be that they need only to turn around to see the door they need to go through or the corridor they need to walk down—but it is just a neater way of introducing the player to your level.

7.2.6.2 Flow

Flow in level design refers to the way in which players move from the beginning of the level to their goal. It is the level designer's job to make the environment flow as best he can to challenge players, keep them moving toward their goal, and keep them engaged. Flow is mostly dictated by the physical layout of the map as described in Section 7.2.5.

Although in the end we all know that the designer is herding the player down a certain path, this need not be revealed to the player immediately. Providing players with numerous paths to take allows them to make decisions in their game play about the way they traverse the map. This creates an illusion of freedom where there is none.

The game developers, Valve, and others use a variety of methods to control the flow through the game. In some areas, you will want the player to run, in others to walk. Breaking the map into narrow areas that make the player feel confined, thus increasing tension in the game play, creates *narrow flow*.

Side rooms are another common technique in 3D environments. They give the map extra areas of interest but are dead ends. The player's reward for exploring these areas is by way of extra weapons, power-ups, and other useful items. Side paths without reward do not encourage the player to explore, and thus the exercise of creating these areas in the map becomes pointless and just extra work for the artists.

7.2.6.3 Trapping

Blocking the exit of a dead end after the player has entered is another way to create tension and panic. You could use this pathway through a map or at the goal location. It should be obvious that if you do trap a player in part of the level, he is able to get out. Most seasoned players would expect that if they become trapped it is the end of the level, they have some puzzle to solve, or very soon they will die or be rescued.

7.2.6.4 Use the Third Dimension

Three-dimensional environments have height as well as depth and width. A map with various height levels allows for the player to get from one place to another via alternate routes. In addition, if players can see that there are multiple heights to a building or terrain, they will expect to be able to get to these heights that could be used as resting or attacking positions.

7.2.6.5 Vantage Points

Ensure that your map has multiple vantage points that the player can use to hide or as an attacking position. Some might be in better locations than others and will provide players with choice and variety in the way they choose to approach the game play.

If you are designing for a multiplayer environment, then multiple vantage points will ensure that play does not become predictable and ultimately boring. In the original *Halo* multiplayer mode, there is one map in which players can teleport between two spacecraft and shoot at each other across the void. There is a nice little nook off to the side of one of the ships with a cloaking shield in it. The same location looks out across the void and is also perfect for using the sniper rifle on your opponent when they are on the other ship. The cloaking field only starts a short time, and therefore it is wise to stand near the cloaking shield until your opponent comes into view on the other ship, pick up the cloak, and start shooting. As you cannot move and use the zoom on the sniper rifle at the same time, having played the map a few times, this strategy fails as your opponent knows where you are shooting from even when he cannot see you.

It is unavoidable that players will eventually explore and use up all the vantage points in a multiplayer map; however, the more variety provided, the longer the game play potential.

Map and level designs are challenging for even the seasoned game developer, and there are many books devoted to the topic. If you are interested in reading up on game and level design, start by reading some books dedicated to the subject, such as *Fundamentals of Game Design* (2nd edition) by Ernest Adams.

7.3 Terrain

Terrains are meshes that make up the ground in an outdoor scene. They usually undulate in height and sport a variety of surface textures to make them look like a real outdoor desert, mountain, and even alien world scenes. The more detailed a terrain, the more polygons from which it will be made as additional vertices are required to give them a real-world smooth appearance. Because large elaborate terrains require a lot of processing, numerous tricks are employed to make the terrain look more detailed.

While there are many available tools for creating terrains, making them look real can be quite a challenge. The best examples come from nature.

FIG 7.5 Mount Fuji.

7.3.1 Drawing a Terrain

As you will find in the next section, although a terrain can be computer generated, the most detailed and realistic terrains are best created by hand. Throughout this chapter, we work with the same terrain, adding differing effects to make it feel as realistic as possible. The terrain will be modeled on a photograph of Japan's Mt. Fuji, as shown in Figure 7.5.

◉ Unity Hands On
Creating a Terrain

Step 1: Open Unity and create a new project. It will contain a Directional Light by default.

Step 2: From the main menu, select GameObject > 3D Object > Terrain. A large flat plane will appear in the scene.

Step 3: To sculpt the terrain, select the terrain in the Hierarchy. A toolset will appear in the Inspector. The operation of the buttons is defined in Table 7.1.

Step 4: For sculpting, select Tool 1 and from the dropdown box below "**Raise or Lower Terrain**." The brush size will affect the area of ground you can sculpt in one stroke, and the opacity and the strength. A higher opacity will cause more of the terrain to be lifted in one stroke. A left click will raise the terrain and holding show the SHIFT key will lower the terrain.

TABLE 7.1 The Terrain Editor Tools

Number	Tool Icon	Use
1		This tool reveals a multitude of functions, including: • Add a texture to the terrain. This brush allows you to paint the terrain with the texture of your choice. • Raise and lower the terrain. The selected brush shape is used to emboss the terrain. Each stroke in the same place lifts the terrain. • Set the terrain height. This allows for the exact altitude of any part of the terrain to be set. A height of 0 is the same level as the default terrain plane. • Smooth the terrain. This brush allows you to smooth the terrain heights between differing levels to get a smoother effect from jagged surfaces.
2		Place trees. Places trees on the surface of the terrain under the brush location.
3		Place flowers, small plants, and rocks. This brush performs the same action as the tree planting brush; however, it places smaller multiple models on the surface of the terrain.
4		Control the overall settings for the terrain. In this area, you can set the distances for level of detail, and whether or not the trees are rendered as billboards instead of 3D objects. These settings are for optimizing the performance of the terrain in the game.

Step 5: Hold down the left mouse button over the terrain and start lifting the surface. At this state, begin with a basic outline of the lake area, as shown in Figure 7.6. To lower the terrain, hold down the shift key with the mouse stroke.

◉ **Note**

You might find it easier to replicate a real-world image if you place it on a plane inside the Editor to use as a reference as shown in Figure 7.6.

Step 6: Using a combination of Tool 1 functions, sculpt and smooth the terrain into an approximate representation of the Mt. Fuji landscape as shown in Figure 7.7.

FIG 7.6 Placing a plane with reference photograph in the scene.

FIG 7.7 Sculpting features to match the reference photograph.

Step 7: Once the basic terrain is constructed, it can be textured. For the texturing, seamless images are required. These images must be placed in the Project. Acquire these textures by searching on online. An excellent seamless texture pack is available at http://www.holistic3d.com/resources/.

Step 8: Click on Tool 1 and set the drop down box to "Paint Texture" to select the terrain painting brush. Before you can start coloring the terrain, the images need to be loaded as terrain textures. Select the Edit Textures button as shown in Figure 7.8 and select Add Texture. A popup window will allow you to select the image and its tile size. The larger the tile size, the more terrain a single copy of the image will cover.

Step 9: Select a texture to be the first and click on Apply to add it to the terrain texture list. The first texture added will automatically cover the entire terrain therefore picking an image that represents the most common surface color saves a lot of texturing work later.

Step 10: Add more images to the texture list, and use the brush size, opacity and target strength settings to paint the terrain. The opacity value sets how much of the underneath texture mixes with the newly added texture, and the target strength is how much of the added texture is placed on the surface. A low opacity will allow a lot of the underneath color to show through. A low target strength will add very little of the current texture to the surface. Experiment with these values to get the effect right. If you make a mistake, it is simple enough to recolor over the mistakes.

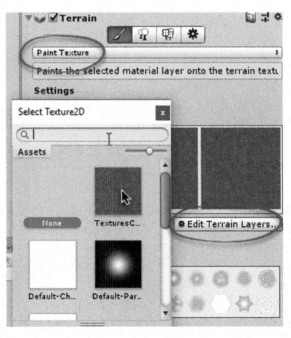

FIG 7.8 Adding a terrain texture.

FIG 7.9 Painting textures on a terrain at differing heights.

Wherever trees will be placed, think about the final effect. If you want the trees to look like lush and forest, a ground color similar to the trees will make it to look denser than it is. An example of the painted terrain is shown in Figure 7.9.
Step 11: Trees can also be painted onto the surface using Tool 2. Currently there will be no trees in the Project. Download the free Extra Terrain Assets package by Unity Technologies available at https://holistic3d.com/resources/ and import into your project.
Step 12: Trees are added to the tree brush in the same way as images are added to the textures. Add a couple of appropriate trees.
Step 13: Examine the photograph of Mt. Fuji. Notice how the trees do not cover the entire landscape? Obviously, they will not be in the lake area, but they are thickest near the water and thin out to a distinct level after which the odd tree is found. In the real world, elevation and soil content at heights make it inhospitable for trees. Therefore, mimicking nature in this way makes the terrain look better.
Step 14: In the picture of Mt. Fuji, there is also a line of reeds and grass around the edge of the lake. Grass and flowers can be added with Tool 3. They are painted in the same way as Trees. Once you have added the trees, take a small texture painting brush, select a grass or flower, and add this detail. It will lift the tree line and create a break between water and land.
Step 15: To add water, import the Environment package supplied in the resources folder supplied with this book. Once imported, search in the Standard Assets folder in the Project for the Water4Advanced prefab. Drag and drop this into the Scene. Resize and reposition such that it wills the lake area in front of the mountain.
Step 16: Remove the plane containing the real photograph of Mt. Fuji and play to enjoy your new creation. An example is shown in Figure 7.10.

FIG 7.10 The final terrain reproduction.

7.3.2 Procedural Terrain

Procedural terrain is generated by a computer algorithm. Most of the methods are based on fractals. A program is written that defines the vertices of a mesh and recursively raises and lowers the points to create altitude. One simple terrain-producing method is the midpoint displacement algorithm.

This algorithm works starting with a flat surface. It divides it into half and then raises or lowers the middle point. Then each half is halved and the midpoints of these are raised or lowered. A 2D representation of this progression is illustrated in Figure 7.11.

Another popular procedural terrain generation algorithm is the Diamond-Square method illustrated in Figure 7.12. Starting with a square mesh with a power of 2 + 1 number of vertices in width and height for example, 257, 513, 1025, all four corners are set to the same initial height (Figure 7.12a). The second step, the diamond step, locates the central vertex where the diagonals from the initial vertices intersect. The third step creates squares

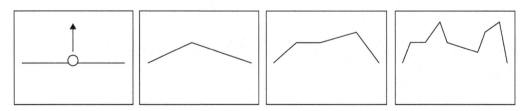

FIG 7.11 Midpoint displacement on a 2D line.

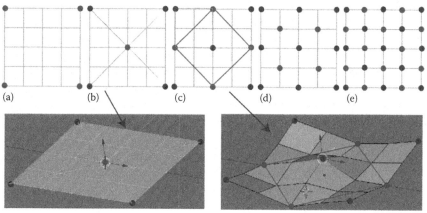

Finding diamond midpoint   Performing squaring and folding

FIG 7.12 The Diamond-Square algorithm.

between the central point and the previous initial points. Now imagine fold lines between the red points and the height values assigned to the blue points as shown in green in Figure 7.12. Blue points determine height, and the green lines are where the mesh is allowed to fold.

The Diamond-Square method continues creating diamonds to find midpoints and squares for lowering and raising until all points in the grid have height values associated with them.

Perlin noise is another popular algorithmic way to generate landscapes. It is used in the next workshop to produce a natural-looking terrain from a plane object in Unity.

◉ Unity Hands On

Generating a Terrain Procedurally

Step 1: Create a new Unity project and import the Character Controller package.

Step 2: Add a plane to the scene and a first person controller (FPC). Position the FPC just above the plane and add a directional light as shown in Figure 7.13. Scale the plane's x and z size to 10.

◉ Note

If you want a smoother, more detailed terrain, you will need to use a plane with more vertices than the one supplied with Unity. To do this, use Blender or your favorite 3D modeling program to create a plane and apply subdivisions to give it the number of polygons you desire.

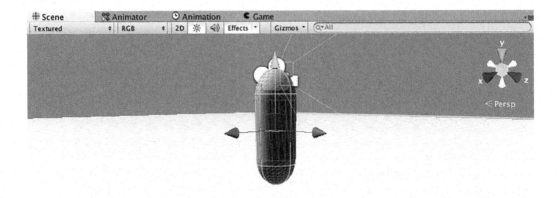

FIG 7.13 A plane and FPC for starting the project.

Step 3: Select the plane in the Hierarchy and remove its Mesh Collider component in the Inspector. We will add a new one shortly after its terrain heights have been modified.

Step 4: Create a C# file called *MakeTerrain.cs*. Add the code shown in Listing 7.1.

Listing 7.1 Script to create random height values on a mesh

```
using System.Collections;
using System.Collections.Generic;
using UnityEngine;

public class MakeTerrain : MonoBehaviour {

    void Start()
    {
        Mesh mesh = this.
            GetComponent<MeshFilter>().mesh;
        Vector3[] vertices = mesh.vertices;
        for (int v = 0; v < vertices.Length; v++)
        {
            vertices[v].y = Random.Range(0f,10f);
        }
        mesh.vertices = vertices;
        mesh.RecalculateBounds();
        mesh.RecalculateNormals();
        this.gameObject.AddComponent<MeshCollider>();
    }
}
```

Step 5: Attach the script to the plane.

Step 6: Play. The terrain will have random heights across its surface. Note that the Mesh Collider is added after the heights have been set. This will ensure that the FPC does not fall through. Switch to the Scene while in Play mode for a better view of the created landscape.

After the mesh vertices are modified in the *y* direction for height, the bounding volume and normals are recreated. The bounding volume is used by the game engine to improve the processing of geometrical operations such as collision detection and overlap. The reason being that in the first instance, computing overlapping volumes is easier than lower level collision detection. Before exact collisions are calculated, determining if there might be a collision between two objects is more efficient with bounding volumes.

In addition, the plane's normals are also recalculated. Because the plane's mesh has changed shape, the normals must be adjusted for the new vertex values for the mesh to be shaded and shadowed correctly.

Using a random function to determine height is not a realistic way to produce rise and fall in a terrain, as the height can change erratically with each vertex. At small height values, it might look all right, but try changing the random range from 0 to 50 and the surface of the plane will become very jagged.

Step 7: To create smoother rises and falls in a surface, a mathematical curve such as sine or cosine can be used. Modify *MakeTerrain.cs* to reflect the changes shown in Listing 7.2.

Listing 7.2 Using a sine function to set the terrain height

```
. . .
    for (int v = 0; v < vertices.Length; v++)
    {
        vertices[v].y = Mathf. Sin(vertices[v].x * 10);
    }
. . .
```

Step 8: Play. The shape of the sine wave will be visually evident. The terrain will be smooth, but too uniform to replicate a natural landscape.

Another way to create a landscape procedurally is to use Perlin noise, a pseudo-random mathematical algorithm that provides smooth gradients between points. This is the method used for landscape generation in *Minecraft. Check out http://bit.ly/holisticminecraft for Unity tutorials showing you how.*

Step 9: Download *Chapter Seven/Perlin.cs* from the website. Add the file to your Project inside a new folder called *Plugins*.

Step 10: Modify *MakeTerrain.cs* to that shown in Listing 7.3.

Listing 7.3 Using Perlin noise to generate terrain heights

```
using System.Collections;
using System.Collections.Generic;
using UnityEngine;

public class MakeTerrain : MonoBehaviour {

    void Start()
    {
        Perlin surface = new Perlin();
        Mesh mesh = this.
            GetComponent<MeshFilter>().mesh;
        Vector3[] vertices = mesh.vertices;
        for (int v = 0; v < vertices.Length; v++)
        {
            vertices[v].y = surface.Noise(
                vertices[v].x * 2 + 0.1365143f,
                vertices[v].z * 2 + 1.21688f) * 10;
        }
        mesh.vertices = vertices;
        mesh.RecalculateBounds();
        mesh.RecalculateNormals();
        this.gameObject.AddComponent<MeshCollider>();

    }
}
```

● Note
Perlin Noise

Perlin noise is the same algorithm used in Photoshop for generating the *Render Clouds* filter. The image created by Perlin noise is grayscale where black indicates the lowest altitude and white the highest as shown in Figure 7.14a.

In fact, you can create a procedurally generated terrain in Unity (shown in Figure 7.14b) by (1) adding a terrain; (2) getting the flat terrain texture with Terrain > Export Heightmap; (3) opening this texture with Photoshop; (4) applying Photoshop's Render Clouds filter; (5) saving the texture in the same raw format; and (6) selecting Terrain > Import Heightmap in Unity to load the heights.

The difference in using a random number for the height and Perlin noise is illustrated in Figure 7.15.

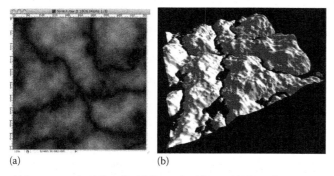

FIG 7.14 (a) A texture created with Photoshop's Difference Clouds Filter and (b) A Unity Terrain with the same texture used as a heightmap.

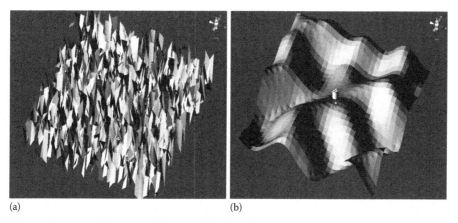

FIG 7.15 (a) A terrain with random height values and (b) A terrain with Perlin noise height values.

7.3.3 Procedural Cities

Generating realistic cities with code is more challenging than landscapes. While terrain can reuse trees, rocks, grass, and dirt textures, reuse of the same building or random street structures can look unrealistic. In the same way that fractals can be used for generating terrain and layout, they can also be used to create objects on the terrain such as trees and buildings.

A Lindenmayer system, or L-system, is a fractal algorithm commonly used for generating trees as it has a natural branching structure. An L-system is constructed from a string representing drawing commands. The string is built through an iterative process where parts of the string are replaced with other strings. An L-system begins with an axiom and a set of rules, thus:

$$F \rightarrow F + F$$

Starting with the axiom as the original string, each character in the string matching a rule is replaced with the rule's string. Therefore, after one iteration, the aforementioned string becomes:

$$F + F$$

Then, each F in the new string is replaced by the rule in the next iteration, thus:

$$F + F + F + F$$

Note that only the character F is replaced, and with F + F, the already existing + carries over to the next string. This is illustrated in Figure 7.16.

After numerous iterations, a string such as F + F + F + F is then interpreted by a drawing algorithm in which the letters represent lines and the + represents a turn to the right (if − is used, it means turn to the left). It is reminiscent of turtle graphics in which a cursor on the screen is given commands to draw a line, turn right, draw another line, and so on. The turn angle is preset. Let us say F represents draw a straight line and + represents turn 90°. The drawn result would be a square as shown in Figure 7.17.

In addition to drawing and turning, an L-system can contain push and pop points. These are represented by square brackets: [ ]. When the drawing algorithm encounters these points, it remembers its location at the opening square bracket and keeps drawing, then returns to the remembered location when it encounters a closing bracket. For example, F[+ F]F where + is 45° would produce the L-system shown in Figure 7.18.

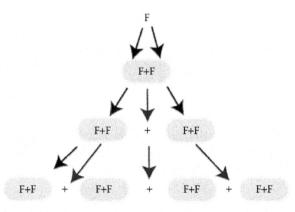

FIG 7.16 L-system rewriting.

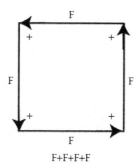

F+F+F+F

FIG 7.17 An L-system that draws a square.

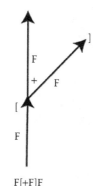

F[+F]F

FIG 7.18 An L-system with remembered locations.

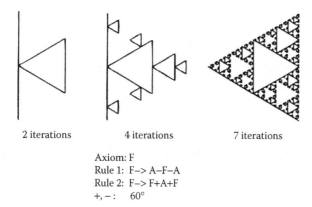

2 iterations   4 iterations   7 iterations

Axiom: F
Rule 1: F–> A–F–A
Rule 2: F–> F+A+F
+, – :   60°

FIG 7.19 Sierpinski triangle.

L-systems become more complex with the addition of extra rules such as the one shown in Figure 7.19. This is a famous fractal called the Sierpinski triangle.

Natural and familiar shapes can be created with L-systems (as shown in Figure 7.20).

Axiom: X
Rule 1: X–> F–[[X]+X]+F[+FX]–X
Rule 2: F–> FF
Angle: 25°

FIG 7.20 An L-system tree.

To produce a procedural map, at least two types of L-systems are required: one for drawing the map layout with the transportation routes and one for creating the buildings. Figure 7.21a illustrates a simple street map using the same L-system as the one for the tree in Figure 7.20 with the angle set to 90°. Figure 7.21b shows how an L-system can be used to create buildings. Simple lines are replaced with 3D blocks. The result in the three iterations shown hints at how compelling a fully finished building could look.

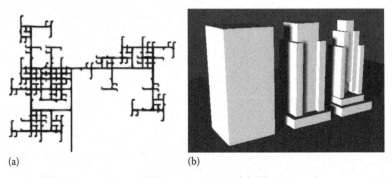

(a)   (b)

FIG 7.21 (a) An L-system street map and (b) L-system progression of a building.

Although the programming of an algorithm to build a 3D L-system city is beyond the scope of this book, it is possible using Perlin noise and existing building models to generate a city. This is the topic of the next workshop.

◉ On the Web
Procedural City Generator

The before mentioned techniques for procedurally generating a city come from the research work of Müller and Parish. Their approach has been packaged into the *CityEngine* software, a 3D-modeling package purposely built to generate vast city landscapes. A free trial can be downloaded from http://www.procedural.com/.

◉ Unity Hands On
Procedural Cities

Step 1: Create a new Unity project and import the Character Controller package.

Step 2: Add a plane to the scene and an FPC. Position the FPC just above the plane and add a directional light as shown in Figure 7.13. Scale the plane's *x* and *z* sizes to 10.

Step 3: Download *Chapter Seven/Perlin.cs* from the website. Add the file to your Project inside a new folder called *Plugins*.

Step 4: Create a C# file named *MakeCity*, reuse the code from Listing 7.3 changing the class name to *MakeCity*.

Step 5: Play. What you should have is the heightened terrain from the previous example. Now instead of heights, we will add buildings.

Step 6: If you put a print statement inside the for loop in *MakeCity.cs* and print out the height values being assigned to the plane, you will notice that they range between −4 and 4. We will use these values to assign buildings instead of terrain heights. Go to TurboSquid and download eight models of various types of houses and buildings. You will also find eight building models already downloaded from TurboSquid on the website as *Chapter Seven/buildings.zip*.

Step 7: Add the buildings to the Project.

Step 8: Add each building into the Scene and position them on the plane. Because different artists created them, their scaling will be different. Resize and rotate each building as you see fit, such that they have reasonable relative sizes and orientations.

Step 9: Create eight prefabs in the Project—one for each building. Drag each building out of the Hierarchy and onto its own prefab.

Step 10: Modify *MakeCity.cs* to that in Listing 7.4.

Listing 7.4 Using building prefabs to create a city based on Perlin noise height values

```
using System.Collections;
using System.Collections.Generic;
using UnityEngine;

public class MakeCity : MonoBehaviour {

    public GameObject[] buildings;

    void Start()
    {
        Perlin surface = new Perlin();

        Mesh mesh = this.GetComponent<MeshFilter>().mesh;
        Vector3[] vertices = mesh.vertices;
        float scalex = this.transform.localScale.x;
        float scalez = this.transform.localScale.z;

        for (int v = 0; v <vertices.Length; v++)
        {
            float perlinValue = surface.
                Noise(vertices[v].x * 2 + 0.1365143f,
                vertices[v].z * 2 + 1.21688f) * 10;

            perlinValue =
            Mathf.Round((Mathf.
                Clamp(perlinValue,0,buildings.Length)));
            Instantiate(buildings[(int)perlinValue],
                new Vector3(vertices[v].x * scalex,
                    vertices[v].y, vertices[v].z * scalez),
                buildings[(int)perlinValue].transform.
                    rotation);

        }
        mesh.vertices = vertices;
        mesh.RecalculateBounds();
        mesh.RecalculateNormals();

        this.gameObject.AddComponent<MeshCollider>();
    }
}
```

FIG 7.22 A procedurally generated city.

Step 11: Select the plane in the Hierarchy and find the MakeCity script in the Inspector. Set the size of Buildings to 8 and drag and drop each building prefab onto the exposed building array elements in the script. Note that you can have any number of buildings and the code will adjust for it.

Step 12: Play. The result will be a small city as illustrated in Figure 7.22.

⊛ **Note**

As Perlin noise creates smooth regions that when drawn as a grayscale graduate between white and black, you can use these values to determine the city density at these locations. For example, white might represent high density and black low or no density. Where the map is densest, use the skyscraper type building models and where it is lower use small houses. This will create a relatively realistic city.

7.3.4 Infinite Terrain

Infinite terrain or endless terrain is a form of procedurally generated landscape. It uses a mathematical equation and the player's current position to create the landscape as the player moves. Small parts of the map are created as needed based on the player's visible distance. Any map outside the visible range is not generated, and therefore not a load on computer memory.

To create undulation of a terrain, a mathematical formula is used for determining the height based on the x and z positions on the terrain for which there will always be a y value no matter the x and z values. For example, the sine or cosine functions can produce values for infinite values of *x* and/or *z* and the result used as the *y* value.

The beauty of using a formula is that the result of *y* for any *x* and *z* values is always going to be the same, thus assuring us that if we return to a previous location on the map that was destroyed after we left but recreated on our return, the height remains the same. In addition, the terrain can be infinitely large, generated entirely by the computer. This means that a human artist is not required to constantly churn out more and more of the landscape. Terrain textures, trees, rocks, and other model objects are used over and over again.

Perlin noise makes for a good choice in infinite terrain generation applications as it produces a random yet smooth undulating surface.

◉ On the Web
An Infinite Terrain Generator
Developing an infinite terrain generator is a tricky business and as such is beyond the scope of this book. However, a generous Unity forum member going by the name of *Quick Fingers* posted a package for one on the Unity website. For this book, the code has been modified to use Perlin noise and place trees and different textures on the terrain at varying heights. You can download the project from the website as Chapter Seven/InfiniteTerrain.zip.

On opening the Infinite Terrain scene, you will find a Terrain Generator object in the Hierarchy. Select this to modify the terrain's parameters in the Inspector. You will notice different terrain textures are used for different altitudes. When rendered, the contrast between the textures is evident. They are not blended in the same way as the Unity paint-on textures in the Unity Terrain Editor. This is because they are placed on the mesh live as the game is playing and the mesh is generated. While a blending algorithm could blend the textures to make them fit together better, it would slow down the generation of the terrain.

As you move around the map, watch the action in the Scene. Only the parts of the map that are within sight of the player's camera are generated and drawn. As you move around, as parts of the map become out of sight, they are destroyed. This keeps the memory usage low and allows you to move infinitely in any direction, totally oblivious to the small mesh your character is standing on.

A view of the infinite landscape is shown in Figure 7.23.

You can find extra online tutorials on procedural and infinite terrains created with Unity here:

- https://youtu.be/dycHQFEz8VI
- https://youtu.be/Vg-V5G2JJNY

FIG 7.23 An infinite landscape generated in Unity.

7.4 Camera Tricks

Cameras are the player's eyes into the game environment. What the camera sees is projected onto the computer screen. Before each pixel is drawn, the game developer can add special treatments to the properties and colors of the pixels by attaching scripts to the camera. This allows for the creation of many different visual effects. For example, a blur effect can be added to the camera when the player is underwater to give the illusion that water is in the player's eyes, or the scene can be rendered in sepia to make it look like an old-time movie.

Many of the following effects come from the domain of image processing and photographic postproduction and can be found readily as filters in Adobe Photoshop. They have found their way into gaming as a way of enhancing the player's visual perception of the environment. Some of the wide ranges of camera effects available in Unity are shown in Figure 7.24.

7.4.1 Depth of Field

Depth of field is the term used to describe how an optical lens focuses on the surrounding environment. It describes the distance between the closest and the farthest objects in view that appear in sharp focus. A shallow depth of field has items only nearest the middle of the view in focus as shown in Figure 7.25.

As the human eye is a lens, it also projects an image with a depth of field. Unlike in a straightforward virtual terrain where all objects are in focus, for humans, our real world tends to become fuzzy in the distance and sometimes close up.

Original scene	Depth of field
Sun shaft	Edge detection
Sepia tone	Fish eye

FIG 7.24 A sample of the camera effects available in Unity.

Adding a depth of field effect to the game view camera gives the scene a higher feel of realism, quality, and 3D effect. The depth of field effect in Unity is shown in Figure 7.24.

7.4.2 Blur

Blur is an effect that makes the entire image look out of focus. It can be used effectively to simulate the look of being underwater.

Setting a pixel's color to the average color of its neighbors creates a blur effect. Within a certain radius, all pixel colors are sampled, added together, and then divided by the number of pixels. Each pixel is then given the same average value. Another familiar blur is Gaussian blur. It adds the pixel colors together to determine an average; however, pixel colors in the center of the

[text partially obscured/blurred]

*to give the illusion water is in the player's eyes or the ...
to make it look like an old-time movie.*

7.3.1. Depth of Field

Depth of field is the term used to describe ho...
rounding environment. It describes the dista...
...ts in view that appear in sharp focus. A...

[blurred text]

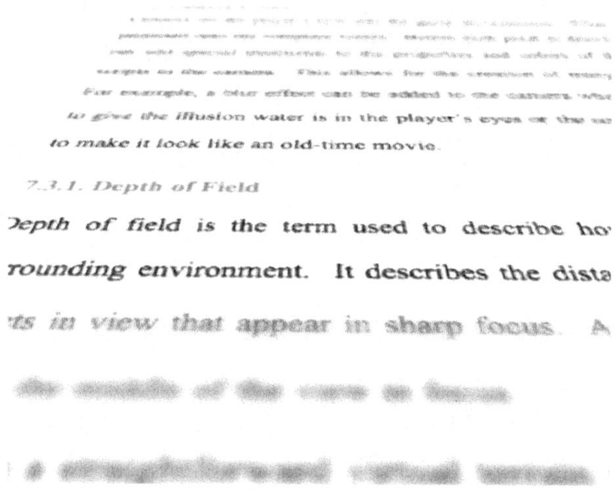

FIG 7.25 A shallow depth of field.

| Original | Average blur | Gaussian blur |

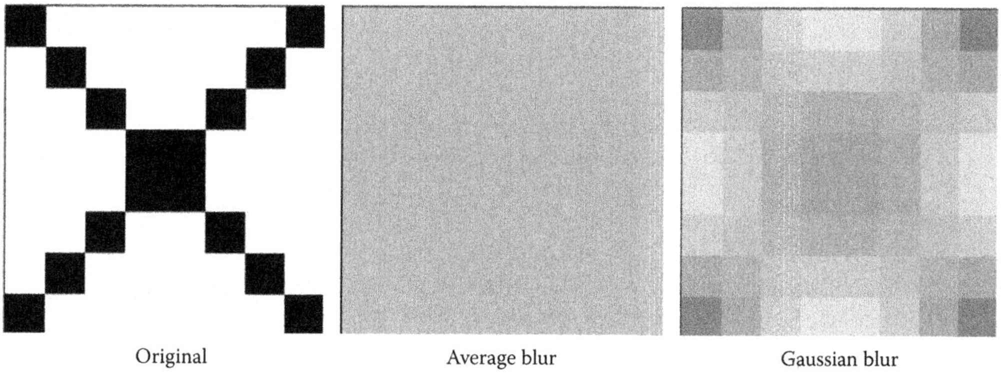

FIG 7.26 Average blur versus Gaussian blur.

selection are given more weight, and therefore the blur appears to radiate outward. The blur effect in Unity is shown in Figure 7.26.

7.4.3 Grayscale

Grayscale reduces colored images down to variations of gray such that it looks like a black and white photograph. The simplest method for creating grayscale from color is the *average* method that takes the red, green, and blue components of a pixel and divides by three. This new value is reassigned to the original pixel. The *lightness* method sets a pixel value to the average of its highest and lowest color components. For example, if a pixel had an RGB value of 255, 45, 60, the highest value 255 and the lowest value 45 would be added together and divided by two. The final method, called *luminosity*, gives the best grayscale result by cleverly weighting the green value to account for human eye sensitivity. The luminosity algorithm is 0.21 R + 0.71 G + 0.07 B.

7.4.4 Motion Blur

Motion blur is an effect used to make something look like it is moving rapidly or to give the player a dreamy view of the environment. The pixels appear to streak across the page in the direction of the motion. In addition, objects can have ghosting effects surrounding them. The effect is achieved by partially leaving the previous frame on the screen while rendering the next one. This effect is also useful in persuading players that their character is disorientated as a result of being drugged or in a dream state. Motion blur is often used in racing games when the scenery is moving past the camera quickly, and in first and third person games when the character is moving quickly.

7.4.5 Sepia Tone

Sepia tone is the brownish tinge seen on old photographs and film. It is achieved using an algorithm similar to that used for grayscale. The red, green, and blue values of a pixel are reset based on the addition of percentages of their original color components, thus

$$\text{Sepia Red} = R \times 0.393 + G \times 0.769 + B \times 0.189$$
$$\text{Sepia Green} = R \times 0.349 + G \times 0.686 + B \times 0.168$$
$$\text{Sepia Blue} = R \times 0.272 + G \times 0.534 + B \times 0.131$$

You may have seen sepia tone used in the cut scenes of games where an event is taking place in the past or in actual environments when the game is set in the past. *The Sims Medieval* uses sepia tones for its world map and storytelling still shots.

Sepia tone applied in Unity is demonstrated in Figure 7.24.

7.4.6 Twirl

The twirl effect takes a portion of the screen pixels and wraps them around a whirlpool-type motion. This effect is usually seen in film footage or cut scenes when one scene is crossing into another. A similar effect can be found in vintage Batman animated cartoons (and other similar productions) where the bat insignia was circled in and out in between acts.

7.4.7 Bloom

Bloom is the glow effect seen around light sources that extend into the environment. It makes an image look overexposed and the colors washed out. It is more prominent the stronger the light source and the dustier the environment.

7.4.8 Flares

Flares are bursts of reflected and refracted light. The most commonly known flare is a lens flare, which causes a series of translucent, rainbow, bright circles on an image from light passing through a camera lens. It is often used in games to give the player the illusion that they are looking into the sun when facing skyward.

Flares can also be caused by bright light passing through partially transparent materials such as glass or reflected off shiny surfaces such as polished metal and water.

7.4.9 Color Correction

Color correction does as its name suggests. It takes certain colors occurring in an image and changes them to another color. For example, a hill covered in green grass could be made to look like a hill of dead brown grass by replacing the color green with brown.

In games, color correction can be used for rendering night vision effects, changing most of the colors to green. Each R, G, B value is matched with a replacement R, G, B value. At any time, color correction, as with all these effects, can be turned off. Using this method, you could simulate the well-known Splinter Cell game play where the main character can use his night vision goggles in dark environments, which changes what the player sees on the screen at a press of a button.

7.4.10 Edge Detection

An edge detection algorithm scans an image for areas where pixels in close proximity contrast in color. Because the difference between individual pixels would produce erratic effects, the algorithm must determine if a pixel is on the edge of an area of similar color by looking at its surrounding pixels. This creates a picture that looks like a sketched outline.

The optimal approach to edge detection is the Canny edge detection algorithm. Further technical details about it can be found at http://en.wikipedia.org/wiki/Canny_edge_detector.

The edge detection algorithm in Unity outlines all objects with a black line as shown in Figure 7.24.

7.4.11 Crease

Creasing is a non-photorealistic effect that increases the visibility of game world objects by drawing a line around the silhouette, much like in comic book images. In a busy game environment with many objects, such as buildings and trees, drawn from similar colors and tones, objects can become difficult to distinguish. By applying creasing at differing depths, the line can distinguish between near and far objects.

7.4.12 Fish Eye

The fish eye effect produces an image as seen in a spherical mirror or through a wide-angle lens. The image produced is hemispherical in nature. Depending on the amount of curvature in the image, it can look completely distorted and inside out as the one from Unity in Figure 7.24. When used in a less exaggerated manner, the effect widens the field of view, showing more of the scene than is in the camera's normal range. However, to fit in the extra parts of the image, at the outer edges the scene starts to bend with the effect, becoming more exaggerated the farther it is from the center.

7.4.13 Sun Shafts

Sun shafts are produced by a bright light source being partially occluded and viewed when passing through atmospheric particles. For example, sun shafts are prominent after a sun shower when the sun is partially blocked by clouds and when the air is heavy with moisture. You might also imagine sun shafts coming through a dusty attic window or between the trees in a rainforest.

This effect as produced in Unity is shown in Figure 7.24.

7.4.14 Vignette

Vignetting is an effect used to focus the viewer's attention on an object in an image by darkening and/or blurring the peripheries. The start of each James Bond movie provides an example where the viewer is looking down the barrel of a gun. The view is restricted to a small circle in the middle of the screen, and the supposed inside of the gun barrel sets the outside to black. Vignetting need not be this dramatic. Instead of the edge darkening abruptly, it might fade to black instead.

In a game view, a vignette can focus the player's attention on an area of the game environment or be used to restrict the player's view.

7.4.15 Screen Space Ambient Occlusion

The screen space ambient occlusion (SSAO) effect approximates shadowing in from ambient light based purely on the image produced by the camera. As it is a postproduction effect, it does not rely on a light source or on information about an object's materials to calculate shadows. It works with the image to emphasize holes, creases, and areas where objects meet. For example, without any lighting in a game environment to provide dynamic or baked shadows, trees stand on the terrain but somehow look disconnected and not in contact. SSAO provides a dusting of shadow around these connection points such that these types of intersections do not appear unnatural.

☉ Unity Hands On
Post-Processing Effects

Step 1: To apply a whole variety of post-processing effects to your game environment, you first need to download the Post Processing Stack from the Unity Asset Store as shown in Figure 7.27. You'll also need a game environment setup to add the post-production effects to. The terrain you created earlier will suffice.

Step 2: Select the main camera in the Hierarchy and then in the Inspector add the Post-Processing Behaviour component as shown in Figure 7.28.

Step 3: This component requires a profile. To create one, right-click in the Project and select Create > Post-Processing Profile as shown in Figure 7.29.

Step 4: If you rename this new profile in the Project and then select it, you'll be able to inspect its properties in the Inspector. These are shown in Figure 7.30. In this case the fog has been turned on and the Ambient Occlusion and Depth of Field set. This profile can be dragged and dropped from the Project Window onto the Post-Processing Behaviour component shown in Figure 7.28 to apply the settings to the camera.

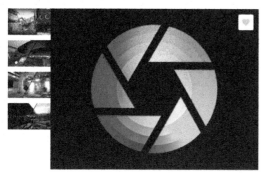

FIG 7.27 Unity's Post Processing Stack plugin.

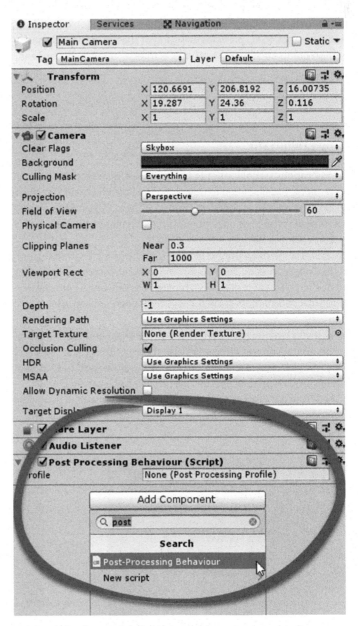

FIG 7.28 Adding the Post-Processing Behaviour component to the camera.

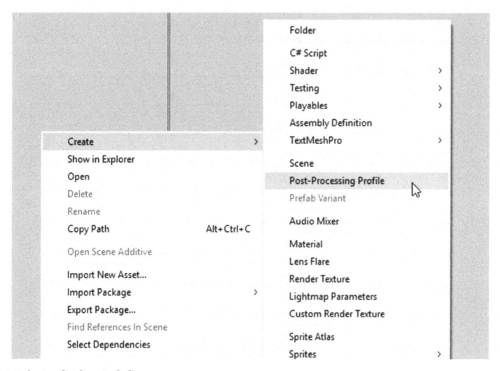

FIG 7.29 Creating a Post-Processing Profile.

Figure 7.31 presents the same terrain with and without the Post-Processing Profile added. The terrain view on the left has fog, ambient occlusion, and depth of field added. Notice how the addition of these simple post-production effects lifts the quality of the scene entirely, making it look far more professional and polished.

This section examined a variety of camera effects. These are added to the rendering postproduction after the camera has determined the scene. As such, they can require a great deal of computer processing and are not recommended for use on platforms without sufficient graphics processing capability (like many mobile devices).

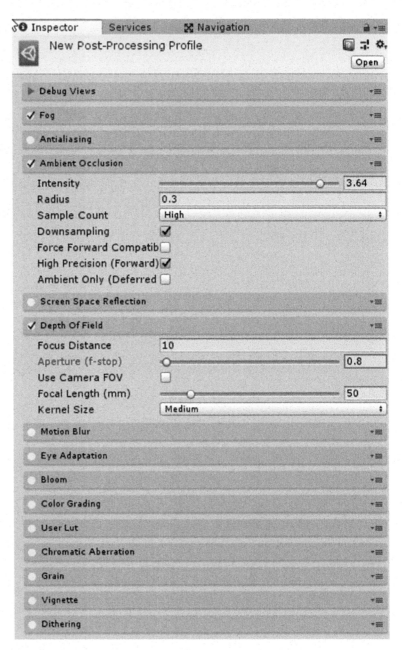

FIG 7.30 Setting the values of a Post-Processing Profile.

FIG 7.31 A game environment without post-processing effects (left) and with (right).

⚪ **On the Web**

Post Processing Stack

For more information on the application of Unity's Post Processing Stack see the following YouTube tutorial:

https://youtu.be/rvdqfUvnzUQ

7.5 Skies

There are a number of ways to create skies for a 3D game environment. The easiest way is to set the background color of the camera to blue. Alternatively, if you want to include fog, setting the fog color to the background color gives the illusion of a heavy mist and provides for landscape optimization as discussed in Chapter 2.

To get clues as to what a game environment sky should look like, we can just look up. Our sky is more than a blue blanket covering the earth. Its color changes throughout the day with the position of the sun, the quality of the air, the weather, and the longitude and latitude.

The daytime sky appears blue due to a phenomenon known as *Rayleigh scattering* (named after the British physicist Lord Rayleigh). As sunlight enters the earth's atmosphere, it interacts with the air and dust particles, which bend the light and scatter the different colors across the sky. The color that is scattered the most is blue. At sunset, the sun rays enter the atmosphere at different angles relative to the viewer and cause more yellow and red light to be scattered. Rayleigh scattering is caused by particles smaller than the wavelength of light.

Particles that are comparable or larger than the wavelength of light also scatter it. This effect is described by the *Mie theory*, developed by physicist Gustav Mie. The theory explains how particles such as water droplets affect the scattering of light. The Mie theory elucidates why clouds are different shades of gray and white.

Another factor influencing the look of the sky is *turbidity*. Turbidity describes the amount of suspended solid particles in a fluid. In the sky, turbidity relates to the quantity of dust, ash, water, or smoke particles in the air. The density of these particles affects both Rayleigh scattering and the Mie theory, as it also adds to light scattering. For example, when the earth experiences a large volcanic event, which spews tons of dust and ash into the air, sunsets appear to last longer and have more vivid colors.

The following sections examine two ways to create skies: one that uses a simple texture and the other that considers the physical theories of light and air interaction described earlier.

7.5.1 Skyboxes

The most common method of creating a sky with cloud textures is to use a Skybox. This is essentially an inside-out cube placed over the camera with seamless images of the sky rendered on it. Because it only requires six planes and six textures, it is a relatively cost-effective way to create a convincing-looking sky. The six textures are referred to by their position on the cube: up, down, front, back, left, and right. An example Skybox is shown in Figure 7.32.

To use your own Skybox, create a folder on your computer containing each of the Skybox textures. Name the textures after the folder name and suffix with their position. For example, if your folder were called *sunset*, then each of the images would be sunset_up.jpg, sunset_down.jpg, sunset_front. jpg, sunset_back.jpg, sunset_left.jpg, and sunset_right.jpg. Drag and drop this folder into the Project. Your custom Skybox will now be available in the Render Settings.

◁ Unity Specifics
Skyboxes
There are numerous Skyboxes available for free on the Unity Asset Store. To use them, simply download and import.

To apply a Skybox to a scene, select the Main Camera and location the Camera component in the Inspector. Set the *Clear Flags* value to *Skybox*. Select Window > Rendering > Lighting Settings from the main menu. Set the Skybox you'd like to use under Scene > Environment > Skybox Material as shown in Figure 7.33.

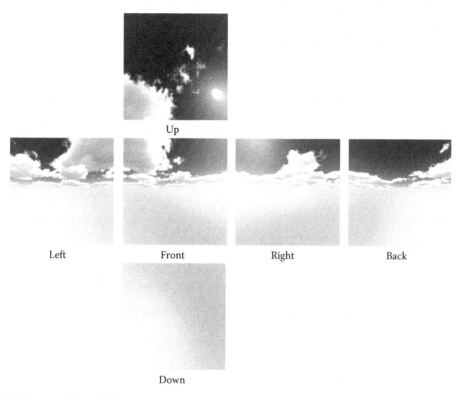

Up

Left   Front   Right   Back

Down

FIG 7.32 The six textures making up a Skybox.

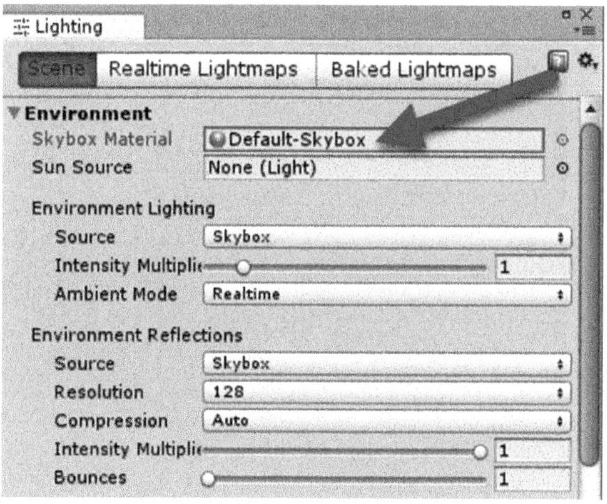

FIG 7.33 Adding a Skybox to a scene.

7.5.2 SkyDomes

A SkyDome, as the name suggests, is a dome mesh placed over the environment with a sky texture stretched across the inside surface as shown in Figure 7.34.

The SkyDome is attached to the player's camera, like an oversized helmet, such that it moves everywhere with the player. Unlike a real helmet, it does not rotate as the camera looks around—it just translates, ensuring that it is always projecting a sky with the player at the center. This ensures that the player never sees the edges of the dome. If the dome is not big enough, as terrain and scenery come into view, they will pop through the dome edges. Strategic sizing and positioning of the dome are critical to ensure that this does not occur.

Because the UVs of the SkyDome are inline in arcs across the sky mesh, it is simple to scroll textures across the mesh in the same way the textures are scrolled across a plane in Chapter 2. This makes it easy to add cloud textures to the dome and move them across the sky.

In the next workshop, a SkyDome package created by Unity Developer Martijn Dekker will be used to place a sky, complete with moving clouds and a sun, around a first person controller. Dekker has taken into consideration Rayleigh scattering and the Mie Theory to produce a truly exceptional SkyDome.

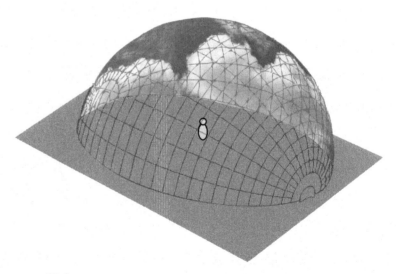

FIG 7.34 A SkyDome.

◉ Unity Hands On

SkyDomes

Step 1: Create a new Unity Project. Import the Character Controller and Terrain Assets from the Environment package.

Step 2: In the scene add a Terrain. Style and texture as you see fit.

Step 3: Add an FPC to the Scene. Position the player over the terrain.

Step 4: Play to ensure that the player is not falling below the terrain. Reposition the player as necessary.

Step 5: Download *Chapter Seven/SkyDome.unitypackage* from the website and import into Unity.

Step 6: From the SkyDome folder created in Project, after the import, drag and drop the SkyDome prefab into the Hierarchy. The SkyDome will appear as a large white sphere in the Scene.

Step 7: Select the SkyDome object in the Hierarchy. Locate the SkyDome Script component in the Inspector and set the Player attribute to the FPC as shown in Figure 7.35.

Step 8: Because the SkyDome object generates its own sun you do not need to add a directional light. However you do need to change the light type to Direction in the code. Modify *SkyDomeScript.cs* to that in Listing 7.5.

Listing 7.5 Set the Sun's light type to directional

```
void Start ()
{
    sunLight = new GameObject("Sun");
    sunLight.AddComponent<Light>();
    sunLight.GetComponent<Light>().type =
        LightType.Directional;
}
```

Step 9: Play. A SkyDome with clouds will fill the sky. The SkyDome has an internal clock, which will cause the sun to move across the sky, making for a day, sunset, night, and sunrise cycle. There are two layers of clouds whose settings are independent.

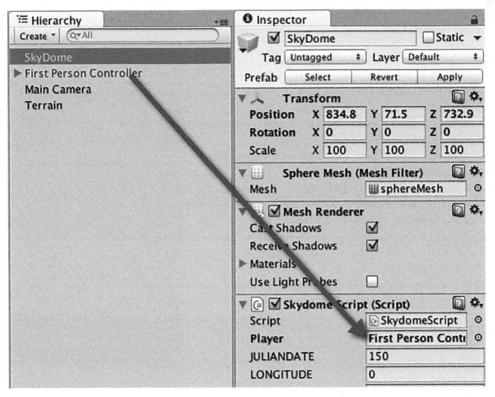

FIG 7.35 The SkyDome Script component and setting the player attribute.

In the SkyDome Script settings in the Inspector, you can modify the specific SkyDome properties for a variety of effects. These include:

- JULIANDATE: Sets the day of the year (with January 1 being day 1)
- LONGITUDE and LATITUDE: Player's position coordinates on the surface
- TIME: The time of day, where 0 is midnight
- Time Speed Factor: The speed at which time passes
- Turbidity: The amount of scattering particles in the air. The higher the turbidity, the longer the sunsets and sunrises last.
- Cloud Speed 1 and 2: The speed at which the clouds move across the sky
- Cloud Height 1 and 2: The relative distance the clouds appear to be from the player
- FRay Factor: The effect of Rayleigh scattering, which determines how blue the sky appears. With a setting of 0 there is no blue (the sky remains black)
- FMie Factor: The effect of the Mie Theory with respect to the brightness of the clouds
- FSun Color Intensity: The brightness of the sun
- For example, if you set the LONGITUDE to 18, the LATTITUDE to 65, and the JULIANDATE to 1, which would position the player somewhere in

Iceland on the 1st of January (winter), you will notice that the days are very short and that the sun stays pretty much in the same position in the sky when it is up. If you set the Turbidity to 10, the sunrise and sunset will be longer and the sun's glare will appear brighter.

7.5.3 Clouds

The previous two sections examined skies with clouds. Clouds on the Skybox were fixed and did not change position or color. Clouds on the SkyDome moved across the sky and exhibited turbulence. While the SkyDome method includes layers of clouds, giving the perception of depth, the player can never get above or in among them. When you want to portray clouds in a 3D fashion such that you can walk around or through them, then you need to explore techniques for generating volumetric fog.

Volumetric fog is a more complex technique than the fog used previously. Although the stock standard fog used in computer graphics applies a faded-out effect over all 3D assets in a scene, volumetric fog is contained within a 3D space. This makes it more processor intensive to render. However, this is not a real issue on today's consoles and desktop machines.

The types of natural effects that can be achieved with volumetric fog include low-lying clouds, mist, and dust as shown in Figure 7.36. You use it whenever you want to look at clouds from above or move through a variety of fog

FIG 7.36 Volumetric clouds.

densities. Whereas the default fog gives a set density, in volumetric fog the player can walk through dense patches and then light patches.

One method for producing volumetric clouds is to use mass instances of billboards with cloud textures on them. The system used to produce the image in Figure 7.36 was developed by Unity developer Julian Oliden and is available for download from https://assetstore.unity.com/packages/tools/particles-effects/cloudstoy-35559. It is also included in the starter project file in the next workshop.

☺ Unity Hands On

Volumetric Clouds

Step 1: Import the free CloudsToy Manager from the Asset Store into a new Unity project.

Step 2: Locate the CloudsToy Mngr prefab in the Project under the Volumetric Clouds prefab.

Step 3: Drag and drop this prefab into the Scene. You will not be able to see it yet as it requires a Terrain to align itself.

Step 4: Add a Terrain to the scene.

Step 5: Sculpt the terrain or import a height map. Paint the terrain as you like.

Step 6: Add a directional light.

Step 7: Select the CloudsToy Mngr in the Hierarchy. Press play. In the Scene, you will be able to see the volume of the clouds over the terrain as shown in Figure 7.37. The CloudsToy Mngr sizes itself correctly to cover the terrain.

FIG 7.37 CloudsToy created clouds.

Step 8: Add an FPC to the Scene. Delete the original main camera.

Step 9: Play.

Step 10: If you have a mountainous terrain, you might want to lower the CloudsToy Mngr object such that it sits with the mountains poking out of the yellow bounding box in the Scene. This will create clouds that the player can walk through and above.

Settings for the CloudsToy Mngr can be changed through the Inspector by selecting the CloudsToy Mngr object in the Hierarchy. Settings begin with Cloud Presets, which allow you to select from Stormy-, Sunrise-, and Fantasy-looking clouds. These are useful to give you an idea of what the package can do, as well as recovering to a more realistic-looking cloud type, should you modify the other settings to the point of no return and end up with pinpoint clouds or no clouds at all!

Of particular note in the settings are the Cloud Creation Size and Disappear Multiplier. The Cloud Creation Size sets the size of the blue box displayed in the Scene. This box is the area in which clouds are spawned. The Disappear Multiplier determines the size of the yellow box. This is the area to which clouds will travel from the yellow box, but beyond which they fade away.

Further down in the settings are cloud colors, sizes, and velocity.

The CloudsToy Mngr can be integrated into your own projects by importing the Chapter Seven/CloudsToy.unitypackage available from the website.

7.6 Weather

The weather affects the look and feel of our environment dramatically. Although players will not be able to feel the cold of virtual snow in a game environment, the correct lighting, coloring, and special effects will make them feel like they are there and add an extra dimension to your scene.

7.6.1 Wind

Wind is one of these elements. Although you cannot see it, it moves environmental objects around. It looks especially good in a 3D world when acting on cloth, trees, and grass.

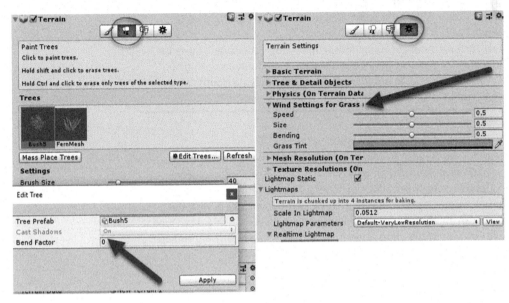

◁ Unity Specifics
Terrain Wind Element

A terrain in Unity can have wind applied through the setting of the bend factor of trees and using a wind zone. To do this, select a tree in the Terrain Editor and click on *Edit Trees*. In the pop-up window you will find a value for *bend* as shown in Figure 7.38. Set this to a value other than zero to make the trees sway in the breeze. Add a wind zone by selecting GameObject > Create 3D Object > Wind Zone, then move the object near the FPC. Play to see the trees move in the wind.

Grass and flower objects will automatically sway with the terrain breeze. The wind settings for this are found in the settings panel of the Terrain Editor as shown in Figure 7.38.

◉ Unity Hands On
Flying the Flag

In this workshop, you will learn how to add wind effects with the Unity physics system.

Step 1: Create a new Unity Project. Add a cube and resize to the shape of a long flagpole.

Step 2: Add a plane to the scene and position it at the top of the flagpole. It will become the flag. Remove its Mesh Renderer and Mesh Collider. The flag will become invisible for the moment.

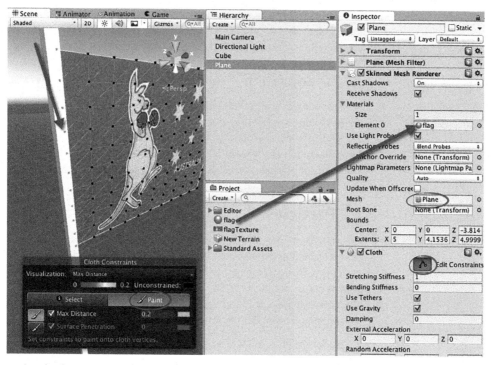

FIG 7.39 Setup for a flag.

Step 3: In the Inspector, use Add Component to add a Physics > Cloth to the plane.

Step 4: Create a new material with a flag texture.

Step 5: Add the flag material to the Skinned Mesh Renderer of the flag. And set its Mesh property to that of the plane as shown in Figure 7.39.

Step 6: Click the Edit Constraints button for the Cloth to bring up the Cloth Constraints window. The vertices of the flag will turn black. Using the paint tool, select the vertices closest to the flagpole. They will turn green indicating that they will now be fixed.

Step 7: Play. The flag will now flop under gravity but remain fixed in the location of the green painted vertices.

Step 8: To add a wind effect to the flag, locate the values for its External Acceleration and Random Acceleration in the Cloth component attached to the plane. Set External Acceleration to (80,5,0) and the Random Acceleration to (100,5,20). These values will place a force on the cloth causing it to push in mostly in the X direction.

The External Acceleration value maintains a constant force in the given direction according to the x, y and z values. The Random Acceleration adds in a fluctuating component that modifies the External Acceleration values.

In this case, the constant force in the *X* direction is 80, but it is randomly modified to values + and −100. Therefore, the *X* direction of the wind can be anything from −20 to +180. This gives the flag a turbulent motion.

7.6.2 Precipitation

Rain and snow add yet another dimension to the game environment. Not only do they look good, but they also add atmosphere and can be used to impair the vision of the player strategically. Precipitation falls into a category of computer graphics special effects called *particle systems*. They rightly deserve a category of their own and as such will be dealt with in the next section.

7.7 Particles

Particle systems are objects constructed from the mass generation of animated billboards. Each billboard represents a single particle. They are used most commonly in games to generate fluidic and fuzzy phenomena such as rain, snow, dust, fire, smoke, and explosions. The CloudsToy implemented previously and the Detonator objects used in other chapters' workshops are examples of particle systems.

A particle system consists of an emitter that spawns the particles at a specific location. As they are created, each particle is given a velocity, size, and life length. The particle begins its life, is scaled to the given size, and travels off at the set velocity for the length of its life. At the end of its life, the particle is destroyed. For extra effect, a particle can be given a rotational velocity, an animated color change, and size changes throughout its life. Several example particle systems are illustrated in Figure 7.40.

Particle systems can be very processor intensive as they may require hundreds or thousands of particles to simulate the desired effect. However, having each particle represented as a 2D billboard helps lower overheads (somewhat).

A number of prefab particle systems are included in Unity packages; however, the best way to get an understanding of their intricacies is to create them from scratch.

⊙ **Unity Hands On**
A Snowy Retreat
Step 1: Download *Chapter Seven/Particles.zip* and open the SnowyRetreat scene in Unity. In it, you will find a snowy landscape, trees and a log cabin.
Step 2: From the main menu, select GameObject > Effects > Particle System. A default particle system will be added to the Scene. Double-click on it to focus on it. It will be an upward spray of little white dots.

Note, you can see a particle system in action, even when the game is not in play, just by highlighting it in the Hierarchy.

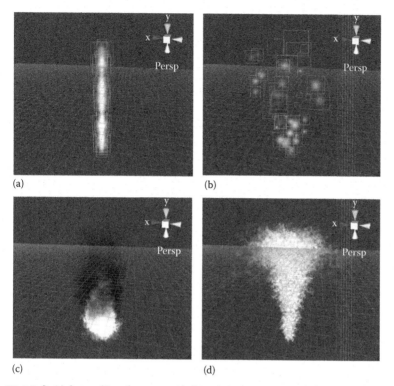

(a)

(b)

(c)

(d)

FIG 7.40 Particle Systems: (a) a uniform system with all particles having a vertical velocity; (b) a vertical system with random x and y velocities, expanding size and changing color; and (c) a fire made with three systems—one for inner glow, one for flames, and one for smoke; and (d) a water fountain.

Step 3: The first particle system we make will be smoke. Position the starting point of the particle system in the cabin's chimney. This starting point is called an emitter. Setting the smoke's transform position to (1190,30,1180) will position it in the correct place.

Step 4: Next, we want to make the smoke particles look like smoke. We can do this by creating a material with a smoke puff texture and adding it to the particle system. Create a new material and apply the smokepuff texture that you will find in the Project. Set the shader for the material to Particles/Additive. Drag and drop the new material onto the Particle System. The small white dots will change to small smoke puffs.

Step 5: With the particle system selected in the Hierarchy, modify its starting particle size to 5 to increase the size of each puff as shown in Figure 7.41. This will look large but that is okay for now.

Step 6: If you observe smoke, you will notice that each apparent puff gets larger the further it is away from the emitter. We can modify the particles size over its lifetime by adding a curve or line to this property in the Inspector. To do this, at the very top of the particle system settings, click on the Open Editor button shown in Figure 7.42.

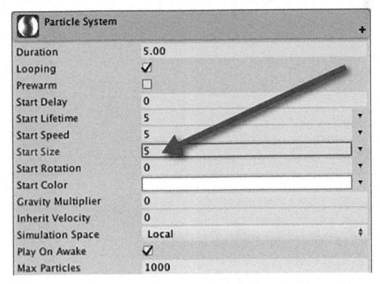

FIG 7.41 Changing the starting size of a particle.

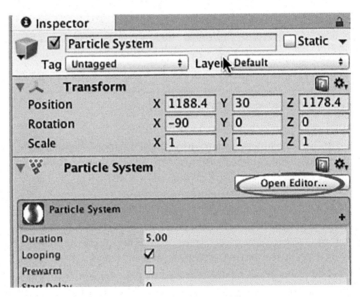

FIG 7.42 Opening the particle editor.

Locate the Size Over Lifetime option and click on the round check box next to it to turn on the option. Next, select the small size diagram to edit the size curve and click on the option shown in Figure 7.43.

The graph determines the scaling of the particle size from its birth to its death. The default for the curve will be to set the particle at a scale

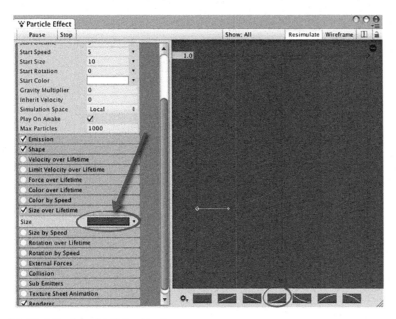

FIG 7.43 Editing the particle lifetime size options.

of 0 of its original size. Move this up to around 0.3 as you want to be able to see the start of the smoke. At the end of its life, you will want the particle to be in full size, and therefore you can leave the end of the curve where it is. Note that you can control the curve anyway you like or even set the size growth to linear. It is totally up to you to achieve the look you are after.

Step 7: Still in the Particle Editor, if you want the smoke to travel higher before it disappears, change the Start Lifetime of the particle to a bigger value. It is the option just above where you changed the Start Size in Step 5. Change this value to 15.

Step 8: To condense the smoke into a narrower stream, you can change the angle at which the particles are emitted. Each emitter takes on its own shape in which particles are created. In this case, it is a cone. To change the angle of the cone, change the value of Angle in the Shape settings shown in Figure 7.44. Set the value to 10. Notice in the Scene how it affects the shape of the smoke.

Step 9: Next, we want to stop the smoke popping out of existence at the top. Each particle lives only for a certain amount of time before it is recycled and reused by the emitter. At the end of its life, it is destroyed. To mask the popping effect when the particle is destroyed, we can have it fade out to nothing over its lifetime and then when it is finally destroyed, it will be transparent and unnoticeable. Turn on the Color Over Lifetime option and then click on the color box. This will bring up a Gradient Editor as shown in Figure 7.45.

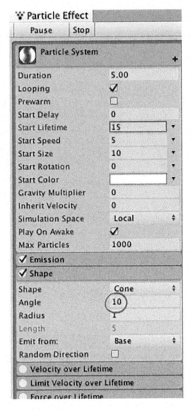

FIG 7.44 Modifying the particle emitter angle.

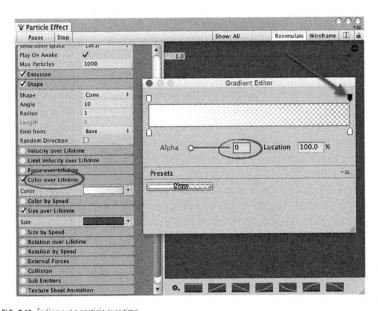

FIG 7.45 Fading out a particle over time.

Select the pointer at the top right of the color chart and set its alpha to 0.

Watch the smoke. It will now fade out of existence rather than popping. This is a much more elegant effect.

Step 10: At this point, the smoke still looks a bit scattered and light. To increase its thickness, increase its Start Size to 20. You will also want to have the smoke start out small at the chimney entrance but grow more rapidly as soon as it is out. To do this, you can modify the Size over Lifetime curve as shown in Figure 7.46. By right-clicking on the curve, a new key can be added that allows you to manipulate the shape of the curve. Try this out for yourself.

Step 11: Last, but not least, we will add a little wind effect to the smoke. There are numerous options for adding a force to a particle system to make it behave in all manner of ways, but for now we will add a little force to the top of it. In other words, toward the end of its life (at the top of the smoke stream), we want the particles to trail away. Manipulation of the force is done in the Force over Lifetime setting as shown in Figure 7.47. Modify the differing effects until you find something you like.

Step 12: Moving away from the smoke effect, we will now make it snow. First add an FPC to the Scene. You will find a prefab for one already in the Project > Standard Assets > Characters > Prefabs folder. Add the FPC near the cabin and then delete the Main Camera that was previously in the scene as you can use the one on the FPC from now on.

Step 13: Add another particle system to the Scene. This time, give it the name Snow in the Hierarchy. In the Inspector, set the X Rotation of the

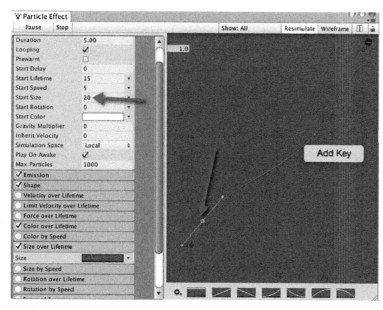

FIG 7.46 Manipulating the particle size curve.

FIG 7.47 Adding a force to the particle system to affect its flow.

system to 90. Open the particle editor and set the Shape of the emitter to Box with an X and Y scale of 20. Set the Start Size to 0.2, the Max Particles to 2000 and the Emission Rate to 200. You can also play with the Force over Lifetime to add a light breeze to blow the particles around. These settings are shown in Figure 7.48.

Step 14: You should now have some decent snow falling in the Scene. The only problem is that if you press Play, you will be able to walk out of

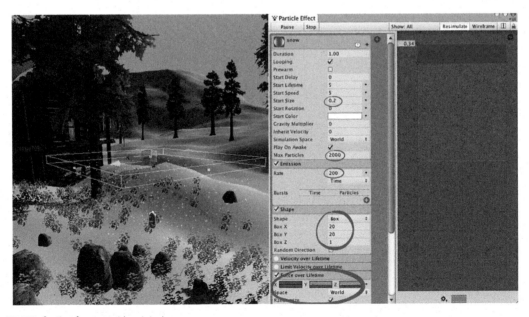

FIG 7.48 Creation of a snow particle emission box.

the area where the snow is falling. To prevent this happening, attach the snow particle system, as a child, to the FPC.

Step 15: As you walk around in the game, if you find the FPC out runs the snow, you will have to make the snow emitter box bigger and add more particles to the Emission Rate. It may take a little playing around with the settings to get the effect you want.

7.8 Summary

This chapter examined the artistic and scientific aspects of the real world in order to recreate similar environments as game environments. So much of real-world physics and mathematics translates into virtual environments, and an understanding of these assists us in making the virtual look and feel as real as possible for a player.

Only through observing the world around us, the types of vegetation, the shapes of rocks, the colors in the sky, and the way things move can we gain a deeper appreciation of the articulation of what can turn a virtual environment into something believable. This chapter has only scratched at the surface of what is possible in developing the aesthetics of a game environment, although it is hoped that you have gained enough knowledge and confidence to go in search of new techniques that you can incorporate in your games to make them look that much more professional and polished.

Reference

Adams, E. (2014). *Fundamentals of Game Design*. Pearson Education, Thousand Oaks, CA.

CHAPTER 8

Mechanics for External Forces

The Force will be with you. Always.

Obi-Wan Kenobi

8.1 Introduction

Designing games is challenging—now more than ever. In addition to the high-end gaming consoles and high-powered desktop graphics cards, there are also low-powered mobile devices and peripherals such as the *Oculus Rift* and *HTC Vive* for which to cater. Of course, if you are designing a game for a mobile device, it is not likely that it will be released on a console. Besides considering the different ways in which art assets are delivered, the designer also has the challenge of coming up with a unique gaming experience.

The flood of mobile devices in the pockets of almost every consumer over nine years of age, has recently seen many small and independent game studios pop up, each battling for the casual gamer's attention.

Human–computer interaction (HCI) technology that once only existed in science fiction is now forefront in the designers' mind. Whether it be the tapping and dragging of a finger across a tablet screen or the tracking of waving arms and legs in front of a screen, the opportunity to create truly unique user experiences has never been more achievable.

Furthermore, as if the challenge of designing for multiple platforms and a diversity of HCI methods were not enough, multiplayer modes have almost become a necessity. Thanks to Twitter, Facebook, and other social media platforms, today's players want to share their gaming experience with their friends, even if it is just to tell them that they beat the other's high score.

This chapter examines the issue of new technologies with relation to game design and development. It examines how to integrate interactive devices, mobile devices, and social networking with your own games.

As the specifications for these external devices are constantly in flux, workshops in this chapter will be kept to a minimum as no printed book can keep up to date with such dynamic content. Instead you will be guided as to the design and use of these technologies, and any exercises given should be taken to be correct at the time of writing and used to further your understanding of how the technology works.

8.2 Mobile

Believe it or not, mobile phones were not originally designed for playing games. However, as games have become more popular on the platform and their hardware and screens have advanced, games that take advantage of all that these devices can offer have grown in numbers. Primarily, these include interacting with touch screens, built-in motion sensors, and location-based services. In this section, these features and how to access them from within Unity will be explained.

Revenue from mobile video games overtook that of consoles in 2015, experiencing 40% growth in the market place. This growth was somewhat due to Google and Apple's domination of the selling space, which made it easy for anyone (with the appropriate skills) to publish a game. Unity realized the potential of mobile games early on and moved to capitalize on the boom by making mobile game development a streamlined process in their software. Today, over 80% of mobile games in the marketplace have been made with Unity.

8.2.1 Design Considerations

Initially, the biggest challenges facing mobile game creators were the lower processing power of the devices and their small screen size. As technology has advanced, however, the processing power is becoming less of an issue and, while it is still important to keep the game highly optimized for performance, the small screen remains.

The design of mobile games is very much focused on HCI, where the player is now coming into direct contact with the game. Without the need for keyboards or controllers, the player is thrust into a gaming experience, in which their haptic senses are able to relate to the environment in a more natural way.

While the principles of design for games and their interfaces, discussed in Chapter 6, still apply for small screens, some elements require more consideration.

8.2.1.1 Text

Text must be kept to a minimum and always be readable. The smallest acceptable size you should consider is 17 px according to Apple and 18 px as recommended by Google. For forms with very obvious labels, you can get away with 14 px and even 11 px, though this should only be used for single words not paragraphs. Note, however, that pixel size does not equate to an individual font's point size (pt) that is used to distinguish between font sizes. As illustrated in Figure 8.1 Arial 18 pt and Georgia 20 pt are both 14 px in height. You will not be able to tell exactly what pixel height a specific font is until you try it out. There are several online tools such as Endmemo

FIG 8.1 Relative font sizes.

(http://www.endmemo.com/sconvert/pixelpoint.php) that convert from point to pixel. They can only provide an approximation, but they are a good starting point.

In addition to font size being an issue with readability, you also need to consider the style of the font. A font with more flourishes is more difficult to read when it gets smaller. Extra decorative strokes on text are called serifs. In Figure 8.1, the serif font Georgia is illustrated with red lines highlighting some of the extra strokes. A font without these flourishes, such as Arial, is called a sans serif, where sans translates to *without*. Sans serif fonts work better on small screens and when used at small point sizes, as their simplistic structure will survive reproduction and smearing, whereas serifs will become blurred.

This restriction on the use of text makes the mobile environment ideal for the use of icons and metaphors. If you examine many of the popular mobile games, you will find less text and more icons.

8.2.1.2 Icons and User Interface Elements
Icons provide the designer with appropriate metaphors to communicate a message quickly. As discussed in Chapter 6, a metaphor can be used in place of text as the old adage, "a picture is worth a thousand words," comes into its own. For example, when there is limited space on the screen, an Information Button takes up much less space than the typed word *Information*. Furthermore, a well-designed icon can be recognized at quite small pixel sizes, whereas text on buttons can become illegible.

Of course, if icons used as buttons, become too small, they will not be usable. Unlike the accuracy a person can get with a mouse cursor on a screen, on a touch device, selection occurs with a finger. According to Apple's Human Interface Guidelines for iOS development, the comfortable minimum tappable size is 44 × 44 px. Microsoft suggests that the size can be smaller at 34 px, whereas Nokia recommends 28 px.

Color is also important to consider when designing an icon. Besides its metaphorical nature, you will also want your icons to stand out from the crowd. Taking a look at some of the more popular icons in use today, you will notice that most of them are blue. This includes Facebook, Twitter, Linked-In, Skype, and Digg. These are well-known brands and easily recognizable; however, to make your own icon stand out, you should select colors that contrast with those making up the majority of existing icons. The ones that work best use limited colors with a highly stylized and simple graphic, such as the orange RSS feed icon illustrated in Figure 8.2.

8.2.1.3 Gameplay
The games dominating the mobile charts are very different from the AAA titles to be found on consoles. Besides the reduction in processing power and

FIG 8.2 Icons, text, and relative sizes on an iPhone 5.

screen size, the context in which mobile devices are used dictates the types of games played on them. A person will use his or her mobile device to play games when in transit. This could mean physically moving, such as traveling from one place to another on a train or airplane, waiting for something or someone, or when in-between activities. This means that a mobile game needs to be easy to pick up and play, require little commitment, and have short reward cycles. A look at the top 10 games in the Apple App Store at the time of writing confirms the popularity of these types of casual games. The list includes card games, slot machine games, tile sliding, and matching games, and tower-defense scenarios.

These casual games lend themselves well to the touch mechanic. They do not require tricky manipulation of a player character or complex hand-to-hand combat scenes. It is just tap and slide. This is the very interface mechanic employed by the highly successful *Angry Birds* franchise.

Such games also make use of icons and 2D art or simplistic cartoon style 3D isometric views. They are cheerful, responsive, charming, and highly polished. They implement the most basic of game mechanics discussed in Chapter 4 using natural human instinct to engage players and keep them coming back. The match-three-in-a-row mechanic employed in *Bejeweled* and very successfully in the *Candy Crush Saga* franchise is evidence.

One of the best ways to investigate as many of the new HCI features used in games as possible is to deploy an application to a mobile device. Unity supports both Android and iOS development with the purchase of an extra plugin.

The next workshop demonstrates deployment to the Android platform as the process is far simpler than for iOS.

◔ Unity Hands On
Your First Android Application

These are the steps required to build an Android application in Unity and put it onto a mobile device. You can build to an Android Device from both Mac and Windows. Every iOS and Android App requires a **Bundle ID** (also called Package Name). The format of a Bundle ID is:

    com DOT your_name_or_company_name DOT app_name

for example,

- com.holistic3d.arapp
- com.penny.mygame

Unity will require one of these to be entered into your project before it will let you build it out to your device. In the Google Play Store ecosystems the Package ID is used to uniquely identify your app. For now, you can make up your own bundle id. Once you have your Bundle ID it will need to be inserted into your Unity Project in the Player Settings.

Note: Steps 1 to 4 aren't necessary for Unity versions 2018.3 and higher as these installs are components that can be added to Unity during installation.

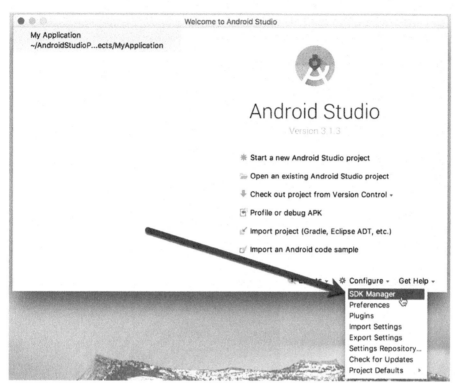

FIG 8.3 The Android Studio SDK Manager.

Step 1: Download the Java Development Kit (Version 8—make sure it is version 8) from https://www.oracle.com/technetwork/java/javase/downloads/jdk8-downloads-2133151.html and install.

Step 2: Install Android Studio by downloading it from here https://developer.android.com/studio/. Follow the instructions from Google for its installation.

Step 3: Open Android Studio and go to the software development kit (SDK) Manager as shown in Figure 8.3.

Step 4: From the Android SDK platforms, select and install the platform you will be building for. In this case, the author's phone has Android 8.0 (Oreo) installed. Take note of the Android SDK Location, as you will need to provide this to Unity. You can find this as per Figure 8.4.

Step 5: You'll need to activate the developer options on your mobile device. To do this, on the device under Settings > About phone > Software Information you can find the Android platform information. While you are on this screen on your device you should activate Developer Mode. To do this tap on the Build Number, as shown in Figure 8.5, seven times.

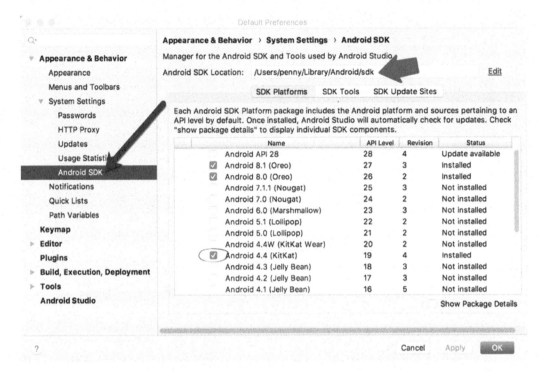

FIG 8.4 Finding the Android SDK installation location.

Step 6: Under Settings on the mobile device there will now be a Developer Options screen. Go into this and scroll down to turn on USB Debugging as shown in Figure 8.6. This will give your computer (and Unity/Android SDK) access to the mobile device. Higher up on this screen is an option to Stay awake. Turn this on to stop the device locking up and going to sleep while you are developing.

Step 7: Download the Android NDK version r13b (64-bit) from https://developer.android.com/ndk/downloads/ or, if you require an older version because Unity insists on it, visit https://developer.android.com/ndk/downloads/older_releases. Extract the *android-ndk* folder to a directory on your computer and note the location (Figure 8.7).

Step 8: Create a new Unity Project. It can be empty with just the Sample Scene.

Step 9: In Unity from the Main Menu select Unity > Preferences (Mac) or Edit > Preferences (Windows). In the Android section add the directories containing the Android SDK, JDK, and NDK that you've just installed.

Step 10: From the Main Menu select File > Build Settings (Figure 8.8a). This will open a Build Settings dialog box where you should ensure the scene/s that you want to build into your app are listed in the top box. If they are not, you can drag them from the Project window (Figure 8.8b).

FIG 8.5 Activating Developer Mode on an Android device.

Then select Android in the Platform box (Figure 8.8c). Finally, click on "Switch Platform" (Figure 8.8d).

Switching the platform will be relatively quick with an empty project. If you already have an application and want to switch the platform, Unity will perform some additional compilation and reimports and this could take a little while depending on the size of your application.

Step 11: The platform you are currently set to will be displayed in the top menu bar of Unity as shown in Figure 8.9.

Step 12: Open the Build Settings window again. (Main Menu > Build Settings) This time click on the "Player Settings" button (Figure 8.10a). In the Inspector add a Company Name (Figure 8.10b), Product Name

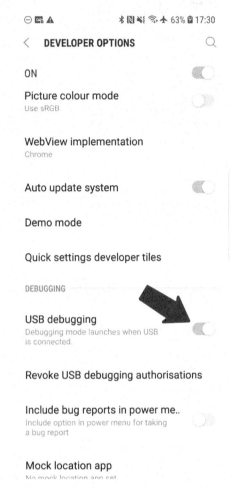

FIG 8.6 Turning on Developer Mode for an Android device.

(Figure 8.10c)—this is the name of the app that will appear on the mobile device below the icon and the Package Name (this will be the same as the Bundle ID if you are also building for iOS) otherwise the format is com.yourname.appname (Figure 8.10d). Click on "Build and Run" to deploy to your mobile device.

Step 13: With your mobile device while you do this, or maybe previously when you plugged the mobile into the computer, a screen asking for USB debugging permission will pop up as shown in Figure 8.11. Select OK when you see this. Make sure you keep an eye on your mobile while building for any messages that might need action, because if Unity fails to build you might not see what the issue was.

Step 14: After the build, the application will run on your mobile device (Figure 8.12).

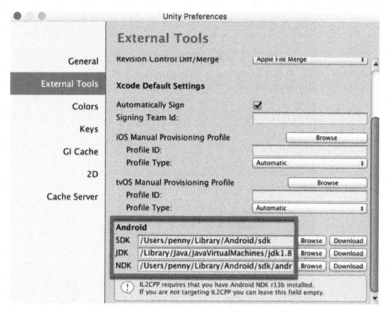

FIG 8.7 Configuring Unity for Android development.

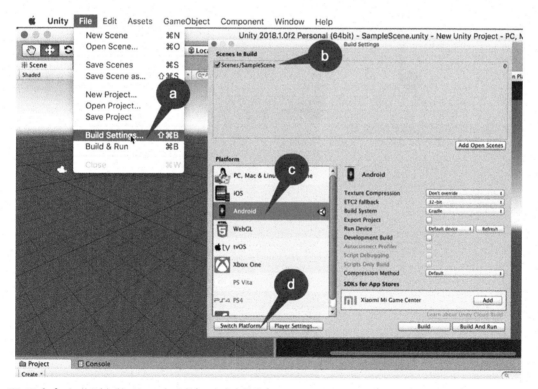

FIG 8.8 Configuring Unity's build settings and switching to the Android platform.

FIG 8.9 Identifying the platform Unity is set to build to.

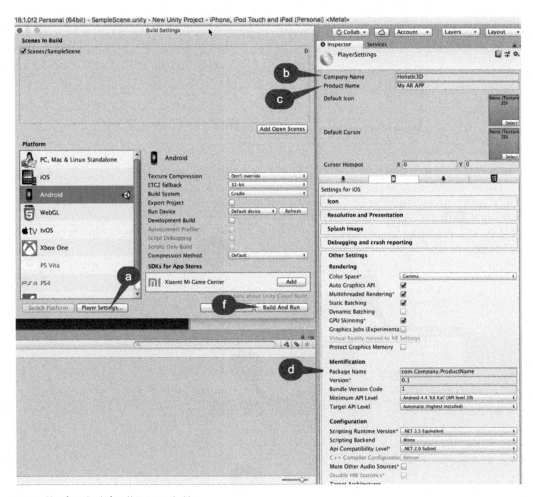

FIG 8.10 Identifying the platform Unity is set to build to.

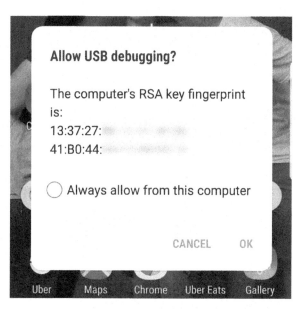

FIG 8.11 Android device prompting for USB debugging privileges.

FIG 8.12 An Android device running a simple Unity Project.

What if it doesn't work or I get strange messages?

1. Make sure your device is plugged in and USB debugging is enabled.
2. Ensure the Android SDK you are building to (on the device) has been downloaded and installed via the SDK Manager in Android Studio.

More Useful Information for Android App Building from Unity

1. https://docs.unity3d.com/Manual/android-sdksetup.html
2. https://docs.unity3d.com/Manual/TroubleShootingAndroid.html
3. https://docs.unity3d.com/Manual/android-BuildProcess.html

8.2.2 Haptics

The game experience encompasses four facets: physical, mental, social, and emotional. The word *haptic* derives from the Greek meaning sense of touch, and it is this sense that enhances the gaming experience when more physical interactions are integrated.

Besides touching a screen, keyboard, controller, or mouse, computer games suffer from a lack of touch. Console controllers introduced haptics to games through vibration. Today, this is still the most commonly used force feedback technology and enhances gameplay through the creation of a deeper physical connection with the game environment. Some of the first game-related peripherals to include vibration as a game feedback include the Nintendo 64 Rumble Pak and Sony PlayStation's Dual Shock analog controller.

◁ **Unity Specifics**
Vibration
You can make an iOS and Android device (with the required capability) vibrate by executing the code:

```
Handheld.Vibrate();
```

8.2.3 Accelerometer

Accelerometers are electromechanical devices that measure acceleration forces. A circuit board, no bigger than a fingernail, can measure its angle of tilt by detecting the downward force of gravity, and how fast it is traveling by sensing motion and vibration. Modern mobile devices have a microelectromechanical systems (MEMS) accelerometer integrated. These consist of a simple cantilever beam attached to a seismic mass sealed in a gas pocket. The beam acts as a bendable needle that moves under accelerative forces. Imagine the pendulum of a grandfather clock on the back of a truck, and how it would move as the truck accelerates. The accelerometer is, in principle, the same. The movement of the beam is measured and reported as acceleration.

These same types of accelerometer are also found in the *Nintendo Wii Remote* and its *Nunchuk* and the *PlayStation 3 Dual Shock 3* controller.

Data from accelerometers can be used in games to change the screen orientation, for example, turning a controller on its side, giving movement commands such as bowling or batting in *Wii Sports* games, or moving a character around in an environment, to name a few. The iPhone version of *Spore Origins*, for example, allows the player to navigate their creature around in the primordial slime by tilting and rotating the device.

Accelerometers report movement in 3D. In the case of Android, while holding the device in upright portrait with the screen facing you, an *x* acceleration will be registered if you tilt the phone forward and back, a *y* acceleration will be registered as the phone is swiveled around its vertical midpoint, and a *z* acceleration registered when the phone is brought toward and away from you. This is illustrated in Figure 8.13.

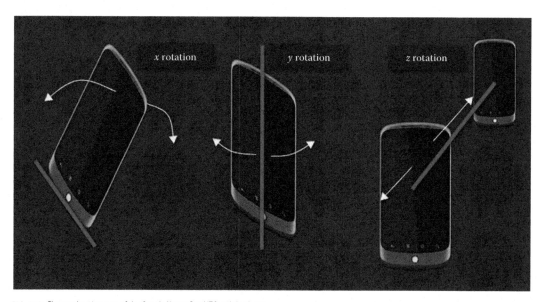

FIG 8.13 The acceleration axes of the Google Nexus One HTC mobile phone.

◁ **Unity Specifics**
Measuring Acceleration

To access a device's acceleration data from within Unity, the *Input* class is used. When played on an iOS or Android enabled device (with an accelerometer) *Input.acceleration* will return the device's acceleration as a Vector3 value. The code in Listing 8.1 can be added to its own C#, attached to the Main Camera, and deployed to a mobile device to display the current acceleration values on the screen. The *x, y,* and *z* values obtained in this example could be used to change the transform data of a game object and thus its position in the game world. Be careful though! The X, Y, and Z of the device do not automatically match the X, Y, and Z of your game world.

Listing 8.1 Unity C# to report on mobile device acceleration

```
float speed = 10.0f;
Vector3 dir = Vector3.zero;

void OnGUI()
{
    GUI.Label (new Rect (10, 10, 100, 20), "x: " + dir.x);
    GUI.Label (new Rect (10, 30, 100, 20), "y: " + dir.y);
    GUI.Label (new Rect (10, 50, 100, 20), "z: " + dir.z);
}

void Update ()
{
    if(Mathf.Abs(Input.acceleration.x) > 1)
        dir.x = Input.acceleration.x;
    if(Mathf.Abs(Input.acceleration.y) > 1)
        dir.y = Input.acceleration.y;
    if(Mathf.Abs(Input.acceleration.z) > 1)
        dir.z = Input.acceleration.z;
}
```

8.2.4 Orientation

As previously revealed, the accelerometer in a device also measures its orientation. As the accelerometer is fixed with respect to the device, it is assumed that its orientation is the same. A device can register one of the following six orientations: facing up, facing down, upright portrait, upright landscape, upside down portrait, and upside down landscape.

◁ **Unity Specifics**

Measuring Orientation

As in the previous section, device orientation can be gathered from the Input class. The orientation value is found in Input. deviceOrientation. Each of the six orientation positions are catered for with the values DeviceOrientation.FaceDown, DeviceOrientation. FaceUp, DeviceOrientation.PortraitUpsideDown, DeviceOrientation. LandscapeLeft, DeviceOrientation.LandscapeRight and DeviceOrientation. Portrait. These orientations relate to the Google Nexus One HTC mobile as shown in Figure 8.14.

Adding the script in Listing 8.2 to a new C# file, attaching it to the Main Camera, and deploying the application to a mobile device will illustrate the reporting of orientation from within Unity. The orientation can then be used to move characters and/or flip the player's view.

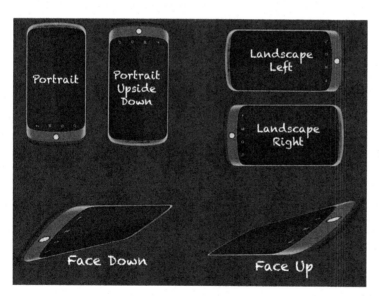

FIG 8.14 The orientations of a Google Nexus HTC mobile phone.

Listing 8.2 Unity C# to report on device orientation

```csharp
using System.Collections;
using System.Collections.Generic;
using UnityEngine;

public class Orient : MonoBehaviour {

    string orientString = "Unknown";
    Vector2 pivotPoint = new Vector2(200,200);
    float rotAngle = 0;
    void OnGUI()
    {
        if (Input.deviceOrientation == DeviceOrientation.
            FaceDown)
        {
            orientString = "Face Down";
            rotAngle = 0;
        }
        if (Input.deviceOrientation == DeviceOrientation.
            FaceUp)
        {
            orientString = "Face Up";
            rotAngle = 0;
        }
        if (Input.deviceOrientation == DeviceOrientation.
            Portrait)
        {
            orientString = "Portrait";
            rotAngle = 0;
        }
        if (Input.deviceOrientation == DeviceOrientation.
            PortraitUpsideDown)
        {
            orientString = "Portrait Upside Down";
            rotAngle = 180;
        }
        if (Input.deviceOrientation == DeviceOrientation.
            LandscapeLeft)
        {
            orientString = "Landscape Left";
            rotAngle = 90;
```

```
        }
        if (Input.deviceOrientation == DeviceOrientation.
            LandscapeRight)
        {
            orientString = "Landscape Right";
            rotAngle = -90;
        }
        GUI.BeginGroup (new Rect (Screen.width / 2 - 200,
            Screen.height / 2 - 200, 400, 400));
        GUIUtility.RotateAroundPivot (rotAngle, pivotPoint);
        GUI.Label (new Rect (0, 0, 400, 400), orientString);
        GUI.EndGroup ();
    }
}
```

8.2.5 Web Services

Access to the Internet is another feature integrated into mobile devices. People use mobile devices to surf the web and to send and receive email. This functionality can be exploited in games to send emails from within a game or to obtain data from a website. For example, extra in-game information may be obtained from a website on as needed. This occurs in *Parallel Kingdom*, when the player wants to look up further information on a monster or item.

◁ **Unity Specifics**
Calling and Retrieving URLs
Unity provides a WWW() function that can make a URL request retrieving the data. As data can be sent and retrieved in any format, it is quite a powerful feature. For calls to websites, the data is collected in raw HTML. You cannot display the webpage as it appears, but rather gather its HTML code. There are XML and HTML Unity parser packages that can be purchased from the Unity Store, should you wish to display a website inside a Unity application.

◎ Unity Hands On

Sending Mail with Device Mail Client

This workshop demonstrates simple methods for sending emails. In the later exercise where a web server is employed, the code could be modified to support the sending of user data to a game server for a multiplayer game. However, WWW calls are notoriously slow with respect to a game server, and this method would not be recommending for live-action games such as real-time car racing.

Step 1: Create a C# file named *Interface* and add the code shown in Listing 8.3.

Listing 8.3 Sending a simple email message from a Unity app

```
void OnGUI()
{
    if(GUI.Button(Rect(10,10,180,30),"Send"))
    {
        Application.OpenURL
        ("mailto:test@email.com?subject=Test
            Email&body=from Unity App");
    }
}
```

Step 2: Attach this code to the Main Camera.

Step 3: This code will not work in the Unity Editor. Build and push the app to a mobile phone.

Step 4: Run the app. When you push the Send button, the email client installed on the device will open with the subject and body lines already included.

Step 5: To send more information from the app to email client, modify Interface.cs to that in Listing 8.4.

Listing 8.4 Prepopulate email data in a Unity app before sending

```
using System.Collections;
using System.Collections.Generic;
using UnityEngine;

public class SendEmail: MonoBehaviour {
```

```
    string toEmail = "test@email.com";
    string nameField = "My Name";
    string messageField = "Message";
    void OnGUI()
    {
        GUI.Label(new Rect(10,10,50,50),"To");
        toEmail = GUI.TextField (new Rect (100, 10, 200,
            50), toEmail);
        GUI.Label(new Rect(10,60,50,50),"Name");
        nameField = GUI.TextField (new Rect (100, 60,
            200, 50), nameField);
        GUI.Label(new Rect(10,120,120,50),"Message");
        messageField = GUI.TextArea(new Rect(100, 120,
            200, 200), messageField);
        if(GUI.Button(new Rect(50,350,180,50),"Send"))
        {
          Application.OpenURL("mailto:" + toEmail + "?" +
              "subject=Test Email&" +
              "body=From: " +
              nameField + "\n" + messageField);
        }
    }
}
```

Step 6: Play. An email form will be created in the Unity app as shown in Figure 8.15. When Send is pressed, the information entered will be sent to the user's email client.

● **Note**

The format for a mailto string should be: mailto:email_address?email _information. The question mark always separates the email address of the recipient with the extra data that is divided into a number of headers separated by ampersands. Each header has a name and its own value set with an equals sign. The headers can include:

- subject: the text that will appear in the subject line
- body: the email message
- cc: the email address of others to send a copy of the message
- bcc: the email address of others who will receive the email but not appear in the send email message of the original

FIG 8.15 A simple email form screen in Unity.

⚙ Unity Hands On

Sending Mail via a Web Server

This method of sending an email from your app may be preferred, as the application will not close to open the mail app. Data are sent straight from the app to the server. You can also use this method for passing other information to a web server.

Step 1: Create a new Unity Project.
Step 2: Create a C# file called *EmailViaServer*, and add the code shown in Listing 8.5. Note that in the code, the server URL is shown in bold. This is where you put the URL of your own server.

Listing 8.5 Sending data from a Unity app to a webserver for the purpose of emailing

```
using System.Collections;
using System.Collections.Generic;
using UnityEngine;
```

```
public class Emailer : MonoBehaviour {

    string toEmail = "test@email.com";
    string nameField = "My Name";
    string messageField = "Message";
    bool showWebMessage = false;
    int emailSuccessful = 1;

    void webMessageScreen()
    {
        GUI.BeginGroup (new Rect (Screen.width / 2 - 50,
            Screen.height / 2 - 50, 100, 100));
        GUI.Box (new Rect (0,0,100,100),"Email Message");
        if(emailSuccessful == 1)
        GUI.Label(new Rect(10,20,100,50),"Sending...");
        if(emailSuccessful == 2)
        GUI.Label(new Rect(10,20,100,50),"Email Sent");
        else if(emailSuccessful == 3)
        GUI.Label(new Rect(10,20,100,50),"Email Failed");
        if (GUI.Button (new Rect (10,50,80,30), "Ok"))
        {
            showWebMessage = false;
        }
        GUI.EndGroup ();
    }

    IEnumerator sendEmail()
    {
        emailSuccessful = 1;
        showWebMessage = true;
        string msgBody = "From: "+ nameField + "\n" +
            messageField;
        WWWForm form = new WWWForm();
        form.AddField("to", toEmail);
        form.AddField("subject", "Email Subject");
        form.AddField("body", msgBody);
        WWW w = new WWW("URL OF YOUR PHP SCRIPT", form);
        yield return w;
        if (w.error != null)
        {
            emailSuccessful = 3;
        }
        else
        {
            emailSuccessful = 2;
        }
    }

    void OnGUI()
    {
        GUI.Label(new Rect(10,10,50,50),"To");
```

```
toEmail = GUI.TextField (new Rect (100, 10, 200,
    50), toEmail);
GUI.Label(new Rect(10,60,50,50),"Name");
nameField = GUI.TextField (new Rect (100, 60, 200,
    50), nameField);
GUI.Label(new Rect(10,120,120,50),"Message");

messageField = GUI.TextArea (new Rect (100, 120,
    200, 200), messageField);
if(GUI.Button(new Rect(50,350,180,50),"Send"))
{
    StartCoroutine(sendEmail());
}
if(showWebMessage)
{
    webMessageScreen();
}
}
}
```

Step 3: Attach this code to the Main Camera. You can test this application in the Unity Editor as it does not require your mail program. It will send the data to a server, and the server will send the email. Remember to check your spam folder for the test email.

Step 4: The server code is written in PHP. The code is very simple. In this case, *emailer.php* is given in Listing 8.6.

Listing 8.6 PHP web emailer

```php
<?php

$to = $_POST["to"];
$subject = $_POST["subject"];
$body = $_POST["body"];
$headers = 'From: mobileEmailTester@someweb.com'. "\r\n".
    'Reply-To: no-reply@someweb.com'. "\r\n".
    'X-Mailer: PHP/'. phpversion();
    if (mail($to, $subject, $body, $headers))
    {
    echo("<p>Message successfully sent!</p>");
    } else
    {
    echo("<p>Message delivery failed...</p>");
    }

?>
```

If you have access to a PHP-enabled web server, try creating your own PHP server file with this code, and redirect your mobile app to it. The full URL of *emailer.php* should appear in `sendEmail()` function of Listing 8.5.

⚉ **Note**

Often when working with WebGL applications built out of Unity, a similar method of writing external files by way of a PHP script on a server is required. If you are interested in how this can be achieved, see the series of YouTube videos created by the author beginning at https://youtu.be/4OZqY1Ukj8I.

8.2.6 GPS

Today's smartphones and tablets come with global positioning system (GPS) receivers. These devices calculate their position on the earth by bouncing signals off the GPS satellites. The GPS was developed by the American Department of Defense (DOD) in 1973 with the first satellites being launched in 1978. In 1993, the DOD decided to make it free for civilian use. The official name of the system is navigation system for timing and ranging (NAVSTAR).

The GPS consists of 30 satellites orbiting the earth within a distance of 20,200 kilometers. The satellites are solar powered and circle the globe two times each day. The configuration of the satellites is such that at any location on the Earth's surface, at least four are visible in the sky.

The GPS receiver in a mobile device calculates its position through analysis of the high-frequency, low-power radio signals emitted by the satellites. It determines its distance from any four of the satellites it is able to detect and works out its position. The process is called trilateration.

Trilateration finds the intersection of a number of circles or spheres. In the case of 3D space and the GPS system, for each detected satellite a sphere can be imagined around each with a radius equal to the distance to the satellite calculated by the GPS device. The location of each satellite is known as the DOD constantly monitors the satellites to ensure they are aligned. With this information from four satellites, and including the earth itself as another sphere in the equation, the location of the GPS device can be restricted to the area in which all spheres intersect. This process is illustrated in Figure 8.16 with just two spheres. The typical accuracy of GPS in mobile devices is around 10 meters.

Possibly the largest GPS-based game is *Geocaching*. It is a worldwide treasure hunt involving the hiding and locating of small boxes of items placed all around the globe. The GPS positions of *geocaches* are registered on the web. Using a GPS navigation system, people scour the earth, arriving at the

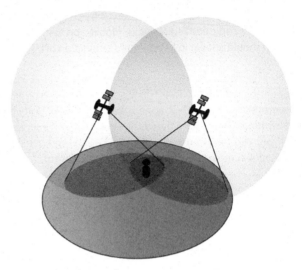

FIG 8.16 Satellite trilateration with two satellites.

correct coordinates and then searching in the vicinity for a box, canister, or jar cleverly hidden under a pile of sticks, behind a brick, or even inside hollow fence poles. When found, the finders record their presences on the logbook inside and leave a small token or gift. More details about the geocaching phenomena can be found at http://www.geocaching.com.

The general genre of games that include geocaching are known as location-based games. Most are in the format of a real-world scavenger hunts such as visiting locations for points or virtual artifacts. *Tourality* (http://www.tourality.com/) is one such game, as shown in Figure 8.17. The goal is to reach as many

FIG 8.17 Tourality.

predefined GPS locations (stored in game sets) in the shortest amount of time. *Tourality* generates game sets based on the location of the player. It is possible to play in a single player or multiplayer mode.

Parallel Kingdom by PerBlue is the first location-based mobile massively multiplayer online role-playing game (MMORPG) played in the real world (http://parallelkingdom.com/). It uses a player's GPS location to superimpose an imaginary fantasy world over the top of a Google Map as shown in Figure 8.18. The player can move around an approximate 1.3 mile radius on the map by tapping on the mobile screen. To move further afield, the player has to physically go to another location in the real world. As with other RPGs, the player fights monsters and collects items while exploring their environment for experience points and leveling up their skills.

My Grove by Kranky Panda is another location-based multiplayer game that creates a virtual world over a map of the real world as shown in Figure 8.19. Players move from one geographical location to another, the goal being to plant and maintain virtual fruit trees to offset carbon emissions. Players compete against each other to be the top fruit producers in their area. They can also sabotage the trees of other players or choose to help other players tend to their trees.

You too can use GPS coordinates in your own games. The next workshop shows you how to obtain a player's location in Unity iOS and Android.

FIG 8.18 *Parallel Kingdom.*

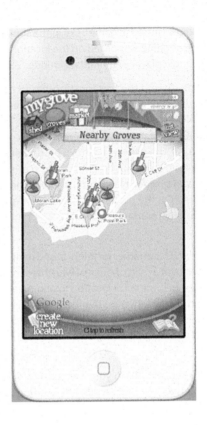

FIG 8.19 *My Grove.*

◎ Unity Hands On

GPS

Step 1: Create a new Unity project. Set it to build for iPhone or Android depending on the device you have.

Step 2: Create a new C# file called *GetGPS*. Add the code shown in Listing 8.7.

Step 3: Play. If your mobile device can access the satellite data, the screen will contain details of your GPS location.

Listing 8.7 Code to obtain GPS information

```
using System.Collections;
using System.Collections.Generic;
using UnityEngine;

public class GetGPS : MonoBehaviour {
```

```
bool locationFound = false;

IEnumerator GetLocation()
{
    Input.location.Start();
    int maxWait = 1;
    while (Input.location.status ==
        LocationServiceStatus. Initializing &&
        maxWait > 0)
    {
        yield return new WaitForSeconds(1);
        maxWait--;
    }
    if (maxWait < 1)
    {
        yield return null;
    }
    if (Input.location.status ==
        LocationServiceStatus.Failed)
    {
        yield return null;
    }
    else
    {
        locationFound = true;
    }
    Input.location.Stop();
}

void Start ()
{
    StartCoroutine(GetLocation());
}

void OnGUI()
{
    if(locationFound)
    {
        GUI.Label(new Rect(10,10,200,30),"Latitude: " +
            Input.location.lastData.latitude);
        GUI.Label(new Rect(10,30,200,30),"Longitude: " +
            Input.location.lastData.longitude);
        GUI.Label(new Rect(10,50,200,30),"Altitude: " +
            Input.location.lastData.altitude);
        GUI.Label(new Rect(10,70,200,30),"Accuracy: " +
            Input.location.lastData.horizontalAccuracy);
        GUI.Label(new Rect(10,90,200,30),"Time: " +
            Input.location.lastData.timestamp);
    }
```

```
        else
        {
            GUI.Label(new Rect(10,10,200,30),
                "Could not initialize location services.");
        }
        if(GUI.Button(new Rect(10,110,80,50),"Quit"))
        {
            Application.Quit();
        }
    }
}
```

8.3 Gestures and Motion

In 2003, Sony released the *EyeToy* for the *PlayStation 2*. This is essentially a webcam that attaches to the gaming console. By processing the image taken by the camera, computer vision and gesture recognition algorithms can estimate the movements of a player.

Although the *Nintendo Wii* took game haptics to a new level with its *Wii Remote*, it was *Microsoft* that broke new ground by releasing the *Kinect* in 2010. Although the player does not feel the game environment with a sense of touch, they are still kinesthetically interacting with it and therefore experiencing a level of immersion not previously experienced in earlier games. The Kinect provides full-body 3D motion capture through by continually projecting an infrared laser in front of the screen in a pixel grid. Depth data are gathered from a monochrome sensor gathering information about the reflections of the laser. Currently, the Kinect is capable of tracking six people simultaneously. The Kinect is also able to perform facial and voice recognition tasks.

The *Kinect* differs from the *PlayStation Move*, a game controller wand with built-in accelerometers and light on top, by sensing the actual 3D data. The Move, also released in 2010, uses a combination of motion sensing with visual recognition from the PlayStation Eye (the successor of the EyeToy) to recognize player movements.

There are numerous groups attempting to make access to the Kinect open source and cross platform, such as *OpenKinect* (http://openkinect.org/wiki/Main_Page).

OpenKinect is a community of developers bringing free programming interfaces for the Kinect to Windows, Linux, and Mac so independent application developers and researchers can implement their own Kinect-based games and applications. The links to their source code and tutorials for installation and use can be found on their website.

Succeeding the technology of the Kinect are systems such as the *Stage System* by *Organic Motion* (https://tracklab.com.au/organic-motion/). Currently used for real-time motion capture, this system has the potential to make games that are projected onto all the walls of a room where the player is positioned right in the center of the action. The Stage System has the ability to capture true full body 3D surround motion and structure with the use of its six cameras. It differs from the Kinect in that the Kinect only captures distances from the device itself to whatever is in front of it and tracks for key human features such as the hands, feet, and head. Technologies such as these are driving games toward full-body immersive systems reminiscent of Star Trek's holodeck.

Besides the full body detection systems, simple mouse and finger swiping gestures have been used in games from the magic casting of *Black & White* to the mobile gesture-based battle against evil in *Darklings*. Matching the swiping action to a specific gesture is an exercise in machine learning. There are numerous methods for recognizing gestures, including Bayesian and neural networks and complex artificial intelligence techniques. In the next hands-on exercise, we will examine a very simple and effective method called the $1 Unistroke Recognizer (http://depts.washington.edu/madlab/proj/dollar/index.html). The recognizer uses a nearest neighbor classifier with Euclidean scoring. In short, this means that it takes a set of known patterns and then determines how closely each coordinate of a new gesture matches any of the known patterns using a distance function.

◎ Unity Hands On

Gesture Recognition

Step 1: Download the starter project Chapter 8/Gestures and open the *gestureRibbon* scene.

Step 2: Add an empty game object to the Hierarchy by right clicking in the Hierarchy window and selecting Create Empty. Rename the new object *Ribbon*.

Step 3: With the Ribbon selected in the Inspector, use the Add Component button to add an Effect > Trail Renderer. Set the values for Time, Start Width, and End Width to 1, 5, and 5, respectively. Attach the provided script *swipeTrail* to the Ribbon, and set its material to white as shown in Figure 8.20.

Step 4: Play. You will be able to draw a white Ribbon on the screen using the mouse. This Ribbon will also work on a mobile device if you build out to one.

Step 5: If you examine the Main Camera, you will notice a script called *gestureRecon* attached. This script contains all the coordinates for known gestures. These gestures can be seen by examining the *trained.png* file included in the project. We now need to link the gestures of the Ribbon with this code. This means capturing all the points on the screen that the Ribbon passes through and giving them to the recognition algorithm. To begin, create a new script called *DetectMotion.cs*, and add the code in Listing 8.8.

Listing 8.8 Detect motion

```
using System.Collections;
using System.Collections.Generic;
using UnityEngine;
using UnityEngine.UI;

public class DetectMotion : MonoBehaviour {

    bool isDown = false;
    bool startPointRecording = false;
    Vector2 lastMousePos = new Vector2(-1,-1);
    ArrayList points = new ArrayList();
    string patternDetected = "";
    Text patternDisplay;

    void OnGUI()
    {
        if(isDown && Input.mousePosition.x !=
            lastMousePos.x &&
            Input.mousePosition.y != lastMousePos.x)
        {
            points.Add(new Vector2(Input.mousePosition.x,
                -Input.mousePosition.y));
            lastMousePos = new Vector2(Input.
                mousePosition.x,
                Input.mousePosition.y);
        }
    }

    void Update ()
    {
        if(Input.GetMouseButtonDown(0))
        {
            isDown = true;
            startPointRecording = true;
            points = new ArrayList();
        }
        else if(Input.GetMouseButtonUp(0))
        {
            isDown = false;
            startPointRecording = false;
                Result result = this.
            GetComponent<GestureRecon>().Detect(points);
            patternDetected = result.Rname + "" + result.
                Rscore;
            patternDisplay.text = patternDetected;
        }
    }
}
```

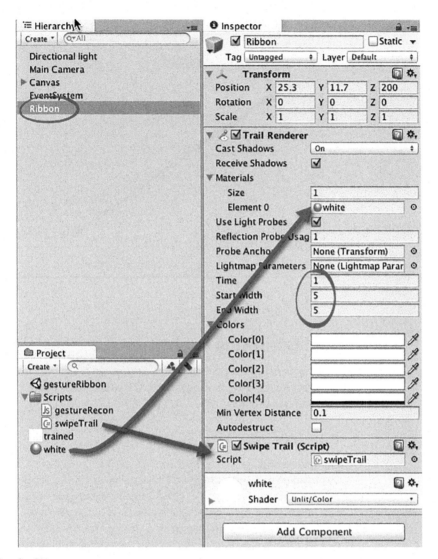

FIG 8.20 Setup for a Ribbon.

Step 6: Save the code and attach the script to the Main Camera.

Step 7: To see which gesture the algorithm has detected, you will need to link up the text on the screen (that currently says *Pattern*) with the *DetectMotion* script. With the camera selected, locate the Pattern Display property of the script and drag and drop the existing text element from the Hierarchy onto it as shown in Figure 8.21.

Step 8: Save, run, and swipe. The algorithm will read your gestures and the closest match will be determined and displayed.

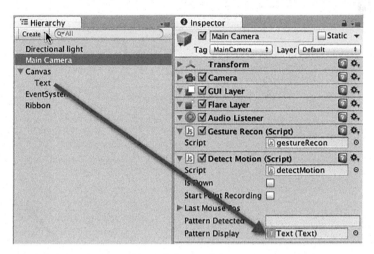

FIG 8.21 Assigning an on-screen text object to display recognized gesture.

8.4 3D Viewing

Viewing virtual objects in three dimensions, otherwise known as stereoscopy or stereoscopics, is a technology that has been around since the beginning of the twentieth century.

8.4.1 Side-by-Side

The earliest displays worked by showing a pair of 2D images in a stereogram. By providing each eye with a different image taken from a slightly different point of view, the brain can be fooled into perceiving depth. This technique for stereoscopy is called side-by-side. One such stereogram is shown in Figure 8.22. The individual images of a stereogram are taken at slightly different angles and distances replicating the natural positioning of our eyes—that is, 15 centimeters apart.

To assist with the viewing process of side-by-side images, a stereoscope is employed to keep the individual eyes focused on the appropriate image. A popular form stereoscope from the nineteenth century, the Holmes stereoscope, is shown in Figure 8.23.

In 2014 Google engineers, David Coz and Damien Henry, revealed a low-cost stereoscope called Google Cardboard. The 3D viewer (shown in Figure 8.24), constructed primarily from cardboard, is an origami project for the game designer wanting to experiment with real-time virtual stereograms.

It employs a mobile device to deliver the interactive 3D content by splitting the screen in two and delivering one half to each eye.

FIG 8.22 "The early bird catches the worm" Stereograph published in 1900 by North-Western View Co. of Baraboo, Wisconsin, digitally restored. Public Domain.

FIG 8.23 A Holmes stereoscope. Public Domain.

FIG 8.24 Google Cardboard. Creative Commons.

The virtual environment being displayed requires two cameras sitting side-by-side and projecting individual images in a split-screen-type configuration.

⊙ **Unity Hands On**

A Google Cardboard Experience

In this activity, we will explore the Google Cardboard plugin for Unity and create a simple environment to view in 3D. To view the final product, you will need a Google Cardboard viewer. These are widely available for purchase on eBay, or you could make your own.

Instructions for building your own virtual reality (VR) experience with Google Cardboard and Unity are available at: https://developers.google.com/vr/develop/unity/get-started-android.

8.4.2 Anaglyphs

Another method for producing stereoscopic images was developed in 1853 by W. Rollmann. The anaglyph is an image constructed by overlaying two offset photographs: one filtered with red and one filtered with cyan. When viewed with red/cyan glasses, each eye perceives a different photograph, thus producing a 3D effect.

The Unity plugin for creating anaglyphs sets up two cameras in the environment and filters one with red and one with cyan. The images from the cameras—which are set 0.04 apart in the X and rotated toward each other by slightly less than one degree to simulate the positions and rotations of

FIG 8.25 A screenshot of the Unity 3D Anaglyph System plugin shows the two cameras and color filters.

the human eyes—are then overlaid. The resulting image from the sample provided with the plugin is displayed in Figure 8.25.

8.4.3 Head-Mounted Displays

In more recent times, head-mounted displays (HMDs) have become popular for 3D viewing. The first commercially available HMDs were the Forte VFX-1 and Sony's Glasstron, which was used in the game *MechWarrior 2* allowing players to see the game world through their own eyes inside their craft's cockpit. Today, the hottest HMD gaining traction in gaming is the Oculus Rift. The Rift was a Kickstarter crowdfunding campaign that saw the release of a developer kit in 2012 (shown in Figure 8.26), with the commercial version released in March 2016. Oculus have also partnered with Samsung to develop the VR Gear, a HMD based on their technology that integrates with smartphone technology.

The Rift (like the other HMDs) works by delivering slightly offset virtual images to each eye. The brain processes them as it does the stereograms and anaglyphs and provides the viewer with the perception of depth. The images are delivered via active screens placed in front of the viewer's eyes. In the case of the second generation Rift, the screens are the same as those in a Samsung Galaxy Note 3.

As is the case with the 3D anaglyph systems, the Rift Unity plugin uses a double camera system to split the perspective of the virtual scene for each eye. When developing, the scene is displayed on the screen showing what each eye is viewing. This is illustrated in Figure 8.27.

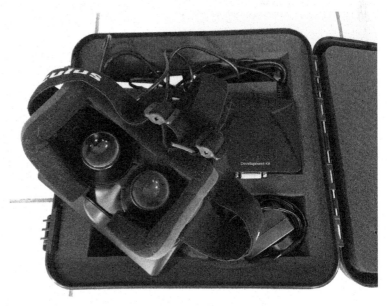

FIG 8.26 The original Oculus Rift developer kit.

FIG 8.27 A view of the Tuscan demo running inside Unity. This was one of the original Oculus Rift demos.

8.5 Augmented Reality

Although augmented reality (AR) technology has been available since 1968, it has only been in the past five or so years that applications have become popular. This is primarily due to the availability of webcams with desktop and laptop computers and cameras coupled with increased processing power in hand-held devices and mobile phones. Technology from the domain of 3D gaming is particularly key with respect to AR, as it allows efficient and seamless integration of high-quality animated virtual objects with AR applications.

AR has slowly been creeping into the field of computer games. Some interactive applications of note include the Sony PlayStation EyeToy and the EyePet and the Nintendo 3DS *Nintendogs*. In these games, players see their real world streamed via a camera onto the screen and superimposed with virtual game characters. The characters are positioned such that they appear to exist in the real world. The player almost feels like they could reach out and touch them.

AR is a multidisciplinary field based on computer science with the goal of providing a viewer with an environment containing both real and virtual objects. With the use of mobile devices with cameras, computer-generated images are projected on top of the physical environment. To ensure correct positioning of virtual objects in the real world, hardware and software are required to determine the viewer's location and orientation (point of view, POV) accurately. The POV can be matched with the location of a camera in a virtual model of the physical location and augmented objects and information projected onto the real-world image. Alternatively, a visual symbol in the real world known as a *fiduciary marker* can have its position relative to the POV determined and used as the location and orientation of a virtual object. It is this latter AR technique that we will examine in this section, as such applications can easily be created for Android mobile devices with Unity and the Vuforia (https://www.vuforia.com/) or Wikitude SDKs (https://www.wikitude.com/).

One very famous AR (and location-based) game created with Unity is *Pokémon Go* (Figure 8.28). It was first released in July 2016 and downloaded some 500 million times by the end of the year. In the game, players must hunt down 150 types of Pokémon that are located somewhere in the real world. By moving to the correct geographical location, the Pokémon is revealed through the use of AR on the player's mobile phone.

Wearable devices that allow virtual content to be projected atop a vision of the real world have been prototyped since the late 1960s; however, the earliest devices required reprocessing of video from the real world with the virtual on top. This same technique is still used for AR on smartphones. A big breakthrough has come about with see-through lenses that only need to process the virtual. Such devices include Google Glass and the Microsoft HoloLens.

Google Glass was released in 2013 as a prototype headset and removed from production in 2015. It consists of a standard pair of glasses with the lenses replaced by a heads-up display as shown in Figure 8.29. Virtual content can be projected onto the lenses, while the user continues to view the real world and thus creating an AR.

FIG 8.28 *Pokémon Go.*

FIG 8.29 Man wearing a Google Glass prototype.

FIG 8.30 A mock-up of the mixed-reality interface provided by Microsoft's HoloLens.

Microsoft's HoloLens is a similar device to Google Glass. The HoloLens projects virtual content atop the real world and provides interactive holographic experiences (illustrated in Figure 8.30). The device includes a microphone, camera for taking photographs and video, as well as an accelerometer, gyroscope, and other haptic interactive technologies.

Without access to such technology, AR development can still be experienced on desktop machines and smartphones. The next hands-on session will introduce you to an easy to use and freely available development kit for creating AR experiences with Unity.

⚉ Unity Hands On

Augmented Reality in Unity with Wikitude SDK

With the Wikitude SDK you can be up and running with your own Augmented Reality application in less than five minutes (Figure 8.31). Follow along with the author's own YouTube tutorial found at *https://youtu.be/Dt3q2URF6b4*.

For readers of this book, there's also a special discount coupon for an entire online AR course developed by the author at https://www.udemy.com/augmented_reality_with_unity/?couponCode=H3DGAMEDEVBOOK.

FIG 8.31 Augmented reality in action showing a virtual character projected onto a fiduciary marker.

8.6 The Social Mechanic

Whether you are playing a game on a mobile device, desktop computer, or console, nowadays it is difficult to escape the social element. From creating personalized 3D avatars on Xbox live to inviting friends to farm virtual pastures in Facebook, the opportunity to boast about your fortunes (or misfortunes) in computer games now expands much farther than your immediate family and friends. Most computer games proudly display the *Twitter*, *Facebook*, *OpenFeint*, and other icons on their menu screens, encouraging you to share your gaming experiences with the wider community.

As online social networks have been developed by other parties, it is not always an easy process to integrate your game with their system. Fortunately, many developers provide application programming interfaces (APIs) for you to use in your own code. These are plug and play functions that you can call in your script to access their system's functionality.

This section looks at two popular social network APIs and how they integrate with Unity. However, before these are covered, an overview of the data encryption process used by these, as well as the Apple App Store and Google Play, will be examined to put the process of connecting Unity apps to an external service in context.

8.6.1 External Application Security Matters

When dealing with Apple, Google, or other external services such as Facebook and Twitter, you will come up against what might seem like a very convoluted system for transferring data back and forth. However, these companies employ such techniques to ensure the safety and validity of the data. First of all, the company needs to give you permission to access their data and services, then you need to prove that you are who you say you are (each time you access their services), and then you should be able to send data securely between your application and theirs. This is where encryption is applied.

Encryption is a method of taking a message and transforming it so that it is incomprehensible. A very simple method is to assign numbers to each of the letters in the alphabet and then to rewrite a text message replacing the alphabetical letters with their numerical equivalents. For example, if $A = 1$, $B = 2$ up to $Z = 26$, then "holistic" encrypted would be "8 15 12 9 19 20 9 3." Such an encoded string is referred to as *cipher text*. Taking the string of numbers and translating them back into the word is the process of decryption. What is known as a *key* is used to encrypt and decrypt the cipher text. To communicate using this method, the first party would use the key to encrypt the original message. On receipt of the encrypted message, the receiver uses the same key to decrypt and reveal the true meaning and content of the original message. This is not the most secure way to transmit sensitive information, as anyone in possession of the key—for example, someone intercepting it—could also decipher the message. If the key is used to encrypt the message, when the key itself is being communicated to the recipient, it is vulnerable. This particular process is referred to as *symmetric cryptography* and illustrated in Figure 8.32.

A more secure technique for encryption is through the use of an *asymmetric key algorithm* known as *public-key cryptography*, in which there are two keys: a public key and a private key. The private key, you will see in many applications, is referred to as the *secret* key. The original sender generates both keys mathematically. The public key can decrypt messages encrypted with the private key, and the private key can decrypt messages encrypted with the public key. The private key remains with the original sender and is used to encode messages to be sent. The public key travels with the message and is used to decipher the message at the other end. As with symmetric cryptography, this specific part of the transaction is not secure. However, the recipient can then use the public key that they received to then encrypt a message intended for the original sender. Only the original sender can decrypt the message with their private key as it was created with their own public key. This process is illustrated in Figure 8.33. This is what sets public-key cryptography apart from symmetric cryptography.

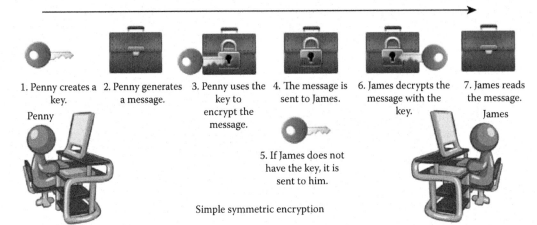

FIG 8.32 Symmetric cryptography.

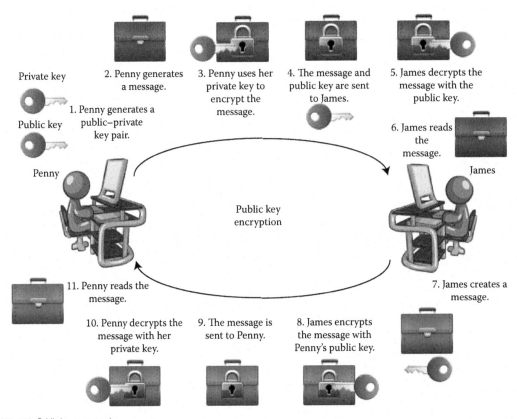

FIG 8.33 Public-key cryptography.

Because the original message and public key can be intercepted during transmission, it is difficult for the receiver to validate the authenticity of the original message. To partially solve this issue, *public-key infrastructures* exist in which third parties known as *certificate authorities* validate key pairs.

Public key encryption is used to create digital signatures. A digital signature is not that dissimilar to a handwritten signature or a wax seal on an envelope. In the case of the wax seal analogy, the private key used to sign the document is the sender's seal stamp: it remains the private property of the sender. However, when the document reaches its destination, the wax seal can be used to identify the sender. An actual digital signature goes one step further, ensuring the integrity of the original message has not been altered. This would be like a protective covering on the wax-sealed document that turned the entire thing purple should someone try and modify the contents.

Before a sender can use a digital signature, they must have a digital identity. This identity consists of a public–private key pair and a digital certificate. The digital certificate proves the sender's credentials and is provided by an independent certificate authority. The process is synonymous with having to produce your passport to prove your identity. The passport is a certificate, and the certificate authority, in this case, would be your country's government. In the case of the wax-sealed letter, the sender who owns the seal would also have to produce an official document provided by, say, the king, to prove that their seal did in fact belong to them.

8.6.2 Twitter

Twitter is a web service allowing people to post a message 280 characters long to a website. The message is not for anybody in particular, though Twitter allows other subscribers to *follow* the messages of another. In a way, it is a method for posting your thoughts at any time into cyberspace for nobody or everybody to read about. The Twitter.com website was founded by Jack Dorsey and launched in July 2006. Since then, it has grown to over 325 million users posting around 500 million messages (called tweets) a day.

Posting messages to Twitter on behalf of a user is a complex process. There are three authentication steps to which you need to adhere. The first step is to send Twitter a message from your application asking for permission to access the user's account. The user's web browser then opens, asking them if it is ok for the application that they are using to access their Twitter account. If the user permits this access, they receive a PIN number. The user enters this PIN number into the application. Following this, the application sends another message to Twitter telling Twitter that the application has the PIN. Once Twitter determines this PIN is correct, it sends personalized authority tokens back to the application. These tokens can be stored inside the application so the user doesn't have to go through the authorization process again. With the tokens, the application can post tweets to the user's Twitter account.

8.6.3 Facebook

The process of user authentication with Facebook is similar to Twitter. Facebook also supplies programming interfaces in C++ and C# for XCode and Visual Studio programming.

The process of authorizing the player's account is done through a series of web-based calls, as is the case with Twitter. Facebook, however, is a far bigger beast, and the amount of data you can obtain is very large. These data are organized into the Facebook Graph. In brief, it is a data network that links your own profile with that of your friends and their friends and their friends.

> ● **Note**
> As Twitter and Facebook control their own APIs and security, they are constantly in flux, which makes the job of keeping your application up to date an arduous task if you've written your own code to hook into their APIs. It is the author's recommendation that if you are keen to explore working with Twitter and Facebook from inside your own Unity application that you check out the following links where more information is available on the process and plugins.
>
> - https://developers.facebook.com/docs/unity/
> - https://developer.twitter.com/en/docs/publisher-tools/twitterkit/overview.html

8.7 Platform Deployment: The App Store, Android Market, and Consoles

In the past, publishing a game was an exercise in self-publicity and tenacity. Small independent developers would have to approach the big publishing houses with their dreams of grandeur, convince the publishers to invest in their game, and then stick to strict milestones and release deadlines, for, in the end, what might amount to 7% royalties. While this situation is still possible nowadays and could lead a small development company to much fame and fortune via the publishers' vast network of marketing resources, small independent developers do have many more options available to them.

8.7.1 Publishing for the App Store and Android Market

The App Store delivers developers' games directly to the consumer, cutting out the middleman. Applications for iOS and Mac OSX+ are listed in the store, and the buyer can purchase over the Internet and download directly to their desktop computer or mobile device.

Applications written for the App Store must be developed with an XCode component. For example, Unity builds its code via XCode when pushing the application to the iPhone or iPad.

Developers wishing to put content in the App Store or on iOS devices must register as an Apple Developer. At the time of writing, this costs $99 per year. For this, the developer gets access to the Apple Development Network, beta releases of Mac operating system updates, and authentication protocols to build and push applications for testing to their mobile devices.

Once a game is ready for deployment, it is submitted to Apple for approval. This process can take up to 2 weeks. Apple has a checklist of the things they look for when approving an application, and it is prudent to check these off yourself before submitting. If there is something wrong with your application, you will have to fix it and resubmit for approval again.

Apple has a fixed pricing scale for all apps. The fees taken by Apple are different in different countries but equate to approximately 30%. For the latest information on the exact procedures, visit http://developer.apple.com/.

The Android Market has a more relaxed approach to app publishing. It currently requires a Gmail account and a small once-off fee of $25 to start selling apps. To get started, visit http://developer.android.com/index.html.

You will require the Android SDK to build applications. It is constantly being updated for new versions of Android, and to ensure your applications are compatible, it is best to update frequently.

To create an Android game, Unity functions in the same way as for iOS. The game is created in the Unity editor, and the final product is built via the Android SDK on its way to the mobile.

8.7.2 Console Publishing

The different game console providers—including Microsoft, Nintendo, and Sony—have a variety of rules and regulations as to who can and cannot publish on their platforms. In the case of Nintendo, a games studio must complete an application form to be authorized as an official developer (http://www.warioworld.com/).

Microsoft supplies the free XNA Game Studio development kit for the creation of Xbox and Windows 7 desktop and mobile games. Independent developers can submit their game to the AppHub (https://dev.windows.com/en-us/develop) for listing in the Xbox Live Marketplace. Access to the AppHub costs $99 per year. All games submitted are peer reviewed, and those listed and sold receive 70% of the revenue.

To become an official developer for PlayStation or Xbox (which means your titles get published on DVD and marketed by the respective publishers) is quite a big hurdle. The application process involves proving to the publishers that you have a quite experienced team and around five AAA published titles under your belt. The development kits start from around $10,000 each.

For the reader interested in pursuing console development, here are some URLs worth checking out:

Microsoft: https://www.xbox.com/en-US/Developers/Home
Sony PlayStation: http://www.scedev.net/
Nintendo: https://developer.nintendo.com/

8.7.3 Download Direct to Player

Last but not least there is the option to self-publish and make your desktop playable game available for download on your own website or via a download client such as Steam or Direct2Drive.

A download client allows players to search through a multitude of titles online and purchase, download, and install directly onto their computer, much in the same way the App Store and Android Market work.

Steam is a platform consisting of a software client that runs on desktop computers and manages distribution, management rights, and multiplayer functionality. It was developed by Valve Corporation (the famous developers of the *Half-Life* games series) and released in 2003. Steam currently manages 781 million titles and has over 75 million active users. It manages games for both large publishing houses and small independent developers. Information on *steam readying* your game can be found at https://partner.steamgames.com/.

Direct2Drive is one of a number of online game stores with their own download clients. They are always looking to list and manage new game titles, even from small, unknown developers. They provide a digital shop front in numerous countries and manage player purchases. Like Steam, they too retain purchase records, so a player can download their game at any time. This is a useful service that means the player is not misplacing DVDs and jewel cases with serial numbers on them. It is all stored online and available as needed. Details of how to distribute through Direct2Drive is at their website: http://www.direct2drive.com/.

8.8 Summary

In this chapter we have examined some of the external mechanics and forces that drive game development in certain directions. If you are an independent developer, there has never been a better time to get your game out into the world on desktop computer, mobile device, or in the Xbox Live Marketplace. Relatively inexpensive high-quality tools, such as Unity, are bringing power to the people and allowing small, inexperienced teams to take their first steps. Online stores are also cutting out the publisher and allowing a more direct line to the consumer. While publishing someday with one of the *big three* might be your dream, there is no reason why your baby steps cannot start now.

The availability of SDKs and game engines that access all the hardware functionality features of new mobile and peripheral devices also means, as a game designer, that you can let your mind run wild. Finding clever new ways to interact kinesthetically with the virtual world could just give you the next big thing in computer games.

8.9 A Final Word

Whichever path you decide to take, know that the face of game design and development has taken a bigger turn in the last ten years than it ever did in the previous 50, and you no longer need to be a computer scientist to work with the technology and create really amazing and visually exciting games.

As I write this, Unity has endured for over ten years. It has grown considerably from a small Apple Mac–based games engine into a successful multi-operating system, cross-platform game development tool. Much of this success can be attributed to the way in which design and code are integrated in the software as a seamless mechanism enabling both artists and programmers to produce exciting content.

Games have become ubiquitous. They are everywhere, on every device and played by everyone. If this final chapter has illustrated anything, it is that technology is growing at break-neck speed. Developing games is no longer a matter of punching out some code and simple graphics. The processes have to change to consider a multitude of platforms and display types. As game artists and programmers, it is imperative that a single technology is never the focus of our efforts or learning. A strong foundation in theory has and always will be critical to see you adapt to the next hardware or software revolution thrown your way.

It is hoped that through the contents of this book you have gained a level of understanding that transcends technology and even the Unity game engine. It is your job now to put this knowledge to work and create the next generation of games and interactive experiences beyond all your teachers' expectations.

Index

Note: Page numbers in italic and bold refer to figures and tables, respectively.

A* algorithm 255; pathfinding with 255–63; testing 260–2
accelerometer 434–6
Adobe Photoshop color picker 16, *16*
Alice Greenfingers 341
alleles 317
anaglyphs 456–7, *457*
AND gate 29, **30**
Android application: Build Settings 428–30, *431, 432*; Bundle ID 426; configuration 428, *431*; Developer Mode 427, *429*; Java Development Kit 427; running *433*; SDK installation 427, *428*; Studio SDK Manager 427, *427*; Switch Platform 428, *431*; USB debugging 428, 430, *430, 433*
Android Market 467
Angry Birds 217, 426
animation: configuration file 184; defined 151; frame 152; humanoid skeletal hierarchy 174, *174*; management 177–84; phi 152; principles of 123–4; secondary 184–7; using vector graphics 152
Anime Studio Pro 162, *163*
anticipation animation 123, 131–2
appealing animation 124
AppHub 467
Apple Mac 469
application programming interfaces (APIs) 462, 466
application structure: Build Settings window 332, *332*; GUI items 331, *331*; MenuController 332–3; player settings *328*; start-up dialog box *329*; 2D Canvas 330, *330*
App Store 466–7
aPrimitive (aP) 51
AR *see* augmented reality (AR)
arcs animation 124

arithmetic operators 43
arrays 54–7
art asset primer: power of two rule 63–8; 3D models 68–72
art, elements of: color 14, 16; direction 11–12; line 9, *9*; point 9; shape 10–11; size 12–13; texture 13–14
Artificial Intelligence: A Modern Approach (book) 255
Assassin's Creed 163, 185, 334
assignment operator 43
asteroid model 69–71, *70*
Astrodude game object: child image, adding *345*; collided with object 346–7; CubeOfDeath 356, *357*; destroy function 348–9; DestroyOnClick 355–6; game objects assignment *348*; inventory counter 350; inventory images display in *346*; prefabs assignment *348*; to stack inventory items 355; 3D items 351–2; 3D prefabs *353*; 2D Canvas *344*
augmented reality (AR): fiduciary marker 459; Google Glass 459, *460*, 461; interactive applications 459; Microsoft's HoloLens 461, *461*; *Pokémon Go* 459, *460*; wearable devices 459; Wikitude SDK 461, *462*
Autodesk's 3D Studio Max 68–72
automatic waypoint collection 271–2
average blur *versus* Gaussian blur 392–3, *393*
Aztec Empire 197

backface culling technique 138
baked 3D animations 163–73
Barnsley fern leaf 5, *6*
Bejeweled 194, 426
belief–desire–intention model 244
Bezier curve 10, *10*

billboards 146–7, *147*
biomechanics 173–7
bit 63
Black & White 244
blob shadows 145–6
bloom 394
blur effect 392–3, *393*
Boolean algebra 29–31
Boolean functions 29
bounciness 62
branching design 368, 370
breadcrumb pathfinding 283–5, 300
breadth-first search (BFS) algorithm 252–3
Bresenham line algorithm 9, *9*
bullet game: fireworks prefab 112, *112*; MoveBullet.cs 106; prefab 106–9, *108*; quad, creating 105, *105*; shoot direction 110; squash and stretch animation 127–9; sticky 129–31; 2D collision detection function 111–12
bump mapping 13–14

C#: Hello World program 4; if-else statement 46; for printing numbers 49; script 26; variables 37–42
camera: bloom 394; blur 392–3, *393*; color correction 395; crease 395; depth of field 391–2, *392, 393*; edge detection *392*, 395; fish eye 396; flares 395; grayscale 393–4; medieval houses 83–6; motion blur 394; orthographic 80, *80, 81, 82*; perspective 80, *81, 82, 82*; post-processing effects 397–401; sepia tone *392*, 394; settings for 82–3, *82–3*; SSAO 396–7; sun shafts *392*, 396; twirl 394; view volume 80; vignette 396
Candy Crush Saga 426
cellular automata 322–3

character mechanics: cellular automata 322–3; decision trees 301–6; flocking 292–300; FSM 269–92; fuzzy logic 306–17; genetic algorithms 317–21; graph theory *250*, 250–1; line of sight *245*, 245–9; waypoints 251–69

chromosome 317

circular motion application 44–5

classical set theory 307, *307*

closest waypoint, NPC 285–91

clouds 407–9

CloudsToy Manager *408*, 408–9, 412

coherence 337–8

colors 335–6; correction 395; depth 64; mapping 13, *15*

compulsive hoarder 197

computer game 190–1

computer graphics: backface culling 138; color 14–16; Lambert shading 92; polygon 10; precipitation 412; scale 12

computer memory: bits 63; color depth 64; variables 34–7

conditional statements: Boolean algebra 46; if-else statement 46–8; loop 48

console: controllers 434; publishing 467–8

contrast, repetition, alignment, and proximity (CRAP) principle 339

creasing effect 395

Creating Procedural Artworks with Processing: A Holistic Guide (book) 7

cross product 77

cube game 116–19

cubeResize: error message 42; game object 41; objScaleX 39–40; save 42

data types 35

decision trees: eating situation 301–4; RTS AI game 304–6

defuzzification 308

degree of freedom (DOF) 176

De Motu Animalium (book) 174

depth-first search (DFS) algorithm 254–5

depth of field effect 391–2, *392*, *393*

development phase, game mechanics: avoidance

227–8; collecting 228–35; feedback 238–42; matching 198–9; racing 223–7; rewards 238; searching 235–8; shooting/hitting/bouncing/stacking 217–23; sorting 199

Diamond-Square method 378–9, *379*

diffuse coloring 13

digital signature 465

dinosaur model 69–71, *70*, *72*

Direct2Drive website 468

directed graph 250, *250*

Dodge Ball 190

Donkey Kong 227

Doom 198

DotFuzzy engine 309

dot product 75–6

draw call 153

Drawing on the Right Side of the Brain (book) 1–2, *2*

Dr. Mario 64 199

Dungeons & Dragons 194, 228

Dutch East India Company 196

dynamic generation 5

eating decision trees: attributes **301**, 301–2, **302**; tree value 303, **303**

edge detection *392*, 395

encryption 463

Endmemo tool 423–4

entity-component system (ECS) 21

environment map 253, *254*

error message 42

Euclidean distance 251, 253

Euclidean vector 11

Euler angles 100, *103*, 103–4

EVE Online 195, 242, 338, 369

exaggeration, animation 124

explicit teleports 360–2

Facebook 466

Far Cry 2 337–8

FBX sequences 165

F.E.A.R 244

feedback mechanisms 342

fiduciary marker 459

field of view (FOV) 82

finite state machines (FSM): breadcrumb pathfinding 283–5; closest waypoint finding 285–91; function

273–82; state transition for **269**, 269–71; waypoint system settings 271–2

first law of motion 116–19

first person controller (FPC) *283*, 379, *380*, 381, 387, 405, 417, 419

first person shooter (FPS) 191, 335

fish eye effect 396

flares 395

flocking: average speed 295–6; behavior 296–7; direct location 298–300; rules 292, *293*; seagulls 294–5; wind value, adding 297

flowcharts 326, *327*

flow level design 371

fog 143

follow-through animation 124

for loop: format 49; printing numbers 50; shortcut arithmetic operations 50, **50**; stacked spheres 51–4

forward kinematics 175, *175*

FPC (first person controller) *283*, 379, *380*, 381, 387, 405, 417, 419

Fracture 6

frames per second (FPS) 18–19

frustum 80

Full Throttle 236

functions 33–4

fuzzification 308

fuzzy logic 306–16

fuzzy rule 307

fuzzy set theory *307*, 307–8

game design: challenges 422; gameplay 424–34; HCI 423; icons/user interface elements 424, *425*; text 423–4

game engine: generic *17*, 17–18; main loop 18–27; in Unity 17

game-level design structures: branching *368*, 370; hub and spokes *368*, 370; linear *368*, 369–70; open *368*, 369

game mechanics: avoidance 197; capturing 196; chancing 194–5; collecting 197–8; conquering 196–7; cycle *191*; defined 190; development phase 198–238; matching 193; mixing 195; progressing

196; searching 192–3; sorting 193–4; timing 195–6

game objects: components 19–21, *20*; definition 58; initialization method 34

Game of Life 322, 322–3

gameplay: Android application 426–34; casual games 425–6; HCI features 426; mobile charts 424–5

game structure 326–34

Gaussian blur 392–3, *393*

genes 317

genetic algorithms 317–21, *321*

Geocaching 445–6

gesture recognition: DetectMotion 451–3; gestureRibbon 451; Kinect 450; OpenKinect 450; Stage System 450–1; text object 453, *454*

gimbal lock *102*, 103

gimbals 101, *102*, 103

GIMP 154, 162

global positioning system (GPS): development 445; geocaching 445–6; information 448–50; *My Grove 447, 448*; *Parallel Kingdom 447, 447*; satellite trilateration 445, *446*; *Tourality 446*, 446–7

Google Cardboard 454, *456*

Google Glass 459, *460*, 461

Google Nexus One HTC mobile: acceleration axes of 435, *435*; orientations of 437, *437*

Gorillas 218

GPS *see* global positioning system (GPS)

Grand Theft Auto 224

graphical user interface (GUI): coherence 337–8; feature exposure 336–7; focus 340; items 331, *331*; layout 339; metaphors 335–6; objects 327; shortcuts 338; state visualization 338; 2D Canvas *330*; user profiling 334–5

graph theory *250*, 250–1

gravity, law of 114–16

grayscale 382, 389, 393–4

Guitar Hero 193

gyroscope 101–2, *102*

Halo 191, 244, 365, 372

H-Anim (Humanoid Animation Working Group) *174*, 175

haptics 434

head-mounted displays (HMDs) 457, *458*

heads-up display (HUD) 325, 334, 339–40, *340*

Hello World program 3–4

help interface 340

heuristic function 255

HMDs (head-mounted displays) 457, *458*

Holmes stereoscope 454, *455*

house model 140–2, *141*

HTC Vive 421

HUD *see* heads-up display

human–computer interaction (HCI) technology 422–3, 426

Humanoid Animation Working Group (H-Anim) *174*, 175

icons 424, *425*

ID3 algorithm 303–4

if-else statement 46–8

The Illusion of Life (book) 123

image texture 64–8

Immediate Mode GUI (IMGUI) 327

implicit teleports 358–60

infinite terrain 389–90, *391*

inventories 343–57

inverse kinematics 175–6, *176*

Jojo's Fashion Show 197

keyboard shortcuts 338

Kinect Sports 224

kinematics 175

Lambert shading 92

lateralization 2

law of gravity 114–16

laws of physics 113–23

layout 339

level of detail (LOD) 140–2

lighting effect model 92, *93*

Lindenmayer system (L-system): natural/familiar shapes 385, *386*; Perlin noise 388–9; with remembered locations 384, *385*; rewriting 384, *384*; Sierpinski triangle 385, *385*; small city 389, *389*; square, drawing 384, *385*; street

map and buildings 386, *386*; string, building 383–4

linear map *368*, 369–70

line of sight *245*, 245–9

local coordinate system 87, *88*, *89*

local variables 52

LOD (level of detail) 140–2

logic gates 28–31

loop 48; *see also* for loop; main game loop/main loop

main game loop/main loop 18–27

male model 145–6

Mamdani style 308

Mandelbrot set 5, *5*

map design: details 366–7; flow 371; focal point 364, *365*; layout 367–70; player's movement 364–5; player starting position 371; scaling 366; third dimension 371–2; trapping 371; vantage points 372

Mario Brothers 228

math operators **43**

The Matrix (movie) 3

maze layout *319*

medieval houses game 83–6

mesh object 11

metaphors 335–6

microelectromechanical systems (MEMS) 435

Microsoft's HoloLens 461, *461*

Microsoft's Xbox 191

Minesweeper 228

mobile: accelerometer 434–6; Android application *see* Android application; design considerations *see* game design; GPS *see* global positioning system (GPS); haptics 434; orientation 436–9; web services 439–45

motion: blur 394; first law of 116–19; perception 152; second law of 120; third law of 121–3

Mt Fuji *373*; features, sculpting 374, *375*; final terrain reproduction 377, *378*; painted terrain 377, *377*; plane, placing 374, *375*; terrain texture 376, *376*

mutation 318
My Grove 447, *448*

navigation mesh (NavMesh): agent
management 267–8;
agent navigation 264,
264; agents movement
269, *269*; agent's speed
settings 268, *268*; AI
controller code 267; area
appearance *266*; navigate
agents *264*; static 264, *265*;
tab 264, *265*; tag 266, *266*
navigation system for timing and
ranging (NAVSTAR) 445
neuromyth 2
Nintendo 64 Rumble Pak 434
Nintendo Wii Remote 435
nodes 250–1
nonplayer characters (NPCs):
breadcrumb 285; closest
waypoint 285–91; DNA
string *320*; field of vision
249; first person controller
settings 283; flocking
see flocking; genetic
algorithms 319; and
players *245*
non-uniform rational basis spline
(NURBS) curve 10, *10*
normalizing vector 75
Nunchuk 435

objects 57–62
Oculus Rift 421, 457, *458*
OpenKinect 450
operant conditioning 239
operators: arithmetic 43; circular
motion 44–5; math **43**;
relational 43–6, **44**;
scripting reference 46
orthographic camera 80, *80*, *81*, *82*
overlapping action 124

paper–rock–scissors game 191–2
Parallel Kingdom 447, *447*
particle systems: CloudsToy 412;
SnowyRetreat 412–19;
velocity/size/life length
412, *413*
patrol game object: A* algorithm
260–2; robot guard 256–9
Perlin noise 379, 382, *383*, 388–90
persistence of vision theory 151
perspective camera 80, *81*, *82*, *82*

photoshop 154
PHP web emailer 444
physics, laws of 113–23
physics materials 121
pig model 69–71, *70*
pirate's treasure map: cross product
77; direction 77; dot
product 75–6; illustration
74; normalized vector 75,
75; Pythagorean theorem
75
pixels 9
plane: animated textures 144–5;
CrumpleMesh 94, *94*;
lighting effect 92, *93*;
normal 92, *92*; polygon 91
player: action *versus* game response
matrix 239–40; feedback
241–2; movement 364–5;
needs, addressing 341–2
player mechanics 325–6; game
interface design 334–42;
game structure 326–34;
inventories 343–57;
teleportation 358–62
PlayStation 3 Dual Shock 3 435
Pokémon Go 459, *460*
polycount 11, 138
polygons: backface culling 138–40;
level of detail 140–2; and
normals 91–5; polycount
11, 138
pose to pose 124
post-processing effects: Behaviour
component 397, *398*;
game environment 399,
401; profile, creating 397,
399; setting values of *400*;
Unity Asset Store 397, *397*
power of two rule 63–8
Princesses 197–8
procedural cities 383–9
procedural generation 5–7
procedural terrain generation:
Diamond-Square method
378–9, *379*; midpoint
displacement algorithm
378, *378*; Perlin noise 382,
383; plane/FPC 379, *380*;
random height values 380;
sine function 381
Project Gotham racing series 195, 224
proximity 339
psychological phenomenon (phi) 152
public-key cryptography 463, *464*, 465

puzzle games: *Bejeweled* 341;
Dr. Mario 64 199;
Machinarium 194

Quake 3 Arena (Q3A) 182
quakebot 182
quaternions 97, 103–13; Euler angles
100; gyroscope 101–2, *102*;
planes, rotation in *103*,
104; 3D space 100, *101*

racing games 223; anticipation 131;
creating 224–7; follow-
through 132; *Grand Theft
Auto* 224; *Kinect Sports*
224; *Project Gotham* 195,
224; *Split Second* 365
Rayleigh scattering 401–2, 404, 406
real-time strategy (RTS) AI game
304–6, **305**
resolution 9
rhythm game 193
robot model: patrol *256*, 256–62;
vectors 78, 78–9
rocket ship game: attack script 96–7;
bullet 105–9; camera 79;
distance test 99–100;
explosion 112, *112*;
shooting 109–10; sprite,
creating 96, *96*; target
game object 98, 98–9;
2D collision detection
function 111–12
Royal Game of Ur 189
RTS (real-time strategy) AI game
304–6, **305**

scaling method 71
screen space ambient occlusion
(SSAO) 396–7
scripting primer: arrays 54–7;
comments 31–3;
conditional statements
46–54; electric circuit *28*,
28–9; functions 33–4;
logic gates 28–31; objects
57–62; operators 43–6;
variables 34–7
searching, game mechanics 192–3
secondary actions 124
secondary animation 184–7
second law of motion 120
sending mail: with device mail client
440–2, *442*; web server
442–5

sepia tone *392*, 394
shaded female model: grass material *67*, 68; mesh hierarchy 65, *65*; texture picker 65, *66*
shader 138–40
shortcuts: arithmetic operations 50, **50**; keyboard 338
Sierpinski triangle 385, *385*
SimCity 322, 368
The Sims 224, 369
The Sims Medieval 195
single-filed 3D animations 182–4
single 2D sprite actions 177–82
skies: clouds 407–9; Rayleigh scattering 401–2; Skyboxes 402, *403*; SkyDomes 404–7; turbidity 402
Skyboxes 402, *403*
SkyDomes 404–7
Skyrim 163
sloping cube model 121–3
slow in and out movement 124
smoking particle system *361*
Snakes and Ladders 228
Snowman 5, *5*
snowy retreat: emitter 415, *416*; Gradient Editor 415, *416*; manipulation 417, *418*; particle editor 413, *414*; particle size 413, *414*; size curve 417, *417*; Size Over Lifetime 414, *415*; smoke particles 413; snow particle emission 417–18, *418*
social mechanic: application programming interfaces 462; Facebook 466; security 463–5; Twitter 465
solid drawing 124
solitaire (card game) 198
Sony PlayStation's Dual Shock analog controller 434
sorting, game mechanics 193–4
Space Invaders 197
Spacewar! 152, *152*
spin program 32
Splinter Cell 131
Split Second 365
spoke and hub *368*, 370
Sporty_Granny game object: amWalking 170; animator controller 166; AnimControls 168; Bool

parameter 170; controller 166; FBX sequences 165; loop pose 169; loop time 169; transitions 170
sprites: animates 157–63; draw call 153; rocket ship 153; UV settings 155–7
squash and stretch animation 123, 125–31
SSAO *see* screen space ambient occlusion
standard assets package 125
StarCraft 196, 336
Start() function 34
state visualization 338
Steam website 468
stereogram 454, *455*
sticky bullet: squash and stretch 129–31; timed explosive devices 131–2
straight-ahead action 124
subtractive color model 14
sun shafts *392*, 396
Super Mario Brothers 198
Super Smash Brothers 195
symmetric cryptography 463, *464*

teleportation: explicit 360–2, *362*; implicit 358–60
terrains: cities 383–9; drawing 373–8; Editor tools **374**; infinite 389–90, *391*; procedural 378–83; utility graph *253*
texture atlas: animated sprite *160*; animation frames 159, *159*; Anime Studio Pro 162, *163*; in GIMP 153–4, *154*; slicing up 158, *159*; sprite mapping *155*, 155–7
textures: animation 144–5; blob shadows 145–6; map 13
third law of motion 121–3
three-dimensional (3D) model: dinosaur model 69–71, *70*, *72*; environments 371–2; for game space optimizing 137–48; pig model 69–71, *70*; polygons/ normals 91–5; robot model *78*, 78–9; space 79; translation/rotation/ scaling 87, 89–91, *90*, *91*; from triangles *11*; 2D games in 95–113

three-dimensional (3D) viewing: anaglyphs 456–7, *457*; HMDs 457, *458*; side-by-side 454–6
tiled strategy game 253, *254*
timing animation 124
Tom Clancy's *Ghost Recon* 235
Tourality 446, 446–7
trapping 371
turbidity 402
TurboSquid 69–72, 177
twirl effect 394
Twitter 465
two-dimensional (2D) model: art assets 63; canvas *330*; space 79; in 3D game engine 95–113

undirected graph 250, *250*
unit vector 75
Unity3D development environment: color 25; cube, creating 22, *23*; download 21; editing 21, *22*; E mode 24; lighting 24; material 26; NewbehaviorScript 26; project, creating 22; R mode 24–5; save 27; W mode 24
Update() functions 33–4
user profiling 334–5
UV mapping process 13, *14*

vantage points 372
variables: C# 37–42; data types 35; defined 34; local 52; in memory allocation 35, *36*; names 36–7; type 35
vectors: magnitude 11, *12*; principles of 74–9
vertices 10
vignette 396
vision persistence 151
visual elements: color 14, 16; direction 11–12; line 9, *9*; point 9; shape 10–11; size 12–13; texture 13–14
volumetric clouds 407, 407–9
Vuforia 459

warehouse model: animated textures 144–5; curtains/wind effects 134–7, *136*; custom shader, loading 138–40; door 132–4, *133*

waypoints 251–2, 271–2; in graph object 257; layout *256*; searching through 252–69

weather: precipitation 412; wind 409–12

web services: Internet access 439; mail, sending 440–5, *442*; mail via

web server, sending 442–5; URLs, calling and retrieving 439

Wei-qi 189

wind: constant force 411–12; description 409; flag, flying 410–11, *411*; grass and flower objects 410, *410*

wireframe model 11

The Witcher 3 73

Wolfenstein 198

world coordinate system 87, *88*, *89*

World of Goo 125

Xbox Kinect 217